RESCUED BY

W0230163

JAVA

Kris Jamsa, Ph.D., MBA

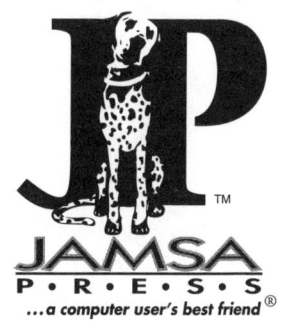

JAMSA
P·R·E·S·S ®
...a computer user's best friend ®

Published by
Jamsa Press
3301 Allen Parkway
Houston, TX 77019
U.S.A.

http://www.jamsapress.com

For information about the translation or distribution of any Jamsa Press book, please write to Jamsa Press at the address listed above.

Rescued by Java

Printed in the United States of America.
98765432

ISBN 1-884133-65-7

Performance Manager	*Technical Advisor*	*Copy Editor*
Kong Cheung	Phil Schmauder	Rosemary Pasco
Composition	*Technical Editor*	*Proofer*
Denise Ruzich	Dr. Robert Barger	Jeanne K. Smith
Helene J. Shin		
Indexer	*Cover Design*	
Kong Cheung	Alan Giana	

Jamsa Press is an imprint of Gulf Publishing Company:

Gulf Publishing Company
Book Division
P.O. Box 2608
Houston, TX 77252-2608
U.S.A.

http://www.gulfpub.com

CONTENTS

Section One

LEARNING THE BASICS

In this section, you will learn basics you must know to create your own Java applets. If you have never created a program before, do not worry, this section starts at step one. By the time you finish the simple lessons this section presents, you will be well on your way to programming in Java! The lessons in this section include:

LESSON 1 INTRODUCING JAVA

LESSON 2 CREATING YOUR FIRST JAVA APPLET

LESSON 3 TAKING A LOOK AT YOUR APPLETS

LESSON 4 JAVA APPLETS VERSUS STANDALONE PROGRAMS

LESSON 5 JAVA APPLETS STORE INFORMATION IN VARIABLES

LESSON 6 SIMPLE MATH OPERATIONS IN JAVA APPLETS

LESSON 7 TEACHING JAVA APPLETS TO MAKE DECISIONS

LESSON 8 TEACHING YOUR APPLETS TO REPEAT ONE
OR MORE STATEMENTS

LESSON 9 USING FUNCTIONS TO SIMPLIFY JAVA APPLETS

LESSON 10 LOOKING AT SEVERAL SPECIAL FUNCTIONS

LESSON 1

INTRODUCING JAVA

Computer programs, or software, are lists of instructions the computer executes to perform a specific task. Programmers create software using a specific programming language, such as BASIC, C, C++, or Java. Historically, programmers used specific languages to create specific types of programs. For example, programmers creating business programs often used COBOL (the Common Business Oriented Language). Programmers creating scientific programs used FORTRAN (the Formula Translator). Likewise, programmers who were creating systems programs used C or C++.

Today, key topics in computing include the Internet, intranets, and the World Wide Web. Java is a programming language with features well-suited to the network environment. This lesson will introduce you to the Java programming language, the computer industry's hottest programming language. You will learn features that make Java well-suited for network operations, and then learn how to download a free copy of the Java Development Kit (JDK) from Sun Microsystems. The Java Development Kit provides you with everything you need to create Java programs. By the time you finish this lesson, you will understand the following key concepts:

- ◆ Java is a programming language with which programmers can create standalone programs and browser-based applets.

- ◆ A standalone Java program does not run within a browser. Instead, a standalone program implements an application the programmer would have otherwise used a programming language such as C++ to compile.

- ◆ A Java applet runs within a browser, such as the Netscape *Navigator* or Microsoft *Internet Explorer*.

- ◆ Java applets are device independent, which means the same applet can execute on a PC running Windows 98 or on a Mac or UNIX-based system.

- ◆ Unlike other programming languages that create programs that are processor specific (such as for the Pentium or Motorola processor), Java creates virtual-machine code that the browser converts to binary code the processor understands.

- ◆ To create a Java applet or standalone program, you must use a special program called the Java compiler.

- ◆ You can get the Java compiler for free by downloading the Java Development Kit from Sun's Web site at *java.sun.com*.

- ◆ The Java Development Kit provides the compiler, utility programs, and many sample applets.

- ◆ Hot Java is a browser written in the Java programming language.

UNDERSTANDING THE NEED FOR JAVA

Over the past few years, the Web has become a very powerful advertising medium. In fact, it is very difficult today to find a television show, motion picture, newspaper, or magazine that does not have a Web page. Many of the most popular Web sites report millions of hits (user visits) each day! Unfortunately, the Web's popularity far exceeds its technological capabilities.

Today, the two fundamental technology issues facing network programmers and engineers are bandwidth and security. Bandwidth specifies the amount of information that can transfer across the network at any time. If you examine current technologies, you will find high-speed lines categorized as T1 through T3 that will transmit data at 1.544

through 45 megabits per second, levels of ISDN lines that transmit data at rates of 64 through 128K bits per second, and standard phone lines over which most users transmit data at 56K bits per second.

To start, keep in mind that most bandwidth speeds are expressed in bits per second, not bytes. Next, consider a 640x480 window that is displaying images in 256 colors (which requires 1 byte per pixel). To display the window's contents requires 307,200 bytes of data, as shown here:

640 pixels x 480 pixels x 1 byte/pixel = 307,200 bytes

To create an animation, programs typically display 15 to 30 different images per second. Given a 640x480 window, 15 to 30 frames per second would require 4,608,000 to 9,216,000 bytes per second. Because most users are surfing the Web using 56K modems, there simply is not enough bandwidth to download animation screens. As a result, most Web sites today resemble (slow) magazines whose images are static (unchanging). However, to satisfy an audience that spends many hours in front of dynamic television images, Internet programmers and engineers must provide a way to animate Web sites. One solution is to download programs that implement the animation. Unfortunately, downloading programs to a user's Web site introduces a second problem: security, as discussed next.

Computer viruses are a major concern users should have any time they download programs from across the Net. As you may know, a *virus* is a program created by malicious programmers to intentionally damage another user's system, typically by destroying the contents of the user's hard drive.

Normally, for a virus to infect your system, you must download and run a program (although there are viruses that can attach themselves to document files such as Word documents and Excel spreadsheets). Your computer cannot get a virus by simply using your browser to download a Web site's text and graphics. As you will learn, Java is a programming language designed to help programmers create animations and other Web applications, but whose programs are safe for other users to download.

JAVA APPLETS DIFFER FROM JAVA STANDALONE PROGRAMS

As discussed, Java is a programming language. Using Java, programmers can create standalone programs similar to those that programmers can develop using C++, and applets that run within a browser. Most of the Java code you will encounter will implement browser-based applets, as opposed to standalone programs.

To address security issues, Java developers had to ensure a programmer could not develop a computer virus using a Java applet, and that an applet could not transfer information about a user's system (such as a file on the user's system) back to the server. You would hate, for example, to be browsing your competition's Web site while their Java applets browsed your hard disk.

To provide such security, the Java developers chose to limit the operations an applet can perform. For example, a Java applet cannot read or write files on the user's system. In this way, an applet cannot store a virus on a user's disk or read information stored on a user's disk. In addition, to prevent an applet from performing file I/O, the Java developers eliminated or changed many features of the C and C++ programming languages, such as pointers, with which advanced programmers could bypass Java's security mechanisms.

As briefly discussed, Java lets programmers create standalone programs and applets. Java standalone programs are similar to the programs that programmers can create using C++. Such standalone programs can read and write files and perform operations that Java restricts applets from performing. A Java applet, on the other hand, only runs within a browser, as discussed next.

JAVA APPLETS RUN WITHIN A BROWSER

As just discussed, Java applets run within a browser, such as the Netscape *Navigator* or Microsoft *Internet Explorer*. Figure 1.1, for example, shows a Java applet running within each browser.

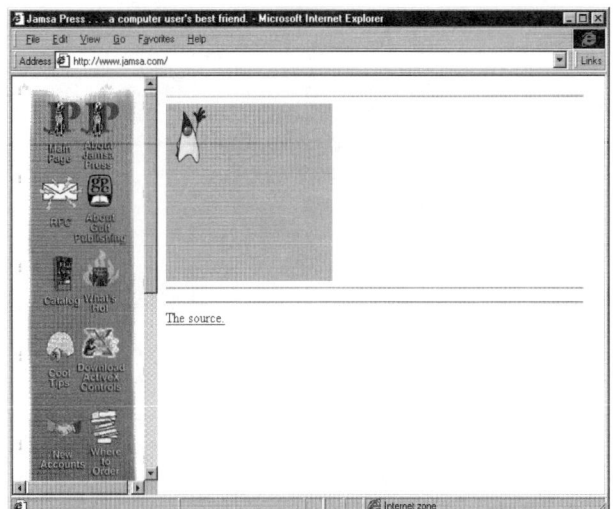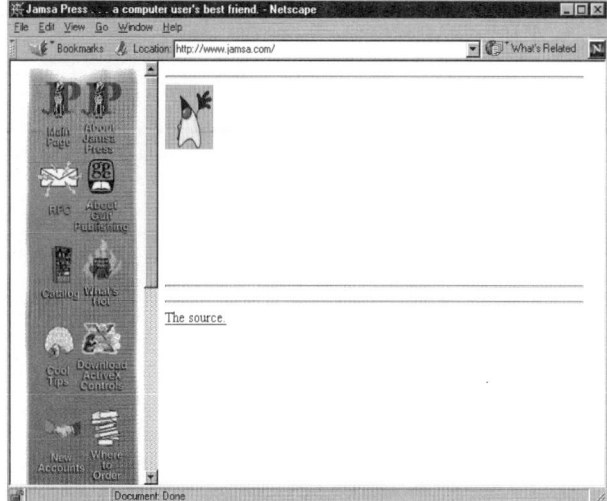

*Figure 1.1 Java applets run within a browser, such as the Netscape **Navigator** or Microsoft **Internet Explorer**.*

If you use the Java Development Kit to create and compile your applets, you can use a special program called the *appletviewer* to start and test your applets quickly. Figure 1.2 shows the same Java applet running within the *appletviewer*.

*Figure 1.2 Running a Java applet within the **appletviewer**, provided with the Java Development Kit.*

JAVA APPLETS ARE DEVICE INDEPENDENT

After the Java developers addressed the speed and security issues, the developers had to determine how to support the different types of systems with which users browse the Web. For example, across the Web, users browse with PCs, Macs, UNIX-based systems, and so on. Because each of these systems uses a different CPU (processor) type, a program written for one system will not run on another. Rather than forcing programmers to create separate programs for each system (one program for Windows, one for the Mac, and so on), the Java developers chose a different technique.

As you know, computers work in terms of ones and zeros. When you write a program, you use a programming language to specify the instructions the program must perform to accomplish a specific task. Next, you use a special program (called a compiler) that converts the programming language statements that you understand into the ones and zeros the computer understands. Figure 1.3 illustrates the process of compiling a program.

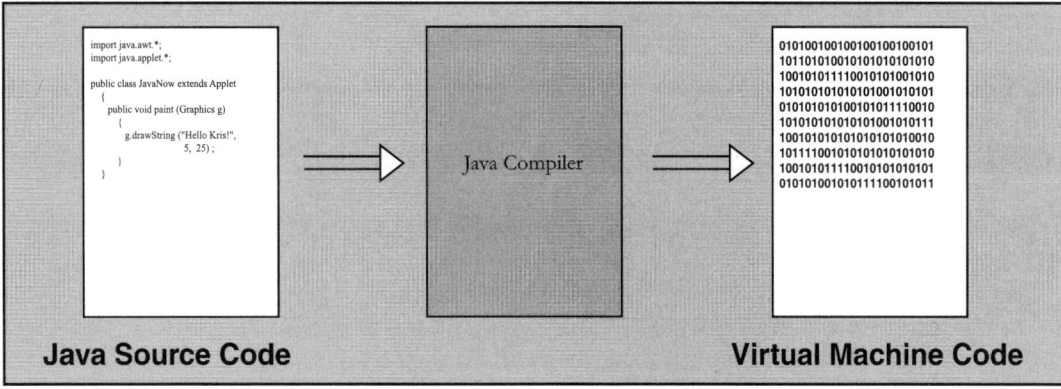

Figure 1.3 *Compiling program statements into ones and zeros the computer can execute.*

When you create programs in other programming languages, such as C++, the ones and zeros the compiler creates are processor specific. In other words, the ones and zeros correspond to an Intel processor or a Motorola processor. The Java compiler, however, is different. Rather than producing processor-specific code, Java produces an intermediate code called virtual-machine code that is not processor specific. Instead, as shown in Figure 1.4, after the browser downloads the applet's virtual-machine code, software within the browser (which programmers refer to as the browser's *virtual machine*) converts the code to ones and zeros the processor understands.

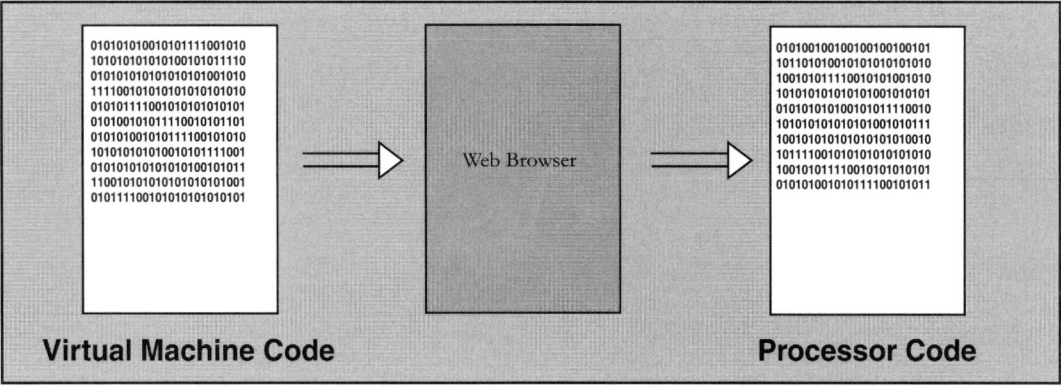

Figure 1.4 *The browser converts virtual-machine code into ones and zeros the processor understands.*

If, for example, a user downloads the applet using a Mac, the Mac-based browser will convert the virtual-machine code into ones and zeros for the Motorola processor. Likewise, if the user is browsing under Windows 98, the browser will convert the virtual-machine code into ones and zeros for the Intel processor. The advantage of using virtual-machine code is that the applet programmer must create only one applet, which a wide range of systems will support.

The problem with virtual-machine code is speed. Because the browser must convert the virtual-machine code into processor-specific code, Java-based programs will not execute as fast as processor-specific code. In fact, if you place equivalent Java and C++ programs side by side, the C++ program (which uses processor-specific code) will execute 10 to 20 times faster! Over time, therefore, you may see Java shift away from virtual-machine code to processor-specific code, simply so Java can compete in terms of speed with other programming languages. Such a shift to processor-specific code would require applet developers to compile their program for each of the processors they want to support. You may also see a change in HTTP (the Hypertext Transfer Protocol), which lets the browser identify its processor type to the Web server so the server can download the correct applet type (Intel, Motorola, and so on) for the user's system.

UNDERSTANDING THE FUTURE OF JAVA

Today, programmers normally use Java to create Web-based or Net-based applications. Because Java is platform independent, many software developers believe that Java is ideal for use in "smart devices," such as a home-monitoring system, a smart TV, as well as a variety of handheld devices. In the future, you may encounter hardware (ROM-based) virtual machines that let smart devices run Java applets. In addition, you will encounter a variety of application program interfaces (APIs) for a variety of hardware devices that programmers can use to simplify their Java program development.

UNDERSTANDING THE JAVA DEVELOPMENT KIT

To create Java applets, you need a special program (called the Java *compiler*) that converts the Java program statements that you understand into the ones and zeros (called virtual-machine code) that your browser executes. When you program in a language such as C++, you have to buy the compiler before you can create programs. Currently, you can download the Java compiler for free from Sun's Web site at *java.sun.com*. Sun's Web page will let you download a Windows-based version of Java (for Windows 95, Windows 98, or Windows NT—not Windows 3.1), a Mac-based version of Java, and a version for UNIX-based systems as well.

Depending on the system you choose to download, the steps you must perform to install the Java Development Kit will differ. In each case, however, you will find instructions at Sun's Web site that will walk you through the installation.

As you have learned, the Java Development Kit provides the Java compiler you will use to create applets. In addition, the kit provides several utility programs, such as the *appletviewer*, that let you run and display applets, a debugger that helps you find and eliminate errors in your applets, and a document generator that simplifies the task of documenting your code. In addition to the compiler and utility programs, the Java Development Kit provides many sample applets whose source code you can study to improve your understanding of Java. In fact, several of the lessons in this book discuss these sample applets.

INSTALLING THE JAVA DEVELOPMENT KIT UNDER WINDOWS

If you are using Windows, perform these steps to install the Java Development Kit on your system:

1. Connect to the Sun's Web page at *java.sun.com* shown in Figure 1.5.

2. From the Web page, download the Windows version of the Java Development Kit. Your system will download the Java Development Kit as a single executable program. When you execute the program, it will extract the Development Kit from within the file, storing the files on your disk.

3. Run the program you downloaded in Step 2. The program will extract the files into subdirectories on your disk.

4. Edit your system's AUTOEXEC.BAT and update the PATH entry to include the BIN subdirectory that resides beneath the JAVA directory. For example, if you installed the Java Development Kit within the root directory on drive C, your PATH statement might appear similar to the following:

    PATH C:\WINDOWS;C:\WINDOWS\COMMAND;C:\JAVA\BIN

5. Review the documentation that accompanied the Java Development Kit to ensure the steps to install the Java Development Kit have not changed since the writing of this book.

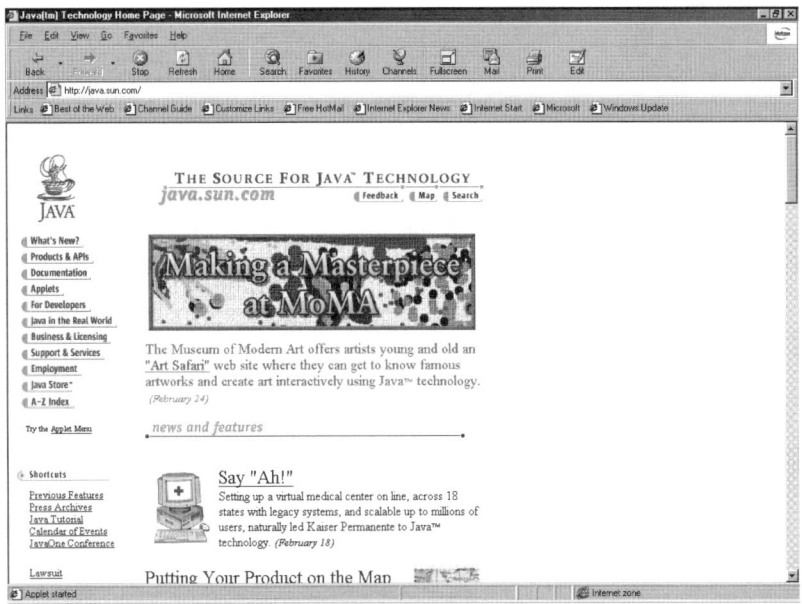

Figure 1.5 Downloading the Java Development Kit from java.sun.com.

WHAT IS HOT JAVA?

Many users who are new to the Java programming language often confuse Java with *Hot Java*, a browser written in Java. In short, Java is a programming language that programmers use to create programs and applets. *Hot Java*, on the other hand, is a browser, much like the Netscape *Navigator*. What makes *Hot Java* unique is that the entire program is written in Java itself! As you start to experiment with Java applets, you might try out the *Hot Java* browser, which you can download from Sun's Web site. Figure 1.6 shows an applet running within the *Hot Java* browser.

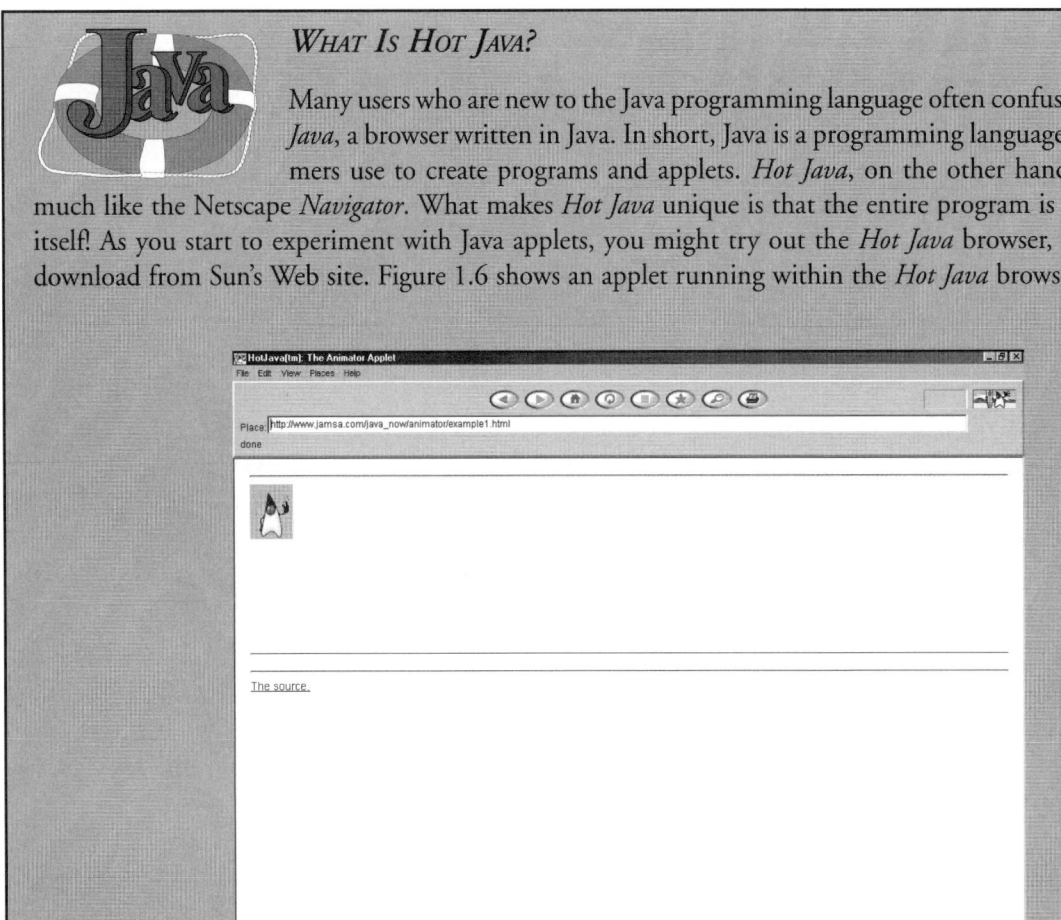

Figure 1.6 Hot Java is a browser created by programmers using the Java programming language.

USING THIS BOOK'S COMPANION CD-ROM

As briefly discussed, the CD-ROM that accompanies this book includes the JBuilder integrated development environment that you can use to create, compile, and test your Java applets. Appendix A, "Using the JBuilder Compiler," examines the *JBuilder* environment in detail. In addition, the CD-ROM contains the Java source code and related HTML file for each program this book presents. As you examine programs throughout this book, take time to run the programs from the companion CD-ROM.

If you copy Java source files from the CD-ROM, you may have to clear the file's readonly attribute before you can change the file's contents. Within Windows, you can clear the readonly attribute by right-clicking your mouse on filename within the Explorer. Windows, in turn, will display a popup menu. Within the popup menu, select the Properties option. Windows will display the Properties dialog box, within which you can clear the file's readonly attribute.

WHAT YOU MUST KNOW

This lesson introduced you to Java and the Java Development Kit. If you have not already downloaded the Java Development Kit, do so now. In Lesson 2, "Creating Your First Java Applet," you will develop your first Java applets. Before you continue with Lesson 2, however, make sure that you understand the following key concepts:

- ☑ Using Java as a programming language, programmers create standalone programs and browser-based applets.

- ☑ Java standalone programs implement applications that, in the past, programmers would have used a programming language such as C++ to compile.

- ☑ Java applets run within a browser.

- ☑ Java applets are device independent, which means the same applet can execute on a PC running Windows 98 or on a Mac or UNIX-based system.

- ☑ Java compiles applets into virtual-machine code that the browser converts to binary code the processor understands.

- ☑ The Java compiler is a special program that converts your Java programming statements into virtual-machine code the browser can execute.

- ☑ By downloading the Java Development Kit from Sun's Web site at *java.sun.com*, you can get the Java compiler for free.

- ☑ In addition to providing the Java compiler, the Java Development Kit provides several utility programs and many sample applets.

- ☑ Hot Java is a browser written in the Java programming language.

LESSON 2

CREATING YOUR FIRST JAVA APPLET

In Lesson 1, "Introducing Java," you learned how to download the Java Development Kit and how to use Sun's *appletviewer,* or your browser, to view Java applets. In this lesson, you will create your own Java applets. In other words, you will create a file that contains the Java programming-language statements that display a message within an applet window. Using the *appletviewer* or your browser, you can run your applet. In fact, if you have a Web site, other users across the Net will be able to run your applet as well.

This lesson presents a lot of material. But do not worry—you should find the pace easy to follow. By the time you finish this lesson, you will understand the following key concepts:

- A Java applet is a file that contains the computer instructions to perform a specific task.

- As a Java programmer, you specify the statements the applet performs to accomplish a specific task.

- To create a Java applet, you use an editor, such as the MS-DOS *EDIT* command or the Windows *Notepad* accessory, to type in the Java programming statements.

- The file that contains your Java statements is called the applet's *source file.* Java source files use the *java* extension, such as *ShowMessage.java.*

- Before the *appletviewer* or a browser can run a Java applet, you must convert the applet's Java programming statements to ones and zeros, called the *virtual-machine code.*

- To convert your source file to virtual-machine code, you use the Java compiler. Sun's Java Development Kit, for example, names its compiler *javac.exe.*

- Like any language, Java has rules (a grammar). If, as you type your Java statements, you violate any of these rules, the Java compiler will display syntax-error messages when you compile your applet.

- Before the Java compiler can successfully compile your applet into virtual-machine code, you must edit your source file and correct all syntax errors.

- If the Java compiler successfully compiles your source file (such as *ShowMessage.java*), the compiler will create an applet file with the same filename, but one that uses the class extension (such as *ShowMessage.class*).

- To run a Java applet, the *appletviewer* or your browser executes the virtual-machine code that resides in the class file.

- To place a Java applet within a Web page that you can view with a browser, or using the *appletviewer,* you place the *<APPLET>* tag within an HTML file.

- The Java programming language and the Java programs, such as the *appletviewer,* are case sensitive, meaning they consider uppercase and lowercase letters as different.

SELECTING AN EDITOR

To create a Java applet, you must type in the Java program statements that describe the task the applet performs. You will store these program statements within a file, called the applet's *source file.* To create your source file, use a text editor such as the *EDIT* command provided with MS-DOS, or the Windows *Notepad* accessory. If you are programming in a UNIX environment, use the *pico* editor.

You should not use a word processor, such as Microsoft *Word*, to create your source file. As you know, word processors let you bold text, align margins, and so on. To perform these formatting operations, most word processors embed special hidden characters within your document file. Although these hidden characters have meaning to your word processor (such as telling the word processor to turn on italics), these characters would cause errors within a Java source file. To avoid such errors, use a text editor—not a word processor—to create your applet's source file.

SELECTING AN APPLET NAME

As you prepare to create your applet, one of your first tasks is to decide on an applet name. Ideally, the name you choose for your applet should correspond to the task your applet performs. For example, if your applet creates a game, you might call the applet TicTacToe or BlackJack. The name you choose for your applet is important. You will use the name for the applet's source file (such as *TicTacToe.java* or *BlackJack.java*) and within your Java programming statements.

In this lesson, you will create your first applet, which displays the message *Rescued by Java!* within an applet window. In this case, you will name the applet *ShowJavaMessage*. Note that the applet name does not include spaces. Instead, the name uses uppercase and lowercase letters to separate the two parts of the name. Remember, Java is case sensitive, which means it considers the names *ShowJavaMessage* and *showjavamessage* as different.

TYPING IN YOUR JAVA STATEMENTS

As discussed, your Java source file contains Java programming statements that the applet performs to accomplish a specific task. As you start out, this book will provide all the statements you must type to create the source file. In very little time, however, you will start changing these applets by editing the existing statements or by adding more statements. To create the *ShowJavaMessage* applet, start your text editor and type in the following statements:

```
import java.awt.*;
import java.applet.*;

public class ShowJavaMessage extends Applet
   {
      public void paint(Graphics g)
         {
            g.drawString("Rescued by Java!", 5, 25);
         }
   }
```

For now, it is not important that you understand these Java programming statements. You will examine each of these statements in Lesson 3, "Taking a Look at Your Applets." As you will learn, these statements instruct your applet to display the message *Rescued by Java!* within the applet window.

As you type in your program statements, pay very close attention to ensure you typed the statements exactly as they appear. If you mistype a statement, possibly by forgetting a semicolon or by typing a lowercase letter when the applet uses uppercase, the Java compiler will encounter errors when you try to compile your applet, as discussed next. Save your Java statements to a source file named *ShowJavaMessage.java*.

COMPILING YOUR APPLET

When you create a Java applet, you work with the applet's source file that contains the Java programming statements. As you have learned, your applet's source file will use the *java* extension, in this case *ShowJavaMessage.java*.

To run your applet, the *appletviewer* or your browser executes the ones and zeros contained in the applet's class file (*ShowJavaMessage.class*). As briefly discussed, these ones and zeros are called virtual-machine code.

USING DIRECTORIES TO ORGANIZE YOUR APPLETS

As the number of applets you create increases, so too will the number of files on your disk. Each applet typically requires at least three files: the Java source-code file, the compiled class file, and the HTML file you use to run the applet. To help you manage your files, you should create directories on your disk. For example, to organize the applets that you create as you read through this book, you might first create a directory named *RBYJAVA* (which is an abbreviation for *Rescued by Java*). Then, within the *RBYJAVA* directory, you can create subdirectories to hold each lesson's applet. For example, you might store the applets for this lesson within the directory *RBYJAVA\LESSON02*. By storing applets in their own directories, you will make your applet files much easier to manage.

To convert your Java program statements into virtual-machine code, your must compile your source file using a special program called the Java compiler. When you downloaded and installed the Java Development Kit in Lesson 1, the Java compiler was one of the files you installed.

In the case of Sun's Java Development Kit, the Java compiler is a program you run from the command line. In this case, to compile the source file, *ShowJavaMessage.java*, that you just created, issue the following command:

```
C:\RBYJAVA\LESSON02> javac    ShowJavaMessage.java    <ENTER>
```

In this case, the *javac* command starts the compiler which, in turn, will compile the source file you specify in the command line. As discussed, remember that Java is case sensitive. You must use the same uppercase and lowercase letters in the source filename that you used within your Java program statements. In other words, if you use the applet name *ShowJavaMessage* within your source file, and the filename *showjavamessage.java* within your command line, the Java compiler will display an error message (you must use the filename *ShowJavaMessage.java*, whose uppercase and lowercase letters match the source-file statements).

If you have typed in the Java statements exactly as they appear within this book, the compiler will not display any error messages. However, if you mistype a line, the compiler will display one or more syntax-error messages, as discussed next.

UNDERSTANDING SYNTAX ERRORS

Every language, be it French, Spanish, English, or even Java, has a set of rules, a grammar. In English, for example, you end sentences with a period, exclamation mark, or a question mark. As you will learn, in Java, you end most statements with a semicolon (;).

When you violate a rule of the Java programming language, the Java compiler will display syntax-error messages on your screen. Before the Java compiler can successfully convert your program into virtual-machine code the *appletviewer* or your browser can execute, you must correct all the syntax errors your source file contains.

As you create your first applet, you will encounter many syntax errors when you compile your source files. Such errors can be subtle. However, to help you locate the errors, the Java compiler will normally display the line that contains the error and a brief description of the problem. For example, if you examine the statements within the *ShowJavaMessage* applet, you will find that the applet's first two statements, the import statements, both end with semicolons. If, for example, you omit the semicolons, the compiler will display the syntax-error messages shown here:

```
C:\RBYJAVA\LESSON02> javac    ShowJavaMessage.java    <ENTER>

ShowJavaMessage.java:1: ';' expected.
import java.awt.*
                 ^
```

```
ShowJavaMessage.java:4: Superclass Applet of class ShowJavaMessage
not found.
public class ShowJavaMessage extends Applet
                                    ^

2 errors
```

In this case, to correct the syntax errors, you must edit the source file *ShowJavaMesssage.java* and type a semicolon at the end of each statement. Then, after you save your changes to the file, you again compile the source file. If other errors remain, the Java compiler will display related error messages. If you have eliminated all of the syntax errors from your source file, the Java compiler will create the applet's class file, as discussed next.

UNDERSTANDING THE CLASS FILE

If, after you successfully compile your Java applet, you perform a directory listing of your files, you will find a file named *ShowJavaMessage.class*. The applet's class file contains the virtual-machine code the *appletviewer* or your browser executes:

```
C:\RBYJAVA\LESSON02> DIR    <ENTER>

 Volume in drive C has no label
 Volume Serial Number is 3B22-17F2
 Directory of  C:\RBYJAVA\LESSON02


.                 <DIR>           04-16-99   2:32p .
..                <DIR>           04-16-99   2:32p ..
SHOWJA~1  CLA            385      04-16-99   3:34p ShowJavaMessage.class
SHOWJA~1  JAV            203      04-16-99   3:33p ShowJavaMessage.java
         2 file(s)              588 bytes
         2 dir(s)     1,375,191,040 bytes free
```

To run your applet, you now must create an HTML file the *appletviewer* or your browser will use to access your applet.

CREATING A SAMPLE HTML FILE

As you know, to build a Web site, developers make extensive use of HTML. Using HTML, Web designers specify the text, graphics, and sounds that correspond to a Web page. In addition, to place a Java applet on a Web page, designers use the *<APPLET>* tag to specify the applet's class file and other settings, such as the applet's window size.

To run the *ShowJavaMessage* applet, create the file *ShowJavaMessage.HTML* that contains the following HTML entries:

```
<HTML><TITLE>ShowJavaMessage Applet</TITLE>
<APPLET  CODE="ShowJavaMessage.class"  WIDTH=300  HEIGHT=200></APPLET>
</HTML>
```

In this case, the HTML *<APPLET>* tag specifies the applet's class file and window size in pixels. Although the filename *ShowJavaMessage.HTML* corresponds to the applet name, you can name the HTML file any name that you would like, such as *Example.HTML*. However, as the number of applets you create increases, you will find that using meaningful HTML filenames make your files easier to manage.

Note: *Under HTML 4.0, many users replace the <APPLET> tag with the <OBJECT> tag.*

USING THE APPLETVIEWER

To run the *ShowJavaMessage* applet using the *appletviewer*, type the following command:

```
C:\RBYJAVA\LESSON02> appletviewer     ShowJavaMessage.HTML     <ENTER>
```

As you can see, the command runs the *appletviewer*, specifying the HTML file that contains the *<APPLET>* tag that corresponds to the *ShowJavaMessage* applet. The *appletviewer* will open an applet window, similar to that shown in Figure 2.1, that displays the *Rescued by Java!* message. To end the applet, you simply close the applet window.

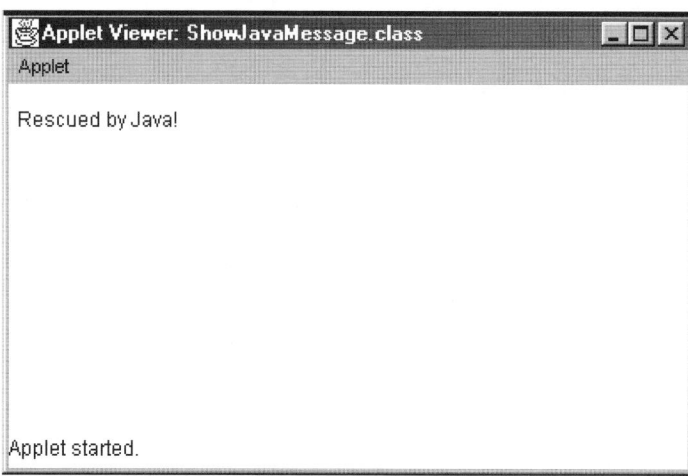

*Figure 2.1 An applet window displaying the **Rescued by Java!** message text.*

USING YOUR BROWSER

To run the *ShowJavaMessage* applet using your browser, you type in the disk location of the HTML file within your browser's address field, preceded by the text *file:///*. For example, if the HTML file resides within a directory named *C:/RBYJAVA/Lesson02/ShowJavaMessage.HTML*, you would type in the URL shown in Figure 2.2.

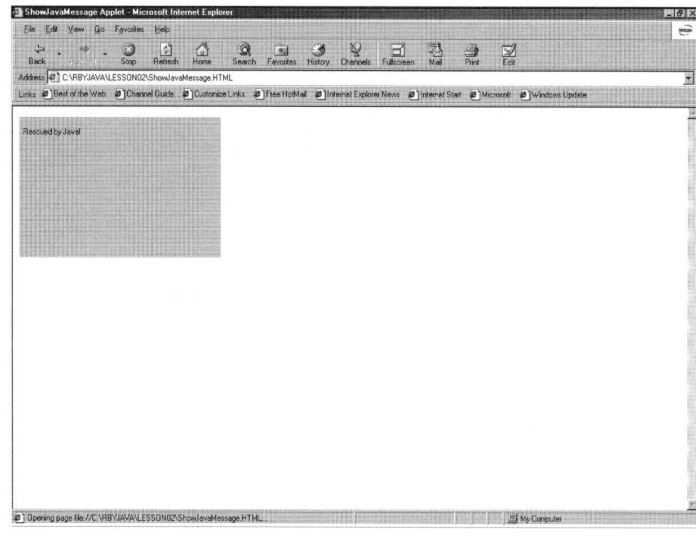

Figure 2.2 Using the applet address FILE:///C:/RBYJAVA/Lesson02/ShowJavaMessage.HTML to run the applet from your hard disk.

CHANGING YOUR APPLET

To change an applet, you must edit the applet's source file and then compile the updated source file to put your changes into effect. In this case, you will change the applet so that it displays your name, as opposed to the message text *Rescued by Java!*. To do so, use your editor to edit the source file *ShowJavaMessage.java*. Next, replace the word *Java!* that appears within the double quotes with your name, as shown here:

```
import java.awt.*;
import java.applet.*;

public class ShowJavaMessage extends Applet
    {
        public void paint(Graphics g)
          {
             g.drawString("Rescued by Kris!", 5, 25);
          }
    }
```

Save your changes to the file and exit your editor. Next, compile the source file to put your changes into effect. In this case, provided that you did not introduce any syntax errors as you made your changes, the compiler will overwrite the previous contents of the applet class file *ShowJavaMessage.class*. If you only edit your source file, but do not compile that file, the *ShowJavaMessage* applet will continue to display the *Rescued by Java!* message text and not your name.

Use the *appletviewer* or your browser to view the contents of the *ShowJavaMessage.HTML* file. You do not have to make any changes to the HTML file for it to display your updated applet. In this case, the *appletviewer* or your browser will display an applet window that contains your name.

CREATING A SECOND APPLET

To ensure that you understand the process of creating and compiling a Java applet, you will now create a second applet named *ChangeMsgFont* that changes the font the applet uses to display the *Rescued by Java!* message. Specifically, the applet displays the message using a 24-point, bold, serif font.

To start, use your editor to create the source file *ChangeMsgFont.java* that contains the following statements:

```
import java.awt.*;
import java.applet.*;

public class ChangeMsgFont extends Applet
    {
        public void paint(Graphics g)
          {
             Font font = new Font("Serif", Font.BOLD, 24);
             g.setFont(font);
             g.drawString("Rescued by Java!", 5, 25);
          }
    }
```

As before, it is not important that you understand programming statements at this point but, rather, that you type in the statements correctly. Next, use the following *javac* command to compile your applet:

```
C:\RBYJAVA\LESSON02> javac   ChangeMsgFont.java   <ENTER>
```

If your applet contains one or more syntax errors, edit your source file and correct them. Make sure you type the statements exactly as they appear here. After you successfully compile your applet, create the following HTML file, *ChangeMsgFont.HTML*, that contains these HTML entries:

```
<HTML><TITLE>ChangeMsgFont Applet</TITLE>
<APPLET  CODE="ChangeMsgFont.class"  WIDTH=300  HEIGHT=200></APPLET>
</HTML>
```

Lastly, to run the applet using the *appletviewer*, use the following command:

```
C:\RBYJAVA\LESSON02> appletviewer   ChangeMsgFont.HTML   <ENTER>
```

The *appletviewer*, in turn, will open an applet window and display the *Rescued by Java!* message using the larger font, as shown in Figure 2.3.

Figure 2.3 Displaying a larger **Rescued by Java!** *message.*

As before, you may want to edit this applet's source file and change the message the applet displays. After you make changes to the source file, you must compile the source file to put your changes into effect.

PUTTING IT ALL TOGETHER—CREATING AND RUNNING A JAVA APPLET

As you have learned, creating, compiling, and running a Java applet is quite straightforward. Regardless of your applet's processing, you will perform these steps to create, compile, and run your applet:

1. Use a text editor to type your Java program statements into a source file.
2. Use the Java compiler (*javac*) to compile the applet.
3. Create an HTML file that contains an *<APPLET>* tag that runs your applet.
4. Use a browser or the *appletviewer* to load the HTML file which will, in turn, run the applet.

16

TAKING A CYBER FIELD TRIP

Throughout this book, several of the lessons will direct you to visit Java-related sites on the Web or to run Java applets that reside at the Jamsa Press Web site at *www.jamsa.com*. In this lesson, you will visit the Gamelan Web site, one the best directories on the Web for Java-related resources. Figure 2.4 shows the Gamelan site at *www.gamelan.com*.

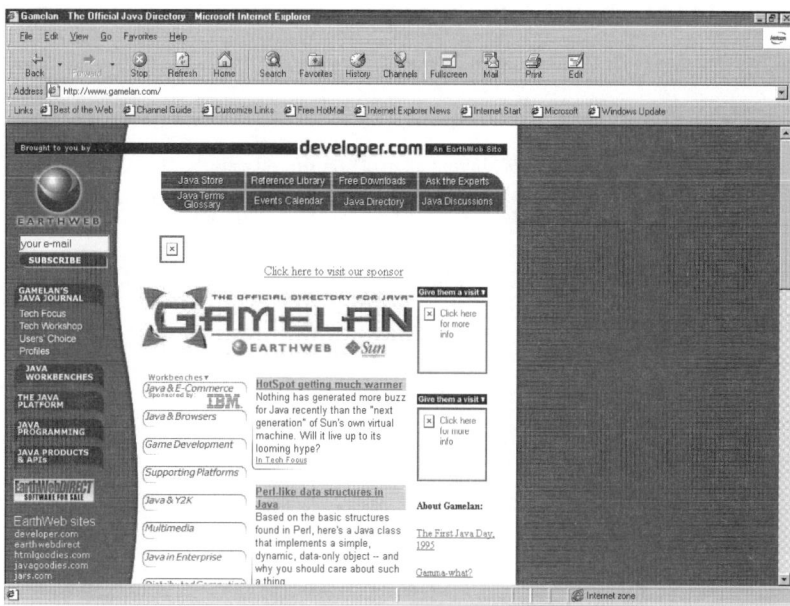

Figure 2.4 *For information on a variety of Java topics, visit the Gamelan Web site at* ***www.gamelan.com****.*

WHAT YOU MUST KNOW

In this lesson, you learned how to create a Java source file using a text editor. You learned how to compile the Java program statements into virtual-machine code that you can execute using *appletviewer* or your browser. In Lesson 3, "Taking a Look at Your Applets," you will examine the actual program statements that make up the *ShowJavaMessage* and *ChangeMsgFont* applets. Before you continue with Lesson 3, however, make sure that you have learned the following key concepts:

☑ Java applets are files, with the *class* extension, that contain the computer instructions to perform a specific task.

☑ To create a Java applet, you use the Java programming language to specify the operations that applet must perform. You place the programming-language statements within a source file.

☑ To create the source file that contains your program statements, use an editor such as the MS-DOS *EDIT* command or the Windows *Notepad* accessory.

☑ Java source files use the *java* extension, such as *ShowJavaMessage.java*.

☑ The *appletviewer* or browsers do not use your Java statements but, rather, they run a file containing ones and zeros, called the *virtual-machine code*.

☑ The Java compiler is a special program that converts your source file to virtual-machine code. You run the Java compiler from the command line, specifying the name of the source file you want to compile.

☑ If your statements violate any Java syntax rules, the Java compiler will display error messages when you compile your applet.

☑ Before the Java compiler can successfully compile your applet into virtual-machine code, you must edit your source file and correct all syntax errors.

☑ When the Java compiler successfully compiles your source file, it will create an applet file that uses the class extension. Using the *appletviewer* or your browser, you can execute the *class* file.

☑ To view a Java applet within a Web browser or the *appletviewer*, you must first place the *<APPLET>* tag for the applet within an HTML file.

☑ The Java programming language and the Java programs, such as the *appletviewer*, are case sensitive, meaning they consider uppercase and lowercase letters as different.

LESSON 3

TAKING A LOOK AT YOUR APPLETS

In Lesson 2, "Creating Your First Java Applet," you learned how to create, compile, and run your first Java applets. In this lesson, you will examine each applet's program statements. In short, Lesson 2 taught you the steps you must perform to create a Java applet. In this lesson, you will start to understand the Java programming statements that make up the applet. By the time you finish this lesson, you will understand the following key concepts:

- ◆ Java is an object-oriented programming language which lets programmers design applets in terms of the objects (things) that make up the system.

- ◆ To simplify your programming, you can take advantage of Java code that other programmers have previously written. Java stores such reusable code within class libraries, which Java programmers often refer to as *packages*.

- ◆ To use a class library within your applet, you specify the class-library name at the start of your applet using an import statement.

- ◆ As your programs increase in size, you will divide each program into smaller, more manageable pieces, which programmers call *functions*. Each function performs a specific task.

- ◆ Each of the Java applets you create will use a special function, named *paint*, that draws the applet's output to the applet window.

- ◆ Using a *Font* object, your applets can customize the font (style, attributes, and size) your applets use to display their output to the applet window.

LOOKING AT THE JAVA NOW! APPLET

In Lesson 2, you used the following statements within the source file *ShowJavaMessage.java* to display the *Rescued by Java!* message within an applet window:

```java
import java.awt.*;
import java.applet.*;

public class ShowJavaMessage extends Applet
   {
      public void paint(Graphics g)
        {
           g.drawString("Rescued by Java!", 5, 25);
        }
   }
```

As you have learned, using Java programming statements, you specify the task you want the applet to perform. Although the Java programming statements may look far from "easy to read and understand," it will not take you long before each of these statements is "old hat." The following sections will examine each of these statements in detail.

JAVA IS AN OBJECT-ORIENTED PROGRAMMING LANGUAGE

As you read books and articles about Java (as well as the lessons that appear in this book), you will learn that Java is an object-oriented programming language. Think of an object as nothing more than a "thing." When programmers design programs, they often start with the things that make up the system. For example, if you consider a school, the "things" consist of students, classes, classrooms, professors, and so on. Programmers first examine the system by trying to identify the operations these "things" perform, as well as the operations that happen to the "things."

For example, a professor object may teach, perform research, or hold office hours. Likewise, a classroom object may be empty or in use. By focusing on the "things" (objects) that make up a system, programmers can better understand and design complex systems.

Think, for a moment, about the "things" or objects users employ as they surf the Web. There is a mouse, keyboard, windows, Web sites, Web addresses, and so on. As programmers create Java applets, they must consider many of these objects. As a user runs your applet, for example, the user may type at the keyboard or move his or her mouse. Your Java applet, in turn, must know how to respond to such events. Unfortunately, the only way your applet will know how to respond to these events is if you provide Java code that tells your applet what to do if the user presses a key or clicks the mouse.

As you can imagine, the code to handle mouse and keyboard operations can become quite complex. Luckily, Java lets you take advantage of code that other Java programmers have created in the past. As you will learn, the programmers who created Java have written code that you can use in your applets to handle mouse, keyboard, and window operations, and more. To use such existing code, your applets normally specify one or more *import* statements, as discussed next.

UNDERSTANDING IMPORT STATEMENTS

In Java applets, you create objects from predefined classes. For example, the applets that you created in Lesson 2 took advantage of the *Applet* class, *Graphics* class (which controls window operations), and the *Font* class. The Java developers created each of these classes for you—which, in turn, simplifies your programming tasks.

To simplify your use of these existing classes, Java programmers store the code for each class in a special file, called a *class library* or *package*. To use a Java package within an applet, you must *import* the package into your applet. If you examine the *ShowJavaMessage* applet, for example, you will find that the applet's first two statements are *import* statements that tell the Java compiler that the applet will use the *awt* and *applet* class libraries:

```
import java.awt.*;
import java.applet.*;
```

As you examine Java applets, you will find that each starts with one or more *import* statements.

UNDERSTANDING THE IMPORT STATEMENT

As you create your applets, you will make extensive use of the code you or other programmers have previously written (often for use by other applets). To make this code easy for your applets to use, the programmers store the code within files called class libraries (or *packages*). Within your applet, you tell the Java compiler that you want to use a specific class library by specifying the class library's name using an *import* statement. Each Java applet you create will begin with one or more *import* statements, as shown here:

```
import java.awt.*;
import java.applet.*;
```

In this case, the applet uses the *awt* and *applet* class libraries. The *awt* class provides code that handles windows and graphics operations. The applet uses *awt* code, for example, to display the *Rescued by Java!* message within the applet window. Likewise, the applet uses the *applet* code to let the browser run the applet.

HOW JAVA USES CLASS LIBRARIES

As you create Java applets, you will make extensive use of Java class libraries, which contain code that other programmers have written for your use. To use these class libraries within your applets, you must use the *import* statement. In short, the *import* statement tells the Java compiler the name of a class library that contains the code you want to use. The Java compiler, in turn, will automatically include the library code your applet requires within the virtual-machine code it stores in your applet's class file. As you examine Java applets, you will find that each applet begins with one or more *import* statements.

WHERE CLASS LIBRARIES RESIDE ON YOUR SYSTEM

As you have learned, a class library is a file that contains code that you can use within your applet to perform a specific task. Depending on your system, your Java class libraries will reside in one of two locations. First, if you examine the Java directory on your disk, you may find a subdirectory named *LIB*, which is short for library. The *LIB* directory, in turn, may have subdirectories that contain the files for specific class libraries. Second, within the *LIB* directory, you may find files that use the *zip* or *jar* extensions, within which Java stores specific class libraries.

As you may know, in a Windows environment, *zip* files store data in a compressed format. Normally, you must use a special program named *WinZip* or *PKUnzip* to decompress a *zip* file into the files it contains. To reduce the amount of disk space class library files consume, early versions of the Java compiler stored class libraries within *zip* files. When you compiled an applet, the Java compiler would extract the class libraries the applet used from this *zip* file (normally named *classes.zip*) automatically, including the class library's contents within the applet's virtual-machine code.

Today, rather than using *zip* files, most Java compilers store class libraries within files that use the *jar* extension, which is short for *Java archive*. Take time now to examine your compiler's *LIB* directory.

UNDERSTANDING THE APPLET CLASS

As you examine Java applets, you will normally find a statement that includes the applet name, as shown here:

```
public class ShowJavaMessage extends Applet
```

As you have learned, when you create an applet, you must include all the program statements that define the task that applet performs. Likewise, as you have learned, Java works in terms of objects. When you create a Java applet, you actually specify program statements that extend the existing *Applet* class. The previous statement, therefore, tells the Java compiler that you are creating an applet named *ShowJavaMessage* that extends the existing *Applet* class. The *public* keyword at the start of the statement lets the Java browser (or *appletviewer*) run your applet. If you omit the *public* keyword, the browser cannot access your applet.

Next, the *class* keyword tells the compiler that you are creating a class object named *ShowJavaMessage* that extends the *Applet* class. When you extend a Java class in this way, you must specify new program statements. In this case, the applet places those statements between the left-and-right braces shown here:

```
public class ShowJavaMessage extends Applet
  {
      public void paint(Graphics g)
        {
```

21

```
        g.drawString("Rescued by Java!", 5, 25);
    }
}
```

In Java, the left and right braces ({}) are *grouping symbols*. Using these braces, for example, you can group the program statements that correspond to a class or, as you will learn, the statements that correspond to a function.

UNDERSTANDING CLASSES

Java is an object-oriented programming language, which means programmers often design their applets around "things" or objects that make up the system. To create an object, Java applets make extensive use of classes. In short, a Java class provides a template that defines the object's characteristics (the object's data and the operations the program can perform on the data). Each Java applet you create will use at least one class, which is the *Applet* class. In later lessons, you will learn how to create and use your own classes.

DIVIDING AN APPLET INTO FUNCTIONS

As you create large Java applets, you can simplify your programming by breaking the applet's statements into related pieces of code, called *functions*. For example, assume that you are creating an accounting program to handle a company's books. To create the applet, you might write one function that performs payroll processing, a second function that manages accounts payable, and a third function that manages accounts receivable. By breaking the large applet into smaller functions, you can focus your programming efforts on specific tasks. In Lesson 9, "Using Functions to Simplify Java Applets," you will examine Java functions in detail.

If you examine the statements that make up the *ShowJavaMessage* class, you will find that the class contains a function named *paint*:

```
public void paint(Graphics g)
    {
        g.drawString("Rescued by Java!", 5, 25);
    }
```

For now, simply understand that the *paint* function contains the *g.drawString* statement that displays the *Java Now!* message within the applet window. In later lessons, you will learn that each time the applet must update its window, the applet executes the statements that the *paint* function contains. In other words, each time the user moves or resizes a window, this applet will use the *paint* function to display the *Rescued by Java!* message.

KEY FEATURES OF THE SHOWJAVAMESSAGE APPLET

The previous sections have looked at different parts of the *ShowJavaMessage* applet. The discussion has briefly touched on the aspects of Java you will examine in detail in later lessons of this book (such as functions and classes). For now, however, it is important that you understand these key concepts:

- Java applets can use existing code that resides in class-library files.

- To use a Java class library within your applet, you must use an *import* statement.

- Each of the Java applets you examine will start with one or more *import* statements.

- Immediately following the *import* statements, you will find a statement that extends the *Applet* class.

- Within the *Applet* class statements, you will find one or more functions that perform specific processing.

LOOKING AT THE *CHANGEMSGFONT* APPLET

In Lesson 2, you used the following statements to implement the *ChangeMsgFont* applet, which displays the *Rescued by Java!* using a 24-point serif font:

```
import java.awt.*;
import java.applet.*;

public class ChangeMsgFont extends Applet
   {
       public void paint(Graphics g)
         {
             Font font = new Font("Serif", Font.BOLD, 24);
             g.setFont(font);
             g.drawString("Rescued by Java!", 5, 25);
         }
   }
```

As you can see, the applet starts with two *import* statements that tell the Java compiler the applet uses the *awt* and *applet* class libraries:

```
import java.awt.*;
import java.applet.*;
```

Next, the applet defines the *ChangeMsgFont* class. As you will recall, the *public* keyword lets the *appletviewer* or your browser access the class statements. As before, the left and right braces group the class statements:

```
public class ChangeMsgFont extends Applet
   {
       public void paint(Graphics g)
         {
             Font font = new Font("Serif", Font.BOLD, 24);
             g.setFont(font);
             g.drawString("Rescued by Java!", 5, 25);
         }
   }
```

Like the *ShowJavaMessage* applet, the *ChangeMsgFont* applet uses the *paint* function to redraw the applet window's contents. As before, each time the applet must update the applet window, it uses the statements that reside in the *paint* function. In this case, the *paint* function creates a *Font* object that corresponds to a 24-point, bold, serif font. The *paint* function uses the *setFont* function to select the font, and the *drawString* function to display the *Rescued by Java!* message. In Lesson 14, "Controlling Fonts within Java Applets," you will examine Java's font capabilities in detail.

TAKING A CYBER FIELD TRIP

In Lesson 1, "Introducing Java," you visited Sun Microsystem's Java Web site to download the Java Development Kit. In this lesson, you will view the Java documentation at Microsoft, which you can view at *www.microsoft.com/java* as shown in Figure 3. From within the Microsoft Web site you can view documentation on the latest Java products from Microsoft. In addition, you can download Microsoft's Java Software Development Kit.

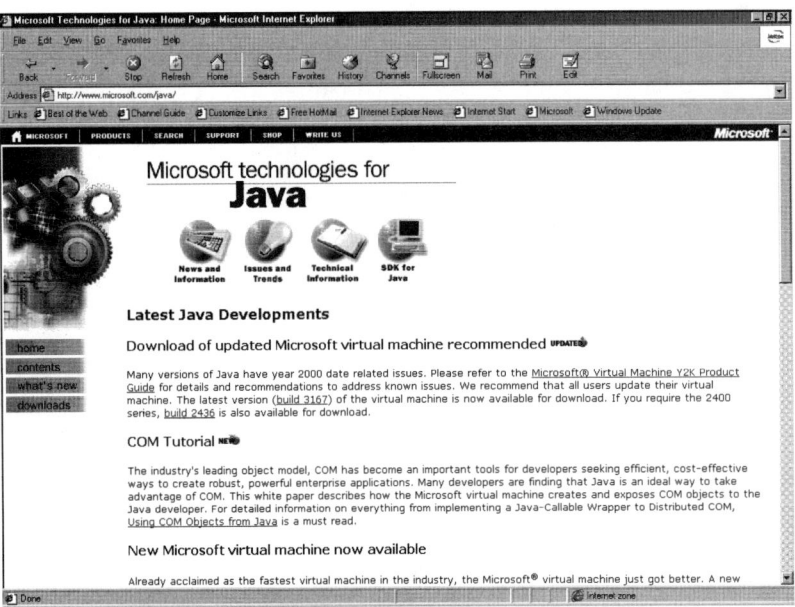

Figure 3 *Viewing information on Java at the Microsoft Web site.*

WHAT YOU MUST KNOW

In this lesson, you examined the statements that make up the *JavaNow* and the *JavaNowFont* applets that you created in Lesson 2. As you have learned, Java applets follow a similar pattern, starting with one or more *import* statements followed by statements that define the *Applet* class.

Throughout this book, we have used the term applet to describe the statements that the *appletviewer* or your browser executes. In Lesson 4, "Java Applets Versus Standalone Programs," you will learn that by using Java, you can create standalone programs that, unlike applets, do not run within the *appletviewer* or your browser. By creating such standalone programs, programmers can use Java to create programs that in the past would have required you to use a programming language, such as C++. Before you continue with Lesson 4, however, make sure that you have learned the following key concepts:

- ☑ Object-oriented programming languages, such as Java, let programmers design applets in terms of the objects (things) that make up the system.

- ☑ By using Java code that other programmers have previously written (class libraries), you can simplify your programming tasks.

- ☑ By using an *import* statement at the start of your applet, you can use a class library.

- ☑ To simplify difficult programming tasks, programmers often divide the program into smaller, more manageable pieces, called functions. Each function performs a specific task.

- ☑ Each of the Java applets you create will use a special function named *paint*, which draws the applet's output to the applet window.

- ☑ To customize the font (style, attributes, and size) your applet uses to display its output to the applet window, your applets use a *Font* object.

LESSON 4
JAVA APPLETS VERSUS STANDALONE PROGRAMS

As you have learned, a Java applet is a small application that you run within the *appletviewer,* or from within a browser, such as Netscape *Navigator* or Microsoft *Internet Explorer.* Most of the applications you create using Java will be applets. However, depending on your application's requirements, there may be times when you will create standalone Java programs—which you run outside of the *appletviewer* or a browser. In this lesson, you will learn how to create standalone Java programs. If you are familiar with the C or C++ programming languages, Java standalone programs will look quite familiar. If you are not familiar with C/C++, do not worry. By the time you finish this lesson, you will understand the following key concepts:

- ◆ Using Java, you can create applets as well as standalone programs.

- ◆ Unlike a Java applet, you cannot run a standalone program within a browser or the *appletviewer.*

- ◆ To run a standalone program, you use the Java interpreter. Depending on the Java compiler you are using, the program name for the Java interpreter will differ. The Sun Java Development Kit names the interpreter program *java.*

- ◆ Standalone Java programs provide capabilities that applets cannot perform, such as the ability to write to a file on disk.

- ◆ The Java interpreter is a special program that converts Java's virtual code into processor-specific (such as Intel or Motorola-specific) binary instructions.

UNDERSTANDING STANDALONE PROGRAMS

As you have learned, Java applets run within the *appletviewer* or a browser. Although the term "standalone program" implies a program that runs on its own, that is not the case for Java programs. Instead, to run a Java program, you use a special program—the Java interpreter. Depending on the compiler you are using, the interpreter's program name may differ. The examples this lesson presents use the *java* interpreter that comes with Sun's Java Development Kit.

To better understand Java programs, create the source file *HelloJava.java*, which contains the following program statements:

```
class HelloJava
   {
     public static void main(String args[])
       {
          System.out.println("Hello, Java!");
       }
   }
```

In this case, the program simply displays the message *Hello, Java!* on your screen display, as opposed to displaying the message within an applet window. To start, you must compile the program by using the Java compiler, just as you did in the previous lesson:

```
C:\RBYJAVA\LESSON04> javac  HelloJava.java  <ENTER>
```

As before, the Java compiler will create a class file that, in this case, is named *HelloJava.class*. By performing a directory listing of the files on your disk, you can display the file's directory entry, as shown here:

```
C:\RBYJAVA\LESSON04> DIR    <ENTER>


 Volume in drive D has no label
 Volume Serial Number is 3142-1BEF
 Directory of D:\RBYJAVA\Lesson04


.                  <DIR>           04-16-99   2:32p .
..                 <DIR>           04-16-99   2:32p ..
HELLOJ~1 CLA           424         04-16-99   2:49p HelloJava.class
HELLOJ~1 JAV           136         04-16-99   2:49p HelloJava.java
         2 file(s)              560 bytes
         2 dir(s)     1,375,514,624 bytes free
```

To run your standalone Java program, use the *java* command, as shown here:

```
C:\RBYJAVA\LESSON04> java   HelloJava   <ENTER>
Hello, Java!
```

The only way you can run the standalone program is to use the Java interpreter in this way. As before, take time to edit the source file to change the program so it displays the message *Rescued by Java,* or a Hello message to your name.

YOU CANNOT BROWSE STANDALONE PROGRAMS

As you have learned, the only way you can run a standalone Java program is to use the Java interpreter. If you create an HTML page with an *<APPLET>* tag for the standalone program, you will find that neither the *appletviewer* nor your browser can run the program. The only way you can run a standalone program is to use the Java interpreter.

WHY STANDALONE JAVA PROGRAMS EXIST

You may be wondering why you would ever create a standalone Java program if users cannot browse the program. The answer lies in flexibility. There are things you can do within a Java standalone program that you cannot do within an applet. Here is why.

One of the major concerns users must have when they download programs from the Web is computer viruses. As you may know, a computer virus is a program that attaches itself to other programs. When you use the Web to download text and graphics, you do not have to worry about viruses—the only way a virus can enter your system is for the virus to attach itself to another program. A virus cannot attach itself to a graphics or text-based HTML file. Should you download programs from the Web, you must be extremely careful to make sure you do not download an infected program.

Should you download and run a program that is infected with a virus, you may unknowingly run the virus itself. Depending on the virus, it may display a message on your screen and freeze your system, forcing you to reboot, or the virus may destroy information that is stored on your disk. Your best defense against computer viruses is simply not to download programs. If, however, you do choose to download programs, make sure you use virus-detection software to examine the programs you download.

When the Java developers first discussed the ability for a browser to download and run a program, one of the first obstacles they faced was how to prevent computer viruses. One way Java reduces the threat of a computer virus is by preventing applets from writing to your disk. By not allowing an applet to write to your disk, an applet cannot attach a virus to files on your system or damage your disk in any way.

When you create a standalone program, on the other hand, you have fewer restrictions. That is because, as you have learned, standalone programs will not run within a browser. Therefore, users who are surfing the Web cannot unknowingly download and run a standalone program within their browsers.

Keep in mind that Java is an object-oriented programming language, much like C++. Ideally, you should be able to use Java to write a wide variety of programs. In this way, you do not have to use Java only for Web-based applets, and then use VisualBasic or Visual C++ to develop your standalone programs. Rather, you can use Java to create both.

LOOKING AT A SECOND EXAMPLE

To ensure that you fully understand the process of creating standalone Java programs, create the source file, *BeepJP.java*, that contains the following statements:

```java
class BeepJP
  {
    public static void main(String args[])
      {
        System.out.println("\007\007\007Visit Jamsa Press on the Web " +
                           "at http://www.jamsa.com");
      }
  }
```

In this case, when you run the program, your computer will beep its built-in speaker three times before displaying the message text, *Visit Jamsa Press on the Web at http://www.jamsa.com*. To compile this program, use the Java compiler, as shown here:

```
C:\RBYJAVA\LESSON04> javac  BeepJP.java  <ENTER>
```

Next, to run the program, use the Java interpreter, as shown here:

```
C:\RBYJAVA\LESSON04> java  BeepJP  <Enter>
Visit Jamsa Press on the Web at http://www.jamsa.com
```

EXAMINING THE PROGRAM STATEMENTS

If you examine the program statements for the *HelloJava* and *BeepJP* programs, you will find neither program uses *import* statements. As you have learned, you use the *import* statement to load Java class libraries. As you create standalone programs, there will be times when you will import one or more Java class libraries. In this case, both programs are so simple that they do not need class libraries.

Like the applets you created in the previous lessons, the standalone programs start by defining a class. However, unlike Java applets that extend the *Applet* class, the standalone programs do not extend the *Applet* class:

```java
class BeepJP
```

In the previous applets, you used the *paint* function to display a message within an applet window. In these standalone applets, you display the program's output to the screen by using the *System.out.println* function:

```java
System.out.println("\007\007\007Visit Jamsa Press on the Web" +
                   " at http://www.jamsa.com");
```

In this case, to avoid line wrapping with the source code, the program broke the one large character string into two strings, using the *plus* operator to append the second string's contents to the first. The characters \007 are a special escape code that sounds the computer's built-in speaker.

UNDERSTANDING INTERPRETERS

As you know, computers perform their processing based on combinations of ones and zeros (binary codes). When you write a program using a programming language such as Visual Basic or Visual C++, the compiler creates binary instructions that are specific to the Intel processor (the PC's electronic brain). If, for example, you wanted to run a program that you created on a PC under Windows on a Mac system, you must compile the program by using a Mac-specific compiler on the Mac system. The Mac-based compiler, in turn, would create its binary instructions specific to the Motorola processor. In short, the binary instructions for an Intel processor are not compatible with those of a Motorola processor. When you compile a Java program, on the other hand, Java does not create binary code that is specific to a processor. Instead, Java creates a *virtual code* that is neither Intel nor Mac.

To run a program's virtual code, you use a browser, the *appletviewer*, or the Java interpreter to run the program. The interpreter does just that—it interprets the virtual code and converts it into binary instructions specific to an Intel, Motorola, or Risc-based processor. The reason Java uses virtual code is because at a Web site, you often do not know if a user who is surfing your site is using Windows 98, a Mac, or some other system. With Java applets, users simply download the virtual code and their browser interprets it. In this way, programmers have to create only one applet which, in turn, all systems can run.

Although the virtual code makes Java very flexible, in that programmer's do not have to worry about writing Mac or Intel-specific code, the virtual code is not without cost. Because the interpreter must examine the code and then convert it to another format (such as Intel machine-code), the process of running a Java applet is much slower than running an executable program that was compiled to a specific processor's machine code. In fact, if you currently place an identical C++ program side-by-side with a Java applet, the C++ program will outperform the Java applet by far. In the future, therefore, you may see Java move away from the virtual code, and instead create processor-specific code that can better compete with the performance of other programming languages.

CREATING A STANDALONE JAVA PROGRAM THAT USES THE ABSTRACT WINDOWING TOOLKIT

In this lesson, you created simple standalone programs that you ran from the command prompt and which displayed their output in a text format. In later lessons, you will learn that Java makes it easy for your programs to display windows, dialog boxes, buttons, and similar objects. As you will learn, using Java you can create standalone programs that use these objects. In addition, depending on your Java compiler, you can also use many Windows-based functions to create a standalone Windows-based executable program, just as you would using programming languages such as Visual C++ and Visual Basic.

TAKING A CYBER FIELD TRIP

Across the Web, programmers make extensive use of Java to create applets. The Java Development Kit, for example, includes an applet named *Animator* which, as shown in Figure 4, shuffles a pile of coffee beans into the letters *Java*. To run the *Animator* applet or to download the applet's source code, visit the Jamsa Press Web site at *www.jamsa.com/ java_demos/animator.html.*

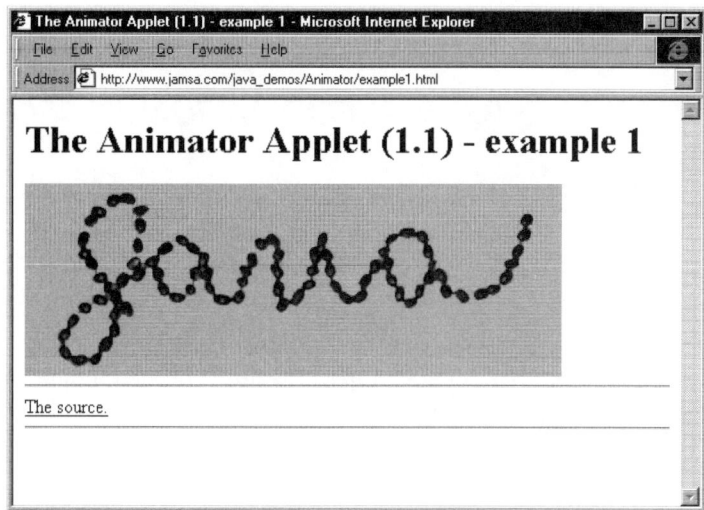

Figure 4 The Animator applet provided with the Java Development Kit.

WHAT YOU MUST KNOW

In this lesson, you learned that Java lets you create standalone programs that users cannot run within a browser or the *appletviewer*. Although all of the Java programs that you create throughout the remainder of this book will be applets (as opposed to standalone programs), it is important that you understand that Java standalone programs give you capabilities applets cannot perform, such as writing to a file on disk. In Lesson 5, "Java Applets Store Information in Variables," you will learn how to use variables within your applets to store information as your applets execute. Before you continue with Lesson 5, however, make sure that you have learned the following key concepts:

☑ The Java compiler lets you create applets as well as standalone programs.

☑ You run a Java applet within a browser or the *appletviewer*.

☑ You cannot run a standalone program within a browser or the *appletviewer*. Instead, to run a standalone program, you use the Java interpreter.

☑ By creating a standalone Java program, as opposed to an applet, you get capabilities such as the ability to write to a file on disk.

☑ The Java interpreter is a special program that converts Java's virtual code into processor-specific (such as Intel or Motorola-specific) binary instructions.

LESSON 5

JAVA APPLETS STORE INFORMATION IN VARIABLES

As your Java applets begin to perform meaningful work, the applets must store information while they execute. For example, an applet that displays images within the applet window needs to know each file's name, as well as the x-and-y window coordinates at which you want to display the images. As they execute, Java applets store such information in your computer's memory. To use specific memory locations, the applets use *variables*. In the simplest sense, a variable is the name of a memory location that can store a specific value. This lesson examines how you create and use variables within your Java applets. By the end of this lesson, you will understand the following key concepts:

◆ Within your applet, you must declare a variable by telling the Java compiler the variable's name and type.

◆ A variable's *type* specifies the kind of value (such as a whole or floating-point number or a string of characters) the variable can store, as well as the operations the applet can perform on the variable.

◆ To assign a value to a variable, you use the Java *assignment operator* (the equal sign).

◆ When you declare variables, use meaningful names to make your applets easier for other programmers to read and understand.

◆ Within your applets, you should place comments that describe the applet's operation to other programmers. In this way, if another programmer must change your applet, your comments describe your applet's operations in detail.

When you assign a value to a variable, think of the variable as a box into which you can place a value. When you later must use the variable's value, the computer simply looks at the value the box contains.

DECLARING VARIABLES WITHIN YOUR JAVA APPLETS

Java applets use variables to store information. Depending on the kind of value you want to store, such as a whole number, letter of the alphabet, or floating-point value, the variable's *type* will differ. In short, a variable's type specifies the kind (type) of value the variable can store, as well as the set of operations (such as addition, multiplication, and so on) the applet can perform on the variable's value. Most Java applets will use the variable types listed in Table 5.1.

Type	Values Stored
boolean	True or false values
byte	Values in the range -128 through 127
char	Alphanumeric (letters, numbers, and symbols) characters based on 16-bit Unicode characters
double	Values in the range -1.7×10^{-308} through 1.7×10^{308}
float	Values in the range -3.4×10^{-38} through 3.4×10^{38}
int	Values in the range $-2,147,483,648$ through $2,147,483,647$
long	Values in the range $-9,223,372,036,854,775,808$ through $9,223,372,036,854,775,807$
short	Values in the range -32,768 through 32,767

Table 5.1 Common Java variable types.

Before you can use a variable, your applet must *declare* the variable. In other words, you must introduce the variable to the Java compiler. To declare a variable in your applet, you must specify the variable's type and the name your applet will use to refer to the variable. Following the opening brace of your applet class, you specify the variable type and name, as shown here:

```
variable_type   variable_name;
```

Normally, the variable's type will be one of the types listed in Table 5.1. The variable name is a meaningful name you choose that describes (to someone reading your applet) the variable's use. For example, your applet might use variables such as *image_name*, *image_size*, and so on. Note the semicolon that follows the variable name. Java considers a variable's declaration a statement. Therefore, you must place a semicolon at the end of the declaration.

The following Java statements declare three variables using the types *int*, *float*, and *long*:

```
import java.applet.*;

public class Variables extends Applet
  {
    int test_score;
    float salary;
    long distance_to_the_moon;
  }
```

It is important to note that these statements do not do anything but declare the variables. If you were to compile and execute this applet, the *appletviewer* would simply display an empty window. As you can see, each variable declaration ends with a semicolon. However, when you declare more than one variable of the same type, Java lets you separate the variable names using a comma between names. The following statement, for example, declares three variables of type *int*:

```
int image_file_size, sound_file_size, user_age;
```

UNDERSTANDING VARIABLES

A variable is the name of a storage location in your computer's memory. During execution, your applet stores information in variables. When you create your applet, you must declare variables by telling the Java compiler the variable's name and type. The following statement, for example, declares a variable named *user_count* of type *int*:

```
int user_count;
```

USE MEANINGFUL VARIABLE NAMES

Each variable you create in your applet must have a unique name. To make your applets easier to read and understand, you should use meaningful variable names. For example, the following statement declares three variables named *x*, *y*, and *z*:

```
int x, y, z;
```

The following variable names are much more meaningful to another programmer who is reading your source code:

```
int image_file_size, sound_file_size, user_age;
```

When you select variable names, you can use a combination of letters, numbers, and underscores (_). The first character of your variable names must be a letter, underscore, or dollar sign. You cannot begin a variable name with a number. Also, the Java compiler considers upper and lowercase letters to be different. As you get started, you might only use lowercase letters within your variable names. As you become more comfortable with Java, you might combine upper and lowercase letters to produce a meaningful name, as shown here:

```
int ImageFileSize, SoundFileSize;
```

In this case, by placing an uppercase letter at key locations throughout the variable name (at the start of each component), the variable name becomes quite easy to read.

JAVA KEYWORDS YOU CANNOT USE FOR VARIABLE NAMES

As you assign variable names, you must know that Java reserves the *keywords,* listed in Table 5.2, that have special meaning to the compiler. You cannot use a Java keyword for a variable name.

abstract	boolean	break	byte	case	catch	char
class	const	continue	default	do	double	else
extends	final	finally	float	for	goto	if
implements	import	instanceof	int	interface	long	native
new	null	package	private	protected	public	return
short	static	super	switch	synchronized	this	throw
throws	transient	try	void	volatile	while	

Table 5.2 Java keywords you cannot use for variable names.

WHY YOUR APPLETS USE VARIABLES

As your applets become more complex, they may perform operations on many different items. For example, if you are writing an applet that displays information about each of your company's products, the applet must process information for each product. In such an applet, you might use variables named *ProductName, ProductId, ProductCost,* and so on. As your applet starts, it will assign information about the first product to these variables. After your applet performs its processing for the first product, it will repeat the process for the next product. To process the second product, the applet will assign that product's information (name, id, and price) to the variables just discussed, and then the applet will perform its processing. In other words, as the applet executes, it assigns different values to the variables which, in turn, change or vary the variables' value.

ASSIGNING A VALUE TO A VARIABLE

As you have read, variables store values as your applet executes. After you declare a variable, you use the Java *assignment operator* (the equal sign) to assign a value to a variable. The following statements assign values to several different variables. Note the use of the semicolon to end each statement:

```
user_age = 32;
user_salary = 25000.75;
distance_to_the_moon = 238857;
```

Note: *The values assigned to the variables do not contain commas (such as 25,000.75 and 238,857). If you include the commas, the Java compiler will generate and display syntax error messages.*

The following Java statements declare the variables just described, and then use the assignment operator to assign values to the variables:

```
import java.applet.*;

public class Variables extends Applet
  {
    int age;
    float salary;
    long distance_to_the_moon;


    age = 35;
    salary = 25000.75;
    distance_to_the_moon = 238857;
  }
```

Again, these statements simply declare and initialize variables. If you compile and run this applet, your browser or the *appletviewer* will display an empty window.

ASSIGNING A VALUE AT DECLARATION

When you declare a variable, it is often convenient to assign the variable's starting value. To make it easy for you to do so, Java lets you assign values when you declare variables, as shown here:

```
int user_age = 32;
float user_salary = 25000.75;
long distance_to_the_moon = 238857;
```

Many of the applets this book presents will assign values to variables at declaration.

ASSIGNING VALUES TO A VARIABLE

Variables store information during an applet's execution. To store a value within a variable, your applets must use the Java assignment operator (the equal sign). The following statement uses the assignment operator to assign the value 5 to the variable *lesson*:

```
lesson = 5;
```

To simplify the assignment of values to variables, Java also lets you assign a value to a variable when you declare the variable, as shown here:

```
int lesson = 5;
```

USING A VARIABLE'S VALUE

After you assign a value to a variable, your applets can use the variable's value simply by referring to the variable's name. The following applet, *ShowVariables.java*, assigns values to three variables and then displays each variable's value by using the *drawString* function:

```
import java.awt.*;
import java.applet.*;

public class ShowVariables extends Applet
  {
    int age = 35;
    double salary = 25000.75;
    long distance_to_the_moon = 238857;

    public void paint(Graphics g)
     {
       g.drawString("Employee age: " + age, 5, 25);
       g.drawString("Employee salary: " + salary, 5, 45);
       g.drawString("Distance to the moon: " + distance_to_the_moon, 5, 65);
     }
  }
```

As you can see, to use the variable's value, you simply refer to the variable's name within your applet. In this case, the applet declares and initializes the three variables following the brace that opens the class definition. Within the *paint* function, the applet displays each variable's value by using the *drawString* function. If you examine the *drawString* function calls, you will find that the first value the applet passes to the function is contained within double quotes. The *drawString* function will display each of the letters contained within the quotes. Next, the function will display the value of the variable that follows the plus sign. In Lesson 15, "Using Java Strings,"

you will learn why you must use the plus sign following the string of characters that appear within the double quotes. As you will recall, the last two values the applet passes to the function specify the x-and-y window coordinates at which the applet displays the message.

To start, if you are using the Java Development Kit, you can compile this applet by using the *javac* compiler, as shown here:

```
C:\> javac ShowVariables.java   <ENTER>
```

Next, create the HTML file, *ShowVariables.HTML*, with these entries:

```
<HTML><TITLE>Show Variables Applet</TITLE>
<APPLET CODE="ShowVariables.class" WIDTH=300 HEIGHT=200></APPLET></HTML>
```

Using the *appletviewer*, display the applet's output, as shown in Figure 5.1.

After you successfully run the *ShowVariables* applet, use your editor to assign different values to the applet's variables. Then, use your Java compiler to compile your changes. When you later run the applet, your browser or the *appletviewer* will display values you assigned to the variables.

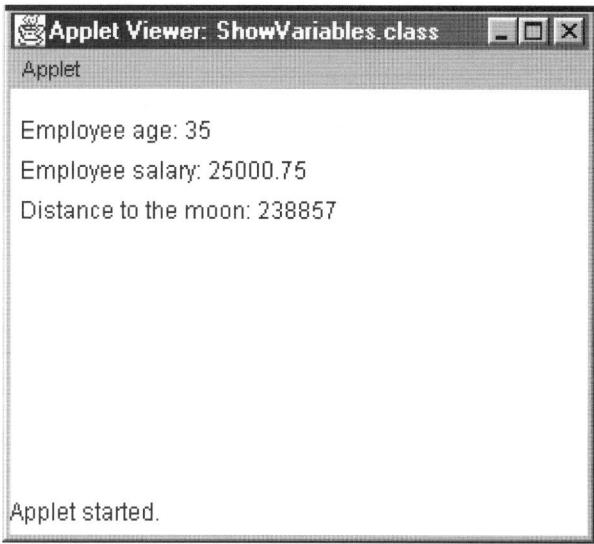

Figure 5.1 Displaying the value of variables within an applet window.

EXCEEDING A VARIABLE'S STORAGE CAPACITY

As you have learned, a variable's type defines the set of values the variable can store. For example, a variable of type *int* can store values in the range –2,147,483,648 through 2,147,483,647. When you assign a value to a variable that is outside of this range, an *overflow* error will occur. For example, the following applet, *OverflowError.java*, illustrates how exceeding a variable's range of values will result in an error. As you can see, the applet assigns values that fall outside of each type's range of values:

```
import java.awt.*;
import java.applet.*;

public class OverflowError extends Applet
  {
    int positive = 1500000000 + 1500000000;
    int negative = -2000000000 - 2000000000;

    public void paint(Graphics g)
      {
        g.drawString("positive contains: " + positive, 5, 25);
        g.drawString("negative contains: " + negative, 5, 45);
      }
  }
```

As before, use the Java compiler to compile this applet. Next, create the following HTML file, *OverflowError.HTML*:

```
<HTML><TITLE>Overflow Error Applet</TITLE>
<APPLET CODE="OverflowError.class" WIDTH=300 HEIGHT=200></APPLET></HTML>
```

When you run the applet by using the *appletviewer*, the applet window will display values for each variable that does not match the values the applet assigned, as shown in Figure 5.2.

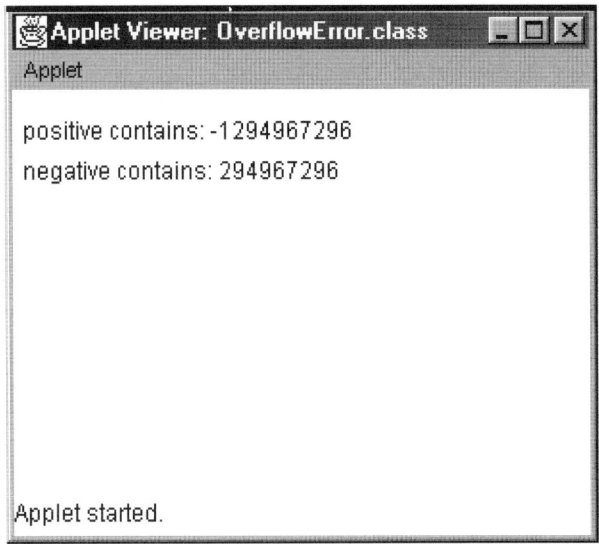

Figure 5.2 Overflow errors are subtle and hard to detect.

As you can see, the *OverflowError* applet assigns values to two variables of type *int* that exceed each type's storage range—producing an overflow error. In the first case, adding the two large positive values results in a negative value. Likewise, subtracting a large value from a negative value results in overflow, which produces a positive result. As you work with variables, you must keep in mind the range of values the variable's type can store. Overflow errors are subtle and can be difficult to detect and correct.

UNDERSTANDING PRECISION

In the previous section, you learned that overflow errors occur when you assign a value to a variable that falls outside of the range of values the variable's type can store. In a similar way, you also must understand that computers do not have unlimited *precision* when they store numbers. For example, when you work with floating-point numbers (values that have a decimal point), there are times when the computer cannot represent the number in its exact format. Such precision errors can be difficult to detect within your applets.

The following applet, *ShowPrecision.java*, assigns a value less than 0.5 to variables of type *float* and *double*. Unfortunately, because the computer has a limited ability to represent numbers, the applet's variables do not actually contain the value assigned but, rather, the value 0.5:

```
import java.awt.*;
import java.applet.*;

public class ShowPrecision extends Applet
  {
    double dbl_not_half = 0.499999990;

    public void paint(Graphics g)
      {
        g.drawString("Double 0.499999990 contains: " + dbl_not_half, 5, 45);
      }
  }
```

As before, compile the applet by using the Java compiler. Next, create the HTML file, *ShowPrecision.HTML,* that contains the following entries:

```
<HTML><TITLE>Show Precision Applet</TITLE>
<APPLET CODE="ShowPrecision.class" WIDTH=300 HEIGHT=200></APPLET></HTML>
```

When you run the applet by using the *appletviewer*, your screen will display an applet window similar to that shown in Figure. 5.3.

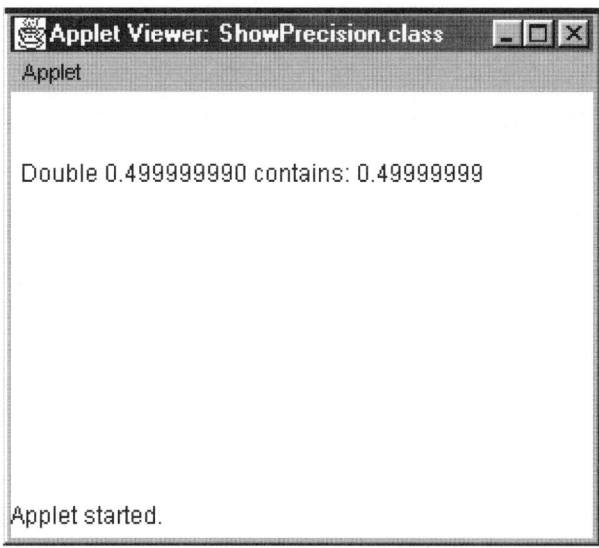

Figure 5.3 *Precision errors prevent your applets from representing numbers exactly.*

As you can see, the values the applet assigns to the variables and the values the variables actually contain are not exactly the same. Such precision errors occur because the computer must represent numbers using a fixed number of ones and zeros. In many cases, the computer can represent numbers exactly. At other times, as shown in this applet, the computer's representation of a number is close, but not exact.

As you create Java applets, you must keep precision in mind. Depending on the values with which your applets are working, precision errors may arise that are difficult to detect.

USE COMMENTS TO IMPROVE YOUR APPLET'S READABILITY

As your applets become more complex, the number of statements they contain may make the applets difficult for other programmers to understand. Because such programmers may eventually have to understand and possibly change your applets, you must write your applets in the most readable manner possible. Ways you can increase your applet's readability include:

- Use meaningful variable names that describe the variable's use

- Maintain proper statement indentation and alignment (see Lesson 6, "Simple Math Operations in Java Applets")

- Use blank lines to separate unrelated statements

- Use comments that explain the applet's processing

As you create applets, you can place notes within your source file that explain the applet's processing. Such notes (called *comments*) not only help other programmers understand your applet, they might help you remember, after you have not looked at the applet for several months, why your applet uses specific statements. The most common way to place a comment within your Java applet is simply to place two forward slashes (//) within your applet statements, as shown here:

```
// This is a comment
```

When the Java compiler encounters the double slashes, the compiler ignores all text remaining on that line. At a minimum, you should place comments at the start of each applet that specify who wrote the applet, when, and why:

```
// Applet: BackgroundMusic.java
// Programmer: Kris Jamsa
// Date Written: 4-15-99
//
// Purpose: Plays background music as the user views a Web page.
```

As your applet performs different processing, you should place comments next to specific statements that explain their purpose. For example, consider the following assignment statement:

```
distance_to_the_moon = 238857;    // Distance in miles
```

The comment to the right of the assignment statement provides additional information to someone reading your applet. New programmers often have difficulty determining when and on what to comment. As a rule, *you cannot have too many comments in your applets*. However, make sure your comments are meaningful. The following comments provide no additional information to a programmer who is reading your code:

```
user_age = 35;              // Assign 35 to the variable user_age
user_salary = 25000.75;     // Assign 25000.75 to the variable user_salary
```

Your goal when using comments is to explain why specific processing occurs.

ADDING COMMENTS TO YOUR APPLETS

As you create your applets, include comments that explain the applet's processing. Should other programmers have to change your applet, they can use your comments to understand your applet's behavior. Java applets normally use the double slashes to indicate a comment:

```
// This is a Java comment
```

When the Java compiler encounters the double slashes, the compiler will ignore all text remaining on the current line that follows the slashes. Good Java applets should be easy to read and understand. Comments and meaningful variable names increase your applet's readability.

Note: In addition to using comments to improve your applet's readability, you should use blank lines to separate unrelated applet statements. When the Java compiler encounters a blank line, the compiler simply skips the line.

OTHER COMMENT FORMATS

As you examine Java applets, you may encounter two other forms of comments. First, you may find comments grouped within forward slashes and asterisks, as shown here:

```
/* This too, is a Java comment */
```

In this case, the asterisk and slash open and close the comment. Java programmers often use this comment format when their comment spans several lines, as shown here:

```
/* Applet: BackgroundMusic.java
   Programmer: Kris Jamsa
   Date Written: 4-15-99

   Purpose: Plays background music as the user views a Web page.  */
```

In this case, after the Java compiler encounters the opening slash and asterisk (/*), the compiler will ignore all of the text that follows (regardless of the number of lines) until it encounters the ending asterisk and slash (*/). Programmers often use this form of comment to "comment out" specific code while they are testing. When the compiler encounters the opening slash and asterisk, the compiler will ignore everything else (code or comments) up to and including the closing asterisk and slash.

Also, you may encounter comments that start with a slash and two asterisks (/**):

```
/** This is a comment */
```

Programmers use this form of comment with the *Javadoc* program to automate the process of documenting their code. As a rule, you should pick one form of comments and stick to it throughout your applet. In most cases, you should use the double slashes (//) for your comments because they only effect one line of code at a time and are easy for other programmers to recognize.

TAKING A CYBER FIELD TRIP

In Lesson 18, "Creating Simple Graphics," you will learn how to draw a variety of shapes, such as circles, squares, and ellipses. As you will learn, using Java's graphics library, you can draw or fill these shapes. To help you get started, the Java Development Kit provides the *ArcTest* applet, which as shown in Figure 5.4, you can use to draw empty or filled arcs. To use the *ArcTest* applet, you simply specify the arc's starting and ending angles and then click your mouse on the Draw or Fill button. To run the applet or to download the applet's source code, visit the Jamsa Press Web site at *www.jamsa.com/java_demos/ArcTest.html*.

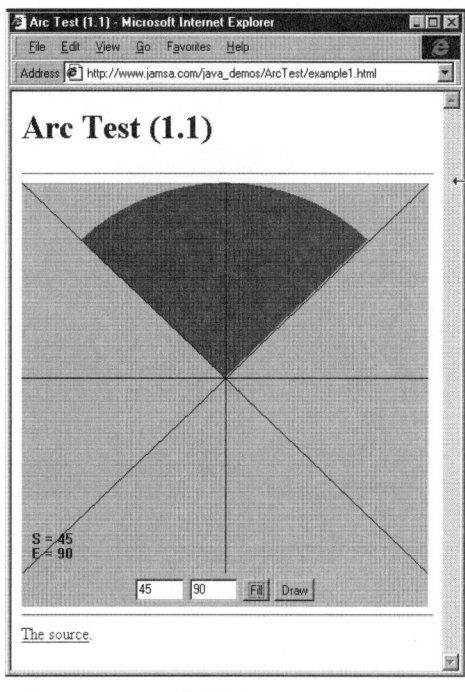

Figure 5.4 *Using the ArcTest applet to draw empty and filled arcs.*

39

WHAT YOU MUST KNOW

In this lesson, you learned that applets store information in variables as they execute. In short, a variable is a name your applets assign to a memory location within which an applet stores information. Before your applets can use a variable, you must declare the variable's name and type. In Lesson 6, "Simple Math Operations in Java Applets," you will learn how to perform simple operations, such as addition and subtraction, on variables. Before you continue with Lesson 6, however, make sure you have learned the following key concepts:

☑ To use variables within your applet, you must declare each variable's type and name.

☑ Within an applet, variable names must be unique and should be meaningful to another programmer who reads your source code. A variable's name should correspond to the variable's purpose.

☑ Variable names must start with a letter, underscore, or dollar sign.

☑ The Java compiler considers upper and lowercase letters within variable names to be different.

☑ A variable's type determines the type of value a variable can hold. Common variable types include *char*, *int*, *float*, and *long*.

☑ Comments improve your applet's readability by explaining the applet's processing. Java applets often represent comments by using double slashes (*//*).

LESSON 6

SIMPLE MATH OPERATIONS IN JAVA APPLETS

In Lesson 5, "Java Applets Store Information in Variables," you learned how to declare and use variables within your applets. As your applets become more complex, they will perform arithmetic operations such as addition, subtraction, multiplication, and division on the values your variables contain. This lesson examines how you use Java arithmetic operators to perform these operations. By the time you finish this lesson, you will understand the following key concepts:

◆ To perform mathematical operations within your applets, you use the Java arithmetic operators.

◆ To ensure Java evaluates arithmetic operations in a consistent manner, Java assigns a precedence to each operator.

◆ Using parentheses within your arithmetic expressions, you can control the order in which Java performs each operation.

◆ Many Java applets add or subtract the value one from variables by using the Java increment (++) and decrement (--) operators.

After you learn to recognize the different Java arithmetic operators, you will find that performing math operations within a Java applet is very easy.

BASIC MATH OPERATIONS

Regardless of your applet's purpose, most Java applets will add, subtract, multiply, or divide values. As you will learn, your applets can perform arithmetic operations on constants (such as 3 * 5) or on variables (such as *payment - total*). Table 6.1 lists the Java basic math operators:

Operator	Purpose	Example
+	Addition	TotalPrice = Cost + Tax;
-	Subtraction	CustomerChange = Payment - TotalPrice;
*	Multiplication	Tax = Cost * TaxRate;
/	Division	Average = Total / Count;

Table 6.1 The Java basic math operators.

The following applet, *ShowMathOperations.java*, uses the *drawString* function to display the result of several simple arithmetic operations:

```
import java.awt.*;
import java.applet.*;

public class ShowMathOperations extends Applet
  {
    public void paint(Graphics g)
      {
```

```
        g.drawString("5 + 7 = " + (5 + 7), 5, 25);
        g.drawString("12 - 7 = " + (12 - 7), 5, 40);
        g.drawString("1.2345 * 2 = " + (1.2345 * 2), 5, 55);
        g.drawString("15 / 3 = " + (15 / 3), 5, 70);
    }
}
```

Take a close look at the applet statements. Note that each expression first appears within quotes, which causes the applet to output the characters (such as 5 + 7 =) with the applet window. You could, for example, replace the characters "12 – 7 = " with the text "The answer is ".

Next, the statement performs each arithmetic operation within parentheses (such as 5 + 7). As you have seen, to display a numeric value with a text string by using the *drawString* function, you use the plus operator, as shown here:

```
g.drawString("This is lesson:" + 5, 10, 25);
```

Based on how you are using the plus operator, the Java compiler determines if you are appending a value to a string or adding two numbers.

After you compile this applet, create the following HTML file, *ShowMathOperations.HTML,* which contains these entries:

```
<HTML><TITLE>ShowMathOperations Applet</TITLE>
<APPLET CODE="ShowMathOperations.class" WIDTH=300 HEIGHT=200></APPLET></HTML>
```

When you run the applet from within the *appletviewer,* the applet window will display the output shown in Figure 6.1.

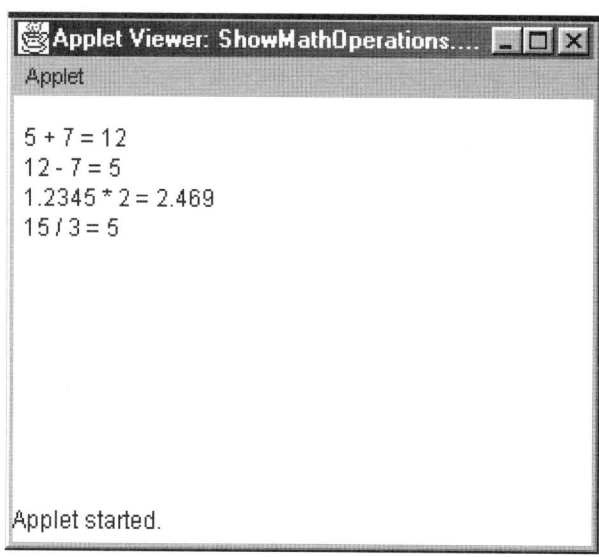

*Figure 6.1 The output of math operations in the applet **ShowMathOperations.java.***

In the previous program, the applet performed arithmetic operations using constant values (numbers) only. The following applet, *MathWithVariables.java,* performs arithmetic operations using variables:

```
import java.awt.*;
import java.applet.*;


public class MathWithVariables extends Applet
    {
```

```
double cost = 15.50;          // The cost of an item
double sales_tax = 0.06;      // Sales tax is 6 percent
double amount_paid = 20.00;   // How much the buyer paid
double tax, change, total;

public void paint(Graphics g)
  {
    tax = cost * sales_tax;
    total = cost + tax;
    change = amount_paid - total;

    g.drawString("Item cost: " + cost, 5, 25);
    g.drawString("Tax: " + tax, 5, 40);
    g.drawString("Total: " + total, 5, 55);
    g.drawString("Customer change: " + change, 5, 70);
  }
}
```

As you can see, the applet uses only floating-point variables to which it assigns values at each variable's declaration. Next, the applet performs arithmetic operations on the variables to determine the amount of sales tax, the total item cost, and the amount of customer change. As before, if you are using the Java Development Kit, you can compile this applet by using the *javac* compiler, as shown here:

```
C:\> javac MathWithVariables.java   <ENTER>
```

Next, create the HTML file, *MathWithVariables.HTML*, which contains these statements:

```
<HTML><TITLE>MathWithVariables Applet</TITLE>
<APPLET CODE="MathWithVariables.class" WIDTH=300 HEIGHT=200></APPLET></HTML>
```

When you execute this applet by using the *appletviewer*, the applet window will display the result of each arithmetic operation, as shown in Figure 6.2.

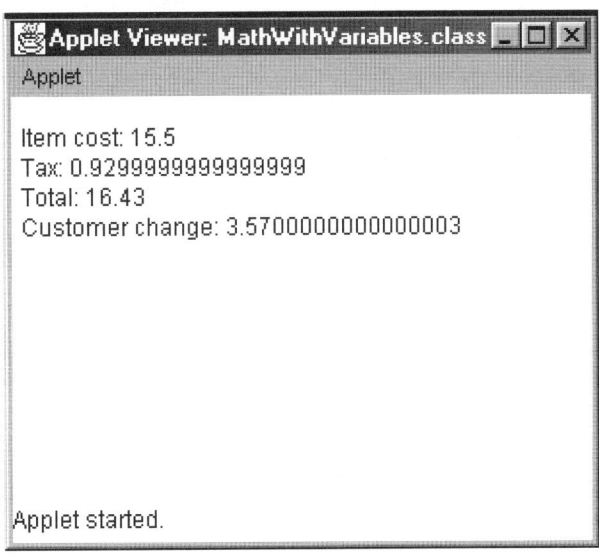

Figure 6.2 Displaying the results of math operations on variables.

43

INCREMENTING A VARIABLE'S VALUE BY 1

Within your Java applets, a common operation you will perform is to add 1 to the value of an integer variable. For example, assume your applet uses the variable named *SongCnt* to keep track of the number of songs the user has played on your Web site's interactive jukebox. Each time the user plays a song, your applet will add 1 to *SongCnt's* current value. Using the Java assignment operator, your applet can increment *SongCnt's* value as follows:

```
SongCnt = SongCnt + 1;
```

In this case, the applet first obtains *SongCnt's* current value and then adds 1 to that value. Next, the applet stores the result of the addition back to the variable *SongCnt*. The following applet, *SongCount.java*, uses the Java assignment operator to increment the variable *SongCnt* (which originally contains the value 1000) by 1 (assigning the result, 1001, to the variable):

```
import java.awt.*;
import java.applet.*;

public class SongCount extends Applet
   {
     public void paint(Graphics g)
       {
         int SongCnt = 1000;

         g.drawString("SongCnt's starting value: " + SongCnt, 5, 10);
         SongCnt = SongCnt + 1;
         g.drawString("SongCnt's ending value: " + SongCnt, 5, 25);
       }
   }
```

Use the following HTML file, *SongCount.HTML*, to run the applet:

```
<HTML><TITLE>SongCount Applet</TITLE>
<APPLET CODE="SongCount.class" WIDTH=300 HEIGHT=200></APPLET></HTML>
```

When you run this applet by using the *appletviewer*, the applet window will display the *SongCnt* variable's starting and ending values, as shown in Figure 6.3.

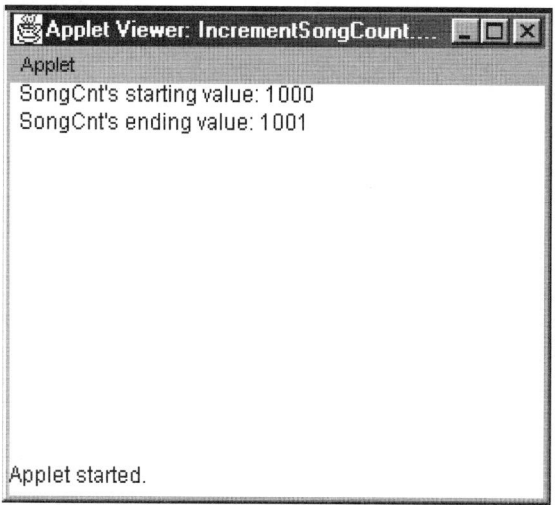

Figure 6.3 Incrementing a variable's value by 1.

Because incrementing a variable's value is a common operation within applets, Java provides an increment operator, the double plus sign (++). The increment operator provides a shorthand way to add 1 to a variable's value. The following statements, for example, both increment the variable *SongCnt's* value by 1:

```
SongCnt = SongCnt + 1;                    SongCnt++;
```

The following applet, *IncrementSongCount.java*, uses the Java increment operator to increment the variable *SongCnt's* value by 1:

```java
import java.awt.*;
import java.applet.*;

public class IncrementSongCount extends Applet
  {
    public void paint(Graphics g)
      {
        int SongCnt = 1000;

        g.drawString("SongCnt's starting value: " + SongCnt, 5, 10);
        SongCnt++;
        g.drawString("SongCnt's ending value: " + SongCnt, 5, 25);
      }
  }
```

This applet works exactly the same as *SongCount.java*, which used the assignment operator to increment the variable's value. When Java encounters an increment operator, Java first gets the variable's value, adds 1 to the value, and then stores the result back into the variable.

UNDERSTANDING PREFIX (BEFORE) AND POSTFIX (AFTER) INCREMENT OPERATORS

When your applets use the *increment* operator, your applets can place the operator before or after the variable, as shown here:

```
++variable;                    variable++;
```

Because the first operator appears in front of the variable, it is called a *prefix* increment operator. Likewise, the second operator that appears after the variable is called a *postfix* increment operator. You must understand that Java treats these two operators differently. For example, consider the following assignment statement:

```
current_count = count++;
```

The assignment statement directs Java to assign *count's* current value to the variable *current_count*. Then, the postfix increment operator tells Java to increment *count's* current value. Using the postfix operator in this case makes the previous statement equivalent to the following two statements:

```
current_count = count;
count = count + 1;
```

Next, consider the following assignment statement that uses the prefix increment operator:

```
current_count = ++count;
```

In this case, the assignment statement tells Java to first increment *count's* value and then assign the result to the variable *current_count*. Using the prefix increment operator makes the previous statement equivalent to the following two statements:

```
count = count + 1;
current_count = count;
```

It is important that you understand the prefix and postfix increment operators, because you will see them in most Java applets. The following applet, *PrefixAndPostfix.java*, illustrates the use of the prefix and postfix increment operators:

```java
import java.awt.*;
import java.applet.*;
public class PrefixAndPostfix extends Applet
  {
    public void paint(Graphics g)
      {
        int small_count = 0;
        int big_count = 1000;
        g.drawString("small_count is " + small_count, 5, 10);
        g.drawString("small_count++ is " + small_count++, 5, 25);
        g.drawString("small_count's ending value is " + small_count, 5, 40);

        g.drawString("big_count is " + big_count, 5, 60);
        g.drawString("++big_count is " + ++big_count, 5, 75);
        g.drawString("big_count's ending value is " + big_count, 5, 90);
      }
  }
```

Use the following HTML file, *PrefixAndPostfix.HTML*, to run the applet:

```html
<HTML><TITLE>PrefixAndPostfix Applet</TITLE>
<APPLET CODE="PrefixAndPostfix.class" WIDTH=300 HEIGHT=200></APPLET></HTML>
```

When you run this applet within the *appletviewer*, the applet window will display the output shown in Figure 6.4.

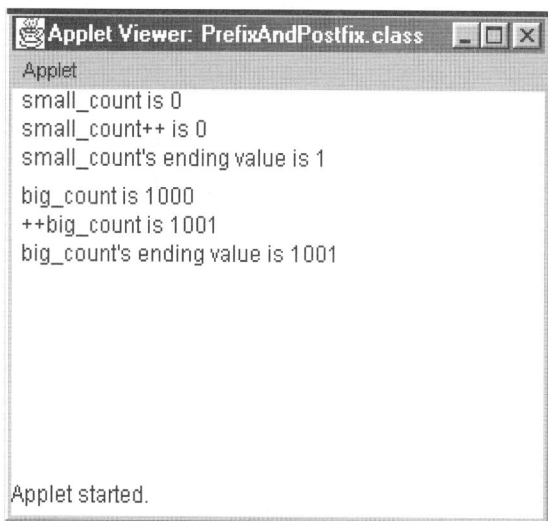

Figure 6.4 Displaying the result of prefix and postfix operations.

The applet uses the postfix increment operator with the variable *small_count*. As a result, the applet displays the variable's current value (0) and then increments the value by 1. The applet uses the prefix increment operator with the variable *big_count*. As a result, the applet first increments the variable's value (1000 + 1) and then displays the result (1001).

Take time now to edit this applet and change the first postfix operator to a prefix operator and the prefix operator to postfix. Compile and execute the applet, noting how changing the operators changes the applet's outputs.

JAVA ALSO PROVIDES A DECREMENT OPERATOR

As you have just learned, the double plus sign (++) is the Java increment operator. In a similar way, the double minus sign (--) is the Java *decrement operator*, which decrements a variable's value by 1. As was the case with the increment operator, Java supports a prefix and postfix decrement operator.

The following applet, *DecrementOperator.java*, illustrates the use of the Java decrement operator:

```java
import java.awt.*;
import java.applet.*;

public class DecrementOperator extends Applet
  {
    public void paint(Graphics g)
      {
        int small_count = 0;
        int big_count = 1000;

        g.drawString("small_count is " + small_count, 5, 10);
        g.drawString("small_count-- is " + small_count--, 5, 25);
        g.drawString("small_count's ending value is " + small_count, 5, 40);

        g.drawString("big_count is " + big_count, 5, 60);
        g.drawString("--big_count is " + --big_count, 5, 75);
        g.drawString("big_count's ending value is " + big_count, 5, 90);
      }
  }
```

Use the following HTML entries to create the file *DecrementOperator.HTML*:

```html
<HTML><TITLE>DecrementOperator Applet</TITLE>
<APPLET CODE="DecrementOperator.class" WIDTH=300 HEIGHT=200></APPLET></HTML>
```

The Java prefix and postfix decrement operators work just as their increment operator counterparts, with the difference being that they decrement the variable's value by 1. When you use the *appletviewer* to execute this applet, the applet window will display the results shown in Figure 6.5.

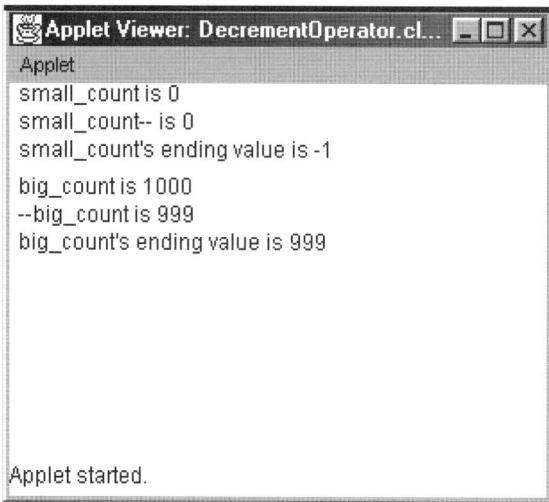

Figure 6.5 *Displaying the result of decrement operations.*

OTHER JAVA OPERATORS

This lesson has focused on the common Java arithmetic operators and the increment and decrement operators. As you examine Java applets, you may encounter one or more of the operators listed in Table 6.2:

Operator	Function
%	Modulo or remainder operator; returns the remainder of an integer division
~	Ones complement operator; inverts a value's bits
&	Bitwise *AND* operator; *ANDs* the ones bits between two values
|	Bitwise *OR* operator; *ORs* the ones bits between two values
^	Bitwise exclusive *OR*; exclusive *ORs* the bits between two values
<<	Bitwise left shift; shifts a value's bits left the number of positions specified
>>	Bitwise right shift; shifts a value's bits right the number of positions specified

Table 6.2 *Other Java operators you might encounter.*

UNDERSTANDING JAVA'S OPERATOR PRECEDENCE

When you perform arithmetic operations within Java applets, you must be aware that Java performs operations in a specific order, based on an operator precedence. For example, Java will perform a multiplication operation before it will perform an addition operation. To understand operator precedence better, consider the following expression:

```
result = 5 + 2 * 3;
```

Depending on the order that Java performs the multiplication and addition operations, different results will occur:

```
result = 5 + 2 * 3;
       = 7 * 3;
       = 21;
```

```
result = 5 + 2 * 3;
       = 5 + 6;
       = 11;
```

To avoid such mix-ups, Java assigns a precedence to each operator that determines the order in which it performs operations. Because Java performs operations in a consistent order, your applets will perform arithmetic calculations in a consistent manner.

Table 6.3 lists the Java operator precedence. The operators that appear in the top box have the highest precedence. Within each box, operators have the same precedence. If you examine the table, you will find that Java assigns a higher precedence to multiplication than addition. You have not seen many of the operators that appear in the boxes. For now, do not worry about these operators. By the time you finish this book, you will have used (and should understand) each of them.

Operator	Name	Example
.	Member selector	object.member_name
[]	Subscript	pointer[element]
()	Function call	expression(parameters)
++	Postfix increment	variable++
++	Prefix increment	++variable
--	Postfix decrement	variable--
--	Prefix decrement	--variable
~	Ones complement	~expression
!	NOT operator	! expression
instanceof	Instance operator	if (object_a instanceof classname)
new	Allocate operator	new type
*	Multiply	expression . expression
/	Divide	expression / expression
%	Modulo	expression % expression
+	Addition	expression + expression
–	Subtraction	expression – expression
<<	Bitwise left-shift	expression << expression
>>	Right-shift operator	expression >> expression
>>>	Zero-fill right-shift operator	expression >>> expression
<	Less-than operator	expression < expression
>	Greater-than operator	expression > expression
<=	Less-than-or-equal-to operator	expression <= expression
>=	Greater-than-or-equal-to operator	expression >= expression

Table 6.3 Java operator precedence. (continued on next page)

Operator	Name	Example
==	Equality	expression == expression
!=	Inequality	expression != expression
&	Bitwise and	expression & expression
^	Bitwise exclusive or	expression ^ expression
|	Bitwise or	expression | expression
&&	Logical and	expression && expression
||	Logical or	expression || expression
?:	if-else	(boolean_expression) ? true_expression: false_expression
operator=	Assignment	variable *= expression;

Table 6.3 Java operator precedence. (continued from previous page)

Controlling the Order in Which Java Performs Operations

As you have learned, Java assigns a different precedence to operators that control the order in which operations are performed. Unfortunately, there may be times when the order in which Java performs arithmetic operations does not match the order in which you need the calculations performed. For example, assume that your applet must add two prices and then multiply the result by a tax rate:

```
cost = price_a + price_b * 1.06;
```

Unfortunately, in this case, Java will perform the multiplication first (price_b * 1.06) and then will add the value of *price_a*. When your applets must perform arithmetic operations in a specific order, you can place expressions within parentheses. When Java evaluates expressions, Java always performs operations grouped within parentheses first. For example, consider the following expression:

```
result = (2 + 3) * (3 + 4);
```

When Java evaluates this expression, Java will do so as follows:

```
result = (2 + 3) * (3 + 4);
       = (5) * (3 + 4);
       = 5 * (7);
       = 5 * 7;
       = 35;
```

By grouping expressions within parentheses in this way, you can control the order in which Java performs arithmetic operations. Given the previous example, your applet can add the two prices within parentheses, as shown here:

```
cost = (price_a + price_b) * 1.06;
```

BE AWARE OF OVERFLOW WITH ARITHMETIC OPERATIONS

In Lesson 5, you learned that when you assign a value to a variable that falls outside of the range of values the variable's type can store, an overflow error occurs. When you perform arithmetic operations, you must keep overflow errors in mind. For example, the following applet, *MathOverflow.java*, multiplies the value 2,000,000 by 3,000,000 and assigns the result to a variable of type *int*. However, because the result of the multiplication exceeds the largest value a variable of type *int* can store, an overflow error occurs:

```
import java.awt.*;
import java.applet.*;

public class MathOverflow extends Applet
  {
    public void paint(Graphics g)
      {
        int result;

        result = 2000000 * 3000000;
        g.drawString("200 * 300 = " + result, 5, 10);
      }
  }
```

Place the following HTML entries within the file *MathOverflow.HTML* to run the applet:

```
<HTML><TITLE>MathOverflow Applet</TITLE>
<APPLET CODE="MathOverflow.class" WIDTH=300 HEIGHT=200></APPLET></HTML>
```

When you compile and run this applet, the applet window displays the errant results, as shown in Figure 6.6.

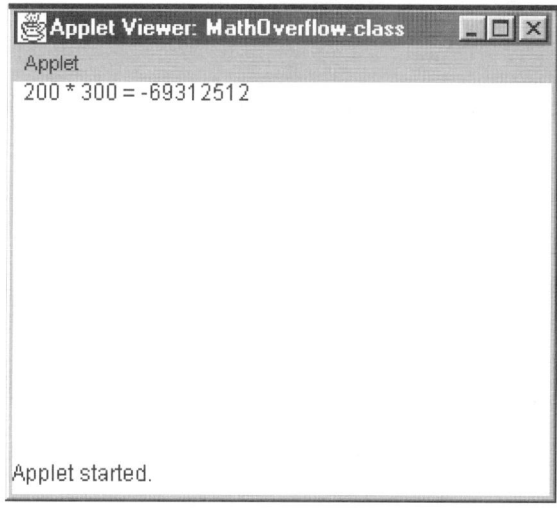

Figure 6.6 Errant results due to a math overflow error.

TAKING A CYBER FIELD TRIP

Multimedia is the use of text, pictures, sound, and video to present information in a meaningful way. As you create Java applets, there may be times when you focus the applet's processing on the manipulation and display of text. To help you get started, the Java Development Kit provides the Blink applet shown in Figure 6.7 that flashes words in different colors within the applet window. To run the applet or to download the applet's source code, visit the Jamsa Press Web site at *www.jamsa.com/java_demos/blink.html.*

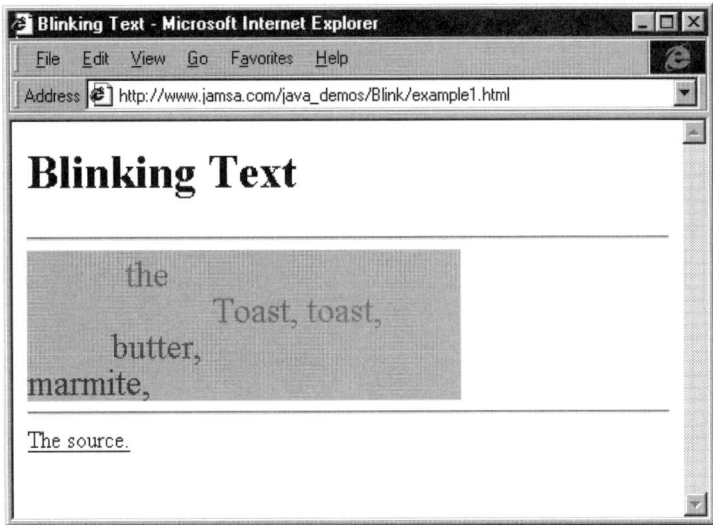

Figure 6.7 *Flashing text in color within a Java applet.*

WHAT YOU MUST KNOW

In this lesson, you examined the common Java arithmetic and increment operators. As you learned, to ensure that your applets perform arithmetic calculations consistently, Java assigns a precedence to each operator that controls the order in which Java performs each operation.

In Lesson 7, "Teaching Java Applets to Make Decisions," you will learn how to use conditional operators within your applets to make decisions. Before you continue with Lesson 7, however, make sure that you have learned the following key concepts:

☑ Java uses the operators +, –, *, and / for addition, subtraction, multiplication, and division.

☑ Java provides prefix (before) and postfix (after) increment operators that add 1 to a variable's value.

☑ Java provides prefix (before) and postfix (after) decrement operators that subtract 1 from a variable's value.

☑ The Java prefix operators direct Java to first increment (++variable) or decrement (--variable) the variable's value, and then to use the value.

☑ The Java postfix operators direct Java to first use the variable's value, and then to increment (variable++) or decrement (variable--) the value.

☑ To ensure that expressions are evaluated consistently, Java assigns a precedence to each operator that controls the order in which operations occur.

☑ If you must control the order in which arithmetic operations are performed, place your expressions in parentheses. Java always evaluates expressions in parentheses first.

LESSON 7

TEACHING JAVA APPLETS TO MAKE DECISIONS

As you have learned, a Java applet contains a list of instructions the computer performs to accomplish a specific task. In each of the simple applets you have created so far, Java starts its execution with the first statement in the applet and executes each statement, in order, until it reaches the end of the applet. As your applets become more complex, there will be times when you will want the applets to execute one set of statements if one condition is *true,* and possibly another set if the condition is *false.* In other words, you will want your applets to make decisions and respond accordingly. This lesson examines the Java *if* statement, which your applets will use to make such decisions. By the time you finish this lesson, you will understand the following key concepts:

- Java applets use *relational operators* to determine if two values are equal, or if one value is larger or smaller than the other.

- Within your applets, you use the Java *if* statement to make decisions.

- Java statements can be *simple* (one operation) or *compound* (multiple operations grouped within right and left braces ({})).

- Your Java applets use the *if-else* statement to perform one set of statements when a condition is *true*, and a second set of statements if the condition is *false*.

- By combining several *if-else* statements, Java applets can test for several different conditions.

- Using the Java AND and OR operators, your applets can test for multiple conditions, such as, *Does the user have a dog AND is the dog a Dalmatian?*

Java applets that make decisions perform *conditional processing*. In other words, based on the outcome of one or more conditions, the applet will execute specific statements. Experiment with the applets in this lesson; your collection of Java tools is now becoming large enough for you to create useful applets.

COMPARING TWO VALUES

When your applets make decisions, they normally perform some type of test. For example, one applet might test if a user's age is at least 18, and a second applet if the cost of an item is more than $50.00. To perform such tests, your applets will use the Java relational operators listed in Table 7. Relational operators let your applets test how one value relates to another. In other words, using relational operators, your applets can test whether one value is equal to, greater than, or less than a second value.

Operator	Test	Example
==	If two values are equal	(user_age == 18)
!=	If two values are not equal	(old != new)
>	If the first value is greater than the second	(cost > 50.00)
<	If the first value is less than the second	(salary < 20000.00)
>=	If the first value is greater than or equal to the second	(stock_price >= 30.0)
<=	If the first value is less than or equal to the second	(age <= 21)

Table 7 Java relational operators.

When your applets use the relational operators to compare two values, the result of the comparison is either *true* or *false*. In other words, two values are either equal (*true*) or they are not (*false*). Each of the *if* statements this book presents will use the relational operators listed in Table 7.

GETTING STARTED WITH THE *if* STATEMENT

The Java *if* statement lets your applets perform a test and then execute statements based on the result of the test. The format of the *if* statement is as follows:

```
if (condition_is_true)
    statement;
```

The *if* statement normally performs a test by using a Java relational operator. If the result of the test is *true*, the *if* statement executes the statement that follows. The following applet, *TestScore.Java*, uses the *if* statement to compare the value stored in the variable *TestScore* to value 90. If the test score is greater than or equal to 90, the applet displays a message that tells the user that his or her score was an A. Otherwise, if the value is less than 90, the applet simply ends:

```
import java.awt.*;
import java.applet.*;

public class TestScore extends Applet
  {
    public void paint(Graphics g)
      {
        int TestScore = 95;

        if (TestScore >= 90)
           g.drawString("Congratulations, you got an A!", 5, 15);
      }
  }
```

As you can see, the applet uses the Java greater-than-or-equal-to relational operator (>=) to perform the test. If the value comparison results in *true*, the applet will execute the statement that follows, in this case, displaying the message by using the *drawString* function. If the comparison results in *false*, the applet does not display the message.

Use the following HTML file, *TestScore.HTML*, to run the applet:

```
<HTML><TITLE>TestScore Applet</TITLE>
<APPLET CODE="TestScore.class" WIDTH=300 HEIGHT=200></APPLET></HTML>
```

When you use the *appletviewer* to run this applet, the applet window will display a message, as shown in Figure 7.1, that tells the user that his or her score was an A.

Experiment with this applet, changing the test score to a value that is less than 90, and note the processing the *if* statement performs. Remember, you must recompile your applet for your changes to take effect.

UNDERSTANDING SIMPLE AND COMPOUND STATEMENTS

When your applets use the *if* statement for conditional processing, there will be times when your applets will want to perform one statement if the condition is *true,* and other times when the applet will perform several statements. When your applet performs only one statement following an *if*, the statement is called a *simple statement*:

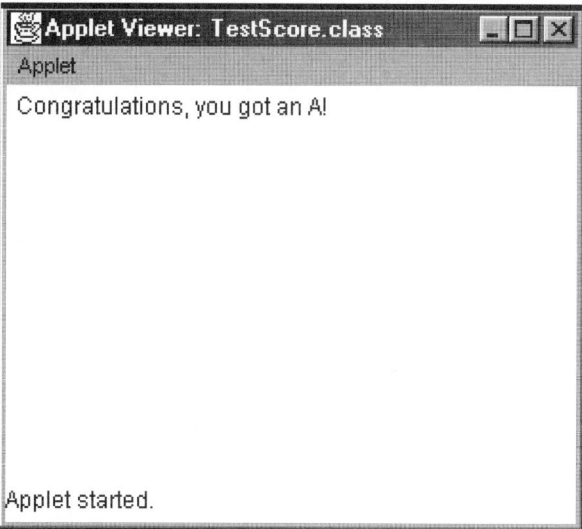

*Figure 7.1 Using an **if** statement to determine a grade.*

```
if (TestScore >= 90)
  g.drawString("Congratulations! You got an A!", 5, 25);
```

When your applet performs several instructions when a condition evaluates as *true*, the group of statements must be grouped within left-and-right braces ({}). The statements that appear within the braces make up a *compound statement*, as shown here:

```
if (TestScore >= 90)
  {
    g.drawString("Congratulations! You got an A!", 5, 25);
    g.drawString("Your test score was " + TestScore, 5, 50);
  }
```

It is not important that you remember the terms simple and compound statements but, rather, that you know that you must group related statements within the left-and-right braces. The following applet, *CompoundStatement.java*, changes the previous applet to display two messages if the test score is greater than or equal to 90:

```
import java.awt.*;
import java.applet.*;

public class CompoundStatement extends Applet
  {
    public void paint(Graphics g)
      {
        int TestScore = 95;

        if (TestScore >= 90)
          {
            g.drawString("Congratulations, you got an A!", 5, 15);
            g.drawString("Your test score was " + TestScore, 5, 30);
          }
      }
  }
```

USING SIMPLE AND COMPOUND STATEMENTS

When your applets perform conditional processing, there will be times when your applets only must perform one statement (a simple statement) when a condition is *true*. At other times, however, your applet must perform multiple statements (a compound statement). When your applets must perform two or more related statements based on a condition, you must group the statements within left-and-right braces, as shown here:

```
if (age >= 21)
   {
     g.drawString("Make sure you remember to vote!", 5, 25);
     g.drawString("Oh yeah, this Bud's for you!", 5, 50);
   }
```

PROVIDING ALTERNATIVE STATEMENTS FOR FALSE CONDITIONS

The previous two applets used an *if* statement to determine whether a test score was greater than or equal to 90. If the condition was *true*, the applets displayed messages to the screen. If the condition was *false*, meaning the test score was less than 90, the applet did not display a message, the applet simply ended. In most cases, your applets will want to specify one set of statements that executes when the condition is *true*, and a second set that executes if the condition is *false*. To provide the statements that execute when the condition is *false*, your applets must use the *else* statement. The format of the *else* statement is as follows:

```
if (condition_is_true)
    statement;
else
    statement;
```

The following applet, *IfElse.Java*, uses the *if* statement to test whether the test score is greater than or equal to 90. If the condition is *true*, the applet displays a message of congratulations. If the condition is *false*, the applet displays a message telling the student to work harder:

```
import java.awt.*;
import java.applet.*;

public class IfElse extends Applet
   {
     public void paint(Graphics g)
        {
          int TestScore = 95;

          if (TestScore >= 90)
             g.drawString("Congratulations, you got an A!", 5, 15);
          else
             g.drawString("You need to work harder next time!", 5, 15);
        }
   }
```

Again, take time to experiment with this application by changing the value the applet assigns to the variable *TestScore*.

COMPOUND STATEMENTS ALSO APPLY TO ELSE

As you have learned, a compound statement is a group of related statements enclosed in left-and-right braces. When your applet uses an *else* statement to specify statements that will be performed when a condition is *false*, you can use a compound statement to specify multiple statements. The following applet, *CompoundElse.java*, uses a compound statement for both the *if* and *else*:

```
import java.awt.*;
import java.applet.*;

public class CompoundElse extends Applet
  {
    public void paint(Graphics g)
      {
        int TestScore = 95;

        if (TestScore >= 90)
          {
            g.drawString("Congratulations, you got an A!", 5, 15);
            g.drawString("Your test score was " + TestScore, 5, 30);
          }
        else
          {
            g.drawString("You should have worked harder!", 5, 15);
            g.drawString("You missed " + (100 - TestScore) + " points",
                          5, 30);
          }
      }
  }
```

Place the following HTML statements within the file *CompoundElse.HTML* to run the applet:

```
<HTML><TITLE>CompoundElse Applet</TITLE>
<APPLET CODE="CompoundElse.class" WIDTH=300 HEIGHT=200></APPLET></HTML>
```

As before, take time to experiment with this applet, changing the *TestScore* variable to values less than and greater than 90.

UNDERSTANDING IF-ELSE PROCESSING

As your applets become more complex, your applets will test different conditions and perform one set of statements when the condition is *true*, and a second set when the condition is *false*. To perform such conditional processing, your applets will use an *if-else* statement, as shown here:

```
if (condition_is_true)
  statement;
else
  statement;
```

If your applets want to perform more than one statement when the condition is *true* or *false*, you must group the related statements within left-and-right braces ({}):

```
    if (condition_is_true)
      {
        first_true_statement;
        second_true_statement;
      }
    else
      {
        first_false_statement;
        second_false_statement;
      }
```

USE INDENTATION TO IMPROVE YOUR APPLET'S READABILITY

If you examine the applets this lesson presents, you will find that the applets indent the statements that follow an *if*, *else*, or left brace. By indenting your statements one or two spaces in this way, you make it easy for someone who is reading your applet to determine related statements, as shown here:

```
if (TestScore >= 90)
  {
    g.drawString("Congratulations, you got an A!", 5, 15);
    g.drawString("Your test score was " + TestScore, 5, 30);
  }
else
  {
    g.drawString("You should have worked harder!", 5, 15);
    g.drawString("You missed " + (100 - TestScore) + " points", 5, 30);
  }
```

As you create your applets, use similar indentation to make your applets more readable. Java does not care about the indentation, but programmers who are reading and trying to understand your code will.

UNDERSTANDING BOOLEAN TYPES

When your applet tests whether a condition is *true* or *false*, your applet is said to perform *Boolean operations*. Depending on your applet's requirements, there may be times when your applet must store a *true* or *false* value. For example, an applet might use a variable named *user_owns_a_dog* to track whether or not the user owns a dog. If the user owns the dog, the variable will store the value *true*. Likewise, if the user does not own a dog, the variable will store the value *false*. Variables that store either the value *true* or *false* are boolean variables. To declare a boolean variable, you use the keyword *boolean*, as shown here:

```
boolean user_owns_a_dog;
```

To assign a value to a boolean variable, you can use the keywords *true* or *false*:

```
user_owns_a_dog = true;
```

Later, to test the variable's value, you can use an *if* statement. For example, the following statements test if the user owns a dog, and display an appropriate message:

```
if (user_owns_a_dog)
   g.drawString("Dogs are great!", 5, 25);
else
   g.drawString("You should buy a puppy!", 5, 25);
```

When you examine Java applets, you may encounter an *if* statement written as follows:

```
if (user_owns_a_dog == true)
   g.drawString("Dogs are great!", 5, 25);
```

In this case, the *if* statement tests whether the value stored in the variable *user_owns_a_dog* is equal to *true*. As it turns out, it is equivalent and easier to simplify the test, as shown here:

```
if (user_owns_a_dog)
   g.drawString("Dogs are great!", 5, 25);
```

In a similar way, you might encounter an *if* statement, similar to the following, that tests for a *false* value:

```
if (user_owns_a_dog == false)
   g.drawString("Dogs are great!", 5, 25);
```

As you will learn, rather than testing for a *false* value in this way, most applets will use the NOT operator, discussed later in this lesson.

Using boolean variables, the following applet, *DogsAndCats.java*, uses the variables *user_owns_a_dog* and *user_owns_a_cat* within *if* statements to determine the types of animals the user owns:

```
import java.awt.*;
import java.applet.*;

public class DogsAndCats extends Applet
  {
    public void paint(Graphics g)
      {
        boolean user_owns_a_dog = true;
        boolean user_owns_a_cat = false;

        if (user_owns_a_dog)
          g.drawString("Dogs are great!", 5, 15);

        if (user_owns_a_cat)
          g.drawString("Cats are great!", 5, 30);
      }
  }
```

Place the following HTML statements within the file, *DogsAndCats.HTML*, to run the applet:

```
<HTML><TITLE>DogsAndCats Applet</TITLE>
<APPLET CODE="DogsAndCats.class" WIDTH=300 HEIGHT=200></APPLET></HTML>
```

Experiment with this applet, assigning the value *true* to both variables, *false* to both variables, and then *true* and *false* to different variables. As you can see, testing two conditions is very easy using Java's logical OR and AND operators.

TESTING TWO OR MORE CONDITIONS

As you have learned, the *if* statement lets your applet test specific conditions. As your applets become more complex, there will be times when you will test more than one condition. For example, your applet might test whether a test score is greater than or equal to 90, and whether a student's grade is currently an A. Likewise, you might test whether a user owns a dog and whether that dog is a Dalmatian. To perform such operations, you will use the Java logical *AND* operator (&&). In addition, if you want to test whether a user owns a dog or a cat, you would use the logical *OR* operator (||).

When your applets use the logical *AND* or logical *OR* operators to test more than one condition, you place each condition within parentheses, as shown here:

```
        Condition One              Condition Two
        _____                _____
             |                          |
if ((user_owns_a_dog) && (dog == dalmatian))
```

As you can see, the applet groups each condition within its own parentheses, which is then contained within an outer set:

```
              Entire Condition
              _____
                     |
if ((user_owns_a_dog) && (dog == dalmatian))
```

When your applets use the logical *AND* operator (&&), all of the conditions tested must be *true* for the entire condition to evaluate as *true*. If any condition is *false*, the entire condition becomes *false*. For example, if the user does not own a dog, the previous condition is *false*. Likewise, if the user's dog is not a Dalmatian, the condition is *false*. In order for the condition to be *true*, the user must own a dog, and that dog must be a Dalmatian.

The following statement uses the logical *OR* operator (||) to determine if a user owns a dog or cat:

```
if ((user_owns_a_dog) || (user_owns_a_cat))
```

For a condition that uses the logical *OR* operator to evaluate as *true*, only one condition need be *true*. For example, if the user owns a dog, the condition is *true*. If the user owns a cat, the condition is *true*. Likewise, if the user owns a dog and a cat, the condition is *true*. The only time the condition would be *false* is if the user does not own a dog or a cat.

The following applet, *DogsOrCats.java,* uses the logical *AND* and the logical *OR* operators to determine what type of pet the user owns:

```java
import java.awt.*;
import java.applet.*;

public class DogsOrCats extends Applet
   {
     public void paint(Graphics g)
       {
           boolean user_owns_a_dog = true;
           boolean user_owns_a_cat = false;

           if (user_owns_a_dog)
              g.drawString("Dogs are great!", 5, 15);
```

```
        if (user_owns_a_cat)
          g.drawString("Cats are great!", 5, 30);


        if ((user_owns_a_dog) && (user_owns_a_cat))
          g.drawString("Dogs and cats can get along", 5,45);


        if ((user_owns_a_dog) || (user_owns_a_cat))
          g.drawString("Pets are great!", 5, 60);
      }
   }
```

Place the following HTML statements within the file, *DogsOrCats.HTML*, to run the applet:

```
<HTML><TITLE>DogsOrCats Applet</TITLE>
<APPLET CODE="DogsOrCats.class" WIDTH=300 HEIGHT=200></APPLET></HTML>
```

When you use the *appletviewer* to run this applet, the applet window will display the messages shown in Figure 7.2.

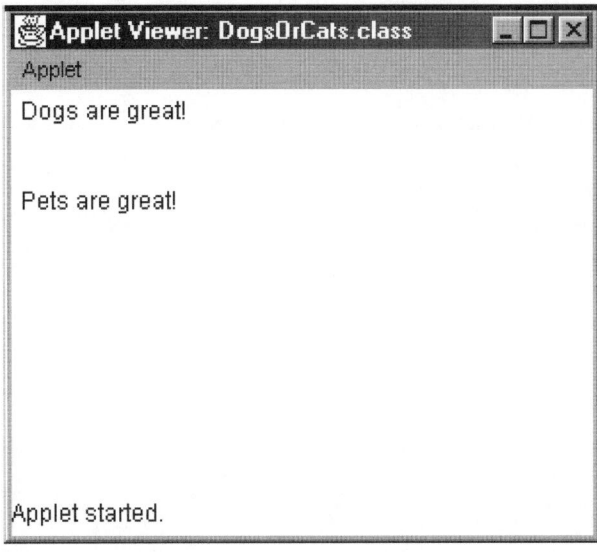

Figure 7.2 *Using logical AND and OR operators within if statements.*

As before, experiment with the program's boolean variables by changing your combinations of *true* and *false* values.

USING THE JAVA NOT OPERATOR

As you have learned, when your applets test for specific conditions, there are times when you want your applets to perform specific statements when a condition is *true*. In a similar way, there may be times when you want your applets to perform a set of statements when a condition is not *true*. The Java *NOT* operator, the exclamation point (!), lets your applets test if a condition is not *true*. For example, the following statement tests whether the user does not own a dog:

```
 if (! user_owns_a_dog)
   g.drawString("You should buy a dog!", 5, 25);
```

The *NOT* operator converts a *false* condition to *true* and a *true* condition to *false*. For example, assume that the user does not own a dog. The variable *user_owns_a_dog* would contain the value *false*. When Java performs the condition using the *NOT* operator, Java uses the variable's current value (*false*), and applies the *NOT* operator. The *NOT* operator makes the *false* value *true*. The entire condition then evaluates as *true*, and Java performs the corresponding statements.

The following applet, *NotOperator.java*, illustrates the use of the *NOT* operator:

```java
import java.awt.*;
import java.applet.*;

public class NotOperator extends Applet
  {
    public void paint(Graphics g)
      {
          boolean user_owns_a_dog = true;
          boolean user_owns_a_cat = false;

          if (! user_owns_a_dog)
             g.drawString("You should buy a dog!", 5, 15);

          if (! user_owns_a_cat)
             g.drawString("You should buy a cat!", 5, 30);
      }
  }
```

Place the following HTML statements within the file, *NotOperator.HTML*, to run the applet:

```html
<HTML><TITLE>NotOperator Applet</TITLE>
<APPLET CODE="NotOperator.class" WIDTH=300 HEIGHT=200></APPLET></HTML>
```

As before, experiment with the values you assign to the variables *user_owns_a_dog* and *user_owns_a_cat* and watch the processing the applet performs. As your applets become more complex, you will use the *NOT* operator on a regular basis. For example, your applet may continue to repeat its processing as long as it has *not* encountered the end of a file.

USING JAVA LOGICAL OPERATORS

As you specify conditions within your applets, there will be times when the conditions have multiple parts. For example, your applet might test if an employee is paid hourly and has worked over 40 hours this week. When your conditions require two parts to be *true* for the condition to be *true*, you use the Java AND operator (&&). To use the AND operator, group each condition within its own parentheses and both conditions within their own parentheses, as shown here:

```java
if ((employee_pay == hourly) && (employee_hours > 40))
   statement;
```

When your condition requires only one of two parts to be *true* for the condition to be *true*, your applets should use the Java OR operator (||). For example, the following condition tests whether the user owns either a car or motorcycle:

```java
if ((vehicle == car) || (vehicle == motorcycle))
   statement;
```

As before, the applet groups each condition within parentheses. In some cases, you may want your applets to perform a statement when a condition is not *true*. In such cases, you should use the Java NOT operator (!). The NOT operator converts a *true* condition to *false*, and a *false* condition to *true*.

The Java AND, OR, and NOT operators are *logical operators*.

HANDLING DIFFERENT CONDITIONS

The applets this lesson has presented thus far have used *if* and *else* to specify one set of statements the applet performs when a condition is *true*, and another set of statements the applet performs if the condition is *false*. There may be times, however, when your applets must test several different related conditions. For example, assume that your applet must determine a student's test grade. To do so, your applet must test for scores greater than or equal to 90, 80, 70, 60, and so on. The following applet, *TestGrade.java*, uses a series of *if-else* statements to do just that:

```
import java.awt.*;
import java.applet.*;

public class TestGrade extends Applet
  {
    public void paint(Graphics g)
      {
        int TestScore = 91;

        if (TestScore >= 90)
          g.drawString("You got an A!", 5, 10);
        else if (TestScore >= 80)
          g.drawString("You got a B", 5, 10);
        else if (TestScore >= 70)
          g.drawString("You got a C!", 5, 10);
        else if (TestScore >= 60)
          g.drawString("Your grade was a D", 5, 10);
        else
          g.drawString("You failed the test!", 5, 10);
      }
  }
```

When the applet performs the first *if* statement, it tests whether the test score is greater than or equal to 90. If so, the applet displays a message saying the user received an A. If the test score is not greater than or equal to 90, the applet performs the following *else-if* statement to test whether the score is greater than or equal to 80. The applet repeats this processing until it determines the correct grade. After Java finds a condition that evaluates as *true*, Java performs the condition's corresponding statements and then resumes its processing at the first statement that follows the last *else* statement. As before, use different test scores to experiment with this applet.

USING THE SWITCH STATEMENT

As you just learned, by combining a series of *if-else* statements, your applets can test multiple conditions. In the previous applet, you used *if-else* statements to determine if a test score fell within a range of values. For cases when your applets must test for specific values, your applets can use the Java *switch* statement.

When you use the *switch* statement, you must specify a condition, and then one or more cases where the applet tries to match the condition. For example, the following applet, *SwitchGrade.java*, uses a *switch* statement to display a message based on a student's current grade:

```java
import java.awt.*;
import java.applet.*;

public class SwitchGrade extends Applet
  {
    public void paint(Graphics g)
      {
        char grade = 'B';

        switch (grade) {
          case 'A': g.drawString("Congratulations on your A!", 5, 10);
                  break;
          case 'B': g.drawString("Not bad, a B is OK", 5, 10);
                  break;
          case 'C': g.drawString("C's are only average", 5, 10);
                  break;
          case 'D': g.drawString("D's are terrible", 5, 10);
                  break;
          default:  g.drawString("No excuses! Study harder!", 5, 10);
                  break;
        }
      }
  }
```

The *switch* statement consists of two parts. The first part of the *switch* statement is the condition that appears after the keyword *switch*. The second part is the possible matching cases. When the applet encounters a *switch* statement, the applet first examines the condition and then tries to find a value that matches within the possible cases. When the applet finds a match, the applet executes the corresponding statements. In the case of the previous applet, the case for a letter grade of 'B' matches the condition. Therefore, the applet displays a message telling the user that a B is not bad. Take time to experiment with this applet, changing the letter grade and watching the corresponding processing. The *default* case provides a "catch all" case that will match any condition.

Note the use of the *break* statement with each case in the previous applet. As it turns out, when Java encounters a case that matches the condition in a *switch* statement, Java considers all the cases that follow to be a match as well. The *break* statement tells Java to end the current *switch* statement, and to continue the applet's execution at the first statement that follows the *switch* statement. If you remove the *break* statements from the previous applet, the applet will display a message not only for the matching case, but for each of the cases that follow (because Java considers all cases as *true* after one case is *true*).

UNDERSTANDING JAVA'S CONDITIONAL ASSIGNMENT OPERATOR

Within Java applets, a common operation you may perform is to assign one of two values to a variable based on a specific condition. For example, the following *if* statement tests the variable *user_age* to determine if a user is 16 or older. If the user's age is 16 or older, the *if* statement assigns the value *true* to the variable, *consider_car_insurance*. If the user is younger than 16, the *else* statement assigns the value *false* to *consider_car_insurance*:

```
if (user_age >= 16)
  consider_car_insurance = true;
else
  consider_car_insurance = false;
```

For cases when you are assigning a value to a variable based on a specific condition, Java lets you use the conditional-assignment operator, whose format is as follows:

```
variable = (condition) ? true_value: false_value;
```

When Java encounters the conditional operator, Java evaluates the corresponding condition. If the condition evaluates as *true*, Java assigns the value that immediately follows the question mark. If the condition evaluates as *false*, Java assigns the value that follows the colon. The following statement uses the conditional-assignment operator to assign a value to the variable *consider_car_insurance* based on the user's age:

```
consider_car_insurance = (user_age >= 16) ? true: false;
```

In a similar way, the following *if-else* statement displays a message to the screen based on the user's age:

```
if (user_age >= 16)
  g.drawString("Buy car insurance.", 5, 45);
else
  g.drawString("You do not need car insurance yet.", 5, 45);
```

The following statement uses the conditional-assignment operator to display the same messages:

```
g.drawString((user_age >= 16) ? "Buy car insurance.":
  "You do not need car insurance yet.", 5, 45);
```

By reducing the number of statements in your applet, you may find that the conditional-assignment operator makes your source code easier to read and understand. The following applet, *ConditionalAssignment.java*, illustrates the use of the conditional-assignment operator:

```
import java.awt.*;
import java.applet.*;


public class ConditionalAssignment extends Applet
  {
    public void paint(Graphics g)
      {
        int TestScore = 95;
        String Passing;
        Passing = (TestScore >= 60) ? "You passed." : "You failed.";
        g.drawString("Test result: " + Passing, 5, 15);
        g.drawString((TestScore >= 90) ?
            "Congratulations, you got an A!" :
            "You need to work harder next time!", 5, 45);
      }
  }
```

Place the following HTML statements within the file, *ConditionalAssignment.HTML*, to run the applet:

```
<HTML><TITLE>ConditionalAssignment Applet</TITLE>
<APPLET CODE="ConditionalAssignment.class" WIDTH=300 HEIGHT=200></APPLET>
</HTML>
```

When you use the *appletviewer* to run this applet, the applet window will display the messages shown in Figure 7.3.

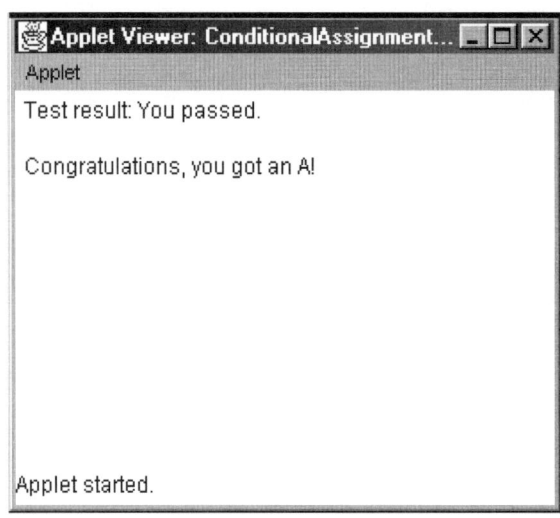

*Figure 7.3 Using logical And and Or operators within *if* statements.*

TAKING A CYBER FIELD TRIP

In Lesson 21, "Using Threads to Create Simple Animations," you will use Java class libraries to determine the current system date and time. Within Lesson 21, you will create an applet that repeatedly shows the current time. In a similar way, the Java Developer's Kit provides the Clock applet, which as shown in Figure 7.4, displays the current system time using an analog clock. To run the Clock applet or to download the applet's source code, visit the Jamsa Press Web site at *www.jamsa.com/java_demos/Clock.html*.

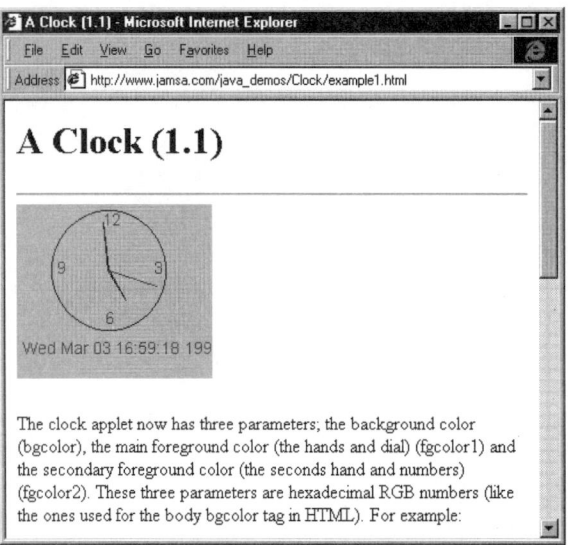

Figure 7.4 Displaying an analog clock using the Clock applet.

WHAT YOU MUST KNOW

In this lesson, you learned how to use the Java *if* statement to perform conditional processing, which lets your applets make their own decisions. As you have learned, your applets can use the *if* statement to perform one set of statements when a condition is *true*, and the *else* statement to specify a different set of statements the applet executes if the condition is *false*.

In Lesson 8, "Teaching Your Applets to Repeat One or More Statements," you will learn how to use Java iterative statements to repeat statements a specific number of times, or until a specific condition is met. For example, you might repeat the same statements 100 times to add up 100 student test scores. Before you continue with Lesson 8, however, make sure that you have learned the following key concepts:

☑ Java relational operators let your applets test whether two values are equal, not equal, or if one value is greater than or less than another.

☑ The Java *if* statement lets your applet test a condition and perform one or more statements if the condition is *true*.

☑ The Java *else* statement lets your applets specify one or more statements that execute when a condition tested by an if statement is *false*.

☑ The Java logical *AND* (&&) and *OR* (||) operators let your applets test for more than one condition.

☑ The Java logical *NOT* (!) operator lets your applets test for conditions that are not *true*.

☑ If your applets must execute more than one statement for an *if* or *else*, you must place the statements within left-and-right braces ({}).

☑ Indent your applet statements to help programmers reading your code determine related statements quickly.

☑ When your programs must test if a condition matches specific values, your applets can use the *switch* statement.

☑ When your applet encounters a matching case within a *switch* statement, Java considers all the cases that follow to be a match as well. Using the *break* statement, you can instruct Java to end the *switch* statement and to continue the applet's processing at the first statement that follows the *switch* statement.

☑ When your applet assigns a value to a variable based on a specific condition, you can use the Java conditional-assignment operator, as opposed to an *if-else* statement.

LESSON 8

TEACHING YOUR APPLETS TO REPEAT ONE OR MORE STATEMENTS

In Lesson 7, "Teaching Java Applets to Make Decisions," you learned how to use the Java *if* statement to make decisions within your applets. Closely related to such decision-making within your applet is the ability to repeat one or more instructions a specific number of times, or until a specific condition is met. In this lesson, you will use the Java *iterative constructs* to repeat one or more statements. By the time you finish this lesson, you will understand the following key concepts:

- ◆ To repeat statements a specific number of times, your applets use the Java *for* statement.

- ◆ The Java *while* statement lets your applets repeat statements as long as a condition is *true*.

- ◆ The Java *do while* statement lets your applet perform statements at least one time and then possibly repeat the statements based on a specified condition.

The ability to repeat statements is a very powerful programming feature. Experiment with the applets presented in this lesson. After you have finished, you will have considerable Java programming capabilities.

REPEATING STATEMENTS A SPECIFIC NUMBER OF TIMES

One of the most common operations your applets will perform is repeating one or more statements a specific number of times. For example, one applet might repeat the same statements to print five copies of a file and a second applet might repeat a set of statements 30 times to determine whether your 30 stocks are gaining or losing value. The Java *for* statement makes it very easy for your applets to repeat one or more statements a specific number of times.

When your applet uses a *for* statement (often called a *for loop*), your applet must specify a variable, called a *control variable*, that keeps track of the number of times the loop executes. For example, the following *for* loop uses the *count* variable to keep track of the number of times your applet has performed the loop. In this case, the loop will execute 10 times:

```
for (count = 1; count <= 10; count++)
   statement;
```

The *for* loop consists of four parts. The first three parts control the number of times the loop executes. To begin, the statement *count = 1;* assigns the control variable's starting value. The *for* loop performs this initialization one time, when the loop first starts. Next, the loop tests the condition *count <= 10*. If the condition is *true*, the *for* loop executes the statement that follows. If the condition is *false*, the loop ends, and the applet continues its execution with the first statement that follows the loop. If the condition is *true* and the *for* loop executes the statement, the loop then increments the *count* variable by using the statement *count++*. Next, the applet tests the condition *count <= 10*. If the condition is still *true*, the statement again executes, and the process of incrementing and then testing the *count* variable repeats.

The following applet, *ForLoop.java*, uses the *for* loop to display the values 1 through 10 on your screen display:

```
import java.awt.*;
import java.applet.*;
```

```
public class ForLoop extends Applet
  {
    public void paint(Graphics g)
      {
        int count;

        for (count = 1; count <= 10; count++)
          g.drawString(" " + count, count*10, 25);
      }
  }
```

As you can see, the *for* loop initializes the variable *count* to the value 1. The loop then tests if *count's* value is less than or equal to 10. If so, the *for* loop executes the corresponding statement and then increments *count*, repeating the test. Experiment with the applet by changing the value 10 to 5, 4, and even -5.

Note the x-coordinate the applet uses within the *drawString* function. The function uses the variable *count* to control the x-coordinate. As you can see, with each iteration of the loop, the function multiplies the variable by 10 to produce a new coordinate. On the first iteration of the loop, the coordinate is 10. On the second iteration of the loop, the coordinate is 20, on the third, 30, and so on. On the final iteration of the loop, the x-coordinate is 100.

To run the applet, place the following HTML statements within the file *ForLoop.HTML*:

```
<HTML><TITLE>ForLoop Applet</TITLE>
<APPLET CODE="ForLoop.class" WIDTH=300 HEIGHT=200></APPLET></HTML>
```

When you run the *ForLoop.java* applet, the applet will display the numbers 1 through 10 on your screen, as shown in Figure 8.1.

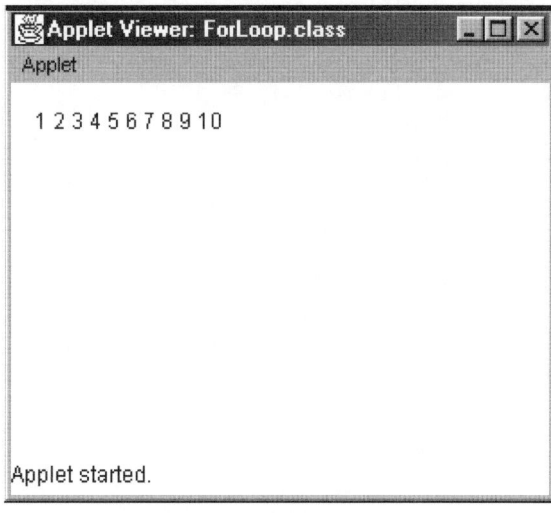

Figure 8.1 *Using a* **for** *statement to repeat a set of statements 10 times.*

In the previous applet, the *for* statement used the value 10 to end the loop. In the following applet, *VariableCount.java*, the *for* loop applet displays the numbers from 1 through the value contained in the variable *ending_count*:

```
import java.awt.*;
import java.applet.*;
```

```
public class VariableCount extends Applet
  {
    public void paint(Graphics g)
      {
        int count;
        int ending_count = 10;

        for (count = 1; count <= ending_count; count++)
          g.drawString(" " + count, count*10, 25);
      }
  }
```

Experiment with this applet by assigning values such as 10, 1, and even 0 to the variable *ending_count*. If you assign the value 0 or a negative value such as −1, the *for* loop will never execute, because the condition *count <= ending_count* immediately fails. As you increase the ending value, pay attention to the spacing between values. You may, for example, have to change the expression **count*10** to **count*15**, or possibly even use an *if* statement to wrap text onto a second line.

JAVA FOR LOOPS SUPPORT COMPOUND STATEMENTS

In Lesson 7, you learned that when your applets perform more than one statement within an *if* or *else*, you must group the statements within left-and-right braces. The same is true for multiple statements and the *for* loop. The following applet, *AddOneToTen.java*, loops through the numbers 1 through 10, displaying and adding each number to a grand total:

```
import java.awt.*;
import java.applet.*;

public class AddOneToTen extends Applet
  {
    public void paint(Graphics g)
      {
        int count;
        int total = 0;

        for (count = 1; count <= 10; count++)
          {
            g.drawString("Adding " + count + " to " + total, 5, count*15);
            total = total + count;
          }
        g.drawString("Ending total is: " + total, 5, count*15);
      }
  }
```

By grouping the statements within braces, the *for* loop can execute multiple statements with each loop (called an *iteration* of the loop). In this case, note how the *drawString* function uses the variable *count* to determine the y-coordinate. On the first iteration of the loop, the y-coordinate is 15. On the second iteration, it is 30, then 45, and so on.

Place the following HTML entries within the file *AddOneToTen.HTML* to run the applet:

```
<HTML><TITLE>AddOneToTen Applet</TITLE>
<APPLET CODE="AddOneToTen.class" WIDTH=300 HEIGHT=200></APPLET></HTML>
```

After you compile and execute this applet, your screen will display an applet window similar to that shown in Figure 8.2.

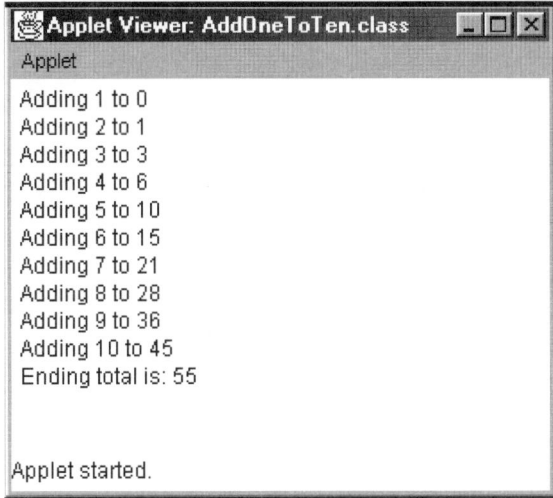

Figure 8.2 *Displaying a count of numbers by using a* **for** *statement.*

CHANGING THE FOR LOOP'S INCREMENT

Thus far, each of this lesson's *for* loops have incremented the loop's control variable by one with each iteration of the loop. However, the *for* loop does not limit your applets to incrementing the variable by one. The following applet, *ForByFives.java*, displays every fifth number from 0 through 50:

```java
import java.awt.*;
import java.applet.*;

public class ForByFives extends Applet
  {
    public void paint(Graphics g)
      {
        int count, y;

        for (count = 0, y = 15; count <= 50; count += 5, y += 15)
          g.drawString("count:" + count, 5, y);
      }
  }
```

When you compile and execute this applet, your screen will display the numbers 0, 5, 10, and so on through 50, as shown in Figure 8.3.

Note the statement the *for* loop uses to increment the variable *count*:

```java
count += 5;
```

71

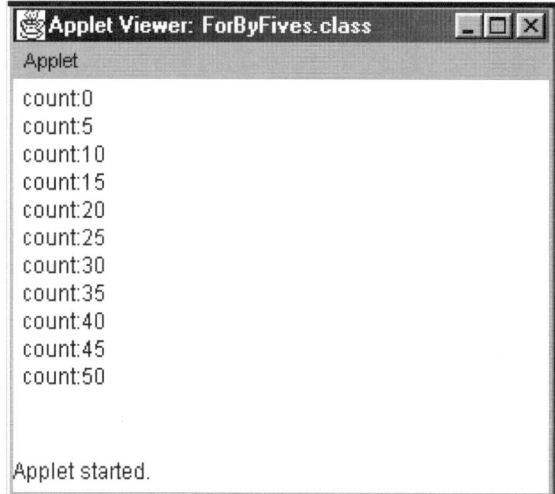

*Figure 8.3 Displaying the numbers 0, 5, 10, … to 50, using a **for** loop.*

When you want to add a value to a variable's current value, and then assign the result to the same variable, Java lets your applets do so in one of two ways. First, assuming your applet must add the value 5 to the variable *count*, your applet can do as shown here:

```
count = count + 5;
```

Second, Java lets you use the shorthand notation shown here to add the value 5 to the variable *count*:

```
count += 5;
```

Because it is easier to write, programmers commonly use this shorthand notation within loops. In addition, this applet uses the *comma* operator within the *for* statement, which lets the applet initialize two variables (*count* and *y*), and later increment both variables. Using the *comma* operator, the applet initializes the variable *count* to 0 and the variable *y* to 15. With each iteration, the *for* loop increments the variable *count* by 5 and the variable *y* by 15. Although you can use the *comma* operator to initialize and increment several variables, your applets will become difficult to read if you try to initialize or increment more than two variables.

When you use a *for* loop, Java does not constrain you to counting up. The following applet, *CountDown.java*, uses a *for* loop to display the numbers 10 down to 1:

```java
import java.awt.*;
import java.applet.*;

public class CountDown extends Applet
  {
    public void paint(Graphics g)
      {
        int count, y;

        for (count = 10, y =15; count > 0; count--, y += 15)
          g.drawString("count: " + count, 5, y);
      }
  }
```

As you can see, the *for* loop initializes the variable *count* to 10 and the variable *y* to 15. With each iteration, the loop decrements the variable *count's* value by 1 and increments the variable *y* by 15 (the code uses the *y* variable to specify the location within the applet window at which the applet will display its next line of output). When the variable *count* contains the value 0, the loop ends.

BE AWARE OF INFINITE LOOPS

As you have learned, a *for* loop provides your applets with a way to repeat related statements a specific number of times. Using a control variable, the *for* loop essentially counts the number of iterations it has performed. When the loop reaches its ending condition, your applet stops repeating the statements and continues its execution at the first statement that follows the *for* loop.

Unfortunately, due to errors within applets, there are times when a loop never reaches its ending condition and, thus, loops forever (or until you end the applet). Such unending loops are called *infinite loops*. In other words, they are loops that have no way of ending. The following *for* statement, for example, creates an infinite loop:

```
for (count = 0; count < 100; wrong_variable++)
    Statements
```

As you can see, the *for* loop uses the *count* variable as its control variable. Within the loop's increment section, however, the applet increments the wrong variable. As a result, the loop never increments the *count* variable, and *count* will never have a value greater than or equal to 100. Thus, the loop becomes a never-ending infinite loop.

It is important to note that *for* loops are not restricted to using values of type *int* as their loop-control variable. The following applet, *ForAlphabet.java*, for example, uses a variable of type *char* to display the letters of the alphabet within one loop, and a variable of type *float* to display floating-point numbers within a second loop:

```
import java.awt.*;
import java.applet.*;

public class ForAlphabet extends Applet
  {
    public void paint(Graphics g)
      {
        int x;
        char letter;
        float value;

        for (letter = 'A', x = 5; letter <= 'Z'; letter++, x += 10)
          g.drawString(" " + letter, x, 25);

        for (value = 0, x = 5; value <= 1.0; value += 0.25, x += 35)
            g.drawString(" " + value, x, 50);
      }
  }
```

When you compile and execute this applet, the applet window will display the output shown in Figure 8.4. Take time to experiment with the applet's *for* statements, changing each loop's starting or ending values. Also, note that each loop uses the variable *x* to control the location within the applet window at which the applet will display the next value.

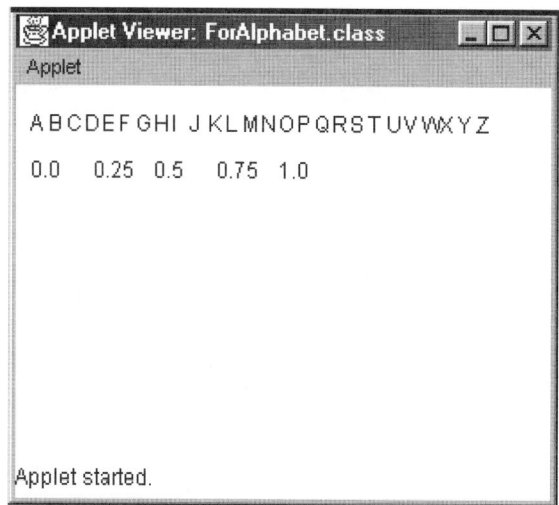

Figure 8.4 Using characters and floating-point variables within for loops.

LOOPING A SPECIFIC NUMBER OF TIMES

One of the most common operations your applets will perform is repeating one or more statements a specific number of times. The Java *for* statement lets your applets do just that. The *for* statement uses a control variable that keeps track of the number of times the loop has executed. The general format of the *for* statement is as follows:

```
for (initialization; test; increment)
    statement;
```

When the *for* loop begins, it assigns the starting value to the loop's control variable. Next, the applet tests the loop's condition. If the condition is *true*, the applet executes the loop's statements. Next, the applet increments the loop's control variable and repeats the condition test. If the condition is *true*, the process repeats. If the condition is *false*, the *for* loop ends, and the applet continues its execution at the first statement that follows the *for* statement.

LOOPING WITH A WHILE LOOP

As you just learned, the Java *for* loop lets your applets repeat one or more statements a specific number of times. In some cases, however, your applets must repeat statements as long as a specific condition is met (is *true*). For example, assume your applet displays buttons the user can select to perform specific processing. Such applets may repeatedly loop until the user clicks on the Exit button. For situations where your applets must loop as long as a specific condition is met, but not necessarily a specific number of times, your applets can use the Java *while* statement. The general format of the *while* statement is as follows:

```
while (condition_is_true)
    statement;
```

When your applet encounters a *while* statement, your applet tests the specified condition. If the condition is *true*, the applet executes the *while* loop's statements. After the last statement in the loop executes, the *while* loop again tests the condition. If the condition is still *true*, the loop's statements repeat, and this process continues. When the condition finally becomes *false*, the loop ends, and your applet continues its execution at the first statement that follows the loop.

Several of the applets presented in the lessons that follow make extensive use of *while* loops. Rather than present such an applet here, whose *while* loop contents may confuse you, we will examine the *while* loop in a later lesson when the loop is first used.

LOOPING UNTIL A SPECIFIC CONDITION OCCURS

As your applets become more complex, there will be times when you must perform a group of related statements until a specific condition occurs. For example, your applet might calculate payroll amounts for all the employees in a company. In this case, the applet would loop until the last employee had been processed. To repeat statements until a specific condition occurs, your applets will normally use a *while* statement:

```
while (condition_is_true)
     statement;
```

When your applet encounters a *while* statement, your applet will evaluate the loop's condition. If the condition is *true*, your applet will execute the *while* loop's statements. After the applet performs the last statement within the loop, the applet tests the condition again. If the condition is *true*, the applet repeats this process, executing the statements and then repeating the condition. When the condition evaluates as *false*, the applet continues its execution at the first statement that follows the *while* statement.

PERFORMING STATEMENTS AT LEAST ONE TIME

As you have just learned, the Java *while* loop lets your applets repeat a set of statements until a specific condition is met. When your applet encounters a *while* statement, the applet first evaluates the condition specified. If the condition is *true*, the applet enters the loop. If the condition is *false*, the *while* loop's statements are never executed. Depending on your applet's purpose, there will be many times when you will want the applet to perform a set of statements at least once, and then, based on some condition, possibly repeat. In such cases, your applets can use the *do while* loop:

```
do {
     statements;
} while (condition_is_true);
```

When your applet encounters a *do while* loop, the applet enters the loop and starts executing the statements the loop contains. The applet then evaluates the specified condition. If the condition is *true*, the applet loops back to the start of the loop:

```
do {
     statements;
} while (condition_is_true);
```

If the condition is *false*, the applet does not repeat the loop's instructions, continuing instead with the first statement that follows the loop. A common use of the *do while* loop is to display menu options and then process the user's selection. You will want your applet to display the menu at least one time. If the user selects any option except Quit, the applet will perform the option and then redisplay the menu (repeating the loop's statement). If the user selects Quit, the loop will end, and the applet will continue its processing at the first statement after the loop.

REPEATING STATEMENTS PROVIDED A CONDITION IS TRUE

Depending on your applet's requirements, there may be times when your applet must perform a set of statements at least one time and then possibly repeat the statements if a specific condition is *true*. In such cases, your applets should use the Java *do while* statement:

```
    do {
        statements;
    } while (condition);
```

When your applet encounters a *do while* statement, your applet immediately performs the statements the loop contains. Then, the applet examines the loop's condition. If the condition is *true*, the applet repeats the loop's statements and the process continues. When the loop's condition becomes *false*, the applet continues its execution at the first statement that follows the *do while* statement.

USING THE BREAK AND CONTINUE STATEMENTS WITHIN LOOPS

As you examine Java programs, you may periodically encounter programs that use the *continue* or *break* statements to control processing within a loop. Normally, when you use a *for*, *while*, or *do while* loop to perform specific processing, your loop has one test that it performs to determine if it should continue or end its processing. If the loop's test is *true*, the Java performs the statements that reside within the loop. If the loop's test is *false*, Java continues your program's execution at the first statement that follows the loop.

Using the *break* and *continue* statements, however, a program can change a loop's standard behavior. In Lesson 7, "Teaching Java Applets to Make Decisions," you used the *break* statement within a *switch* statement to indicate the last statement Java should perform when one of the *switch* statement's cases matched a specific condition. As it turns out, you can use the *break* statement within a loop to immediately end a loop's processing. When Java encounters a *break* statement within a loop, Java will continue the program's execution at the first statement that follows the loop. The following applet, *BreakOnThree.java*, uses a *break* statement to terminate a *for* loop's processing when the loop's control variable equals the value 3:

```java
import java.awt.*;
import java.applet.*;


public class BreakOnThree extends Applet
  {
    public void paint(Graphics g)
      {
        int i;
        for (i = 1; i <= 10; i++)
          {
            if (i == 3)
              break;
            g.drawString(" " + i, i*10, 25);
          }
        g.drawString("Done.", 5, 50);
      }
  }
```

To run the applet, place the following HTML statements within the file *BreakOnThree.HTML*:

```html
<HTML><TITLE>BreakOnThree Applet</TITLE>
<APPLET CODE="BreakOnThree.class" WIDTH=300 HEIGHT=200></APPLET></HTML>
```

When you run the *BreakOnThree* applet, your applet window will display the numbers 1 and 2, followed by the message *Done*, as shown in Figure 8.5.

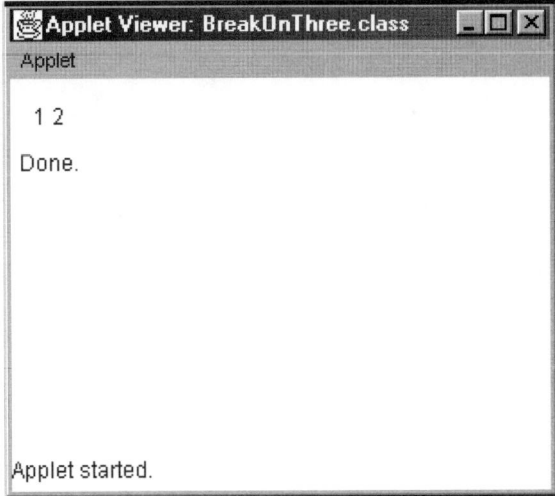

Figure 8.5 *Using a* **break** *statement to control a loop's execution.*

In most cases, if you find yourself placing a *break* statement (or a *continue* statement, for that matter) within a loop, you should examine your loop's code and determine a better way to state the loop's test condition. In the case of the *BreakOnThree.java* applet, you could achieve the same processing without the *break* statement using the following *for* statement:

```
for (i = 1; i <= 2; i++)
    g.drawString(" " + i, i*10, 25);
```

The following applet, *Continue.java*, uses a *continue* statement to control a *for* loop's processing. When Java encounters a *continue* statement within a loop, Java skips the loop's remaining statements and immediately performs the loop's test. If the test is *true*, Java starts the loop's next iteration. If, instead, the test is *false*, Java continues its processing at the first statement following the loop. In the case of the *Continue.java* applet, the code uses the *continue* statement to skip the loop's statement when the loop counter's value is even, which causes the loop to display only odd values, as shown in Figure 8.6.

The following statements implement the *Continue.java* applet:

```
import java.awt.*;
import java.applet.*;


public class Continue extends Applet
   {
     public void paint(Graphics g)
       {
         int i, count = 0;


         for (i = 1; i <= 10; i++)
           {
             if ((i % 2) == 1)
                continue;
             g.drawString(" " + i, ++count*10, 25);
           }
       }
   }
```

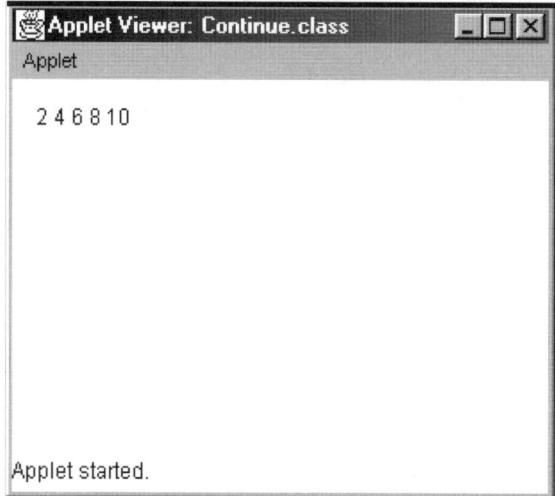

Figure 8.6 *Using a* **continue** *statement to control a loop's processing.*

As briefly discussed, if you are using a *continue* statement within a loop, there is often a better way you can write your code which eliminates the *continue* statement's use and which makes your code easier to understand. In the case of the *Continue.java* applet, you could use the following *for* loop to display odd values:

```
for (i = 1; i <= 10; i++)
  if ((i % 2) == 1)
    g.drawString(" " + i, ++count*10, 25);
```

Within a Java applet, it is not uncommon to find one loop within a second loop. Java programmers refer to the inner loop as a *nested loop*. The following applet, *NestedLoop.java*, for example, uses a nested *for* statement to display the numbers 1 through 10 three times within the applet window, as shown in Figure 8.7.

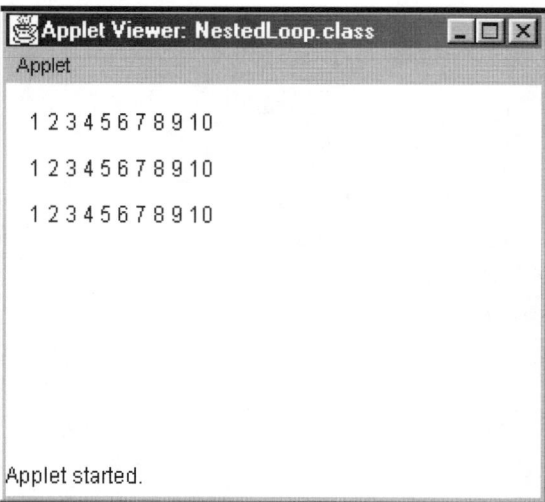

Figure 8.7 *Using a nested* **for** *statement.*

The following statements implement the *NestedLoop.java* applet:

```
import java.awt.*;
import java.applet.*;
```

```
public class NestedLoop extends Applet
  {
    public void paint(Graphics g)
      {
        int i, j;
        for (i = 1; i <= 3; i++)
          for (j = 1; j <= 10; j++)
            g.drawString(" " + j, j*10, 25*i);
      }
  }
```

To run the applet, place the following HTML statements within the file *NestedLoop.HTML*:

```
<HTML><TITLE>NestedLoop Applet</TITLE>
<APPLET CODE="NestedLoop.class" WIDTH=300 HEIGHT=200></APPLET></HTML>
```

When you place a *break* or *continue* statement within a nested loop, the statement controls the innermost loop's processing. For example, the following applet, *NestedBreak.java*, uses a *break* statement to end the innerloop when the control variable *i* contains the value 2. As a result, the applet skips the inner row of numbers, as shown in Figure 8.8.

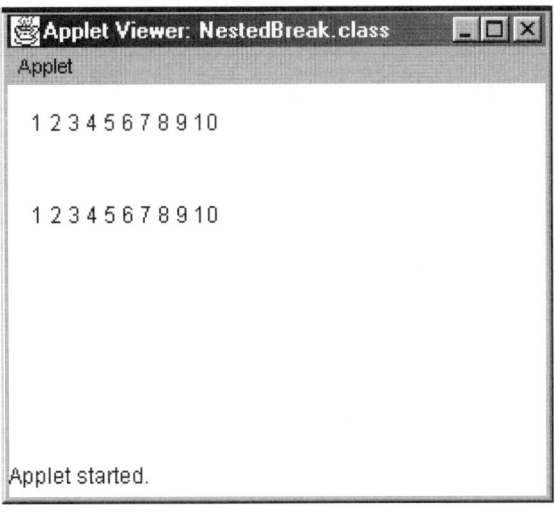

Figure 8.8 *Using a **break** statement within a nested loop.*

The following statements implement the *NestedBreak.java* applet:

```
import java.awt.*;
import java.applet.*;


public class NestedBreak extends Applet
  {
    public void paint(Graphics g)
      {
        int i, j;
        for (i = 1; i <= 3; i++)
          for (j = 1; j <= 10; j++)
            {
```

```
            if ((i % 2) == 0)
              break;
            g.drawString(" " + j, j*10, 25*i);
        }
      }
    }
```

To run the applet, place the following HTML statements within the file *NestedBreak.HTML*:

```
<HTML><TITLE>NestedBreak Applet</TITLE>
<APPLET CODE="NestedBreak.class" WIDTH=300 HEIGHT=200></APPLET></HTML>
```

Depending on a loop's processing, there may be times when you want a *break* or *continue* statement to affect a specific loop, as opposed to the inner loop. In such cases, Java lets you assign a label (a name) to the loop and then specify the label name within the *break* or *continue* statement. To create a label, you simply place an identifier (a name) within your code, followed by a colon (label:). The following applet, *LabeledLoop.java*, uses a labeled loop with a *break* statement:

```
import java.awt.*;
import java.applet.*;


public class LabeledLoop extends Applet
  {
    public void paint(Graphics g)
      {
        int i, j;
        done:
        for (i = 1; i <= 3; i++)
          for (j = 1; j <= 10; j++)
            {
              if ((i % 2) == 0)
                break done;
              g.drawString(" " + j, j*10, 25*i);
            }
        }
    }
```

To run the applet, place the following HTML statements within the file *LabeledLoop.HTML*:

```
<HTML><TITLE>LabeledLoop Applet</TITLE>
<APPLET CODE="LabeledLoop.class" WIDTH=300 HEIGHT=200></APPLET></HTML>
```

Again, as previously discussed, if you examine the applets that use the *continue* and *break* statements within a loop, you should find that you could easily rewrite the code to eliminate the statements and to produce code that is easier for other programmers to read and understand.

TAKING A CYBER FIELD TRIP

If you use programs such as Excel, you may have used bar charts or pie charts to present data in a meaningful way. In a similar way, the Java Development Kit provides the Bar Chart applet, which as shown in Figure 8.9, displays a labeled bar chart. To run the applet or to download the applet's source code, visit the Jamsa Press Web site at *www.jamsa.com/java_demos/Barchart.html.*

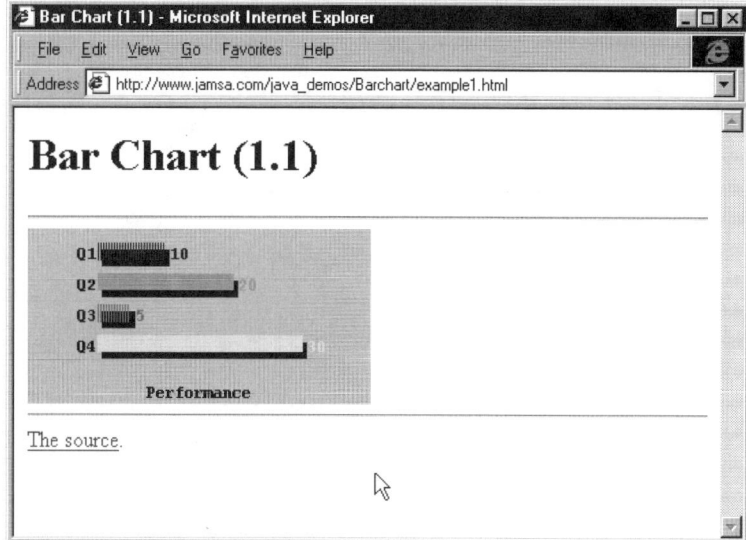

***Figure 8.9** Displaying a barchart within a Java applet.*

WHAT YOU MUST KNOW

Iterative processing is the ability of an applet to repeat one or more statements. This lesson presented the Java iterative (or looping) statements. As you have learned, the *for* statement lets your applet repeat one or more statements a specific number of times. The *while* statement lets your applets repeat statements as long as a specific condition is *true*. Lastly, the *do while* statement lets your applets perform statements at least one time, possibly repeating them if a specified condition is *true*. In Lesson 9, "Using Functions to Simplify Java Applets," you will learn how to break larger applets into smaller, more manageable pieces, called *functions*. Before you continue with Lesson 9, however, make sure you have learned the following key points:

- ☑ The Java *for* statement lets your applets repeat one or more statements a specific number of times.

- ☑ The *for* statement consists of four parts: an initialization, a test condition, the statements that are to repeat, and an increment.

- ☑ The *for* statement does not require your applets to increment the loop's control variable by 1, nor does the *for* statement require your applets to count upward.

- ☑ The Java *while* loop lets your applets repeat statements as long as a specific condition is *true*.

- ☑ Programs often use the *while* loop to read the contents of a file until the end of the file is encountered.

- ☑ The Java *do while* statement lets your applets perform one or more statements at least once, possibly repeating them based on a specific condition.

- ☑ Programs often use *do while* statements for menu processing.

- ☑ When the tested condition in the *for*, *while*, or *do while* loops become *false*, the applet continues its execution at the first statement that follows the loop.

LESSON 9

USING FUNCTIONS TO SIMPLIFY JAVA APPLETS

As your applets increase in size and complexity, you should break them up into smaller, more manageable pieces called *functions*. Each function within your applet should perform a specific task. For example, if you are writing a multimedia applet, you might create one function that displays a background image, a second function that plays background music, a third function to rotate the company logo, and so on. When your applet must perform a specific task, the applet *calls* the corresponding function, providing the function with information it needs to perform its processing, such as the filename of a graphics image or sound file. This lesson will teach you how to create and use functions within your Java applets. By the time you finish this lesson, you will understand the following key concepts:

- ◆ Within your applets, functions group related statements that perform a specific task.

- ◆ To use a function, your applet calls the function by specifying the function's name followed by parentheses, such as *beep()*.

- ◆ When they complete their processing, many functions return a value of a specific type, such as *int* or *float*, that your applets can test or assign to a variable.

- ◆ Your applets pass parameters (information) to functions, such as a filename, x-and-y coordinates, or a username, by including the parameters within the parentheses that follow the function name.

As your applets become larger and more powerful, your use of functions will become essential. As you will find, however, creating and using functions in Java is very easy.

CREATING AND USING YOUR FIRST FUNCTIONS

As you create your applets, you should design each function to perform a specific task. If you find that a function is performing more than one task, you should divide the function into two or more functions. Each function you create within your applets must have a unique name. As was the case with variable names, the function names you choose should correspond to the operation the function performs. For example, by simply looking at the function names listed in Table 9, you have a good idea as to each function's purpose.

Function Name	Function Purpose
PlayBackgroundMusic	Plays an audio file in the background as the user traverses the Web page
DisplayBackgroundImage	Loads and displays a background image
GetUserName	Prompts the user for his or her name
PrintDocument	Prints the specified document file

Table 9 Examples of meaningful function names.

Each Java function you will create will be similar in structure to the *paint* function you have been using in all of the previous applets. In other words, the function name is preceded by a type and followed by a parameter list that appears within parentheses. You group the function's statements within left-and-right braces, as shown here:

```
return_type   function_name(parameter_list)
  {
      variable_declarations;

      statements;
  }
```

Consider, for example, how this function structure corresponds to the following *paint* function:

```
type name(parameter_list)
  {
      variable_declarations;

      statements;

  }
```

```
public void paint()
  {
    int count;

      for (count = 0; count < 10; count++)
        g.drawString(" " + count, count*15, 5);
  }
```

The following statements, for example, define a function named *paint* that displays a message to the applet window:

```
public void paint(Graphics g)
  {
    g.drawString("Rescued by Java", 5, 10);
  }
```

To use a function, your applet *calls* the function. Within this *paint* function, for example, you can see that the statements call the *drawString* function to actually display the message. In most cases, your applet will call functions in this way. At other times, however, the *appletviewer* or your browser will call the function. For example, as you have learned, when the browser must update the applet window, the browser calls the applet's *paint* function.

As you may remember from Lesson 2, "Creating Your First Java Applet," the keyword *void* that precedes the function name specifies the function does not return a value. Likewise, the keyword *public* lets other classes (or the browser) call the *paint* function. Lesson 25, "Local Variables and Scope," will examine the *public* keyword in detail.

In most of the applets you have examined throughout this book, you have used the *paint* function to display messages to the applet window. To display the messages, the *paint* function specified each of the *drawString* function calls. The following applet, *ShowMessage.java*, creates a function named *ShowMessage* that displays a message on the screen. In this case, when the applet starts, the browser calls the *paint* function to update the applet window. The *paint* function, in turn, calls the *ShowMessage* function to display a series of messages:

```
import java.awt.*;
import java.applet.*;

public class ShowMessage extends Applet
  {
    public void paint(Graphics g)
      {
        ShowMessage(g);
      }

    public void ShowMessage(Graphics g)
      {
```

```
        g.drawString("Book: Rescued by Java", 5, 15);
        g.drawString("Lesson: 9", 5, 30);
        g.drawString("Lesson title: Using Functions to Simplify Java Applets",
                5, 45);
    }
}
```

Place the following HTML entries within the file *ShowMessage.HTML* to run the applet:

```
<HTML><TITLE>ShowMessage Applet</TITLE>
<APPLET CODE="ShowMessage.class" WIDTH=300 HEIGHT=200></APPLET></HTML>
```

After you compile and execute this applet, your screen will display an applet window similar to that shown in Figure 9.1.

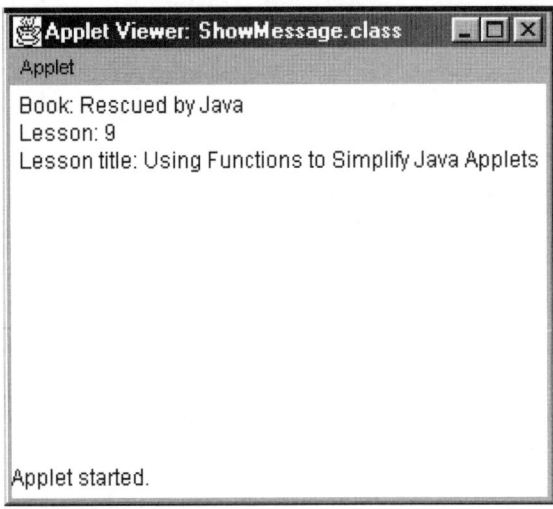

*Figure 9.1 Displaying messages from within the **ShowMessage** function.*

In this case, the applet could have written these same messages from within the *paint* function. The applet uses the *ShowMessage* function simply to help you understand the steps you must perform to create and later call a function. As you can see, the *paint* function calls *ShowMessage* by placing the variable *g* within the parentheses that follow the *ShowMessage* function name. As you will learn, *g* is a parameter or a value passed to the function. In this case, the *g* parameter provides the *ShowMessage* function a graphics context that it uses to display the message. You will examine graphics contexts in detail in Lesson 9.

When the applet encounters the *ShowMessage* function call within *paint*, the applet begins executing the statements that reside within the *ShowMessage* function. After the applet executes all the statements the function contains (in other words, the function completes), the applet's execution continues at the statement that immediately follows the function call.

To help you better understand how the applet moves its execution from the *paint* function to *ShowMessage* and then back to *paint*, the following applet, *ShowFunctionCalls.java*, places statements within the *paint* function that precede and follow the *ShowMessage* call:

```
import java.awt.*;
import java.applet.*;
```

```
public class ShowFunctionCalls extends Applet
  {
    public void paint(Graphics g)
      {
        g.drawString("About to call the function", 5, 15);
        ShowMessage(g);
        g.drawString("Back from the function", 5, 75);
      }

    public void ShowMessage(Graphics g)
      {
        g.drawString("Book: Rescued by Java", 5, 30);
        g.drawString("Lesson: 9", 5, 45);
        g.drawString("Lesson title: Using Functions to Simplify Java" +
                     "Applets", 5, 60);
      }
  }
```

Place the following HTML statements in the file *ShowFunctionCalls.HTML* to run the applet:

```
<HTML><TITLE>ShowFunctionCalls Applet</TITLE>
<APPLET CODE="ShowFunctionCalls.class" WIDTH=300 HEIGHT=200></APPLET>
</HTML>
```

After you compile and execute the applet, your screen will display an applet window similar to that shown in Figure 9.2.

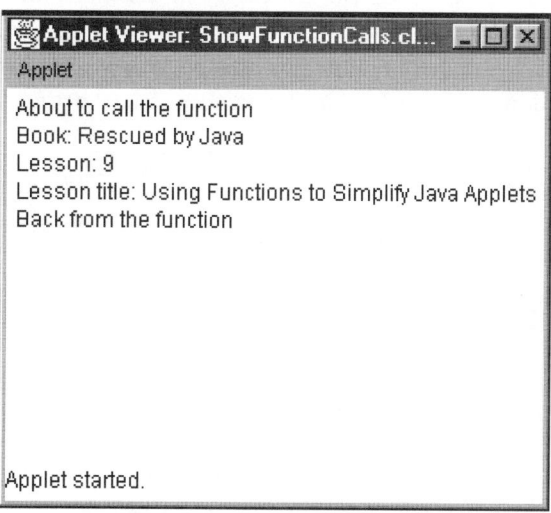

*Figure 9.2 Showing the flow execution from **paint** to **ShowMessage** and back to **paint**.*

In this case, the browser calls the *paint* function to update the applet window. Within the *paint* function, the applet executes the first statement, which displays a message to the user that the applet is about to call the *ShowMessage* function. Next, the applet encounters the function call and starts executing the statements in *ShowMesssage*. After the applet executes the function's statements, the applet continues its execution back in *paint*, at the statement that immediately follows the function call. In this case, the applet displays a message telling the user that it has returned from the function call and then ends.

The following applet, *TwoMessageFunctions.java*, uses two functions, *ShowTitle* and *ShowLesson*, to display information about this book:

```java
import java.awt.*;
import java.applet.*;

public class TwoMessageFunctions extends Applet
   {
     public void paint(Graphics g)
       {
          ShowTitle(g);
          ShowLesson(g);
       }

     public void ShowTitle(Graphics g)
       {
          g.drawString("Book: Rescued by Java", 5, 30);
       }

     public void ShowLesson(Graphics g)
       {
          g.drawString("Lesson 9: Using Functions to Simplify Java Applets",
                       5, 45);
       }
   }
```

When the applet's execution begins, the browser will first call *paint* which, in turn, will call the *ShowTitle* function that displays a message that contains this book's title. When *ShowTitle* ends, the applet continues its execution within *paint*, which then calls the *ShowLesson* function, which displays a message about this lesson. When the *ShowLesson* function ends, the applet's execution continues within the *paint* function. Because there are no more statements in *paint*, the applet ends.

Place the following HTML statements in the file *TwoMessageFunctions.HTML* to run the applet:

```html
<HTML><TITLE>TwoMessageFunctions Applet</TITLE>
<APPLET CODE="TwoMessageFunctions.class" WIDTH=300 HEIGHT=200></APPLET>
</HTML>
```

When you compile and execute this applet, your screen will display an applet window similar to that shown in Figure 9.3.

The functions presented in this lesson have performed very simple tasks. In each case, your applet could have easily performed the same processing without the use of the functions by simply including the function's statements within *paint*. However, the purpose of the applet's functions was to show you how your applet defines and later calls a function. As your applets become more complex, you will use functions to simplify large tasks by breaking your applet into smaller, more manageable pieces. As you create functions, you will find that because they contain fewer lines of code than one large applet, your functions are easy to understand and easy to change. In addition, you will find that, in many cases, you can use a function that you created for one applet in a second applet, with no changes. By creating a library of functions, you will reduce the amount of time you spend coding and testing similar functions in the future.

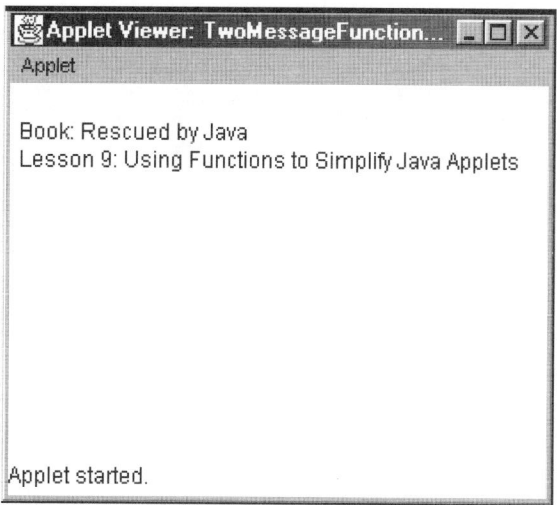

Figure 9.3 *Using two functions to display messages.*

CALLING A FUNCTION

A function is a collection of related statements that perform a specific task. By creating functions within your applets, you can break large tasks into smaller, more manageable pieces. Your applets execute a function's statements by *calling* the function. To call the function, your applets simply reference the function's name followed by parentheses, as shown here:

```
function_name();
```

When your applet passes information (parameters) to the function, your applet will place the information within the parentheses, separated by commas:

```
StartMusic("MUSIC.AU", Volume, RepeatOption);
```

After the last statement in the function completes, the applet's execution continues at the first statement that follows the function call.

APPLETS CAN PASS INFORMATION TO FUNCTIONS

To increase the capability of your functions, Java lets your applets pass information (parameters) to your functions. When a function uses parameters, you must tell Java each parameter's type, such as *int*, *float*, *char*, and so on. For example, the following function, *ShowNumber*, uses two parameters. The first parameter is a *Graphics* object that provides the graphics context with which the function will display a message. The second parameter is a value of type *int*:

```
void ShowNumber(Graphics g, int value)
  {
    g.drawString("The parameter's value is: " + value, 5, 25);
  }
```

When your applet invokes the *ShowNumber* function, your applet must now pass a value to the function, as shown here:

```
ShowNumber(g, 1001);
```

Java, in turn, will substitute the value passed for each occurrence of the parameter names *g* and *value* within the function, as shown here:

```
ShowNumber(g, 1001);


    void ShowNumber(Graphics g, int value)
      {
         g.drawString("The parameter's value is: " + value, 5, 25);
      }


        void ShowNumber(g, 1001)
          {
               g.drawString("The parameter's value is: " + 1001, 5, 25);
          }
```

As you can see, because Java substitutes the parameter values, the function *ShowNumber* displays the value 1001.

The following applet, *UseParameters.java*, slightly changes the function *ShowNumber* to support a third parameter named *y* that specificies the y-coordinate at which the function displays its message. The applet then calls the function several times to display different values:

```
import java.awt.*;
import java.applet.*;

public class UseParameters extends Applet
  {
    public void paint(Graphics g)
      {
        ShowNumber(g, 1001, 15);
        ShowNumber(g, 9, 30);
        ShowNumber(g, -33, 45);
        ShowNumber(g, 4431, 60);
      }

    public void ShowNumber(Graphics g, int value, int y)
      {
        g.drawString("The number is: " + value, 5, y);
      }
  }
```

Place the following statements within the HTML file, *UseParameters.HTML,* to run the applet:

```
<HTML><TITLE>UseParameters Applet</TITLE>
<APPLET CODE="UseParameters.class" WIDTH=300 HEIGHT=200></APPLET></HTML>
```

After you compile and execute this program, your screen will display an applet window similar to that shown in Figure 9.4.

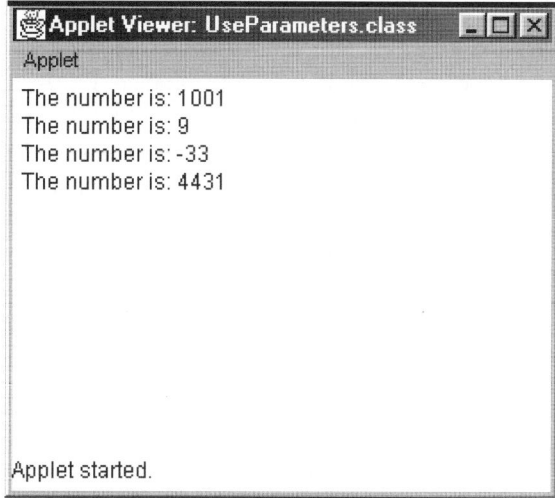

Figure 9.4 *Passing parameter values to the **ShowNumber** function.*

As you can see, each time the applet invokes the function, Java assigns the correct number to the variable *value*. Take time to experiment with this applet, changing the values *paint* passes to the function and noting the result.

Each function parameter is a specific type. In the case of the *ShowNumber* function, the first parameter value must be type *Graphics* and the second type *int*. If you try to pass a value of a different type to the function, such as a floating-point value to the parameter, the compiler will generate an error.

In most cases, your applets will pass several values to a function. For each parameter passed, your function must specify a name and type.

PASSING PARAMETERS TO FUNCTIONS

When your functions use parameters, your functions must specify a unique name and type for each parameter. When your applet invokes the function, Java will assign the parameter values to the function parameter names from left to right. Each function parameter has a specific type, such as *int*, *float*, or *char*. The values your applet passes to a function using parameters must match each parameter's type.

FUNCTIONS CAN RETURN A RESULT TO THE CALLER

A function should perform a specific task for your applet. In many cases, a function will perform some type of calculation. The function will then return its result to the caller. When a function returns a value, you must tell Java the value's type, such as *int*, *float*, *char*, and so on. To inform Java of the function's return type, you simply precede the function name with the corresponding type. For example, the following function, *AddValues*, adds its two integer parameters and returns a result of type *int* to the calling applet:

```
public int AddValues(int a, int b)
  {
    int result;

    result = a + b;

    return(result);
  }
```

In this case, the word *int* that appears before the function name specifies the function's *return type*. Functions use the *return* statement to return a value to their caller. When your applet encounters the *return* statement, the applet returns the value specified and the function's execution ends, returning control to the applet. Within the applet, you can use the return value, as shown here:

```
result = AddValues(1 + 2);
```

In this case, the applet assigns the function's return value to the variable *result*. Your applet can also directly print the function's return value by using *drawString*, as shown here:

```
g.drawString("Sum of values is: " + AddValues(500, 501), 5, 25);
```

The previous implementation of the *AddValues* function used three statements to make the function's processing easier to understand. You can, however, reduce the function to a *return* statement, as shown here:

```
public int AddValues(int a, int b)
 {
   return(a+b);
 }
```

The following applet, *AddValues.java*, uses the *AddValues* function to add several different values:

```
import java.awt.*;
import java.applet.*;

public class AddValues extends Applet
  {
    public void paint(Graphics g)
     {
        g.drawString("5 + 5 = " + AddValues(5, 5), 5, 15);
        g.drawString("500 + 15 = " + AddValues(500, 15), 5, 30);
        g.drawString("35 + -35 = " + AddValues(35, -35), 5, 45);
        g.drawString("54 + 45 = " + AddValues(54, 45), 5, 60);
     }

    public int AddValues(int x, int y)
      {
        return(x + y);
      }
  }
```

Take time to experiment with this applet, changing the values the applet passes to the function. You might try passing very large values to the function, such as 2000000000 and 3000000000. As you might guess, the function (which returns a value of type *int*) will experience an overflow error.

Not all functions will return the type *int*. The following function, *AverageValue*, returns the average of two integer values, which can be a fractional value, such as 3.5:

```
double AverageValue(int a, int b)
  {
    return((a + b) / 2.0);
  }
```

In this case, the keyword *double*, which precedes the function name, specifies the function's return type.

FUNCTIONS THAT RETURN VALUES

If a function does not return a value, you precede the function name with the type *void*. Otherwise, you should precede the function name with the type of value the function returns, such as *int, float, char*, and so on. To return a value to the caller, the function uses the *return* statement. When your applet encounters a *return* statement, the function's execution ends, and the value specified is returned to the caller. There may be times when you will encounter a *return* statement within a function that does not return a value:

```
return ;
```

In this case, the function is of type *void* (does not return a value) and the *return* statement simply ends the function's execution.

Note: If statements appear in a function after the **return** *statement, the statements will not execute. As discussed, when your applet encounters a* **return** *statement within a function, the applet returns the corresponding value, the function ends, and the applet's execution continues at the first statement that follows the function call.*

USING A FUNCTION'S RETURN VALUE

When a function returns a value, the caller can assign the return value to a variable by using the assignment statement, as shown here:

```
payroll_amount = payroll(employee, hours, salary);
```

In addition, the caller can simply reference the function. For example, the following statement displays the function's return value by using *drawString*:

```
g.drawString("The employee made " + payroll(employee, hours, salary),
     5, 25);
```

Also, the caller can use the return value within a condition, as shown here:

```
if (payroll(employee, hours, salary) < 500.00)
    g.drawString("This employee needs a raise", 5, 25);
```

As you can see, an applet can use a function's return value in many different ways.

YOU CANNOT CHANGE A PARAMETER'S VALUE

When you pass parameters to a function, the function may, as a part of its processing, change the parameter's value. However, when a function changes a parameter's value, the change lasts only until the function ends. When the calling function resumes its processing, the parameter will have the same value it did prior to the function call. In other words, a function cannot make a permanent change to a parameter's value.

For example, the following applet, *NoChange.java*, passes two parameters, named *big* and *small*, to the function *DisplayValues*. The function *DisplayValues*, in turn, assigns both parameters the value 1001 and then displays each parameter's value. When the *DisplayValues* function ends, the *paint* function resumes and displays the parameters' values.

```
import java.awt.*;
import java.applet.*;

public class NoChanges extends Applet
   {
     public void paint(Graphics g)
        {
           int big = 2002;
           int small = 0;

           g.drawString("Values before function call " + big + " and " +
                     small, 5, 15);
           DisplayValues(g, big, small);
           g.drawString("Values after function call " + big + " and " +
                     small, 5, 45);
        }

     public void DisplayValues(Graphics g, int x, int y)
        {
           x = 1001;
           y = 1001;

           g.drawString("Values in function: " + x + " and " + y, 5, 30);
        }
   }
```

Place the following HTML statements within the file, *NoChanges.HTML*, to run the applet:

```
<HTML><TITLE>NoChanges Applet</TITLE>
<APPLET CODE="NoChanges.class" WIDTH=300 HEIGHT=200></APPLET></HTML>
```

After you compile and execute this applet, your screen will display an applet window similar to that shown in Figure 9.5.

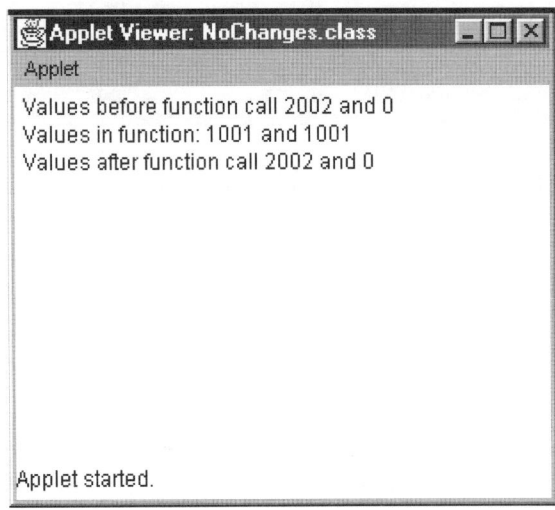

Figure 9.5 Functions cannot make permanent changes to parameter values.

As you can see, within the *DisplayValues* function, the parameter values have been changed to 1001. However, when the function ends, the values of the variables *big* and *small* within *paint* have not changed. To understand why the change to the parameters did not affect the variables *big* and *small* within *paint*, you must understand how Java passes parameters to functions.

By default, when your applets pass a parameter to a function, Java makes a copy of the parameter's value and places the copy into a temporary memory location, called the *stack*. The function then uses the *copy* of the value to perform its operations. When the function ends, Java discards the stack contents and any changes the function has made to the copy of the parameter value.

As you know, a variable is a name your applet assigns to a location in memory that stores a value of a specific type. Assume, for example, that the variables *big* and *small* reside at memory locations 10 and 12. When you pass the variables to the function *DisplayValues*, Java will place copies of the variables' values on the stack. As Figure 9.6 shows, the function *DisplayValues* will then use the copies of the variables' values.

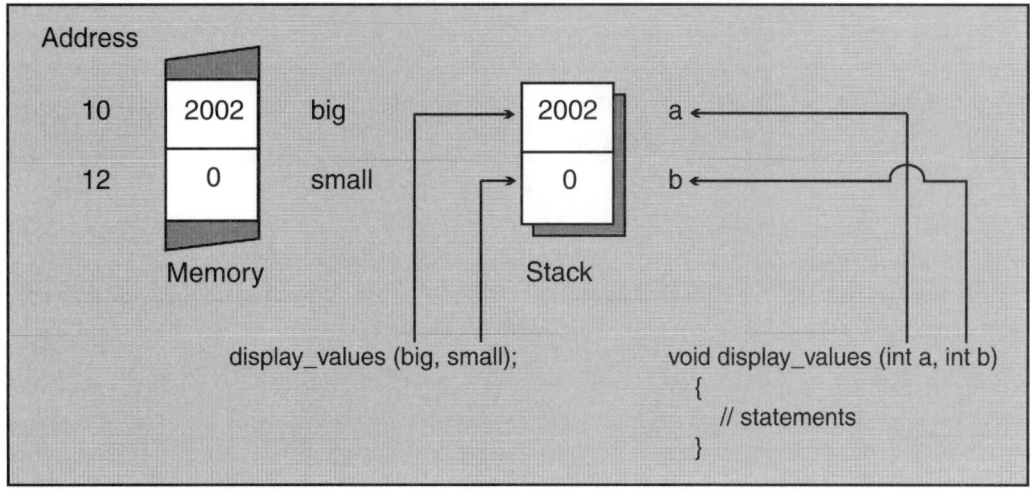

Figure 9.6 *Java places copies of parameter values in a temporary storage location called the stack.*

As you can see, the function *DisplayValues* has access to the contents of the stack, which contains copies of the values 2002 and 0. Because the function *DisplayValues* has no knowledge of the *big* and *small* variables' memory locations (address 10 and 12), the function has no way to change the variables' actual values.

WHY JAVA FUNCTIONS NORMALLY CANNOT CHANGE PARAMETER VALUES

When you pass parameters to a function, Java places copies of the parameter values in a temporary storage location, called the stack. Any changes the function makes to the parameters appear only within the stack. When the function ends, Java discards the stack's contents, along with any changes the function makes to the parameters. Because the function has no knowledge of the parameters' memory address, the functions cannot change the values the parameters store.

JAVA FUNCTIONS CAN CHANGE CLASS AND ARRAY VARIABLES

As you will learn in later lessons, Java functions can change parameters that correspond to class objects or array variables. If you are familiar with the C and C++ programming languages, you may have used pointers in the past to change parameters within functions. However, the Java programming language does not support pointers. Therefore, for simple parameters such as variables of type *int* or *float*, you cannot change the parameters' values within a function.

TAKING A CYBER FIELD TRIP

By now, you have learned enough Java that you may be feeling quite comfortable with your programming skills. To keep you humble, the Java Devloper's Kit provides the Jumping Box applet that tests your mouse skills. When you run the applet, your screen will display a small box, as shown in Figure 9.7. Your task is simply to click your mouse on the box. However, as you move your mouse toward the box, the box will jump away, so you have to be quick. To run the Jumping Box applet or to download the applet's source code, visit the Jamsa Press Web site at *www.jamsa.com/java_demos/JumpingBox.hml.*

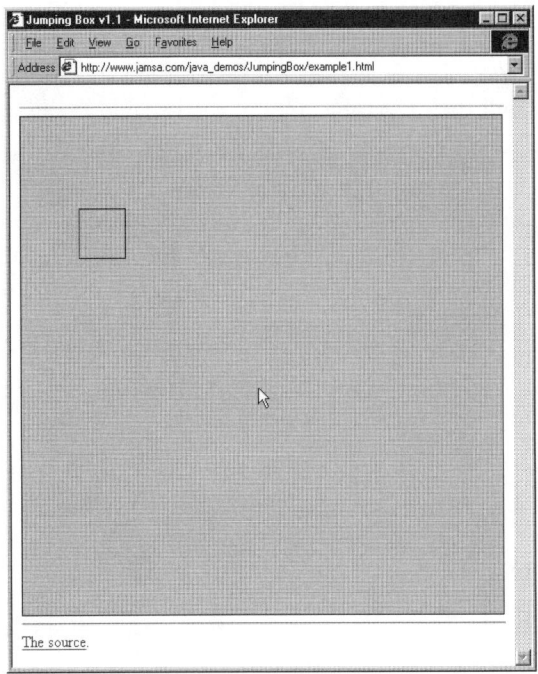

Figure 9.7 Try to click your mouse on the jumping box.

WHAT YOU MUST KNOW

In this lesson, you learned how to use functions within your Java applets. This lesson covered a lot of key material, such as parameters, return types, and function prototypes. You might want to spend a few more minutes now experimenting with the sample applets. In Lesson 10, you will examine several special functions you will encounter in most Java applets, such as *paint*, *init*, and *start* . Before you continue with Lesson 10, however, make sure that you have learned the following key concepts:

☑ As your applets become larger and more complex, you should break your applets into smaller, more manageable pieces, called functions.

☑ Each function must have a unique name. Assign names to your functions that meaningfully describe the task the function performs.

☑ Functions can return a value to the caller. If a function returns a value, you must specify the function's return type (*int*, *char*, and so on) before the function name; otherwise, you should precede the function name with *void.*

☑ Applets pass information to functions by using parameters. If the function receives parameters, you must specify a unique name for each parameter and a type.

LESSON 10
LOOKING AT SEVERAL SPECIAL FUNCTIONS

In Lesson 9, "Using Functions to Simplify Java Applets," you examined how functions let you break your applet into smaller, more manageable pieces. For example, throughout this book, you have made extensive use of the *paint* function within your applets to draw your applet-window contents. As it turns out, there are several key functions whose names you will encounter in most Java applets. This lesson will give you a brief overview of each of these functions. By the time you finish this lesson, you will understand the following key concepts:

◆ Most of the Java applets you examine will define the *init*, *start*, *run*, and *paint* functions.

◆ When you run an applet, Java automatically calls the applet's *init* function.

◆ Your applets should use the *init* function (which is short for initialize) to assign initial values to key variables and objects.

◆ After the *init* function completes its processing, Java will automatically call the applet's *start* function.

◆ Within the *start* function, most applets will create one or more *Thread* objects.

◆ To start a *Thread* object's execution, the applet calls the *Thread* object's *start* function which, in turn, calls the object's *run* function. Before an applet can call the *run* function, the applet must implement the *Runnable* interface.

◆ To stop an applet, the browser calls the applet's *stop* function.

◆ When the browser unloads an applet, the browser will call the applet's *destroy* function.

◆ To update the applet window, the browser will call the applet's *paint* function.

◆ If the applet itself wants to update the applet window, the applet can call *repaint* which, in turn, will call *paint*.

UNDERSTANDING THE INIT FUNCTION

As your applets become more complex, they will initialize image files, audio files, fonts, and other objects. Because your applets will normally only initialize these items one time, Java lets you group these operations within a special function named *init*:

```
public void init()
  {
   // Statements here
  }
```

Each time your applet starts, the applet automatically calls the *init* function. As you create your applet, use the *init* function only to initialize your applet's variables. In other words, your applet should not perform its actual processing within *init*. Your applet should perform its actual processing in other functions, such as the *start* function, discussed next. As you have seen, an applet does not have to define the *init* function. However, as your applets become larger, other programmers who read your code will expect to find an *init* function within your applet that initializes key variables.

UNDERSTANDING THE START FUNCTION

After the applet runs the *init* function, the applet will call a special function named *start,* the purpose of which is to begin (start) the applet's processing. In most Java applets, the *start* function will create one or more threads of execution (as discussed in Lesson 21, "Using Threads to Create Simple Animations") which, in turn, will perform the applet's processing. The following statements illustrate a sample *start* function that creates and runs a thread:

```
Thread someThread = null;


public void start()
   {
       if (someThread == null)
         {
             someThread = new Thread(this);      // Create the thread object
             someThread.start();                 // Start the thread object
         }
   }
```

For now, it is not important that you understand these *start* function statements. Rather, it is important that you understand that after the applet calls the *init* function, the applet will call *start*. In a similar way, when an applet ends, the applet will call the *stop* function, discussed next.

UNDERSTANDING THE STOP FUNCTION

Depending on your browser and the contents of the Web page that contains the applet, there may be times when a browser will stop an applet if the user scrolls the applet from view. Later, if the user scrolls the applet back into view, the browser will start the applet again. To start and stop the applet in this way, the browser will use the applet's *start* and *stop* functions.

As your applets become more complex, they will take advantage of threads that perform different tasks. For example, one thread may play different background sounds, while a second thread spins the company's logo, and a third thread moves an animated object across the screen. When your applets use multiple threads, you may need a way to control the order in which the threads stop as the brower stops the applet. Otherwise, the applet may continue to move an object across the screen after the music stops or vice versa—making your applet stop sloppily.

Each time the browser stops your applet, the browser calls a special function named *stop*. Within the *stop* function, your applet can stop each of the threads in the order you desire. Otherwise, if your applet does not manually shut down the threads in this way, Java may stop the threads in the order it chooses. The following statements, for example, illustrate how you might use the *stop* function to end one or more threads:

```
public void stop()
   {
       if (someThread != null)
         {
             someThread.stop();
             someThread = null;
         }
   }
```

In this case, the *if* statement tests if the thread SomeThread is active (if the applet has not started the thread or if the applet has already stopped the thread, the thread variable will contain the value *null*). If the thread is active, the statement stops the thread using the *stop* method and then assigns the *null* value to the thread variable. Later, by searching for variables with the *null* value, Java can discard unused objects as it performs its garbage collection. Should the browser later start the thread, the *start* function can test for the *null* value and create and start a new thread, as required.

As before, it is not important that you understand these statements but, rather, you must know that your browser will call the *stop* function to stop your applet.

UNDERSTANDING THE PAINT FUNCTION

As you have learned, each time the browser must update the applet window, the browser calls the *paint* function. For example, when your browser first displays your applet, the applet automatically calls the *paint* function. Likewise, if the user sizes or moves the window, the browser will call *paint*.

Throughout this book, your applets have used the *paint* function to display their output to the applet window, as shown here:

```
public void paint(Graphics g)
  {
     g.drawString("Rescued by Java", 5, 15);
  }
```

Within the *paint* function, your applet must redraw each item it has previously written to the window. For example, assume that your applet draws a rectangle in the applet window, and the user then minimizes the window. When the user later restores the applet window, the *paint* function must redraw the window's previous contents (in this case, the rectangle). In other words, neither your browser nor Windows keeps track of the applet window's contents. Instead, *paint* must keep the window's contents up-to-date. If, for example, the applet window has a background image, *paint* must redraw that image. If the window contains text, *paint* must restore the text. In short, the *paint* function has full control of the applet window's contents.

Depending on the processing your applet performs, there may be times when the applet must update the window's contents. In such cases, the applet can call the *repaint* function which, in turn, will call *paint*:

```
repaint();
```

UNDERSTANDING THE GRAPHICS CONTEXT

Java applets run in a graphical environment and display their output within an applet window. Each applet, therefore, must manage its own applet window. In other words, when the applet displays text to the window, the applet must know the current font, font color, and screen coordinates at which the text should appear. To keep track of this information, the applet uses a *Graphics* class object, which maintains the applet's *graphics context*.

For example, if you examine the *paint* function, you will find that *paint* receives a *Graphics* object as a parameter. The *paint* function, in turn, uses this object to display text or graphics:

```
public void paint(Graphics g)
  {
     g.drawString("Rescued by Java", 5, 15);
  }
```

In addition to tracking font and color information, *Graphics* objects provide functions such as *drawstring* and *drawRect* that perform device-independent graphics operations. This means that your applets can use the same set of functions to perform graphics, regardless of whether the applet is running on a Mac, or a UNIX workstation, or under Windows 98 on a PC.

UNDERSTANDING THE DESTROY FUNCTION

As you have learned, Java provides the *init* function that lets your applets initialize key variables. In a similar way, Java lets your applets use a *destroy* function to get rid of objects as your applet ends. For example, an applet might use the *destroy* function to release memory the applet had previously allocated to store an array:

```
public void destroy()
  {
      // Statements
  }
```

Think of the Java *destroy* function as your applet's one-time chance to manage the release of resources.

TAKING A CYBER FIELD TRIP

In Lesson 18, "Creating Simple Graphics," you will learn to draw lines using the Graphics class *drawLine* function. Likewise, in Lesson 19, "Using Java's Built-In Functions," you will learn how to use trigonometric functions to perform sine and cosine operations. As it turns out, the Java Development Kit provides the Simple Graph applet that combines Java's graphics and math capabilities. As shown in Figure 10, the applet displays a simple graph. To run the applet or to download the applet's source code, visit the Jamsa Press Web site at *www.jamsa.com/java_demos/ SimpleGraph.html.*

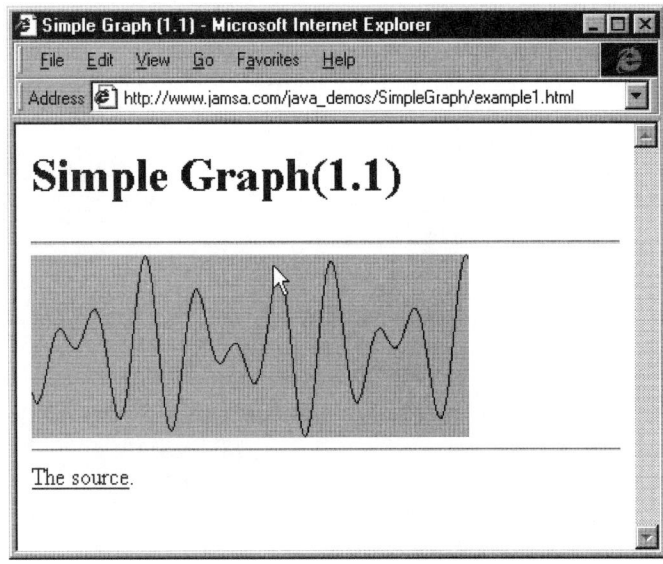

Figure 10 Drawing a simple line graph within a Java applet.

WHAT YOU MUST KNOW

As you examine Java applets throughout this book's lessons, and within other books and magazines, you will encounter many key functions on a regular basis. In this lesson, you examined these key functions. In Lesson 11, "Overloading Functions," you will learn how you can *overload* a function's definition by providing two or more function definitions for the same function name. In this way, if you have a function that performs a specific task, but which may require a different number of (or different types of) parameters, you can use the same function name with a different set of parameters. Before you continue with Lesson 11, however, make sure that you have learned the following key concepts:

☑ As you examine Java applets, you will frequently encounter the *init, start, run,* and *paint* functions.

☑ When the browser first loads an applet, the browser automatically calls the applet's *init* function.

☑ Within the *init* function, your applets should initialize key variables and objects.

☑ After the *init* function completes its processing, Java will automatically call the applet's *start* function.

☑ Within the *start* function, most applets will create one or more *Thread* objects.

☑ When the browser must stop an applet, such as when the user scrolls the applet off the screen, the browser calls the applet's *stop* function.

☑ When the browser unloads an applet, the browser will call the applet's *destroy* function.

☑ When the browser must update the applet window, the browser will call the applet's *paint* function.

☑ When the applet must update the applet window, the applet can call the *repaint* function which, in turn, will call *paint.*

Section Two

INTERMEDIATE JAVA

In this section, you will learn the topics you must know to create object-oriented programs, control fonts, work with arrays and strings, and more. By the time you finish the lessons this section presents, you will have developed very solid Java programming skills. The lessons in this section include:

LESSON 11

OVERLOADING FUNCTIONS

When you define functions within your applets, you must specify the function's return type, as well as the number and type of each parameter. In the past (for example, if you programmed in the C programming language), if you had a function named *AddValues* that worked with two integer values and you wanted to use a similar function to add three integer values, you had to create a function that used a different name. Therefore, you might use the *AddTwoValues* and *AddThreeValues* functions.

Likewise, if you wanted to use a function to add two values of type *float*, you needed yet another function with its own name. To eliminate your need to duplicate functions, Java lets you define multiple functions with the same name. During compilation, the Java compiler examines the number of arguments each function uses, and then calls the correct function. The process of providing multiple functions for the compiler to select is called *overloading*. This lesson examines how you can overload functions within your applets. By the time you finish this lesson, you will understand the following key concepts:

◆   Function overloading lets you use the same function name with different types of parameters.

◆   To overload functions within your applet, you simply define two functions of the same name and return type that differ by their number or type of parameters.

◆   To distinguish between two functions that have the same name, Java examines the number and type of the parameters your applet is passing to the function. Java refers to the parameter information as the function's *signature*.

As you will learn, overloading functions is convenient and can improve your applet's readability.

GETTING STARTED WITH FUNCTION OVERLOADING

Function overloading lets your applets define multiple functions with the same name and return type. The following applet, *OverloadAddValues.java,* for example, overloads the function *AddValues*. The first function definition adds two values of type *int*. The second function definition adds three values. During compilation, the Java compiler determines the correct function to use:

```java
import java.awt.*;
import java.applet.*;

public class OverloadAddValues extends Applet
   {
     int AddValues(int a, int b)
       {
         return(a + b);
       }


     int AddValues(int a, int b, int c)
       {
         return(a + b + c);
       }
```

```
    public void paint(Graphics g)
      {
         g.drawString("1 + 2 = " + AddValues(1, 2), 5, 15);
         g.drawString("1 + 2 + 3 = " + AddValues(1, 2, 3), 5, 30);
      }
   }
```

As you can see, the applet defines two function definitions named *AddValues*. The first definition adds two values of type *int*, while the second adds three values. You do not have to do anything special to warn the compiler about overloading; just do it. The compiler, in turn, will determine which definition of the function to use, based on the parameters the applet supplies.

To run the applet, place the following HTML entries in the file *OverloadAddValues.HTML*:

```
<HTML><TITLE>OverloadAddValues Applet</TITLE>
<APPLET CODE="OverloadAddValues.class" WIDTH=300 HEIGHT=200></APPLET>
</HTML>
```

After you compile and run this applet, your screen will display an applet window similar to that shown in Figure 11.1.

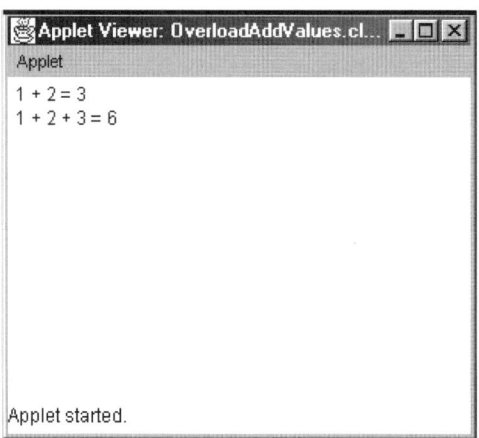

Figure 11.1 Overloading the AddValues function.

In a similar way, the following applet, *OverloadShowMessage.java*, overloads the *ShowMessage* function. The first function displays the message passed and the second displays two messages:

```
import java.awt.*;
import java.applet.*;

public class OverloadShowMessage extends Applet
   {
      void ShowMessage(Graphics g, String Message)
        {
           g.drawString(Message, 5, 15);
        }

      void ShowMessage(Graphics g, String first, String second)
        {
           g.drawString(first + second, 5, 30);
        }
```

```
    public void paint(Graphics g)
      {
         ShowMessage(g, "Rescued by Java");
         ShowMessage(g, "Rescued by Java", " is really easy");
      }
  }
```

To run the applet, place the following HTML entries within the file *OverloadShowMessage.HTML*:

```
<HTML><TITLE>OverloadShowMessage Applet</TITLE>
<APPLET CODE="OverloadShowMessage.class" WIDTH=300 HEIGHT=200></APPLET>
</HTML>
```

After you compile and execute this applet, your screen will display an applet window similar to that shown in Figure 11.2.

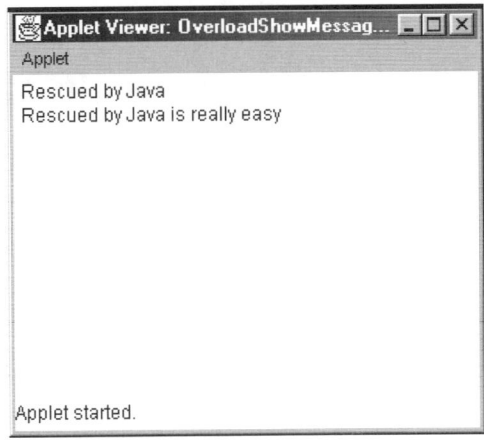

*Figure 11.2 Overloading the **ShowMessage** function.*

In Lesson 14, "Controlling Fonts within Java Applets," you will learn how to use different fonts to display text within an applet window. Using function overloading, you might create a version of the *ShowMessage* function to which you can pass a specific font as a parameter.

WHEN TO USE OVERLOADING

One of the most common uses of overloading is to use a function to obtain a result, even though parameter types might differ. For example, assume your applet has a function named *DayOfWeek*, which returns the current day of the week (0 for Sunday, 1 for Monday, . . . , 6 for Saturday). Your applet might overload the function so that the function returns the correct day of the week if the applet passes a Julian day as a parameter, or if the applet passes a day, month, and year:

```
  int DayOfWeek(int julian_day)
   {
     // Statements
   }

  int DayOfWeek(int month, int day, int year)
   {
     // Statements
   }
```

As you examine Java's object-oriented capabilities presented in later lessons, you will use function overloading to increase your applet's capabilities.

TAKING A CYBER FIELD TRIP TO LOOK AT NERVOUS TEXT

As discussed throughout this book, the Java Development Kit provides many different applets that may give you ideas for your own future applets, or whose source code you want to examine to learn how to manipulate text, sounds, and images. As you work with text within your applets, you should check out the *Nervous Text* applet, which displays a string's contents by jumping its letters around the screen, as shown in Figures 11.3a and 11.3b. To run the applet or to download the applet's source code, visit the Jamsa Press Web site at *www.jamsa.com/java_demos/ NervousText.html.*

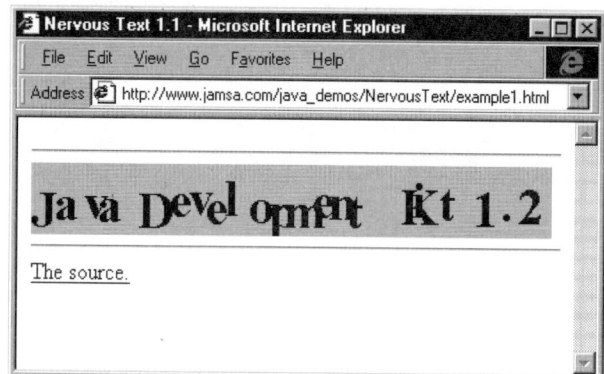 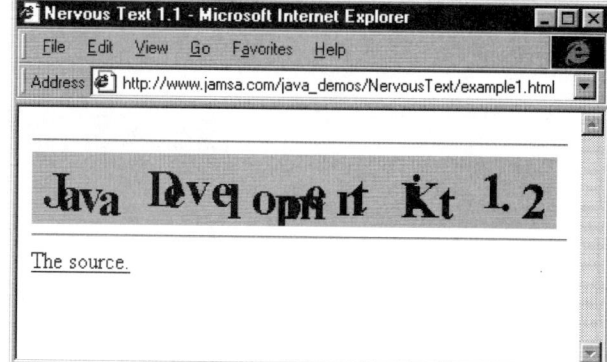

Figures 11.3a and 11.3b Displaying Nervous Text.

WHAT YOU MUST KNOW

Function overloading lets your applets specify multiple definitions for the same function. When you compile the applet, the Java compiler will determine which function to use, based on the number and type of parameters (the function's signature). In this lesson, you learned that it is easy to overload functions within your applets.

In Lesson 12, "Getting Started with Java Classes," you will examine Java classes, a key concept for object-oriented programming. Before you continue with Lesson 12, however, make sure that you have learned the following key concepts:

☑ Function overloading lets your applets provide multiple "views" to the same function within your applet.

☑ To overload a function within your applet, you simply define two or more functions with the same name and return type that differ only by the number or type of parameters they support.

☑ During compilation, the Java compiler will determine which function to invoke based on the number and type of parameters passed.

☑ Function overloading simplifies programming by letting programmers work with only one function name when their applets must accomplish a specific task.

LESSON 12

GETTING STARTED WITH JAVA CLASSES

The *class* is the primary tool in Java for object-oriented programming. As you will learn in this lesson, a class groups members that correspond to an object's data, as well as functions that operate on the data (called *methods*). As you will learn, an object is a *thing*, such as a telephone, an employee, a menu, or a dialog box. A Java class lets your applets define all the attributes for an object. In the case of a telephone object, the class might contain data members, such as the phone's number and type (tone or rotary), and functions that operate on the phone, such as *dial*, *answer*, and *hang_up*.

By grouping an object's data and functions into one variable, you simplify programming and increase your code reuse. Often, you can use the class you created for one applet, such as a *menu* class, within a second applet with few or no changes. This lesson introduces Java classes. By the time you finish this lesson, you will understand the following key concepts:

- ◆ To define a class, your applet must specify the class name, the class data members, and the class functions (methods).

- ◆ A class definition provides a template with which your applets can create objects of that class type, much like your applets create variables from the types *int*, *char*, and so on.

- ◆ To create an instance of an object, you must use the *new* operator.

- ◆ Your applets assign values to class-data members by using the dot operator.

- ◆ Your applets invoke class-member functions by using the dot operator.

UNDERSTANDING OBJECTS AND OBJECT-ORIENTED PROGRAMMING

In the simplest sense, an *object* is a thing. When you create an applet, the applet normally uses variables to store information about different real-world things, such as employees, books, and even files. When you perform object-oriented programming, you focus on the things that make up a system and the operations you must perform on those things. For example, given a file object, you might have operations that print, display, delete, or change the file. In Java, you use a class to define your objects. Your goal is to include as much information about the object within the class as you can. In this way, you can pick up a class that you created for one applet and use it in many different applets.

A class lets your applet group data and functions that perform operations on the data. Most books and articles on object-oriented programming refer to the class functions as *methods*. A Java class must have a unique name, followed by an opening brace, one or more members, and a closing brace:

```
class class_name {
   int data_member;          // Data member
   void show_member(int);    // Function member
     {
         // Function statements
     }
};
```

After you define a class, you can declare variables of the class type (called *objects*), as shown here:

```
class_name object_one, object_two, object_three;
```

In Java, all objects are dynamic, which means you must use the *new* operator to create the object. If you simply declare an object, the Java compiler will know the object name, but an actual object does not yet exist, and will not until you use the *new* operator to create one.

The following definition creates an *Employee* class that contains data variables and method definitions:

```
class Employee
  {
    public String Name;
    public long EmployeeId;
    public int OfficeNumber;
    public double Salary;
    public void ShowEmployee(Graphics g, int x, int y)
      {
        g.drawString("Name: " + Name, x, y);
        g.drawString("Office: " + OfficeNumber, x, y+20);
        g.drawString("Employee Id: " + EmployeeId, x, y+40);
        g.drawString("Salary: $" + Salary, x, y+60);
      }
  }
```

In this case, the class contains four variable members and one function member. Note the use of the *public* label within the class definition. As you will learn in Lesson 25, "Local Variables and Scope," class members can be *private, protected, public,* or *private protected,* which controls how your applets can access the members. In this case, all of the members are *public,* which means your applet can access any member by using the dot operator. After you define the class within your applet, you can declare objects (variables) of the class type, using the class name and *new* operator, as shown here:

```
Employee Boss = new Employee();
Employee TopDog = new Employee();
Employee Worker = new Employee();
```

Using Class Members

A class lets your applet group information, called members, into one variable. To assign a value to a member or to access a member's value, you use the Java *dot operator* (.). For example, the following statements assign values to different members of a variable named *worker* of the type *employee*:

```
Worker.Name = "Stephanie";
Worker.OfficeNumber = 111;
Worker.EmployeeId = 10;
Worker.Salary = 9999.99;
```

To access a class member, you specify the variable name, followed by a dot and member name. In a similar way, to access a class-member function, you again use the dot operator. For example, the following statement will call the *ShowEmployee* member function for the *worker* object:

```
Worker.ShowEmployee(g, 10, 25);
```

USING A CLASS WITHIN AN APPLET

The following applet, *EmployeeClass.java*, creates three *employee* objects. Using the dot operator, the applet assigns values to the data members. The applet then uses the *ShowEmployee* member to display the employee information:

```java
import java.awt.*;
import java.applet.*;

class Employee
  {
      public String Name;
      public long EmployeeId;
      public int OfficeNumber;
      public double Salary;
      public void ShowEmployee(Graphics g, int x, int y)
        {
          g.drawString("Name: " + Name, x, y);
          g.drawString("Office: " + OfficeNumber, x, y+20);
          g.drawString("Employee Id: " + EmployeeId, x, y+40);
          g.drawString("Salary: $" + Salary, x, y+60);
        }
  }


public class EmployeeClass extends Applet
   {
     public void paint(Graphics g)
        {
          Employee Boss = new Employee();
          Employee TopDog = new Employee();
          Employee Worker = new Employee();

          Boss.Name = "Debbie";
          Boss.OfficeNumber = 123;
          Boss.EmployeeId = 1;
          Boss.Salary = 15000.00;

          TopDog.Name = "Happy";
          TopDog.OfficeNumber = 124;
          TopDog.EmployeeId = 101;
          TopDog.Salary = 25000.00;

          Worker.Name = "Stephanie";
          Worker.OfficeNumber = 111;
          Worker.EmployeeId = 10;
          Worker.Salary = 9999.99;

          Boss.ShowEmployee(g, 5, 20);
          TopDog.ShowEmployee(g, 5, 120);
          Worker.ShowEmployee(g, 5, 220);
        }
   }
```

109

As you can see, the applet declares three *Employee* objects: *Boss*, *TopDog*, and *Worker*. The applet then uses the dot operator to assign values to the members and to invoke the *ShowEmployee* function, which displays information about an employee.

Note that the applet declares the *Employee* class outside of the *Applet* class definition. Originally, the Java compiler did not let you define one class (called an inner class) within a second class. Starting with Java 1.1, however, the compiler does support inner classes. Also note that the applet does not precede the class name with the *public* keyword. If you precede a class definition with a *public* keyword, you must place the class definition within its own source file, which has the same name as the class. For now, simply understand that if only this applet uses your class definition, and you define the class within the same source file as the applet, then you do not precede the class definition with the *public* keyword. When you compile this applet, the Java compiler will create two .class files: *EmployeeClass.class* for the applet and *Employee.class* for the *Employee* class.

Place the following HTML entries within the file *EmployeeClass.HTML* to run the applet:

```
<HTML><TITLE>EmployeeClass Applet</TITLE>
<APPLET CODE="EmployeeClass.class" WIDTH=400 HEIGHT=300></APPLET></HTML>
```

After you compile and execute this applet, your screen will display an applet window similar to that shown in Figure 12.1.

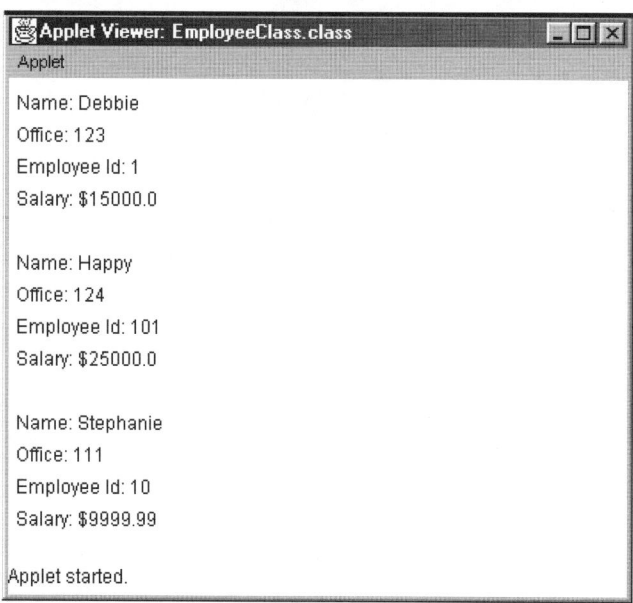

*Figure 12.1 Creating and using an **Employee** class.*

The following source code, *InnerEmployeeClass.java*, moves the *Employee* class definition within the code that extends the applet:

```
import java.awt.*;
import java.applet.*;

public class InnerEmployeeClass extends Applet
  {
    class Employee
      {
        public String Name;
        public long EmployeeId;
        public int OfficeNumber;
```

```
    public double Salary;
    public void ShowEmployee(Graphics g, int x, int y)
      {
         g.drawString("Name: " + Name, x, y);
         g.drawString("Office: " + OfficeNumber, x, y+20);
         g.drawString("Employee Id: " + EmployeeId, x, y+40);
         g.drawString("Salary: $" + Salary, x, y+60);
      }
  }


  public void paint(Graphics g)
    {
      Employee Boss = new Employee();
      Employee TopDog = new Employee();
      Employee Worker = new Employee();

      Boss.Name = "Debbie";
      Boss.OfficeNumber = 123;
      Boss.EmployeeId = 1;
      Boss.Salary = 15000.00;

      TopDog.Name = "Happy";
      TopDog.OfficeNumber = 124;
      TopDog.EmployeeId = 101;
      TopDog.Salary = 25000.00;

      Worker.Name = "Stephanie";
      Worker.OfficeNumber = 111;
      Worker.EmployeeId = 10;
      Worker.Salary = 9999.99;

      Boss.ShowEmployee(g, 5, 20);
      TopDog.ShowEmployee(g, 5, 120);
      Worker.ShowEmployee(g, 5, 220);
    }
  }
```

UNDERSTANDING OBJECTS

Most Java applets represent real-world entities, or objects. In the simplest sense, an object is a thing, such as a car, a dog, a clock, and so on. An object normally has several attributes and operations that your applet must perform on the attributes. For example, in the case of a clock, attributes might include the current time and the alarm time. Operations your applet might include on the clock include setting the time, setting the alarm, or turning the alarm off. When your applets perform object-oriented programming, your applets focus on objects and operations on those objects.

LOOKING AT A SECOND EXAMPLE

The following applet, *Pedigree.java*, creates a *dogs* class, which contains several data fields and the function *ShowDog*. The applet creates two *dogs* objects and displays information about each dog:

```java
import java.awt.*;
import java.applet.*;

public class Pedigree extends Applet
   {
     class dogs
       {
         public String Breed;
         public int AverageWeight;
         public int AverageHeight;
         public void ShowDog(Graphics g, int x, int y)
           {
             g.drawString("Breed: " + Breed, x, y);
             g.drawString("Average Weight: " + AverageWeight, x, y+20);
             g.drawString("Average Height: " + AverageHeight, x, y+40);
           }
       }

     public void paint(Graphics g)
       {
         dogs Happy = new dogs();
         dogs Matt = new dogs();

         Happy.Breed = "Dalmatian";
         Happy.AverageHeight = 58;
         Happy.AverageWeight = 24;

         Matt.Breed = "Shetland Sheepdog";
         Matt.AverageHeight = 12;
         Matt.AverageWeight = 15;

         Happy.ShowDog(g, 5, 20);
         Matt.ShowDog(g, 5, 120);
       }
   }
```

To run this applet, place the following HTML entries within the file *Pedigree.HTML*:

```html
<HTML><TITLE>Pedigree Applet</TITLE>
<APPLET CODE="Pedigree.class" WIDTH=400 HEIGHT=300></APPLET></HTML>
```

Passing Class Objects to a Function

In Lesson 9, "Using Functions to Simplify Java Applets," you learned how to pass parameters to Java functions. The parameters you pass to functions can be values (such as the number 1001), simple variables (such as a variable of type *int* or *float*), class variables, and arrays (discussed in Lesson 17, "Using Arrays to Store Multiple Values"). As you learned in Lesson 9, when you pass a simple value to a function, the function cannot make a permanent change to the parameter's value. In other words, when a function changes a simple parameter's value, the change only exists until the function's execution ends. At that time, the parameter's original value takes effect.

However, when your applets pass a class variable to a function, the function can make permanent changes to the class-member variables. For example, the following applet, *ChangeClass.java*, uses the *AssignDogAttributes* function to assign values to *dogs* class objects:

```java
import java.awt.*;
import java.applet.*;

 public class ChangeClass extends Applet
   {
     class dogs
       {
         public String Breed;
         public int AverageWeight;
         public int AverageHeight;
         public void ShowDog(Graphics g, int x, int y)
           {
             g.drawString("Breed: " + Breed, x, y);
             g.drawString("Average Weight: " + AverageWeight, x, y+20);
             g.drawString("Average Height: " + AverageHeight, x, y+40);
           }
       }

     public void AssignDogAttributes(dogs Dog, String breed, int weight,
                                     int height)
       {
         Dog.Breed = breed;
         Dog.AverageWeight = weight;
         Dog.AverageHeight = height;
       }

     public void paint(Graphics g)
       {
         dogs Happy = new dogs();
         dogs Matt = new dogs();

         AssignDogAttributes(Happy, "Dalmatian", 58, 24);
         AssignDogAttributes(Matt, "Shetland Sheepdog", 12, 15);

         Happy.ShowDog(g, 5, 20);
         Matt.ShowDog(g, 5, 120);
       }
   }
```

Place the following HTML entries within the file *ChangeClass.HTML* to run the applet:

```
<HTML><TITLE>ChangeClass Applet</TITLE>
<APPLET CODE="ChangeClass.class" WIDTH=400 HEIGHT=300></APPLET></HTML>
```

When you run this applet, it will call the *AssignDogAttributes* function to initialize the *dogs* objects. In this case, the applet presents the *AssignDogAttributes* function to show you that you can change class-member variables within a function. Because the *AssignDogAttributes* function only works with objects of the class type *dogs*, you would ideally define the function within the *dogs* class, as shown here:

```
class dogs
  {
      public String Breed;
      public int AverageWeight;
      public int AverageHeight;
      public void ShowDog(Graphics g, int x, int y)
        {
          g.drawString("Breed: " + Breed, x, y);
          g.drawString("Average Weight: " + AverageWeight, x, y+20);
          g.drawString("Average Height: " + AverageHeight, x, y+40);
        }
      public void AssignDogAttributes(String breed, int weight, int height)
        {
          Breed = breed;
          AverageWeight = weight;
          AverageHeight = height;
        }
  }
```

In Lesson 13, "Understanding Constructor Functions," you will examine class-constructor functions that provide you with the correct way to initialize object-member variables.

REVIEWING KEY TERMS

One of the most difficult aspects of learning object-oriented programming is keeping the terms straight. Therefore, this section provides a brief review of the key object-oriented programming terms you will encounter.

Class A class provides a template with which your applets can later declare objects (variables) that have the class attributes. Within your applets, you define one or more classes. Each class contains one or more attribute variables and member functions.

Object An object is a class variable. For example, given a class named *pedigree*, your applet might create objects (variables) named *WatchDog*, *BigDog*, and *LapDog*.

Object Instance An object instance (or instance) is simply another name for an object. When an applet creates an instance of a class using the *new* operator, the applet declares a variable (an object) of that class type.

Instance Variables An instance variable is another term for a member variable that is unique for each object. For example, given two objects of the *pedigree* class, each object will have different attribute variables. For example, one dog's weight may be 15 pounds, while another's is 50 pounds. Each object stores its weight in a member variable that is unique to each instance.

Methods A method is a function specific to a class. For example, the *pedigree* class defines the *ShowDog* method.

Class Library A class library is a file that contains one or more class definitions with which your applet can declare an object. For example, each of the applets you have created throughout this book have used the *java.applet* class library from which you have extended the *Applet* class.

TAKING A CYBER FIELD TRIP

In Lesson 18, "Creating Simple Graphics," you will learn how to draw lines using the *drawLine* method. To help you get started with graphics operations, the Java Development Kit provides the Draw Test applet. Using the applet, you can draw colored lines and points, as shown in Figure 12.2. To run the applet or to download the applet's source code, visit the Jamsa Press Web site at *www.jamsa.com/java_demos/DrawTest.html*.

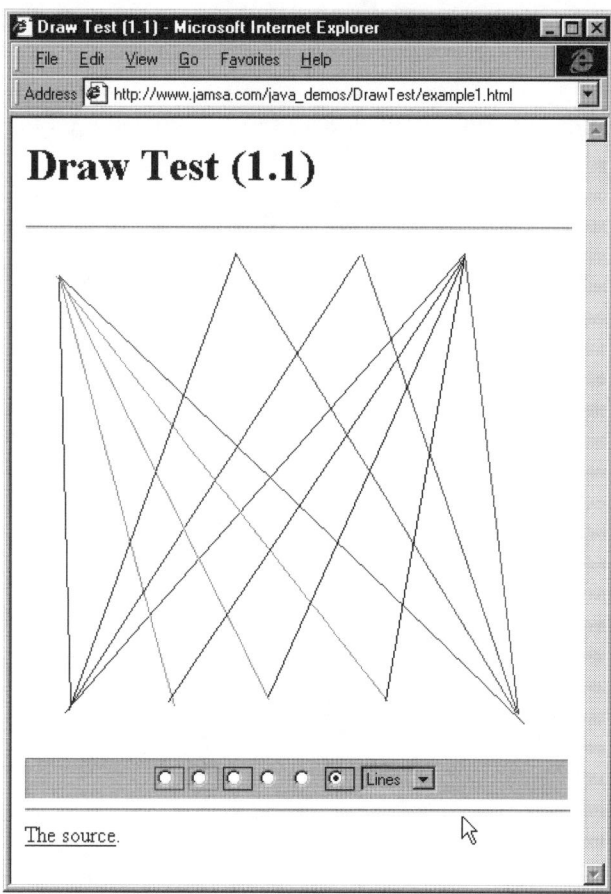

Figure 12.2 Drawing images using the Draw Test applet.

WHAT YOU MUST KNOW

Java applets make extensive use of classes. In short, a class lets your applet group an object's data and the methods (functions) that operate on that data into one variable. Java classes provide the basis for object-oriented programming. The following lessons will expand on the different capabilities classes provide. As this lesson briefly discusses, the *public* label that appeared in the class definitions made the class members available throughout the entire applet. In Lesson 13, you will learn about class-constructor functions that let you initialize class member variables. Before you continue with Lesson 13, however, make sure that you have learned the following key concepts:

☑ In the simplest sense, an object is a thing upon which your applet performs different operations.

☑ Java applets use a class to represent objects.

☑ A Java class contains members. Class members can store information (data) or be functions that operate on the data (called methods).

☑ Each class has a unique name.

☑ After you define a class, you can declare objects of that class by using the class name as a type.

☑ To create an instance of a class variable, you must use the *new* operator.

☑ To access class members (either data or functions), your applets use the dot operator.

☑ Within a function, you can change the values stored by a class-member variable.

LESSON 13
UNDERSTANDING CONSTRUCTOR FUNCTIONS

When you create objects, one of the most common operations your applets will perform is to initialize the object's data members. To simplify the process of initializing class-data members, Java provides a special *constructor* function that runs for each object you create. This lesson examines constructor functions in detail. By the time you finish this lesson, you will understand the following key concepts:

- Constructor functions are class methods that make it easy for your applets to initialize class-data members.

- Constructor functions have the same name as the class. A class named *Telephone*, for example, would use a constructor function named *Telephone*.

- Constructor functions do not return a type. However, you do not precede the constructor function name with the type *void* as you would a standard function that does not return a value.

- Each time your applet creates a class variable, Java calls the class-constructor function that you can use to initialize the class member values (provided you have defined a constructor function for the class).

- If constructor parameter names conflict with class-member names, simply precede the class-member names with the *this* keyword when you want to assign or use a member's value.

- Unlike the C++ programming language, Java does not provide destructor functions that execute when you discard an object. However, before Java destroys an object, Java will call a special class function named *finalize*.

Do not let the term *constructor* intimidate you. Instead, think of a constructor function as a function that helps you build (construct) an object.

CREATING A SIMPLE CONSTRUCTOR FUNCTION

A *constructor function* is a class method that has the same name as the class itself. For example, if you are using a class named *employee*, the constructor function will be named *employee*. Likewise, for a class named *dogs*, the constructor will be named *dogs*. If your class defines a constructor function, Java will automatically invoke the function each time you create an object of that class type. The following statements create a class named *employee*. The class definition provides a constructor function named *employee* that assigns the object's initial values. A constructor function cannot return a value; however, you do not declare the function as *void*. Instead, you simply do not specify a return type. Within your applet, you simply define the constructor function, just as you would any class method:

```
class Employee
  {
    public String Name;
    public long EmployeeId;
    public int OfficeNumber;
    public double Salary;
    public void ShowEmployee(Graphics g, int x, int y)
      {
```

```
        g.drawString("Name: " + Name, x, y);
        g.drawString("Office: " + OfficeNumber, x, y+20);
        g.drawString("Employee Id: " + EmployeeId, x, y+40);
        g.drawString("Salary: $" + Salary, x, y+60);
    }

    public Employee(String EmpName, int Id, int Office,
                    double AnnualSalary)
    {
      Name = EmpName;
      EmployeeId = Id;
      OfficeNumber = Office;
      Salary = AnnualSalary;
    }
}
```

As you can see, the constructor function does not return a value to the caller and the applet does not precede the constructor function name with the type *void*. The following statements implement the *EmployeeConstructor.java* applet. To help you focus on the *Employee* class and its constructor function, the source code defines the *Employee* class outside of the applet class (as you learned in Lesson 12, "Getting Started with Java Classes," Java lets you define a class within or outside of another class):

```
import java.awt.*;
import java.applet.*;

class Employee
 {
    public String Name;
    public long EmployeeId;
    public int OfficeNumber;
    public double Salary;
    public void ShowEmployee(Graphics g, int x, int y)
      {
        g.drawString("Name: " + Name, x, y);
        g.drawString("Office: " + OfficeNumber, x, y+20);
        g.drawString("Employee Id: " + EmployeeId, x, y+40);
        g.drawString("Salary: $" + Salary, x, y+60);
      }

    public Employee(String EmpName, int Id, int Office,
                    double AnnualSalary)
      {
        Name = EmpName;
        EmployeeId = Id;
        OfficeNumber = Office;
        Salary = AnnualSalary;
      }
 }
```

```
public class EmployeeConstructor extends Applet
  {
    public void paint(Graphics g)
      {
        Employee Boss = new Employee("Debbie", 1, 123, 15000.0);
        Employee TopDog = new Employee("Happy", 101, 124, 25000.0);
        Employee Worker = new Employee("Stephanie", 10, 111, 9999.99);

        Boss.ShowEmployee(g, 5, 20);
        TopDog.ShowEmployee(g, 5, 120);
        Worker.ShowEmployee(g, 5, 220);
      }
  }
```

Place the following HTML entries within the file *EmployeeConstructor.HTML* to run the applet:

```
<HTML><TITLE>EmployeeConstructor Applet</TITLE>
<APPLET CODE="EmployeeConstructor.class" WIDTH=400 HEIGHT=300></APPLET>
</HTML>
```

After you compile and execute this applet, your screen will display an applet window similar to that shown in Figure 13.1.

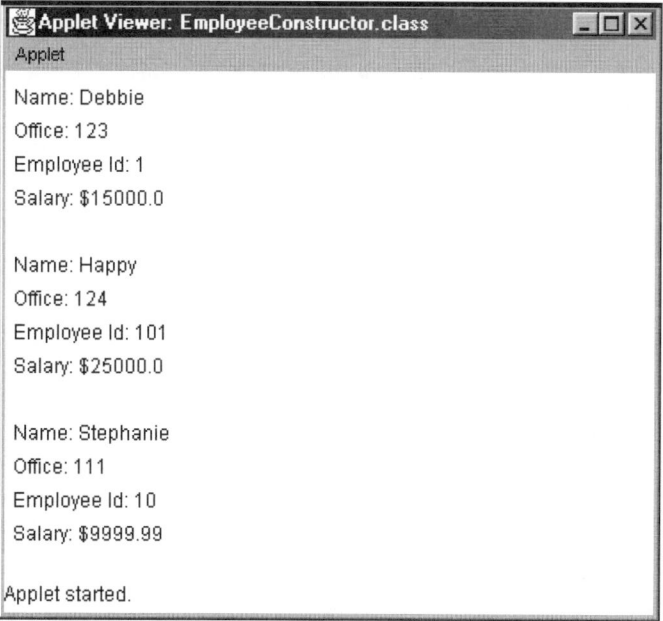

Figure 13.1 *Using a constructor function to initialize class-member variables.*

Note that the applet follows the declaration of each object with parentheses and the object's initial values, just like a function call. When you use constructor functions, you pass parameters to the function when you declare an object:

```
Employee Boss = new Employee("Debbie", 1, 123, 15000.0);
```

A constructor function is a special function Java automatically invokes each time you create an object. The most common use of a constructor is to initialize the object's data members. Constructor functions have the same name as the object class. A class named *GraphicsFile*, for example, uses a constructor named *GraphicsFile*. You define constructor functions within your applet, just as you would any class method. The only difference is that for constructor functions you do not specify a return type. When you later declare an object, you can pass parameters to the constructor, as shown here:

```
class_name  object(value1, value2, value3);
```

The following applet, *PedigreeConstructor.java*, uses the *dogs* constructor function to initialize members of the *dogs* class:

```java
import java.awt.*;
import java.applet.*;


public class PedigreeConstructor extends Applet
  {
    class dogs
      {
        public String Breed;
        public int AverageWeight;
        public int AverageHeight;
        public void ShowDog(Graphics g, int x, int y)
          {
            g.drawString("Breed: " + Breed, x, y);
            g.drawString("Average Weight: " + AverageWeight, x, y+20);
            g.drawString("Average Height: " + AverageHeight, x, y+40);
          }
        dogs(String DogBreed, int DogWeight, int DogHeight)
          {
            Breed = DogBreed;
            AverageWeight = DogWeight;
            AverageHeight = DogHeight;
          }
      }
    public void paint(Graphics g)
      {
        dogs Happy = new dogs("Dalmatian", 58, 24);
        dogs Matt = new dogs("Shetland Sheepdog", 12, 15);
        Happy.ShowDog(g, 5, 20);
        Matt.ShowDog(g, 5, 120);
      }
  }
```

Place the following HTML entries within the file *PedigreeConstructor.HTML* to run the applet:

```
<HTML><TITLE>PedigreeConstructor Applet</TITLE>
<APPLET CODE="PedigreeConstructor.class" WIDTH=400 HEIGHT=300></APPLET>
</HTML>
```

USING THE THIS KEYWORD

In this lesson's previous examples, the constructor functions have used parameter names that are different from the class-variable names. For example, the class uses the member-variable *Name*, and the constructor function uses the parameter *EmpName*. To improve the readability of your code, you may want to use the same names for constructor parameters as you use for class-member names. When the parameter names and class-member names conflict, the Java compiler will give parameter names priority. In other words, if you reference the name within the function, the Java compiler will assume you are referencing the parameter name, as opposed to the class member name.

To tell the compiler which names correspond to class members and which correspond to parameters, precede the class-member names with the *this* keyword, as shown here:

```
public Employee(String Name, int EmployeeId, int OfficeNumber,
               double Salary)
  {
    this.Name = Name;
    this.EmployeeId = EmployeeId;
    this.OfficeNumber = OfficeNumber;
    this.Salary = Salary;
  }
```

By preceding class member-variable names with the *this* keyword, other programmers who are reading your code, as well as the Java compiler, can readily determine which names correspond to parameters and which to class members.

OVERLOADING CONSTRUCTOR FUNCTIONS

As you learned in Lesson 11, "Overloading Functions," Java lets your applets overload function definitions by specifying alternative functions for different parameter types. In this same way, Java also lets you overload constructor functions. The following applet, *ConstructorOverload.java*, overloads the *Employee* constructor function. The first function definition requires the applet to specify an employee name, identification number, and salary. The second function definition assigns default values for the *OfficeNumber*, *EmployeeId*, and *Salary*:

```
import java.awt.*;
import java.applet.*;

class Employee
  {
    public String Name;
    public long EmployeeId;
    public int OfficeNumber;
    public double Salary;
```

```
        public static int default_office = 200;
        public static int default_id = 300;
        public static double default_salary = 10000.0;

        public void ShowEmployee(Graphics g, int x, int y)
          {
            g.drawString("Name: " + Name, x, y);
            g.drawString("Office: " + OfficeNumber, x, y+20);
            g.drawString("Employee Id: " + EmployeeId, x, y+40);
            g.drawString("Salary: $" + Salary, x, y+60);
          }

        public Employee(String Name, int EmployeeId, int OfficeNumber,
                        double Salary)
          {
            this.Name = Name;
            this.EmployeeId = EmployeeId;
            this.OfficeNumber = OfficeNumber;
            this.Salary = Salary;
          }

        public Employee(String Name)
          {
            this.Name = Name;
            EmployeeId = default_id++;
            OfficeNumber = default_office++;
            Salary = default_salary;
          }
   }

public class ConstructorOverload extends Applet
  {
    public void paint(Graphics g)
      {
        Employee Boss = new Employee("Debbie");
        Employee TopDog = new Employee("Happy", 101, 124, 25000.0);
        Employee Worker = new Employee("Stephanie");

        Boss.ShowEmployee(g, 5, 20);
        TopDog.ShowEmployee(g, 5, 120);
        Worker.ShowEmployee(g, 5, 220);
      }
  }
```

As you can see, within the *Employee* class definition, you will find two definitions of the *Employee* class-constructor function. The first function definition uses parameters for each of the class members. The second function provides default values.

If you examine the class-member statements, you will find that the default values are preceded by the *static* keyword. When you precede a class-member variable with the *static* keyword, each instance of the class shares that variable. As a result, when one object increments one of the variable's values, such as *default_office*, all of the other class objects will immediately see the updated value.

Each time the applet creates an *Employee* object by specifying only an employee name, the applet calls the constructor function that assigns the default values. Within the constructor, the function code assigns the current *default_id* and *default_office* and then increments each variable in preparation for the next employee. The function also assigns the *default_salary*.

Place the following HTML entries within the file *ConstructorOverload.HTML* to run the applet:

```
<HTML><TITLE>ConstructorOverload Applet</TITLE>
<APPLET CODE="ConstructorOverload.class" WIDTH=400 HEIGHT=300></APPLET>
</HTML>
```

After you compile and execute this applet, your screen will display an applet window similar that shown in Figure 13.2.

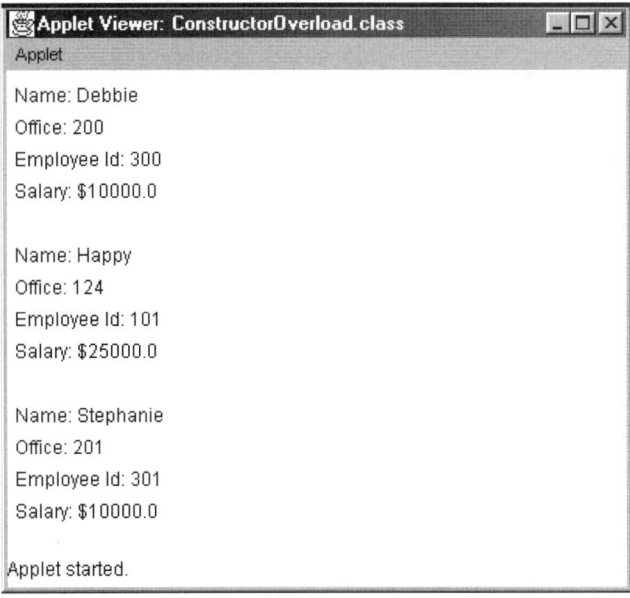

Figure 13.2 Overloading a constructor function.

JAVA DOES NOT SUPPORT DESTRUCTOR FUNCTIONS

Unlike the C++ programming language, Java does not support *destructor* functions, which automatically execute each time your applet destroys an object. Instead, Java itself controls the operations that occur when you destroy an object. As it turns out, before Java destroys an object, Java calls a special class function named *finalize*:

```
protected void finalize()
   {
      // Statements
   }
```

The difference between this function and a C++ *destructor* function is that you have no control over when Java executes this function. If your class extends another class (such as the *Applet* class), the final statement in your *finalize* function should be class *super.finalize()*:

```
protected void finalize()
  {
      // Statements
      super.finalize();
  }
```

In Lesson 26, "Understanding Inheritance," you will examine the purpose of the *super* keyword.

TAKING A CYBER FIELD TRIP

In Lesson 18, "Creating Simple Graphics," you will learn how to create simple graphics that consist of squares, rectangles, and ellipses. To help you get started with graphics operations, the Java Development Kit provides the Graphics Test applet, which as shown in Figure 13.3, lets you draw a variety of shapes. To run the applet or to download the applet's source code, visit the Jamsa Press Web site at *www.jamsa.com/java_demos/GraphicsTest.html*.

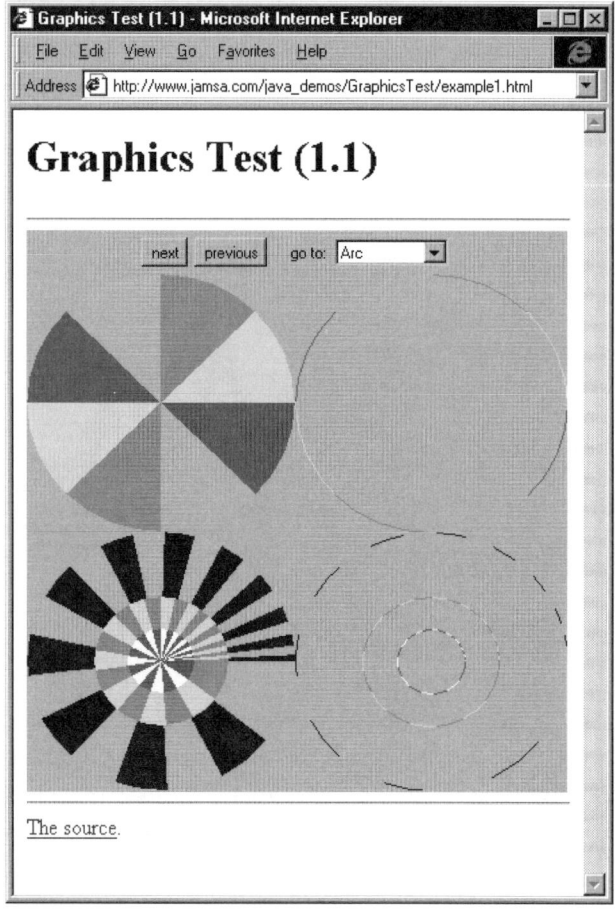

Figure 13.3 Drawing shapes using the Graphics Test applet.

WHAT YOU MUST KNOW

Constructors are special class functions your applet automatically invokes each time the applet creates a class object. Most applets use constructor functions to initialize class-data members. In Lesson 14, "Controlling Fonts within Java," you will learn how to control fonts within your applet by creating *Font* objects. Before you continue with Lesson 14, however, make sure that you have learned the following key concepts:

☑ A constructor function is a special function your applet automatically invokes each time you create an object. Constructor functions have the same name as the *object* class.

☑ Constructor functions do not return a value, but you do not define them as type *void*. Instead, you simply do not specify a return-value type.

☑ When your applets create an object, your applets can pass parameters to the constructor function during the object's declaration.

☑ Java lets you overload constructor functions and provide default parameter values.

LESSON 14

CONTROLLING FONTS WITHIN JAVA APPLETS

As you have learned, Java improves a Web site's appearance by integrating text, graphics, sounds, and animation. An often-overlooked aspect of Java is its support for fonts. In this lesson, you will learn how to use fonts to improve your applet's appeal. You will learn how to use a *Font* object to change the current font, font size, and color. By the time you finish this lesson, you will understand the following key concepts:

◆ To control fonts within your applet, you create a *Font* object.

◆ After your applet defines a *Font* object, you use the *Graphics* class *setFont* function to put the font into use.

◆ Java lets your applets select plain, **bold**, or *italic* fonts.

◆ Using the *getSize().width* member, your applets can determine the applet window's width in pixels.

◆ To determine specifics about the current font, such as its size or leading, your applet uses a *FontMetrics* object.

◆ To set the current text color, use the *Graphics* class *setColor* method.

USING THE FONT CLASS

To control fonts within a Java applet, you use a *Font* object. The class library *java.awt.Font* defines the *Font* class. To use this class library, place one of the following *import* statements near the top of your source file:

```
import java.awt.*;                    import.java.awt.Font;
```

Within your applet, you create a *Font* object by using the *new* operator. When you create a *Font* object, you pass the *Font* constructor function the font name, style, and font size you desire:

```
Font font = new Font("Serif", Font.BOLD, 18);
```

In this case, the applet will create an 18-point, bold font with serifs (the curly tips on the edges of each letter). Older Java applets used to use specific font names, such as Helvetica (a sanserif font) and TimesRoman (a serif font). Newer Java applets, however, should use font names such as Dialog, SanSerif, Serif, Monospaced, and DialogInput.

In addition to selecting the font type, such as SansSerif, the *Font* object lets you specify font attributes such as bold or italics, or a combination of styles. To specify a font style, you use the *Font.PLAIN*, *Font.BOLD*, and *Font.ITALIC* attributes.

When you specify font attributes, you must use uppercase letters. In addition, Java lets your applets combine attributes by using the plus sign, as shown here:

```
Font font = new Font("Serif", Font.BOLD + Font.ITALIC, 18);
```

After you create a *Font* object, you use the *Graphics* class *setFont* method to put the font in use:

```
g.setFont(font);
```

The following applet, *FontDemo.java*, demonstrates several different fonts:

```
import java.awt.*;
import java.applet.*;


public class FontDemo extends Applet
   {
     public void paint(Graphics g)
        {
           Font Serif = new Font("Serif", Font.BOLD, 18);
           Font SansSerif = new Font("SansSerif", Font.BOLD, 18);
           Font Dialog = new Font("Dialog", Font.BOLD, 18);
           Font Monospaced = new Font("Monospaced", Font.BOLD, 18);
           Font DialogInput = new Font("DialogInput", Font.BOLD, 18);

           g.setFont(Serif);
           g.drawString("Serif bold 18-point", 5, 30);

           g.setFont(SansSerif);
           g.drawString("SansSerif bold 18-point", 5, 90);

           g.setFont(Dialog);
           g.drawString("Dialog bold 18-point", 5, 150);

           g.setFont(Monospaced);
           g.drawString("Monospaced bold 18-point", 5, 210);

           g.setFont(DialogInput);
           g.drawString("DialogInput bold 18-point", 5, 270);
        }
   }
```

To run the applet, place the following HTML entries within the file *FontDemo.HTML*:

```
<HTML><TITLE>FontDemo Applet</TITLE>
<APPLET CODE="FontDemo.class" WIDTH=400 HEIGHT=300></APPLET></HTML>
```

After you compile and execute this applet, your screen will display an applet window similar to that shown in Figure 14.1.

UNDERSTANDING FONT METRICS

As your use of fonts within Java applets increases, there will be times when you will need specifics about the current font, such as the font's height or the pixel width of a string that your applet will display using the font. For example, to center a string within the applet window, you must know the string's pixel width. To obtain such font information, your applet creates a *FontMetrics* object, as shown here:

```
Font font = new Font("SanSerif", Font.PLAIN, 18);
FontMetrics fontMetrics = getFontMetrics(font);
```

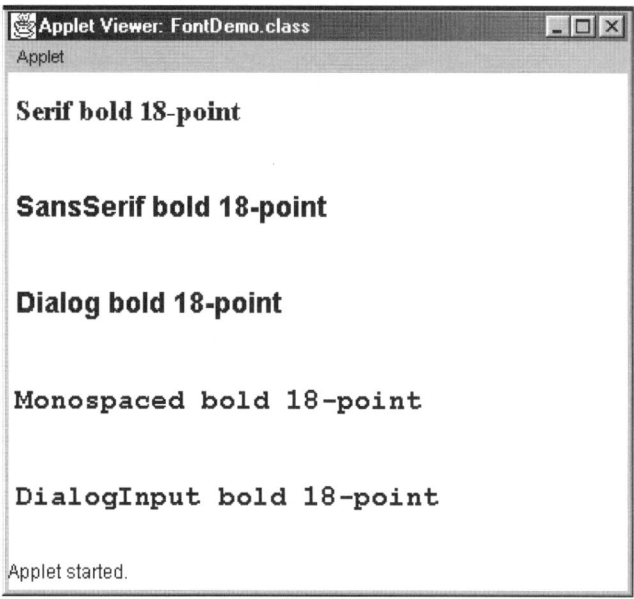

Figure 14.1 *Selecting fonts within a Java applet.*

Next, using the *FontMetrics* class methods, your applet can determine specifics about the font, as shown here:

```
pixelWidth = fontMetrics.stringWidth("Rescued by Java");
characterWidth = fontMetrics.charWidth('A');
Ascent = fontMetrics.getAscent();
Descent = fontMetrics.getDescent();
Leading = fontMetrics.getLeading();
Height = fontMetrics.getHeight();
```

The following applet, *CenterString.java*, uses the *FontMetrics* objects to center the string, "Rescued by Java," within the applet window:

```java
import java.awt.*;
import java.applet.*;

public class CenterString extends Applet
  {
    public void paint(Graphics g)
      {
        int FontSize, y, window_width;

        FontMetrics fontMetrics;
        Font BigFont = new Font("Serif", Font.BOLD, 36);
        Font LittleFont = new Font("Serif", Font.PLAIN, 14);
        window_width = getSize().width;

        g.setFont(BigFont);
        fontMetrics = g.getFontMetrics();
        FontSize = fontMetrics.stringWidth("Rescued by Java Big Font");
```

```
    g.drawString("Rescued by Java Big Font",(window_width-FontSize)/2, 50);
    g.setFont(LittleFont);

    fontMetrics = g.getFontMetrics();
    FontSize = fontMetrics.stringWidth("Rescued by Java Small Font");

    g.drawString("Rescued by Java Small Font",(window_width-FontSize)/2, 150);
  }
}
```

As you can see, the applet uses *getSize().width* to determine the applet window's width. After the function knows the window's width, the function uses the *FontMetrics* class *stringWidth* function to determine the string's pixel width. Knowing the window and string width, the function can then center the string, as shown in Figure 14.2.

Figure 14.2 Centering strings within the applet window.

To run the applet, place the following HTML entries within the file *CenterString.HTML*:

```
<HTML><TITLE>CenterString Applet</TITLE>
<APPLET CODE="CenterString.class" WIDTH=600 HEIGHT=300></APPLET></HTML>
```

GETTING OTHER FONT SPECIFICS

Depending on your applet's processing, there may be times when you must know specifics about the current font, such as if the font is italic, bold, or plain. Likewise, before a function changes the current font to display a message, the function should save the current font so the function can later restore the font after it displays its text. To determine such font information, your applets can use the *Graphics* and *Font* class methods shown here:

```
Font CurrentFont = g.getFont();          // Graphics class function
String FontName = font.getName();
int FontSize = font.getSize();
int FontStyle = font.getStyle();
boolean IsPlain = font.isPlain();
boolean IsBold = font.isBold();
boolean IsItalic = font.isItalic();
```

129

SETTING THE TEXT COLOR

In addition to working with font styles, your applets can use the *Graphics* class *setColor* function to change font colors. The easiest way to change the color by using the *setColor* function is to use one of the predefined color values shown here:

Color.black	Color.blue	Color.cyan
Color.darkGray	Color.gray	Color.green
Color.lightGray	Color.magenta	Color.orange
Color.pink	Color.red	Color.white
Color.yellow		

For example, the following statement sets the current color to red:

```
g.setColor(Color.red);
```

The following applet, *FontColors.java*, uses the *setColor* function to select several different colors for text display:

```java
import java.awt.*;
import java.applet.*;

public class FontColors extends Applet
  {
    public void paint(Graphics g)
      {
        Font font = new Font("Serif", Font.BOLD, 18);

        g.setFont(font);
        g.setColor(Color.red);
        g.drawString("Red Red Red", 5, 30);

        g.setColor(Color.blue);
        g.drawString("Blue Blue Blue", 5, 60);

        g.setColor(Color.green);
        g.drawString("Green Green Green", 5, 90);

        g.setColor(Color.yellow);
        g.drawString("Yellow Yellow Yellow", 5, 120);
      }
  }
```

To run the applet, place the following HTML entries within the file *FontColors.HTML*:

```html
<HTML><TITLE>FontColors Applet</TITLE>
<APPLET CODE="FontColors.class" WIDTH=400 HEIGHT=300></APPLET></HTML>
```

After you compile and execute this applet, your screen will display an applet window similar to that shown in Figure 14.3.

Figure 14.3 Displaying fonts using different colors.

TAKING A CYBER FIELD TRIP TO PLAY TIC-TAC-TOE

If you are ready for a break from studying Java code, you might take time now to play the Tic-Tac-Toe game provided by Sun's Java developers in the Java Development Kit. As shown in Figure 14.4, the applet lets you play Tic-Tac-Toe against the computer. To run the applet or to download the applet's source code, visit the Jamsa Press Web site at *www.jamsa.com/java_demos/TictTacToe.html.*

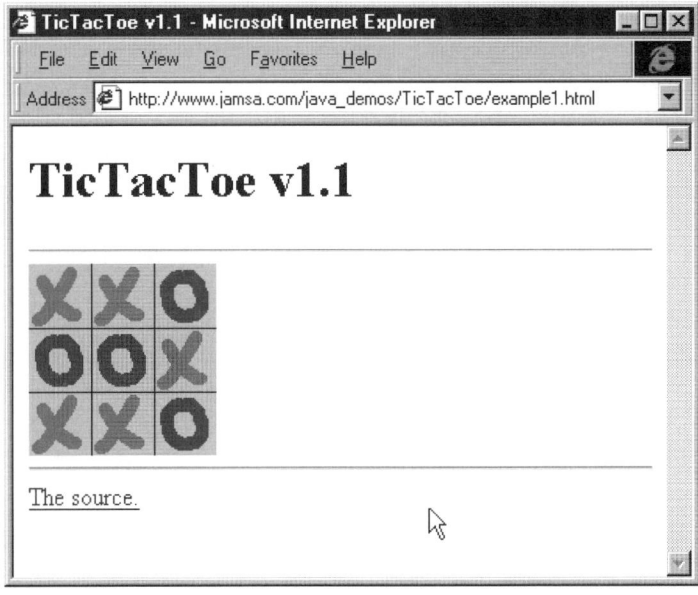

Figure 14.4 A Java-based Tic-Tac-Toe game.

WHAT YOU MUST KNOW

In this lesson, you learned how to control font attributes within your applets by creating *Font* objects. In Lesson 15, "Using Java Strings," you will learn how to create *String* objects that let you store letters, digits, and punctuation symbols. Before you continue with Lesson 15, however, make sure that you have learned the following key concepts:

☑ Using a *Font* object, your applets can control font attributes.

☑ The *Graphics* class *setFont* method lets your applets put a specific font into use.

☑ When you create a *Font* object, Java lets you select plain, **bold**, or *italic* attributes.

☑ The *getSize().width* member contains the applet window's width in pixels.

☑ Using a *FontMetrics* object, your applet can determine specifics about the current font, such as its size or leading.

☑ Using the *Graphics* class *setColor* method, your applets can control the current font color.

LESSON 15
USING JAVA STRINGS

In Lesson 5, "Java Applets Store Information in Variables," you learned how to declare variables of type *int*, *double*, *long*, and so on. As your applets start to perform useful tasks, they must store such information as a username, filename, company name, and so on. As you can imagine, such information can consist of letters, spaces, digits, and even punctuation symbols. To store such information, your applets use a special *String* class. This lesson examines the *String* class in detail. By the time you finish this lesson, you will understand the following key concepts:

◆ To store alphanumeric characters within a variable, your applets use a *String* object.

◆ *String* objects can store letters, digits, spaces, and punctuation symbols.

◆ Unlike strings within the C and C++ programming languages, you do not use a NULL character (ASCII zero) to indicate the end of a Java *String* object.

◆ To determine the number of characters a *String* object contains, you use the *length* method.

◆ Using the plus operator (+), you can concatenate (append) one string's contents to another.

◆ Java provides a special function, named *toString*, that converts values of type *int*, *float*, *double*, and so on into a character-string equivalent.

◆ Within the classes you create, you may want to implement a *toString* function to simplify your output of the class-member values.

DECLARING A STRING OBJECT

Declaring a *String* object within your applet is much like declaring any object or variable within Java—you specify the *String* type and a variable name. For example, the following statement declares a *String* object named *BookTitle*:

```
String BookTitle;
```

Later, to assign a value to a *String* variable, you use the assignment operator, as shown here:

```
BookTitle = "Rescued by Java";
```

When your applet works with string literals (such as the book title *Rescued by Java*), you must place the characters within double quotes. The following applet, *StringObject.java*, creates a *String* object named *BookTitle* and assigns the variable the character string "Rescued by Java". The applet then uses the *drawString* function to display the variable's contents within the applet window:

```
import java.awt.*;
import java.applet.*;

public class StringObject extends Applet
  {
    public void paint(Graphics g)
      {
        String BookTitle = "Rescued by Java";
```

```
        g.drawString(BookTitle, 5, 15);
    }
}
```

To run the applet, place the following HTML entries within the file *StringObject.HTML*:

```
<HTML><TITLE>StringObject Applet</TITLE>
<APPLET CODE="StringObject.class" WIDTH=300 HEIGHT=200></APPLET></HTML>
```

After you compile and execute this applet, your screen will display an applet window similar to that shown in Figure 15.1.

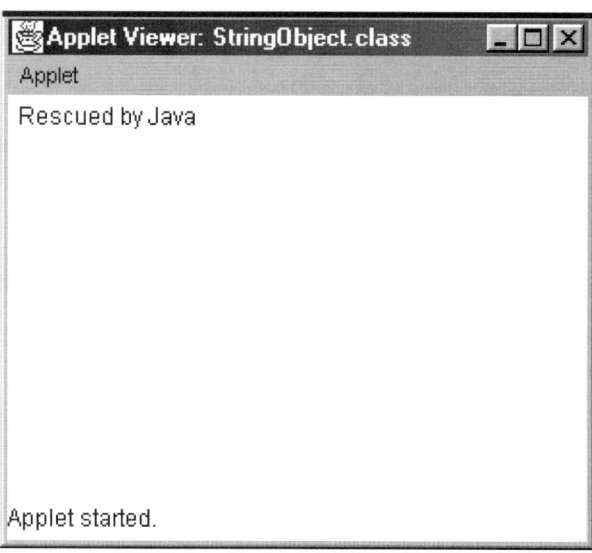

Figure 15.1 Using drawString to display a String object's contents.

DETERMINING A STRING OBJECT'S LENGTH

Depending on the processing your applet performs, there may be times when your applet must know the number of characters the string contains. For example, to center a *String* object's characters on a page, you must know the number of characters the *String* contains. To determine the number of characters in a *String* object, you use the object's *length* method, as shown here:

```
NumberOfCharacters = SomeString.length();
```

The following applet, *StringLength.java*, uses the *String* class *length* method to display the number of characters several different *String* objects contain:

```
import java.awt.*;
import java.applet.*;

public class StringLength extends Applet
    {
    public void paint(Graphics g)
        {
```

```
        String BookTitle = "Rescued by Java";
        String BookLesson = "Using Java Strings";
        String OneLetter = "A";


        g.drawString(BookTitle + " contains " + BookTitle.length() +
                " characters", 5, 15);
        g.drawString(BookLesson + " contains " + BookLesson.length() +
                " characters", 5, 30);
        g.drawString(OneLetter + " contains " + OneLetter.length() +
                " characters", 5, 45);
    }
}
```

To run the applet, place the following HTML entries within the file *StringLength.HTML*:

```
<HTML><TITLE>StringLength Applet</TITLE>
<APPLET CODE="StringLength.class" WIDTH=300 HEIGHT=200></APPLET></HTML>
```

After you compile and execute this applet, your screen will display an applet window similar to that shown in Figure 15.2.

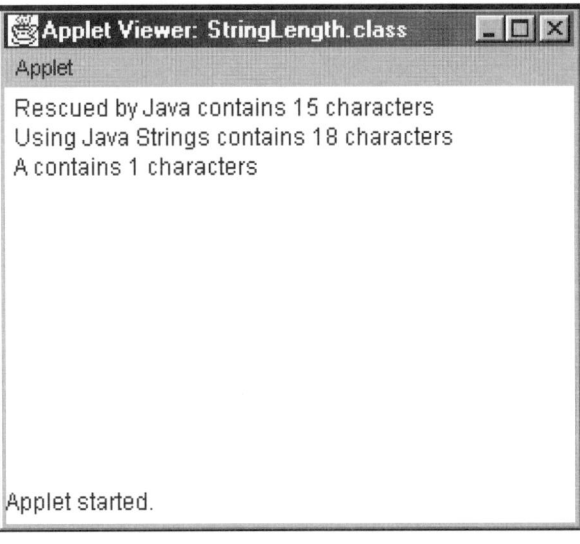

Figure 15.2 Using the String class length method to determine the number of characters a string contains.

ADDING ONE STRING'S CONTENTS TO ANOTHER

Several of the applets you have created throughout this book have used the plus operator (+) to add a value to a character string. For example, the previous applet used the plus sign to add the *String* object's length to the text displayed by the *drawString* function:

```
g.drawString(OneLetter + " contains " + OneLetter.length() +
        " characters", 5, 45);
```

When your applet adds a value to a character string in this way, the applet is said to *concatenate* (append) the value to the string. For example, the following statements concatenate the characters that contain this lesson's title to a *String* object that contains the characters that correspond to this book's title, to produce a third string:

135

```
String BookTitle, LessonTitle, BookInfo;

BookTitle = "Rescued by Java";
LessonTitle = "Using Java Strings";
BookInfo = BookTitle + " " + LessonTitle;
g.drawString(BookInfo, 5, 25);
```

As you can see, the statements declare three *String* variables: *BookTitle*, *LessonTitle*, and *BookInfo*. The statements then assign strings to the variables *BookTitle* and *LessonTitle*. Next, using the plus operator, the statements concatenate (append) the contents of the variable *LessonTitle* to the contents of *BookTitle*, assigning the resulting string to the variable *BookInfo*.

UNDERSTANDING STRING CONVERSIONS

In many of the previous applets, you have used the plus operator (+) to concatenate a numeric value to a character string. For example, the following statement uses the plus operator to add this book's lesson number to a character string named *Lesson*:

```
String Lesson = "Lesson number: ";

Lesson = Lesson + 8;
g.drawString(Lesson, 5, 10);
```

As it turns out, when you use the plus operator with a numeric value in this way, Java calls a special function named *toString* that converts the value to its character-string representation. In other words, the function converts the value from its binary representation, such as 14, to the corresponding ASCII characters, "14". Java provides a *toString* function specific to each of the common types, such as *int*, *float*, and *double*. The following applet, *ToString.java*, illustrates the use of the built-in *toString* function for values of type *int* and *double*:

```
import java.awt.*;
import java.applet.*;
public class ToString extends Applet
  {
    public void paint(Graphics g)
      {
        String NameAndAge = "John Smith, ";
        String NameAndSalary = "Jane Doe, ";

        NameAndAge = NameAndAge + 35;
        NameAndSalary = NameAndSalary + 45000.75;
        g.drawString(NameAndAge, 5, 15);
        g.drawString(NameAndSalary, 5, 30);
      }
  }
```

To run the applet, place the following HTML entries within the file *ToString.HTML*:

```
<HTML><TITLE>ToStringApplet</TITLE>
<APPLET CODE="ToString.class" WIDTH=300 HEIGHT=200></APPLET></HTML>
```

After you compile and execute this program, your screen will display an applet window similar to that shown in Figure 15.3.

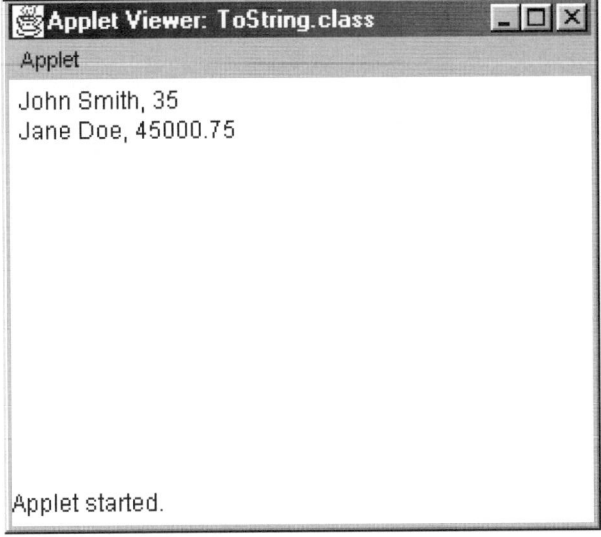

*Figure 15.3 Using the built-in **toString** functions.*

DEFINING YOUR OWN TOSTRING FUNCTION

As you create your own classes, you can define a *toString* method for each class that converts the class value to a character-string representation. For example, the following applet, *DateToString.java*, defines a *Date* class. Within the class definition, the class provides a *toString* function:

```java
import java.awt.*;
import java.applet.*;


class Date
  {
    int month;
    int day;
    int year;

    Date(int month, int day, int year)
      {
        this.day = day;
        this.month = month;
        this.year = year;
      }

    public String toString()
      {
        return("" + month + "/" + day + "/" + year);
      }
  }
```

```
public class DateToString extends Applet
  {
     public void paint(Graphics g)
      {
        Date Today = new Date(4, 15, 99);
        g.drawString("Today is: " + Today, 5, 15);
      }
  }
```

As you can see, the *Date* class defines the *toString* function, which converts the *Date* class-member variables into a *String*. Using the *toString* function behind the scenes, the applet simplifies the output of the *Date* class objects. As you can see, the *toString* function returns the type *String*. Within the *toString* function, the code uses the plus operator to append the date characters to an empty string ("").

To run the applet, place the following HTML entries within the file *DateToString.HTML*:

```
<HTML><TITLE>DateToString Applet</TITLE>
<APPLET CODE="DateToString.class" WIDTH=300 HEIGHT=200></APPLET></HTML>
```

After you compile and execute this applet, your screen will display an applet window similar to that shown in Figure 15.4.

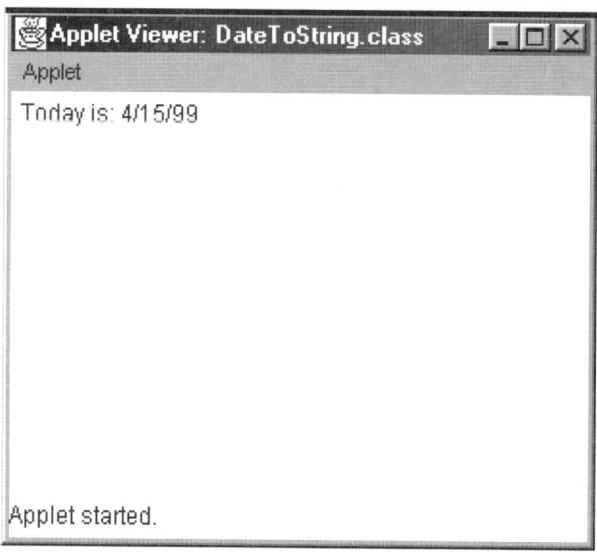

*Figure 15.4 Using the **toString** function to display a **Date** object's value .*

The previous *DateToString* applet simply assigned the fixed date 4/15/99 to an applet-defined *Date* class object. Within your applets, there will be times when you must know the current system date. In such cases, you can use the Java *Date* class that resides in the *java.util.Date* class library. The following applet, *GetSystemDate.java*, uses the Java *Date* class to display the current system date. The applet displays the *Date* class object using the *drawString* method. When Java encounters the *Date* class within the *drawString* function call, Java calls the *Date* class *toString* method to convert the date into a *String* format:

```
import java.awt.*;
import java.applet.*;
import java.util.Date;
```

```
public class GetSystemDate extends Applet
  {
    public void paint(Graphics g)
     {
       Date Today = new Date();

       g.drawString("Today is: " + Today, 5, 15);
     }
  }
```

TAKING A CYBER FIELD TRIP TO DRAW FRACTALS USING JAVA

Fractals are graphic images that programs often draw by taking advantage of repeating geometric shapes. As you surf the Web, you may find many sites that let you view complex fractal images. When Sun's Java developers put together the Java Development Kit, they included a fractal application that draws an image similar to that shown in Figure 15.5. To run the applet or to download the applet's source code, visit the Jamsa Press Web site at *www.jamsa.com/java_demos/Fractal.html.*

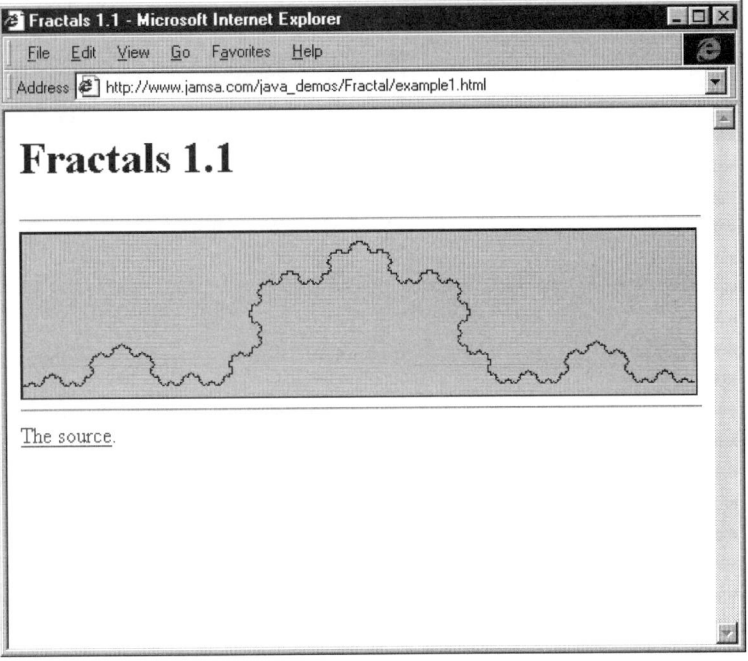

Figure 15.5 Displaying a fractal image within a Java applet.

WHAT YOU MUST KNOW

In this lesson, you learned how to create *String* objects that let you store letters, digits, and punctuation symbols. Your applets will use *String* objects to store usernames, filenames, and so on. In Lesson 16, "Interacting with HTML," you will learn how to use HTML <APPLET> entries to control your applet's execution. Before you continue with Lesson 16, however, make sure that you have learned the following key concepts:

☑ Using *String* objects, your applets can store alphanumeric characters within a variable.

☑ You do not use the NULL character to indicate the end of a Java *String* object, as you would in C or C++. Instead, the *String* object itself keeps track of the number of characters it contains.

☑ Using the *String* class *length* method, your applet can determine the number of characters a *String* object contains.

☑ The plus operator lets your applet concatenate (append) one string's contents to another.

☑ When you concatenate a numeric value, such as a value of type *int*, *float*, or *double*, Java calls a special function named *toString* that converts the value into a character-string equivalent.

☑ To simplify the output of class-member variables, you may want to implement a *toString* function for the classes you create.

LESSON 16

INTERACTING WITH *HTML*

As you know, to run a Java applet, you place entries within an HTML file that your browser or the *appletviewer* uses to determine the applet name, window size, and so on. In this lesson, you will examine the additional HTML entries you can use to control how the browser displays your applet. You will also learn how your applet can get parameter values from within the HTML file by using the *getParameter* function. By the time you finish this chapter, you will understand the following key concepts:

◆ Within an HTML *APPLET* entry, there are several additional attribute settings you can use to control how the browser displays an applet.

◆ Using the *PARAM* attribute, you can place entries within the HTML file whose values the applet can access using the *getParameter* function.

◆ By placing values within the HTML file, you make your applet easier for the end-user to modify. By allowing the end-user to change an applet's behavior using HTML, you reduce the end-user's reliance on Java programmers.

EXAMINING *HTML APPLET*-TAG ENTRIES

Throughout this book, you have used HTML entries similar to the following to run your applet:

```
<HTML><TITLE>ArrayFunction Applet</TITLE>
<APPLET CODE="ArrayFunction.class" WIDTH=300 HEIGHT=200></APPLET></HTML>
```

As you have learned, the *CODE* attribute specifies the applet's class filename. Likewise, the *WIDTH* and *HEIGHT* attributes specify the pixel-size of the applet window. As it turns out, there are several other attribute fields you can use within the *APPLET* tag. The following sections examine each of these attributes in detail.

Note: The HTML 4 standard replaces the <APPLET> tag with an <OBJECT> tag. As you surf the Web, you may find HTML files that use either tag.

USING THE *CODEBASE* ATTRIBUTE

The *CODEBASE* attribute specifies an applet's URL (Uniform Resource Locator). The applet's URL can be an absolute address, such as *www.jamsa.com*, or it can be relative to the directory that contains the current HTML file, such as */AppletPath/AppletName*. If your HTML file does not specify a *CODEBASE* attribute, the browser will use the same URL as that of the HTML file. The following entry, for example, specifies *www.jamsa.com/java_demo* as the *CODEBASE* for an applet:

```
<HTML><TITLE>ArrayFunction Applet</TITLE>
<APPLET CODE="ArrayFunction.class" CODEBASE="www.jamsa.com/java_demo"
WIDTH=300 HEIGHT=200></APPLET></HTML>
```

USING THE ALT ATTRIBUTE

Although Java applets are the hottest thing going on the Web, there may be a time, when for some unknown reason, a user's browser does not support Java applets. Using the *ALT* attribute within your HTML file, you can specify a text message that the browser will display when it encounters an *APPLET* tag, should the browser not support Java applets.

The following entry, for example, uses the *ALT* entry to direct the browser to display the message "Java Not Supported", should the browser not support Java applets:

```
<HTML><TITLE>ArrayFunction Applet</TITLE>
<APPLET CODE="ArrayFunction.class" ALT="Java Not Supported"
WIDTH=300 HEIGHT=200></APPLET></HTML>
```

USING THE ALIGN ATTRIBUTE

Within an HTML document window, you can use the *ALIGN* attribute to control where the applet displays an applet window. Like the HTML *<IMG>* tag, the values you can specify for the *ALIGN* attributes are *TOP*, *MIDDLE*, and *BOTTOM*. The following entry, for example, uses the *ALIGN* attribute to direct the browser to display an applet window at the middle of the current document window:

```
<HTML><TITLE>ArrayFunction Applet</TITLE>
<APPLET CODE="ArrayFunction.class" ALIGN=MIDDLE
WIDTH=300 HEIGHT=200></APPLET></HTML>
```

USING THE VSPACE AND HSPACE ATTRIBUTES

Depending on your applet window and the HTML document's contents, there may be times when you will want the browser to display a margin around the applet window. The *VSPACE* and *HSPACE* attributes let you specify, in pixels, the vertical and horizontal margins the browser displays around the applet window. For example, the following entry uses the attributes to place a 50-pixel margin above and below the applet window, and a 25-pixel margin to the window's left and right:

```
<HTML><TITLE>ArrayFunction Applet</TITLE>
<APPLET CODE="ArrayFunction.class" VSPACE=25 HSPACE=50
WIDTH=300 HEIGHT=200></APPLET></HTML>
```

USING THE NAME ATTRIBUTE

The *NAME* attribute lets you assign a specific name to this instance of the applet. When a browser runs two or more applets at the same time, the applets can refer to each other by name, possibly to exchange messages. If you omit the *NAME* attribute, the applet name will correspond to the applet's class name. The following entry, for example, uses the *NAME* attribute to name this applet instance *Client*:

```
<HTML><TITLE>ArrayFunction Applet</TITLE>
<APPLET CODE="ArrayFunction.class" NAME="Client"
WIDTH=300 HEIGHT=200></APPLET></HTML>
```

USING THE *PARAM* ATTRIBUTE

As your applets become more complex, one of your programming goals will be to make the applets as generic as possible. In other words, you want to make it very easy for end-users and programmers to use the applet to support many different tasks. One way you can make your applets more generic is to let the applet get information from the HTML file.

Assume, for example, that you have created an applet that scrolls a company's name across the screen. To make your applet more generic, you should let the applet get the text it is to scroll from the HTML entry. In this way, to support another company's logo, you need only to update the HTML entry, as opposed to the Java applet itself.

To specify parameters within an HTML file, you use the *PARAM* attribute. The format of the *PARAM* entry is as follows:

```
PARAM Name="SomeName" Value="Desired Value"
```

The following HTML entry, for example, uses the *PARAM* attribute to specify two parameters: one that contains this book's title, and a second that contains this lesson title:

```
<HTML><TITLE>ArrayFunction Applet</TITLE>
<APPLET CODE="ArrayFunction.class" WIDTH=300 HEIGHT=200>
<PARAM NAME=TITLE VALUE="Rescued by Java">
<PARAM NAME=LESSON VALUE="Interacting with HTML"> </APPLET></HTML>
```

Within your Java applet, you use the *getParameter* function to get an HTML parameter's value. For example, the following statement uses the *getParameter* function to assign the book's title to a variable named *BookTitle*:

```
String BookTitle = getParameter("TITLE");
```

If, for some reason, the HTML file does not specify a value for the parameter, the *getParameter* function returns the *null* value, which your applet can test for as shown:

```
String BookTitle = getParameter("TITLE");

if (BookTitle == null)
  BookTitle = "Title Unknown";
```

The following applet, *GetParameters.java*, uses the *getParameter* function to get the value for several HTML parameters:

```
import java.awt.*;
import java.applet.*;

public class GetParameters extends Applet
  {
    String BookTitle;
    String BookLesson;

    public void init()
      {
        BookTitle = getParameter("BookTitle");

        if (BookTitle == null)
          BookTitle = "Unknown";
```

```
        BookLesson = getParameter("BookLesson");

        if (BookLesson == null)
          BookLesson = "Unknown";
      }

   public void paint(Graphics g)
      {
        g.drawString("Book Title: " + BookTitle, 5, 15);
        g.drawString("Book Lesson: " + BookLesson, 5, 45);
      }
   }
```

To run this applet, place the following entries within the HTML file *GetParameters.HTML*:

```
<HTML><TITLE>GetParameters Applet</TITLE>
<APPLET  CODE="GetParameters.class"WIDTH=300  HEIGHT=200>
<PARAM NAME=BookTitle Value="Rescued by Java">
<PARAM NAME=BookLesson Value="Interfacing with HTML">
</APPLET></HTML>
```

As you can see, the HTML file provides values for each parameter the program retrieves by using the *getParameter* function. After you compile and execute this applet, your screen will display an applet window similar to that shown in Figure 16.1.

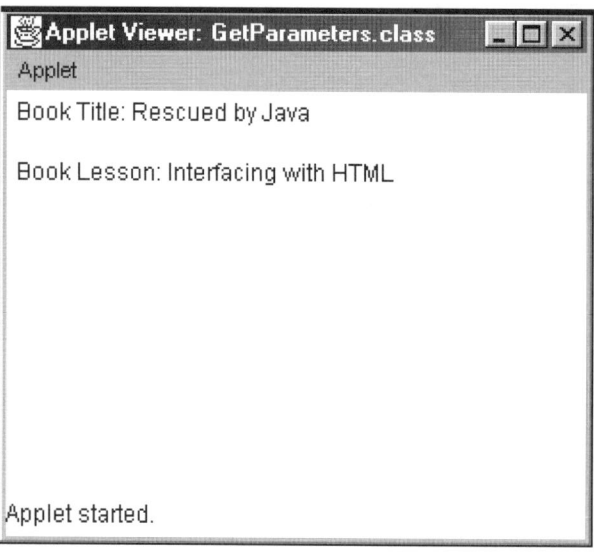

Figure 16.1 *Using the **getParameter** function to retrieve HTML parameters.*

Take time to edit the HTML file, changing the values it assigns to one or more parameters, or simply deleting a parameter. When you run the applet, the applet window will immediately reflect your change.

LOOKING AT A SECOND EXAMPLE

In Lesson 21, "Using Threads to Create Simple Animations," you will create the *MarqueeMessage.java* applet that scrolls a text message across the applet window. As you have learned, one of the advantages of using the *PARAM* attribute within the *APPLET* tag is that you can make your applets more generic. The following applet, *MarqueeParameter.java*, uses the *getParameter* function to get the message the user wants to scroll across the screen. If the user does not specify a value for the *Message* parameter within the HTML file, the applet uses the string *Rescued by Java* as its default:

```java
import java.awt.*;
import java.applet.*;

public class MarqueeParameter extends Applet implements Runnable
  {
    Thread MarqueeThread = null;
    String Message;
    Font font = new Font("TimesRoman", Font.BOLD, 18);
    int x, y;

    public void init()
      {
        x = getSize().width;
        y = getSize().height / 2;

        Message = getParameter("Message");
        if (Message == null)
          Message = "Rescued by Java";
      }

    public void start()
      {
        if (MarqueeThread == null)
          {
            MarqueeThread = new Thread(this);
            MarqueeThread.start();
          }
      }

    public void run()
      {
        while (true)
          {
            x = x - 5;
            if (x == 0)
              x = getSize().width;

            repaint();

            try
              {
                MarqueeThread.sleep(500);
              }
            catch (InterruptedException e)
              {
              }
          }
      }
```

```
    public void paint(Graphics g)
      {
        g.setFont(font);
        g.drawString(Message, x, y);
      }
  }
```

TAKING A CYBER FIELD TRIP TO WATCH TUMBLING DUKE

As you have learned, the Java Development Kit provides many different example programs whose source code you can study, or with which you can experiment. One of the more entertaining applets provided in the JDK is *Tumbling Duke,* which just happens to load values from the HTML file. When you run the *Tumbling Duke* applet, your screen will display a small animated image of "Duke," as shown in Figure 16.2.

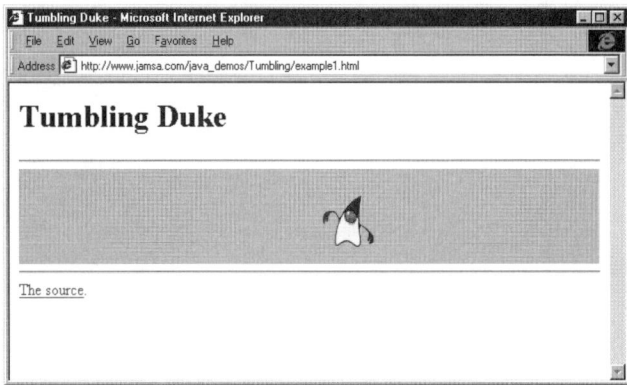

Figure 16.2 *The Java Development Kit* **Tumbling Duke** *applet.*

Every few seconds, Duke will wake up and tumble across the applet window. As you examine the applet's source code, first note how the applet uses the *getParameters* function to get information from the HTML file. Next, examine how the applet implemented the animation. To run the *Tumbling Duke* applet, or to download the applet's source code, visit the Jamsa Press Web site at *www.jamsa.com/java_demos/Tumbling.html.*

WHAT YOU MUST KNOW

As your Java applets become more complex, you can increase the number of tasks the applet can support by using HTML-based parameters. By using the *PARAM* attribute to specify applet values, you make the applet easy for an end-user to modify. In this way, should the user need a simple change to an applet, he or she may be able to change the HTML file as opposed to having to wait for a programmer to change the applet's source code.

In Lesson 17, "Using Arrays to Store Multiple Values," you will learn how to store multiple values of the same type within a data structure called an array. Before you continue with Lesson 17, however, make sure you have learned the following key concepts:

☑ As you create your applet's HTML file, keep in mind that there are several attribute settings you can use to control how the browser displays an applet.

☑ Using the *getParameter* function, your applets can access values the user has placed within the HTML file by using the *PARAM* attribute.

☑ As you create applets, you should make it easy for an end-user to modify your applet's behavior by placing entries within an HTML file. By allowing the end-user to change an applet, you reduce the end-user's reliance on Java programmers.

LESSON 17
USING ARRAYS TO STORE MULTIPLE VALUES

As you know, your programs store information in variables as they execute. Until now, the variables within your applets have only stored one value at a time. In many cases, however, your applets must store multiple values, such as 50 test scores, 100 book titles, or 1,000 filenames. When your applets must store multiple values, your applets use a special data structure called an *array*. To declare an array, your applets specify the array type, name, and number of items the array will store. This lesson examines how your applets declare and later store and access information within an array. By the time you finish this lesson, you will understand the following key concepts:

- An array is a data structure that lets a single variable store multiple values.

- To declare an array, you must specify the type of value the array will store, as well as the number of items (called *array elements*).

- Each element within an array must be the same type, such as *int*, *float*, or *char*.

- To specify the number of items an array can store, you use the Java *new* operator.

- To store a value within an array, you specify the element number within the array at which you want to store the value.

- To access a value stored within an array, your applets specify the array name and the element number.

- To determine the number of items an array can store, you can use the array's special attribute variable, named *length*.

- Your applets can pass array variables to functions just as they would any parameter. Within a function, a Java applet can change the values an array stores.

DECLARING AN ARRAY VARIABLE

An *array* is a variable capable of storing one or more values. Like the variables your applets have used in the previous lessons, an array must have a type (such as *int*, *char*, or *float*) and a unique name. In addition, you must specify the number of values the array will store. All of the values you store in an array must be the same type. In other words, your applet cannot place values of type *float*, *char*, and *long* in the same array. The following declaration creates an array, named *TestScores*, that can hold 100 integer test scores:

```
int TestScores[] = new int[100];
```

When the Java compiler encounters the *new* operator within the variable declaration, the compiler will allocate enough memory to hold 100 values of type *int*. The values stored in an array are called *array elements*. In this case, the left-and-right brackets that follow the *TestScores* variable name indicate to the compiler that variable is an array.

ARRAYS STORE MULTIPLE VALUES OF THE SAME TYPE

As your applets become more complex, they will often work with multiple values of the same type. For example, your applet might store the prices for 50 parts, the ages of 100 employees, or 25 stock prices. Rather than forcing your applet to work with 50, 100, or 25 uniquely-named variables, Java lets your applets define a single variable (an array) that can store multiple, related values.

To declare an array, you must specify the array type, a unique name, and the number of elements the array will hold. For example, the following statements declare three different arrays:

```
float PartCost[] = new float[50];
int EmployeeAge[] = new int[100];
float StockPrices[] = new float[25];
```

MOVING THE BRACKETS IS OK

As you have learned, to declare an array, you specify the right-and-left brackets following the array name:

```
type ArrayName[] = new type[];
```

As it turns out, Java lets you place the brackets following the type name as opposed to the variable name, as shown here:

```
type[] ArrayName = new type[];
```

As you examine Java applets, you will encounter applets that place the brackets following the array type, while others place the brackets after the array name.

ACCESSING ARRAY ELEMENTS

As you have learned, an array lets your applets store multiple values within the same variable. To access specific values within an array, you use an *index value* that points to the desired element. For example, to access the first element in the array *test_scores*, you would use the index value 0. To access the second element, you would use an index of 1. Likewise, to access the third value, you would use an index of 2. As shown in Figure 17.1, the first array element is always indexed by 0, and the last array element is indexed by a value 1 less than the size of the array.

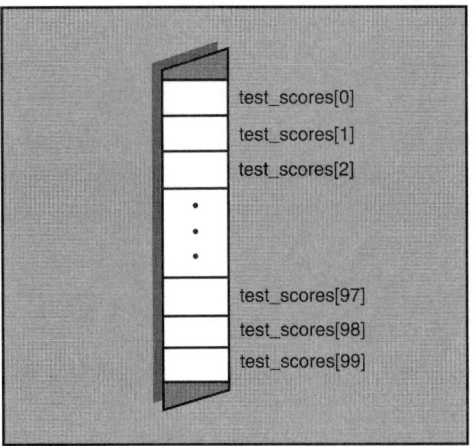

Figure 17.1 How Java indexes array elements.

It is important you remember that Java always uses 0 to index the first array element, and the array size minus 1 for the last element.

The following applet, *UseArray.java*, creates an array (named *values*) that holds five integer values. The applet then assigns the elements the values 100, 200, 300, 400, and 500:

```java
import java.awt.*;
import java.applet.*;

public class UseArray extends Applet
  {
    int Values[] = new int[5];

    public void init()
      {
        Values[0] = 100;
        Values[1] = 200;
        Values[2] = 300;
        Values[3] = 400;
        Values[4] = 500;
      }

    public void paint(Graphics g)
      {
        g.drawString("The array contains the following values", 5, 15);
        g.drawString("Values[0] = " + Values[0], 5, 30);
        g.drawString("Values[1] = " + Values[1], 5, 45);
        g.drawString("Values[2] = " + Values[2], 5, 60);
        g.drawString("Values[3] = " + Values[3], 5, 75);
        g.drawString("Values[4] = " + Values[4], 5, 90);
      }
  }
```

As you can see, the applet assigns the first value to element 0 (*Values[0]*). Also, the applet assigns the last value to element 4 (the array size (5) minus 1).

Place the following HTML entries within the file *UseArray.HTML* to run the applet:

```html
<HTML><TITLE>UseArray Applet</TITLE>
<APPLET CODE="UseArray.class" WIDTH=300 HEIGHT=200></APPLET></HTML>
```

After you compile and execute this applet, your screen will display an applet window similar to that shown in Figure 17.2.

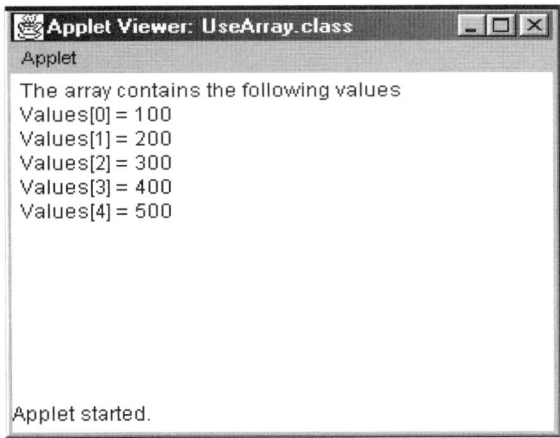

Figure 17.2 *Displaying array values within an applet.*

USE AN INDEX VALUE TO ACCESS ARRAY ELEMENTS

An array lets your applets store multiple values within the same value. To access specific values within the array, your applets use an index value. In short, the index value specifies the array element you desire. All Java arrays start with element 0. The following statement, for example, assigns the value 100 to the first element of an array named *Scores*:

```
Scores[0] = 100;
```

When your applet declares an array, your applet specifies the number of elements the array can store. For example, the following statement declares an array capable of storing 100 values of type *int*:

```
int Scores[] = new int[100];
```

In this case, the array elements are *Scores[0]* through *Scores[99]*.

USING AN INDEX VARIABLE

When your applets use arrays, a common operation is to use an *index variable* to access the array elements. For example, assuming the variable *i* contains the value 3, the following statement assigns the value 400 to *Values[3]*:

```
Values[i] = 400;
```

The following applet, *ShowArray.java*, uses the index variable *index* within a *for* loop to display the array elements. The *for* loop initializes the *index* to 0 so that it can reference element *Values[0]*. The *for* loop ends when the *index* is greater than 4 (the array's last element):

```
import java.awt.*;
import java.applet.*;

public class ShowArray extends Applet
   {
     int Values[] = new int[5];
```

```
   public void init()
     {
       Values[0] = 100;
       Values[1] = 200;
       Values[2] = 300;
       Values[3] = 400;
       Values[4] = 500;
     }


   public void paint(Graphics g)
     {
       int index;
       g.drawString("The array contains the following values", 5, 15);

       for (index = 0; index < 5; index++)
          g.drawString("Values[" + index + "] = " + Values[index], 5,
                     (index + 2)*15);
     }
   }
```

Each time the *for* loop increments the *index* variable, the applet can access the next array element. Take time to understand the *for* loop's processing and how the loop uses the expression (**index + 2**) * **15** to get the y-coordinate values 30, 45, 60, 75, and 90.

Experiment with this applet by changing the *for* loop, as follows:

```
for (index = 4; index >= 0; index--)
  g.drawString("Values[" + index + "] = " + Values[index], 5, (index + 2)*15);
```

In this case, the applet will display the array elements from highest to lowest (from *Values[4]* to *Values[0]*). In a similar way, the following *for* statement uses an index variable to initialize the array values:

```
for (index = 0; index < 5; index++)
   Values[index] = (index + 1) * 100;
```

INITIALIZING AN ARRAY DECLARATION

As you have learned, when you declare a variable, Java lets you use the assignment operator to initialize the variable. For example, the following statement declares a variable of type *int*, named *index,* and initializes the variable to 1:

```
int index = 1;
```

In a similar way, when you declare an array, Java lets you initialize the array elements. When you declare an array in this way, you do not use the *new* operator, and you do not specify an array size. Instead, the Java compiler will determine the array size from the number of element values you specify. The following statement, for example, creates and initializes the *Values* array:

```
int Values[] = {100, 200, 300, 400, 500};
```

In this case, the Java compiler will allocate an array capable of storing five values. If you change the initialization to, say, 10 values, the compiler will allocate sufficient space to store the array.

DETERMINING AN ARRAY'S LENGTH

When you declare an array, the *new* operator specifies the number of items the array can hold. When your applet uses the items the array holds, the applet often must know the array's size. To determine an array's size, your applet can use a special array-variable attribute named *length,* as shown here:

```
array_length = Values.length;
```

The following applet, *UseArrayLength.java*, uses the *length* attribute variable within a *for* loop to control the applet's processing of the array elements:

```
import java.awt.*;
import java.applet.*;

public class UseArrayLength extends Applet
  {
    int Values[] = { 100, 200, 300, 400, 500 };

    public void paint(Graphics g)
      {
        int index;
        g.drawString("The array contains the following values", 5, 15);

        for (index = 0; index < Values.length; index++)
          g.drawString("Values[" + index + "] = " + Values[index], 5,
                           (index + 2)*15);
      }
  }
```

As you can see, the applet no longer uses a constant within the *for* statement but, rather, the variable *Values.length*. By using the *length* attribute in this way, you make the applet easier to change in the future. For example, if you change the array size to 10 elements, you do not have to change the *for* loop in any way. Because the *for* loop now uses the *length* attribute, it will automatically support the larger array.

PASSING ARRAYS TO FUNCTIONS

Like most variables, your applets will pass arrays to functions. The function might initialize the array, add up the array values, or display the array entries on your screen. When you pass an array to a function, you must specify the array type. You do not need to specify the array size. Instead, as you have learned, the function can use the variable's *length* attribute to determine the number of elements in the array:

```
void some_function(int array[])
```

The following applet, *ArrayFunction.java*, passes arrays to the function *ShowArray*, which uses a *for* loop to display the array values:

```
import java.awt.*;
import java.applet.*;

public class ArrayFunction extends Applet
  {
    int Values[] = { 100, 200, 300, 400, 500 };

    public void ShowArray(Graphics g, int SomeArray[])
      {
        int index;
        g.drawString("The array contains the following values", 5, 15);

        for (index = 0; index < SomeArray.length; index++)
          g.drawString("SomeArray[" + index + "] = " + SomeArray[index], 5,
                    (index + 2)*15);
      }

    public void paint(Graphics g)
      {
        ShowArray(g, Values);
      }
  }
```

As you can see, the applet simply passes the array to the function by name:

```
ShowArray(g, Values);
```

CHANGING AN ARRAY'S VALUE WITHIN A FUNCTION

In Lesson 9, "Using Functions to Simplify Java Applets," you learned that you cannot permanently change the value of a simple parameter, such as a parameter of type *int* or *double,* within a function. Java, however, will let a function change array values within a function. For example, the following applet, *FillArray.java*, uses the function *FillArrayValues* to assign three values to the *Values* array:

```
import java.awt.*;
import java.applet.*;

public class FillArray extends Applet
  {
    int Values[] = { 0, 0, 0, 0, 0 };

    public void FillArrayValues(int SomeArray[])
      {
        SomeArray[0] = 100;
        SomeArray[1] = 200;
        SomeArray[2] = 300;
      }
```

```
    public void paint(Graphics g)
      {
        int index;

        g.drawString("The array initially contains the following values",
                     5, 15);

        for (index = 0; index < 5; index++)
          g.drawString("Values[" + index + "] = " + Values[index], 5,
                       (index + 2)*15);

        FillArrayValues(Values);

        g.drawString("The array now contains the following values", 5,
                     115);

        for (index = 0; index < 5; index++)
          g.drawString("Values[" + index + "] = " + Values[index], 5,
                       (index + 2)*15 + 100);
      }
    }
```

As you can see, the applet passes the array to the function by name. The function, in turn, assigns the array elements.

UNDERSTANDING MULTI-DIMENSIONAL ARRAYS

Each of the arrays you have created within this lesson have been one-dimensional arrays that you can view as a single row or column of data. Java, however, like C and C++, supports multi-dimensional arrays. The following statement, for example, creates a 3 by 3 array named TicTacToeBoard:

```
int TicTacToeBoard[] = new int[3][3];
```

In this case, the Java compiler will allocate an array with three rows and three columns, whose values you will access using the index values 0 to 2. The following statement, for example, assigns the value 0 to the array's center element:

```
TicTacToeBoard[1][1] = 0;
```

Although Java supports an almost unlimited number of array dimensions, you will find that as the number of dimensions in your array increases, so too will the difficulty most users will have reading your code.

USING COMMAND-LINE ARGUMENTS IN A STANDALONE JAVA PROGRAM

In Lesson 4, "Java Applets Versus Standalone Programs," you learned that a standalone Java program runs outside of a browser or the *appletviewer*. When you run a standalone program, you use the Java interpreter. Depending on your program's purpose, there may be times when you will want the user to include specific information within the command line when he or she starts the program. For example, assume that you have created a standalone program named *RemotePrint* that will print a file on a remote-network printer. When the user runs the program, he or she specifies the name of the file to print, as shown here:

```
C:\> java   RemotePrint   SampleFile.Java   <ENTER>
```

To access command-line arguments, your programs access a special array of string variables the Java interpreter will pass to the *main* function:

```
public static void main(String args[])
```

The following program, *ShowArguments.java*, displays your program's command-line arguments by looping through the elements of the *args* array:

```
class ShowArguments
  {
    public static void main(String args[])
      {
        int i;

        for (i = 0; i < args.length; i++)
           System.out.println(args[i]);
      }
  }
```

Use the Java compiler to compile this program, and then invoke the program by using different command-line arguments, as shown here:

```
C:\> java   ShowArguments   Hello   World   Let's   Java   <ENTER>
Hello
World
Let's
Java
```

Note: If you are using a Unix-based system, you may need to group each of the command-line arguments within double quotes for the previous program to execute correctly.

In Lesson 16, "Interacting with HTML," you learned that Java applets (as opposed to standalone programs) can get run-time parameters from the HTML file by using the *getParameter* method.

TAKING A CYBER FIELD TRIP

When you work with arrays within Java applets, a common operation you will perform is to sort the array's contents, either from lowest to highest or vice versa. To get you started with sorting operations, the Java Development Kit provides the Sorting Algorithm Demo that, as shown in Figure 17.3, demonstrates several different sorting techniques. To run the applet or to download the applet's source code, visit the Jamsa Press Web site at *www.jamsa.com/java_demos/SortDemo.html*.

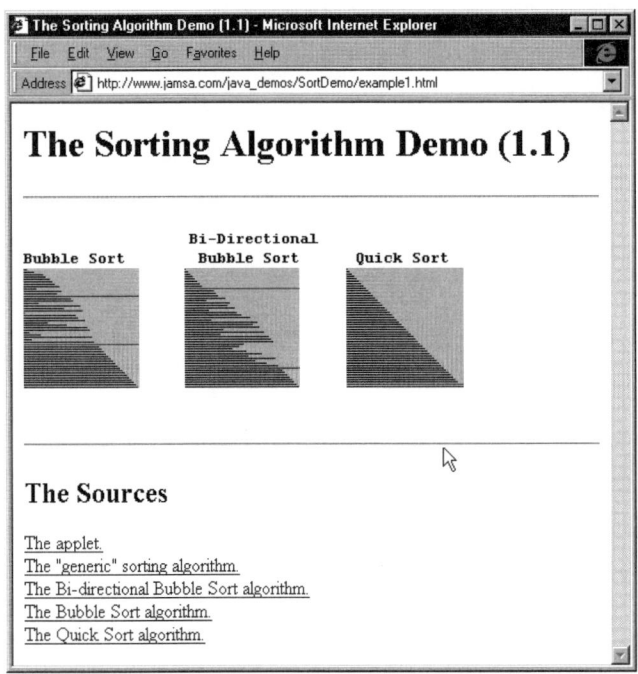

Figure 17.3 Sorting array values within a Java applet.

WHAT YOU MUST KNOW

In this lesson, you learned that your applets can store multiple values of the same type within an array. Java applets make extensive use of arrays. In Lesson 18, "Creating Simple Graphics," you will learn how to draw simple graphics shapes within your applets, such as rectangles, ovals, and arcs. Before you continue with Lesson 18, however, make sure that you have learned the following key concepts:

☑ An array is a variable that can store one or more values of the same type.

☑ To declare an array, you must specify a type, an array name, and the number of values the array is to store.

☑ Values within the array are called array elements.

☑ The first array element is stored at the 0 element (*array[0]*); the last array element is indexed by a value 1 less than the array size.

☑ Programs often use index variables to access array elements.

☑ When a function receives an array as a parameter, the function must specify the array type and name, but not the array size.

☑ To determine the number of items an array can store, your applet can use the *length* attribute.

☑ Within a function, your applet can change the values that the array contains.

☑ Within a standalone Java program, you can access command-line arguments by using an array of strings the Java interpreter passes to the *main* function.

LESSON 18
CREATING SIMPLE GRAPHICS

One of Java's key features is its support for graphics and animation. In this lesson, you will examine the primitive (basic) graphics functions your applets can use to draw circles, squares, polygons, and other shapes. Using the functions this lesson presents, you can create simple or complex images. By the time you finish this lesson, you will understand the following key concepts:

- To display a graphics image within an applet window, you must specify the x-and-y coordinates at which you want the image displayed.

- Java assigns the x-and-y coordinates (0,0) to the upper-left corner of the applet window.

- In addition to specifying an image's x-and-y coordinates, many of the Java graphics-based functions require you to specify the image width and height.

UNDERSTANDING GRAPHICS COORDINATES

As you draw graphics images within an applet window, you must specify the shape's starting and ending locations. To specify these locations, your applet specifies x-and-y coordinates. The graphics functions that you will examine in this lesson use the coordinates (0,0) as the upper-left window coordinates. As you work with the graphics functions, you must always think in terms of these coordinates.

DRAWING SOME SIMPLE SHAPES

The *Graphics* class functions make it very easy for you to draw lines, rectangles, circles, and ellipses. To draw a line, for example, you use the *drawLine* function, specifying the line's starting and ending coordinates, as shown here:

```
g.drawLine(25, 25, 125, 125);
```

Likewise, to draw a rectangle, you use the *drawRect* function, specifying the rectangle's upper-left window coordinates, followed by the box width and height:

```
g.drawRect(50, 50, 100, 100);
```

To draw an oval, you use the *drawOval* function, specifying the upper-left window coordinates and width and height for an imaginary rectangle that frames the oval:

```
g.drawOval(50, 50, 200, 200);
```

In addition to drawing empty shapes, the *Graphics* class functions let you fill your shapes using the current color. For example, the following statements draw a filled rectangle and oval:

```
g.fillRect(50, 50, 100, 100);
g.fillOval(125, 125, 225, 225);
```

The following applet, *SimpleGraphics.java*, uses these graphics functions to create simple images:

```
import java.awt.*;
import java.applet.*;

public class SimpleGraphics extends Applet
  {
    public void paint(Graphics g)
      {
          g.drawRect(25, 25, 50, 50);
          g.drawOval(75, 100, 100, 150);
          g.fillRect(250, 25, 100, 25);
          g.fillOval(205, 125, 100, 100);
      }
  }
```

To run the applet, place the following HTML entries within the file *SimpleGraphics.HTML*:

```
<HTML><TITLE>SimpleGraphics Applet</TITLE>
<APPLET CODE="SimpleGraphics.class" WIDTH=500 HEIGHT=300></APPLET></HTML>
```

After you compile and run this applet, your screen will display an applet window similar to Figure 18.1.

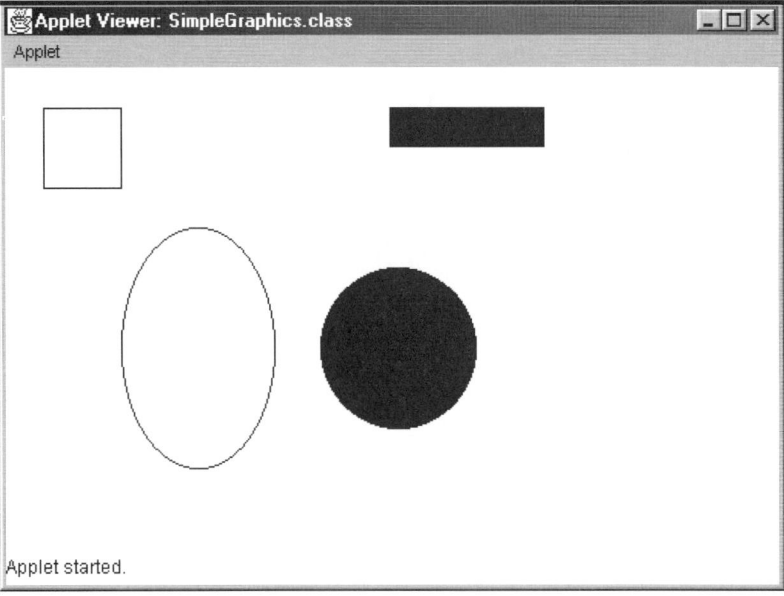

Figure 18.1 *Using the Java **Graphics** class to draw simple images.*

In Lesson 14, "Controlling Fonts within Java Applets," you learned how to use the *setColor* method to select the current font color. In a similar way, when you use the Java graphics functions, you can use the *setColor* method to select the drawing color. The following applet, *ColoredGraphics.java*, changes the previous applet slightly to draw each shape using a different color:

```
import java.awt.*;
import java.applet.*;
```

```
public class ColoredGraphics extends Applet
  {
    public void paint(Graphics g)
     {
        g.setColor(Color.blue);
        g.drawRect(25, 25, 50, 50);

        g.setColor(Color.red);
        g.drawOval(75, 100, 100, 150);

        g.setColor(Color.yellow);
        g.fillRect(250, 25, 100, 25);

        g.setColor(Color.green);
        g.fillOval(205, 125, 100, 100);
     }
  }
```

To run the applet, place the following HTML entries within the file *ColoredGraphics.HTML*:

```
<HTML><TITLE>ColoredGraphics Applet</TITLE>
<APPLET CODE="ColoredGraphics.class" WIDTH=500 HEIGHT=300></APPLET></HTML>
```

DRAWING FANCY RECTANGLES

In the previous section, you learned how to draw simple filled rectangles. By taking advantage of two graphics functions, you can create 3-D rectangles, as well as rectangles with rounded corners:

```
g.draw3DRect(25, 25, 25, 25, true);           //pushed out
g.draw3DRect(150, 150, 50, 50, false);        //pushed in
g.drawRoundRect(225, 225, 100, 100, 20, 20);
g.fillRoundRect(275, 275, 150, 100, 10, 10);
```

The last two parameters to the *drawRoundRect* and *fillRoundRect* functions control the curvature of the rectangle's angles. The two parameters define the width and height of a box whose corners control where the corners of the rectangle start to curve.

The following applet, *FancyRectangles.java*, illustrates the use of these functions:

```
import java.awt.*;
import java.applet.*;

public class FancyRectangles extends Applet
  {
    public void paint(Graphics g)
     {
```

159

```
        g.setColor(Color.yellow);
        g.draw3DRect(25, 25, 75, 75, true);
        g.draw3DRect(75, 150, 50, 50, false);
        g.drawRoundRect(205, 25, 100, 50, 20, 20);
        g.fillRoundRect(205, 125, 200, 100, 30, 30);
    }
  }
```

To run the applet, place the following HTML entries within the file *FancyRectangles.HTML*:

```
<HTML><TITLE>FancyRectangles Applet</TITLE>
<APPLET CODE="FancyRectangles.class" WIDTH=500 HEIGHT=300></APPLET></HTML>
```

Depending on the current color, the 3-D rectangles may not appear to be 3-D. Therefore, you may have to experiment with several different colors until you find one that creates the 3-D image.

OTHER GRAPHICS CLASS FUNCTIONS

In addition to the functions this lesson has discussed, your applets can use the *drawArc* and *fillArc* functions to draw an arc:

```
g.drawArc(25, 25, 50, 50, 180);
g.fillArc(150, 150, 100, 100, 90);
```

Like the *drawOval* function, the first four parameters to these functions define an imaginary rectangle that frames the arc. The last parameter specifies the number of degrees the arc sweeps.

As your shapes become more complex, you can use the *drawPolygon* and *fillPolygon* functions. In short, you pass each of these functions two arrays. The first array contains the image's x-coordinates. The second array contains the corresponding y-coordinates. The last parameter to both functions specifies the number of points in each array.

The following applet, *PolygonShapes.java*, illustrates the use of these functions to draw a simple airplane image:

```
import java.awt.*;
import java.applet.*;

public class PolygonShapes extends Applet
  {
    public void paint(Graphics g)
      {
        int plane_x[] = { 100, 130, 200, 230, 260, 225, 100 };
        int plane_y[] = {  50,  30,  30,  10,  10,  50,  50 };

        int wing_x[] = { 145, 175, 175 };
        int wing_y[] = {  40,  80,  40 };

        g.drawPolygon(plane_x, plane_y, plane_x.length);
        g.setColor(Color.blue);
        g.fillPolygon(wing_x, wing_y, wing_x.length);
      }
  }
```

To run the applet, place the following HTML entries within the file *PolygonShapes.HTML*:

```
<HTML><TITLE>PolygonShapes Applet</TITLE>
<APPLET CODE="PolygonShapes.class" WIDTH=400 HEIGHT=200></APPLET></HTML>
```

When you compile and execute this applet, your screen will display an applet window similar to that shown in Figure 18.2.

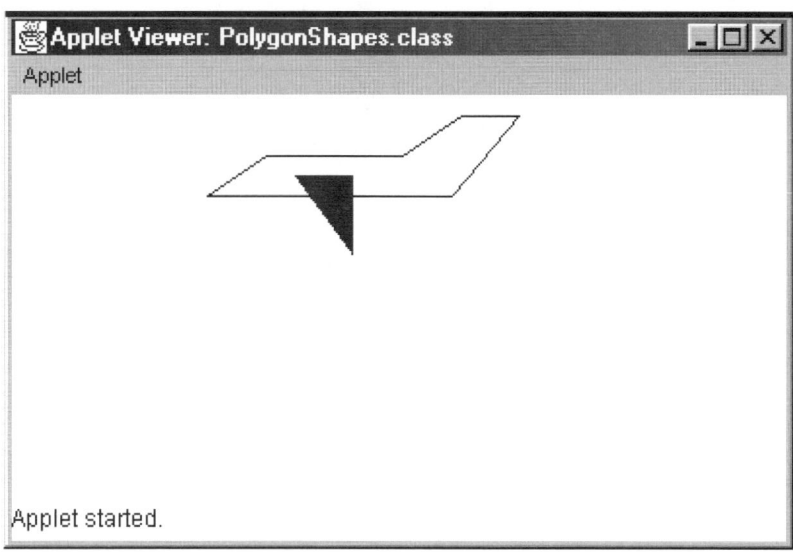

Figure 18.2 *Displaying polygon objects.*

LOOKING AT A FEW MORE EXAMPLES

Earlier in this lesson, you learned how to use the *drawLine* method to draw a line from one screen location to another. The following applet, *ColorBars.java*, repeatedly draws a series of random color bars using the *drawLine* method. The applet uses the *setColor* function to select the current color based on a random number returned by the *Math* class *random* method. The applet multiplies the random number by 13 to create an integer value in the range 0 to 12 that it can use as an index value into the *colors* array, whose elements correspond to the available colors:

```
import java.awt.*;
import java.applet.*;

public class ColorBars extends Applet
  {
    Color colors[] = { Color.black, Color.blue, Color.cyan,
                       Color.darkGray, Color.gray, Color.green,
                       Color.lightGray, Color.magenta, Color.orange,
                       Color.pink, Color.red, Color.white, Color.yellow };

    public void paint(Graphics g)
      {
        int CurrentColor = (int) (Math.random() * 13);

        int x;
```

```
        while (true)
          {
            for (x = 50; x < 350; x++)
              {
                g.setColor(colors[CurrentColor]);
                CurrentColor = (int) (Math.random() * 13);
                g.drawLine(x, 50, x, 200);
              }
          }
      }
  }
```

To run the applet, place the following HTML entries within the file *ColorBars.HTML*:

```
<HTML><TITLE>ColorBars Applet</TITLE>
<APPLET CODE="ColorBars.class" WIDTH=400 HEIGHT=200></APPLET></HTML>
```

When you compile and execute this applet, your screen will display an applet window similar to that shown in Figure 18.3.

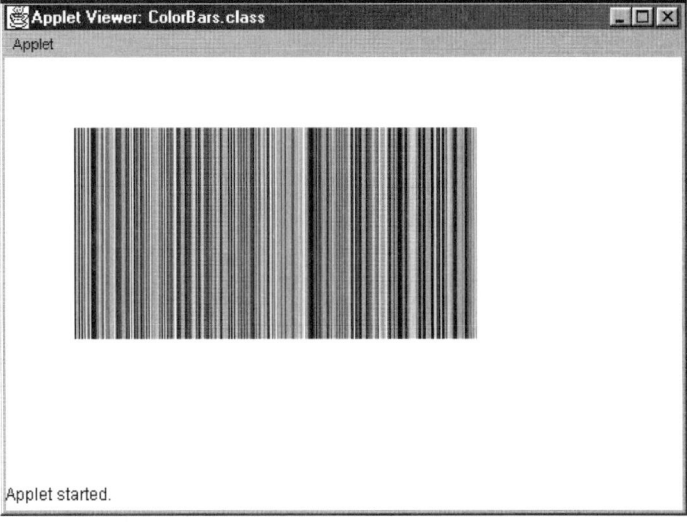

Figure 18.3 Displaying a series of random color bars.

In a similar way, the following applet, *ColorOvals.java*, continually draws a series of repeatedly smaller ovals, which creates an illusion of rotating circles. The program uses a *while* statement to repeat the processing until you close the *appletviewer* and a *for* statement to draw the colored ovals:

```
import java.awt.*;
import java.applet.*;

public class ColorOvals extends Applet
  {
    Color colors[] = { Color.black, Color.blue, Color.cyan,
                       Color.darkGray, Color.gray, Color.green,
                       Color.lightGray, Color.magenta, Color.orange,
                       Color.pink, Color.red, Color.white, Color.yellow };
```

```
    public void paint(Graphics g)
      {
        int CurrentColor = (int) (Math.random() * 13);
        int x;

        while (true)
          {
            for (x = 0; x < 50; x++)
              {
                g.setColor(colors[CurrentColor]);
                CurrentColor = (int) (Math.random() * 13);
                g.drawOval(100+x, 100, 100-(2*x), 100);
              }
          }
      }
  }
```

To run the applet, place the following HTML entries within the file *ColorOvals.HTML*:

```
  <HTML><TITLE>ColorOvals Applet</TITLE>
  <APPLET CODE="ColorOvals.class" WIDTH=400 HEIGHT=200></APPLET></HTML>
```

When you compile and execute this applet, your screen will display an applet window similar to that shown in Figure 18.4.

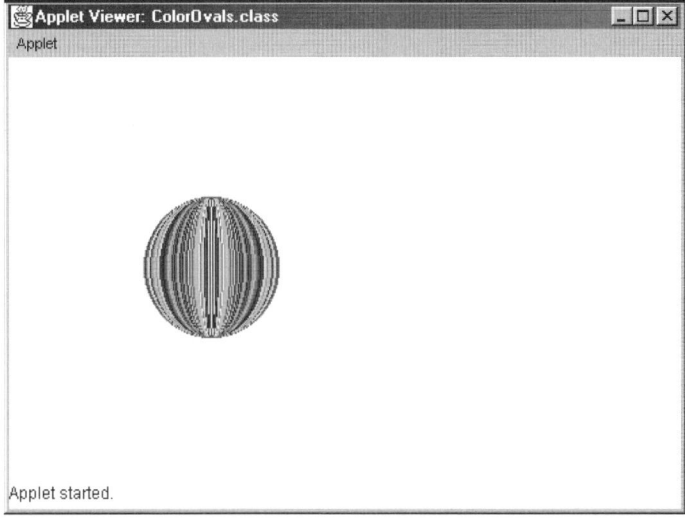

Figure 18.4 *Displaying a series of random color ovals.*

TAKING A CYBER FIELD TRIP TO LOOK AT GRAPHICS

In this lesson, you learned how to create simple graphics images using the Java *Graphics* class. Each of the graphics functions you examined are two-dimensional functions, that let you specify x and y coordinates. As your shapes increase in complexity, however, you may want to draw three-dimensional images. To help you get started with 3D graphics, the Java Development Kit provides the Wire Frame applet, which, as shown in Figure 18.5, draws a 3D image. If you drag your mouse over the image, you can rotate the image about its x, y, or z axis. To run the applet or to download the applet's source code, visit the Jamsa Press Web site at *www.jamsa.com/java_demos/WireFrame.html*.

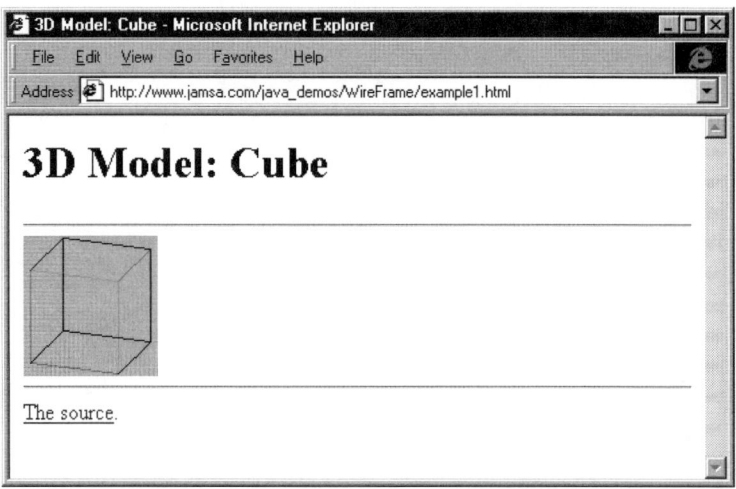

Figure 18.5 *Graphics shapes within the JDK **GraphicsTest** applet.*

WHAT YOU MUST KNOW

In this lesson, you learned how to use Java's graphics primitives (most basic functions) to create simple images within your applet window. In Lesson 19, "Using Java's Built-In Functions," you will learn how to use functions the Java libraries provide. Using such built-in functions, for example, your applets can perform complex arithmetic operations or get the current system date and time. Before you continue with Lesson 19, however, make sure you have learned the following key concepts:

☑ When your applet displays a graphics image within an applet window, the applet must specify the x-and-y coordinates.

☑ Within the applet window, Java assigns the x-and-y coordinates (0,0) to the upper-left corner.

☑ Using the *setColor* method, your applets can select the current drawing color.

☑ For most graphics-based functions, you must specify the image's x-and-y coordinates, as well as the image width and height.

LESSON 19

USING JAVA'S BUILT-IN FUNCTIONS

In Lesson 9, "Using Functions to Simplify Java Applets," you learned how to break your applets into functions, each of which performs a specific task. As you create applets, you will find that you can often use a function that you create for one applet within a second, unrelated applet. To help you create powerful applets quickly, Java predefines many functions for you that you can use within your own applets. This lesson examines several of those built-in functions. By the time you finish this lesson, you will understand the following key concepts:

- ◆ To determine the current system date and time, you can use the Java *Date* class.

- ◆ Java provides the *Math* class whose members you can use to perform many common arithmetic operations.

- ◆ To determine information about the user's country, you can use the Java *Country* class.

- ◆ To determine a class's methods (the class functions), you can use the *getMethods* function.

- ◆ To determine a class's data members, you can use the *getFields* function.

DETERMINING THE CURRENT SYSTEM DATE

Within your many Java applets, you may have to know the current date or time. You might, for example, have to "date and time stamp" various operations or you may want to display the current system date or time within your applet window. To determine the current system date and time, you can use the Java *Date* class. The following applet, *DateDemo.java*, displays the current system date and time within the applet window:

```
import java.awt.*;
import java.applet.*;
import java.util.*;

public class DateDemo extends Applet
  {
    public void paint(Graphics g)
      {
        Date CurrentDateTime = new Date();

        g.drawString(CurrentDateTime.toString(), 5, 15);
      }
  }
```

To run this applet, place the following HTML entries within the file *DateDemo.HTML*:

```
<HTML><TITLE>DateDemo Applet</TITLE>
<APPLET CODE="DateDemo.class" WIDTH=300 HEIGHT=200></APPLET></HTML>
```

When you run the *DateDemo* applet, your screen will display an applet window that contains the current system date and time, as shown in Figure 19.1.

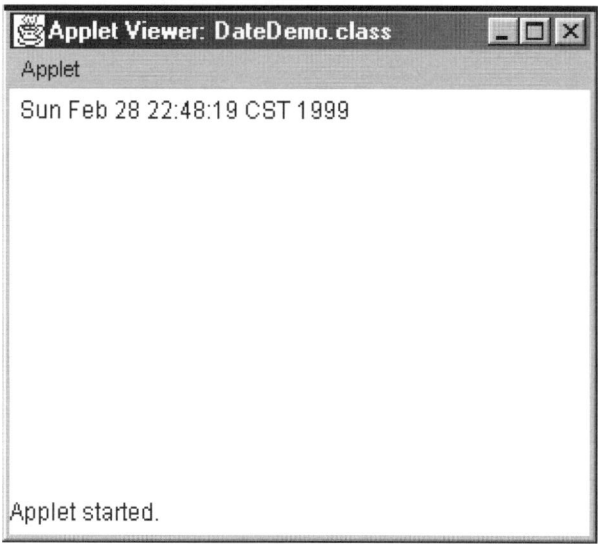

Figure 19.1 *Using the Java* **Date** *class to determine the current system date and time.*

USING JAVA'S MATH-CLASS FUNCTIONS

Depending on your applet's processing, there will often be times when you must perform a variety of arithmetic operations. For example, many graphics-based applets make extensive use of trigonometric functions such as *sine* and *cosine* to rotate objects on the screen. To help you perform such operations, Java provides a *Math* class whose methods implement a variety of common arithmetic functions. The following applet, *MathDemo.java*, uses the *Math* class to perform several operations:

```
import java.awt.*;
import java.applet.*;
import java.lang.*;

public class MathDemo extends Applet
  {
    public void paint(Graphics g)
      {
        g.drawString("Maximum of 5 and 25 is " + Math.max(5, 25), 5, 15);
        g.drawString("Sine of pi/2 is " + Math.sin(Math.PI/2.0), 5, 30);
        g.drawString("The number 7 in binary is " +
                    Long.toBinaryString(7), 5, 45);
      }
  }
```

To run this applet, place the following HTML entries within the file *MathDemo.HTML*:

```
<HTML><TITLE>MathDemo Applet</TITLE>
<APPLET CODE="MathDemo.class" WIDTH=300 HEIGHT=200></APPLET></HTML>
```

When you run the *MathDemo* applet, your screen will display an applet window that contains the result of different arithmetic functions, as shown in Figure 19.2.

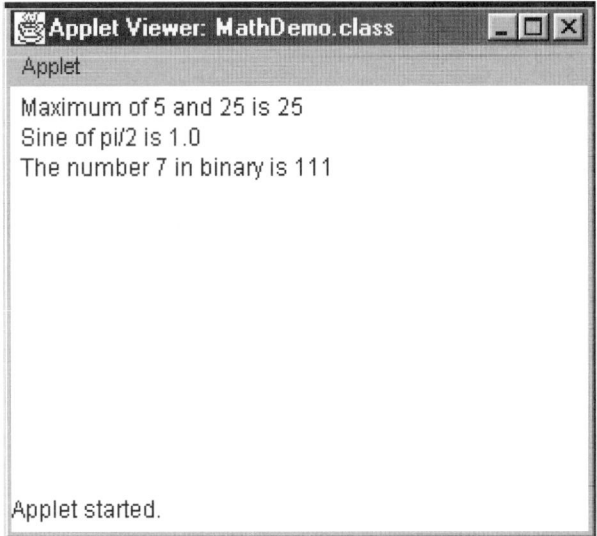

Figure 19.2 *Using the Java **Math** class to perform arithmetic operations.*

DISPLAYING INFORMATION ABOUT THE CURRENT COUNTRY

As you have learned, Java's platform independence lets your applets run on a variety of systems. When you place a Java applet on the Web, your applet may be run by users from around the world. Depending on the processing your applet performs, there may be times when you will want to customize the applet's processing for the user's country. The following applet, *ShowCountry.java*, uses Java's *Country* class to display information about the user's country:

```
import java.awt.*;
import java.applet.*;
import java.util.*;

public class ShowCountry extends Applet
  {
    public void paint(Graphics g)
      {
        Locale Country = Locale.getDefault();

        g.drawString("Country code is " + Country.getCountry(), 5, 15);
        g.drawString("Country name is " + Country.getDisplayCountry(), 5, 30);
        g.drawString("Language is " + Country.getDisplayLanguage(), 5, 45);
      }
  }
```

To run this applet, place the following HTML entries within the file *ShowCountry.HTML*:

```
<HTML><TITLE>ShowCountry Applet</TITLE>
<APPLET CODE="ShowCountry.class" WIDTH=300 HEIGHT=200></APPLET></HTML>
```

When you run the *ShowCountry* applet, your screen will display an applet window that displays specifics about the current country, as shown in Figure 19.3.

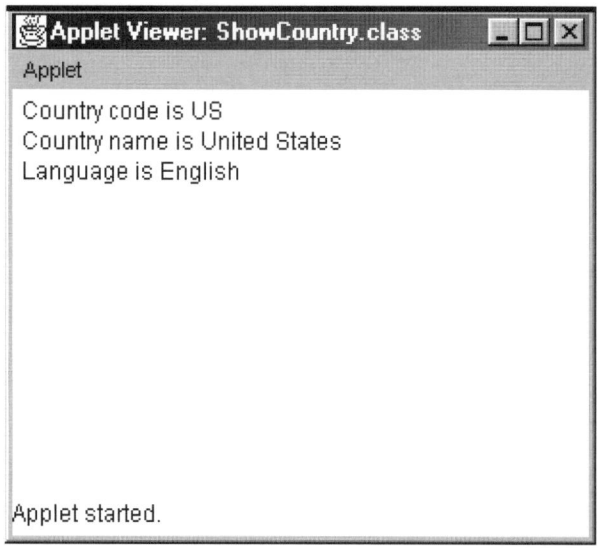

*Figure 19.3 Using the Java **Country** class to display country-specific information.*

DISPLAYING A CLASS' METHODS

As you learned in Lesson 12, "Getting Started with Java Classes," a class consists of data members and methods (class functions). As you work with Java's predefined classes, there may be times when you want to determine the methods the class provides. In such cases, you can use the *getMethods* member to determine the class's members. The following program (standalone program, as opposed to applet), *ShowMethods.java*, uses the *getMethods* method to determine the *String* and *Math* class methods:

```java
import java.lang.reflect.*;

class ShowMethods
  {
    public static void main(String args[])
      {
        Method[] methods;

        methods = String.class.getMethods();

        for (int i = 0; i < methods.length; i++)
          System.out.println("String: " + methods[i]);

        methods = Math.class.getMethods();

        for (int i = 0; i < methods.length; i++)
          System.out.println("Math: " + methods[i]);
      }
  }
```

As you can see, the *getMethods* function returns an array of *String* objects, each of which describes a class-method signature.

To run the *ShowMethods* program, invoke the *java* interpreter from the command-line, as discussed in Lesson 4, "Java Applets Versus Standalone Programs." The program, in turn, will display a list of the methods that reside within the *String* and *Math* classes.

```
C:\RBYJAVA\LESSON19> java   ShowMethods   <ENTER>
```

DISPLAYING A CLASS' DATA MEMBERS

In the previous *ShowMethods* program, you used the *getMethods* function to determine a class's methods. In a similar way, you can use a class's *getFields* method to determine the class's data members. The following program, *ShowFields.java*, uses the *getFields* method to determine the *String* and *Math* class data members:

```java
import java.lang.reflect.*;

class ShowFields
  {
    public static void main(String args[])
      {
        Field[] fields;

        fields = String.class.getFields();

        for (int i = 0; i < fields.length; i++)
          System.out.println("String: " + fields[i]);

        fields = Math.class.getFields();

        for (int i = 0; i < fields.length; i++)
          System.out.println("Math: " + fields[i]);
      }
  }
```

To run the *ShowFields* program, invoke the *java* interpreter from the command-line. The program, in turn, will display a list of the data members that reside within the *String* and *Math* classes.

```
C:\RBYJAVA\LESSON19> java   ShowFields   <ENTER>
```

TAKING A CYBER FIELD TRIP

In the future, Web sites will use Java applets to model products from cars and houses to modern medicine. To give you a feel for Java's graphics capabilities, the Java Development Kit provides the Molecule Viewer applet, shown in Figure 19.4. If you drag your mouse over the molecule image, the applet will rotate the molecules about the x, y, or z axis. To run the applet or to download the applet's source code, visit the Jamsa Press Web site at *www.jamsa.com/java_demos/Molecule.html*.

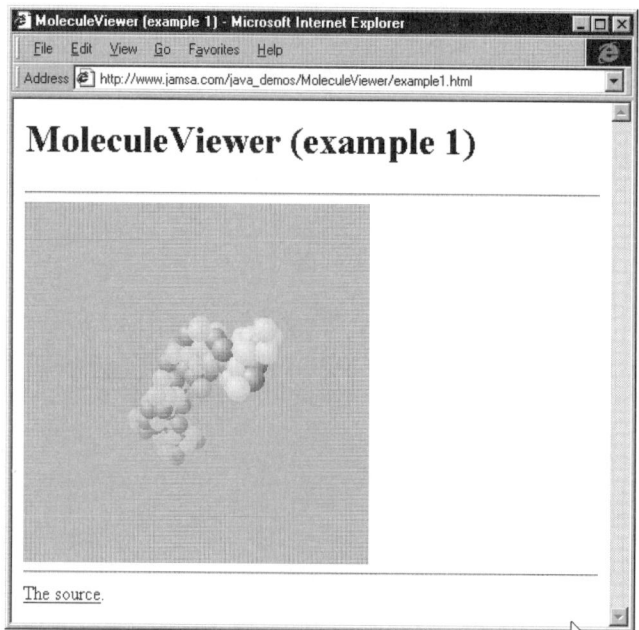

Figure 19.4 Rotating molecules about the x, y, and z axis.

WHAT YOU MUST KNOW

In this lesson, you learned how to use functions the Java library provide. In Lesson 20, "Using Java Archive Files (JARs)," you will learn how to store your applets within a compressed Java archive (JAR) file to reduce the number of download operations your browser must perform. Before you continue with Lesson 20, however, make sure you have learned the following key concepts:

- ☑ Java provides the *Date* class that you can use to determine the current system date and time.

- ☑ To perform many common arithmetic operations, you can use the Java *Math* class.

- ☑ To determine information about the current country, you can use the Java *Country* class.

- ☑ To determine a class's data members and methods, you can use the *getFields* and *getMethods* members.

LESSON 20
USING JAVA ARCHIVE FILES (*JARS*)

As you have learned, when a browser encounters a Java applet on a Web page, the browser must first download the applet file before the browser can run the applet's code. If the applet uses additional files, such as graphics images or audio clips, the browser must download each file as the applet loads the corresponding object—a slow process. To reduce the amount of time the browser must spend downloading files, most browsers let you store an applet's files in a compressed Java archive (JAR) file. Because the JAR file stores the applet files in a compressed format, the browser can download the files faster than a traditional applet. Later, when the applet loads various objects, the browser will decompress then load the object from the JAR file. This lesson examines JAR files in detail. By the time you finish this lesson, you will understand the following key concepts:

◆   When a browser encounters a Java applet within an HTML file, the browser downloads the applet. Then, if the applet requires additional files, such as a graphics image, the browser individually downloads each file.

◆   To reduce download operations, you can place an applet and its required files within a Java archive file that uses the *jar* extension.

◆   To create a JAR file, you use the Java Development Kit *jar* utility.

◆   To use a JAR file, you place an *ARCHIVE* field within the HTML file's *<APPLET>* entry.

◆   To load an image or audio-clip from a JAR file, your applet must use the *getClass().getResource("Filename")* method.

CREATING A *JAR* FILE

As you have learned, by compressing files using a Java archive file, you can reduce the amount of time a browser spends downloading an applet and its corresponding files. To help you get started with JAR files, consider the simple *ShowVariables.java* applet that you created in Lesson 5, "Java Applets Store Information in Variables:"

```java
import java.awt.*;
import java.applet.*;

public class ShowVariables extends Applet
  {
    int age = 35;
    double salary = 25000.75;
    long distance_to_the_moon = 238857;

    public void paint(Graphics g)
      {
        g.drawString("Employee age: " + age, 5, 25);
        g.drawString("Employee salary: " + salary, 5, 45);
        g.drawString("Distance to the moon: " + distance_to_the_moon, 5, 65);
      }
  }
```

Using the *jar* utility, you can create the file *ShowVar.jar*, that includes the *ShowVariables.class* file:

```
C:\RBYJAVA\LESSON20> jar  cf  ShowVar.jar  ShowVariables.class <ENTER>
```

Next, within the applet's HTML file, *ShowVar.HTML*, you reference the JAR file, as shown here:

```
<HTML><TITLE>ShowVariables Applet</TITLE>
<APPLET CODE="ShowVariables.class" ARCHIVE="ShowVar.jar" WIDTH=600
HEIGHT=400></APPLET></HTML>
```

As you can see, the HTML *<APPLET>* entry specifies the applet's class file (*ShowVariables.class*) and the applet's archive file (*ShowVar.jar*). In this case, the archive file contains only the Java class file. In the examples that follow, the JAR file will contain the applet and its related files, such as its graphics images or audio clips. When you load the *ShowVar.HTML* file, your browser will display the output shown in Figure 20.1.

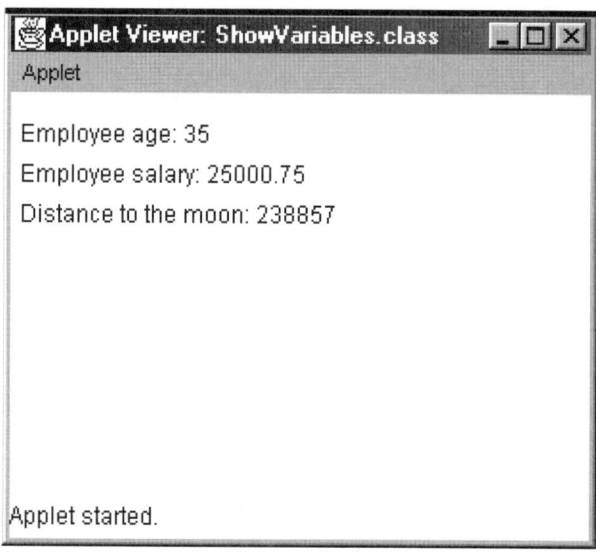

Figure 20.1 Using a JAR file to store an applet's class file.

USING A *JAR* TO STORE AN APPLET AND A GRAPHICS IMAGE

In Lesson 22, "Loading Graphics Images," you will learn how to load and display an image within a Java applet. At that time, you will create the *BackgroundImage.java* applet that displays the GIF image shown in Figure 20.2.

The *BackgroundImage.java* applet loads and displays the image stored in the *Image.GIF* file. Normally, to run the applet, a browser would first download the *BackgroundImage.java* file. Then, when the applet loads the GIF image, the browser would then download the graphics file. To reduce download operations, you can compress the applet and graphics file into a Java archive (JAR) file. In this case, you might name the JAR file *BackgroundImage.jar*. To create the JAR file, you use the *jar* utility, as shown here:

```
C:\RBYJAVA\LESSON20> jar  cf  BackgroundImage.jar  BackgroundImage.class
Image.gif  <ENTER>
```

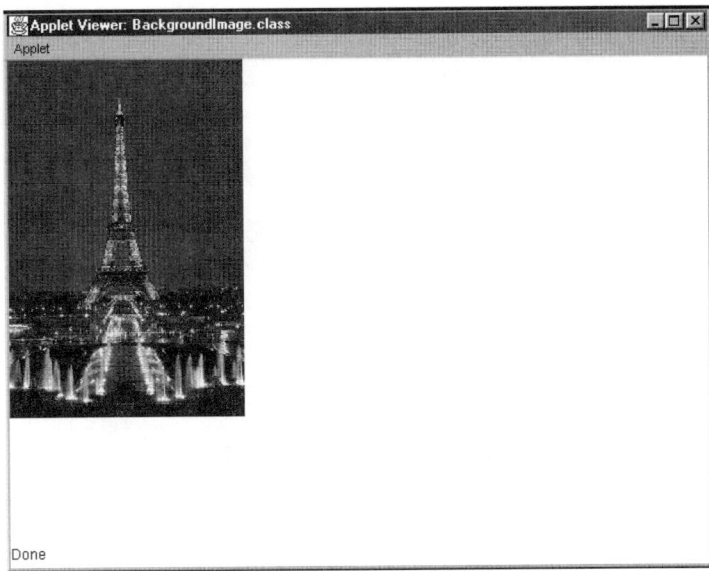

Figure 20.2 Displaying a GIF image within a Java applet.

Next, within the applet's HTML file, you reference the JAR file, as shown here:

```
<HTML><TITLE>BackgroundImage Applet</TITLE>
<APPLET CODE="BackgroundImage.class" ARCHIVE="BackgroundImage.jar"
WIDTH=600 HEIGHT=400></APPLET></HTML>
```

The following code implements a JAR-based version of the *BackgroundImage.java* applet. If you compare this code to the applet Lesson 22 presents, you will find subtle differences. Specifically, to load an image file or audio file from a JAR archive, your applet must use the *getClass().getResource("Filename")* method to get a URL that corresponds to the object within the JAR file, as shown here:

```
import java.awt.*;
import java.applet.*;
import java.net.URL;

public class BackgroundImage extends Applet
  {
    Image picture, offScreenImage;
    boolean ImageLoaded = false;
    boolean ImageNotFound = false;
    public void init()
      {
        URL imageURL = getClass().getResource("Image.gif");

        picture = getToolkit().getImage(imageURL);

        if (picture == null)
          ImageNotFound = true;
        else
```

```
            {
                offScreenImage = createImage(getSize().width,
                                        getSize().height);
                Graphics offScreenGC = offScreenImage.getGraphics();
                offScreenGC.drawImage(picture, 0, 0, this);
            }
    }


    public void paint(Graphics g)
      {
        if (ImageNotFound)
          g.drawString("Image.gif not found", 5, 15);
        else
          {
            if (ImageLoaded)
              {
                g.drawImage(picture, 0, 0, null);
                showStatus("Done");
              }
            else
              showStatus("Loading image");
          }
      }


    public boolean imageUpdate(Image img, int infoflags, int x, int y,
                                int w, int h)
      {
        if (infoflags == ALLBITS)
          {
            ImageLoaded = true;
            repaint();
            return false;
          }
        else
          return true;
      }
}
```

USING A JAR TO STORE AN APPLET AND AUDIO FILES

In Lesson 23, "Getting Started with Sounds," you will learn how to play audio files from within a Java applet. In that lesson, you will create the *SoundDemo.java* applet that plays back the sounds stored in the file *Sample.AU*. To reduce the browser's download operations, you can create a JAR file that contains the applet and the audio file:

```
C:\RBYJAVA\LESSON23> jar  cf  SoundDemo.class  Sample.AU   <ENTER>
```

To run the applet, place the following HTML entries within the file *SoundDemo.HTML*:

```
<HTML><TITLE>SoundDemo Applet</TITLE>
<APPLET CODE="SoundDemo.class" ARCHIVE="SoundDemo.jar"
WIDTH=300 HEIGHT=200></APPLET></HTML>
```

The following applet, *SoundDemo.java*, implements a JAR-based version of the applet you will examine in Lesson 23. As discussed, to access the audio clip file from the JAR file, the applet uses the *getClass().getResource("Filename")* method:

```
import java.awt.*;
import java.applet.*;
import java.net.URL;

public class SoundDemo extends Applet
  {
    public void paint(Graphics g)
      {
        URL url = getClass().getResource("Sample.au");

        AudioClip audioClip = getAudioClip(url);

        if (audioClip == null)
          g.drawString("Audio clip sample.au not found", 5, 15);
        else
          {
            g.drawString("Sound Demo!", 5, 15);
            audioClip.loop();
          }
      }
  }
```

UNDERSTANDING ZIP AND CAB FILES

As you examine HTML files, you may periodically encounter *ARCHIVE* entries that reference *Zip* or *Cab* files. As you may know, users often compress files using the Zip-file format. In fact, early versions of Java stored class libraries within Zip files. A *Cab* (which is short for cabinet) file is a compressed file created by the Microsoft *cabarc* utility. To use a Zip or Cab file, you simply specify the applet name using the *CODE* entry and the Zip or Cab filename using the *ARCHIVE* entry.

TAKING A CYBER FIELD TRIP

As you have learned, the Java programming language is well suited for a variety of applications. For example, the Java Development Kit includes the Spreadsheet applet which, as shown in Figure 20.3, implements a simple four row by three column spreadsheet. Within each cell, you can type a value or a function. To type a value, type the letter v followed by the number you desire. To type a function, type the letter f followed by the function you desire. To run the applet or to download the applet's source code, visit the Jamsa Press Web site at *www.jamsa.com/ java_demos/Spreadsheet.html*.

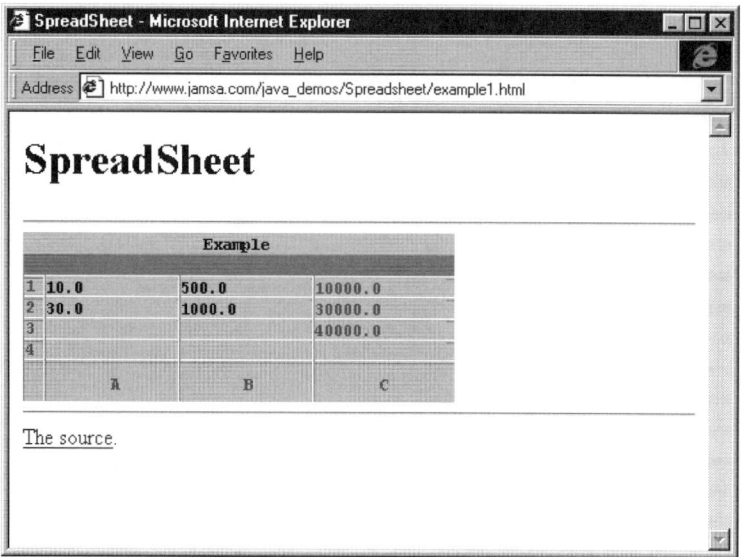

Figure 20.3 *Implementing a simple spreadsheet using Java.*

WHAT YOU MUST KNOW

In this lesson, you learned how to use Java archive (JAR) files to reduce the amount of time a browser spends dowloading an applet and its related files. Using the Java Development Kit *jar* utility, you can store files in a compressed format within a JAR file. In Lesson 21, "Using Threads to Create Simple Animations," you will learn how to use multiple threads of execution within an applet—a key to building animations using Java. Bcforc you continue with Lesson 21, however, make sure you have learned the following key concepts:

☑ To run an applet, a browser first downloads the applet. If the applet uses additional files, such as an audio clip, the browser individually downloads each file.

☑ By storing an applet and its required files within a Java archive (JAR) file, you can reduce the number of download operations the browser must perform.

☑ The Java Development Kit provides the *jar* utility with which you can create JAR files.

☑ To use a JAR file, you place an *ARCHIVE* field within the HTML file's *<APPLET>* entry.

☑ To load an image or audio-clip from a JAR file, your applet must use the *getClass().getResource("Filename")* method.

ADVANCED TOPICS

In this section, you will examine advanced topics that will round out your Java programming toolkit. You will learn how to display graphics, play sounds, use multiple threads to create animations, and more. By the time you finish the lessons this section presents, you will have the skills necessary to create professional-quality applets. The lessons in this section include:

Section Three

LESSON 21

USING THREADS TO CREATE SIMPLE ANIMATIONS

When your applet runs, the browser executes the virtual code that corresponds to your applet's statements. Programmers often refer to the instructions that the browser executes as the applet's *thread of execution*. Depending on the task your applet performs, one applet's thread of execution will obviously differ from that of a second applet. As your applets become more complex, there will be times when you will want the applet to perform two or more tasks at the same time. For example, you may want the applet to spin a company's logo as it flashes names of company products on the screen. In such cases, your applet can use multiple threads of execution. One thread, for example, may spin the company's logo, while a second thread flashes the product names within the applet window.

When your applets use multiple threads, the threads appear to execute at the same time. As it turns out, however, the browser very quickly switches from one thread to another behind the scenes as your applet executes. By letting one thread run briefly, and then letting the other thread run, the browser gives the appearance that both threads are executing at the same time. This lesson examines how you create threads within a Java applet. By time the time you finish this lesson, you will understand the following key concepts:

- The statements an applet executes to perform specific tasks define the applet's thread of execution.

- A multi-threaded applet is an applet that runs two or more threads of execution at the same time.

- To create the illusion that the threads are running at the same time, the browser quickly switches from running one thread to another.

- To create a thread of execution within your applet, you declare a *Thread* object, passing the *Thread* class-constructor function an object whose statements you want the thread to execute.

- To run a *Thread* object, your applet calls the *Thread* class *start* function. The *start* function, in turn, will call the object's *run* function.

CREATING A THREAD OBJECT

Like most of the items that make up a Java applet, a thread is an object that corresponds to a class definition. You declare a thread within your applet by declaring a *Thread* object, as shown here:

```
Thread someThread = null;
```

In this case, the declaration creates a *Thread* object named *someThread*. Next, the statement initializes the object to *null* to indicate to subsequent applet code that the applet has not yet created an object instance of the *Thread* class using the *new* operator. By assigning the *null* value to an object variable, the applet's code can test within the *start* and *stop* functions whether or not the thread exists. If the thread exists, the variable will contain a value other than *null*; otherwise, if the thread does not exist, the variable will contain the *null* value.

To create and start an instance of the *Thread* object, you use the *new* operator (normally within the *start* function), as shown here:

```
void public start()
   {
       if (someThread == null)
          {
```

```
        someThread = new Thread(this);
        someThread.start();
    }
}
```

As you can see, the *start* function first tests if the *Thread* object is *null* (meaning the applet has not yet created an instance of the *Thread* object). If the thread does not exist, the code uses the *new* operator to create an instance of the *Thread* object. As discussed in Lesson 13, "Understanding Constructor Functions," Java defines the *this* keyword to correspond to the current object, which, in this case, is the current *Applet* object. Using the *this* keyword, the applet creates a thread of execution that corresponds to the applet. In other words, when you create a thread, you pass to the *Thread* class-constructor function an object whose statements the new thread will execute. If, for example, your applet has a class named *SpinLogo* that spins a company logo, you could pass the *Thread* class-constructor function a *SpinLogo* object. By using the *this* keyword, the statements the new thread will execute correspond to the current object, which is the *Applet* object.

As you can see, the *start* function calls the thread's *start* method which, in turn, will call the *Thread* object's *run* method that you defined within the applet. Within the *run* function, you specify the actual processing the thread will perform.

The following applet, *MarqueeMessage.java*, creates a *Thread* object that moves the text message, *Rescued by Java!*, across the applet window, as shown in Figures 21.1 and 21.2.

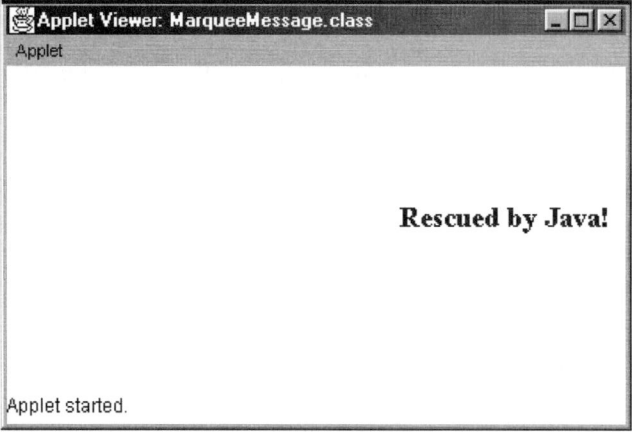

Figure 21.1 *Using a **Thread** object to scroll marquee text.*

Figure 21.2 *Scrolling text across the applet window.*

The following Java statements implement the *MarqueeMessage.java* applet:

```java
import java.awt.*;
import java.applet.*;

public class MarqueeMessage extends Applet implements Runnable
  {
    Thread MarqueeThread = null;
    String Message = "Rescued by Java!";
    Font font = new Font("Serif", Font.BOLD, 18);
    int x, y;

    public void init()
      {
        x = getSize().width;
        y = getSize().height / 2;
      }

    public void start()
      {
        if (MarqueeThread == null)
          {
            MarqueeThread = new Thread(this);
            MarqueeThread.start();
          }
      }

    public void run()
      {
        while (true)
          {
            x = x - 5;
            if (x == 0)
              x = getSize().width;

            repaint();
            try
              {
                MarqueeThread.sleep(500);
              }
            catch (InterruptedException e)
              {
              }
          }
      }

    public void paint(Graphics g)
      {
        g.setFont(font);
        g.drawString(Message, x, y);
      }
  }
```

The applet's processing is really quite straightforward. As you learned, when Java starts an applet, Java first calls the *init* function, within which you can initialize key variables. In this case, the *init* function simply determines the height and width (y and x) of the current applet window. As discussed in Lesson 10, "Looking at Several Special Functions," after the *init* function completes its processing, it calls the *start* function which, in this case, creates and runs the thread that displays the marquee message. Within the *start* function, the code calls the *MarqueeThread.start* method which, in turn, calls the object's *run* function. In this case, because the object corresponds to the applet, the code calls the applet's *run* function.

To run this applet, place the following HTML entries within the file *MarqueeMessage.HTML*:

```
<HTML><TITLE>MarqueeMessage Applet</TITLE>
<APPLET CODE="MarqueeMessage.class" WIDTH=400 HEIGHT=200></APPLET></HTML>
```

If you examine the applet's source code closely, you will find that the applet's class definition has changed to implement a *Runnable* interface, as shown here:

```
public class MarqueeMessage extends Applet implements Runnable
```

When you use threads within an applet, you must change the applet's class definition so the class *implements* the *Runnable* interface, which means the class will provide a *run* function. Lesson 28, "Understanding Class Interfaces," discusses interfaces in detail. For now, simply understand that to use threads, you must change your applet's class definition to include the *implements Runnable* keywords, as shown. Next, you must define a *run* function within the class, which will very likely perform most of the thread's processing:

```
public void run()
   {
      while (true)
         {
            x = x - 5;
            if (x == 0)
               x = getSize().width;

            repaint();
            try
               {
                  MarqueeThread.sleep(500);
               }
            catch (InterruptedException e)
               {
               }
         }
   }
```

Within the *run* function, the applet simply loops forever (or until the user closes the applet window). Within the loop, the applet updates the x-and-y coordinates that the *drawString* function uses to display the *Java Now!* message text. Each time the function updates the message coordinates, the function calls the *repaint* function which, in turn, calls *paint* to update the screen. Next, to control the speed at which the applet scrolls the message text, the applet uses the *thread.sleep* function to suspend the thread's execution for 500 milliseconds (one half of a second). As discussed in Lesson 24, "Using Exceptions to Catch Errors," if, for some reason, the *sleep* function is interrupted unexpectedly, the function will throw the *InterruptedException* exception. In this case, the function simply catches and ignores the exception, should it occur.

LOOKING AT A SECOND EXAMPLE

The following applet, *ShowTime.java*, uses a thread to continuously display the current date-and-time within an applet window, as shown in Figure 21.3.

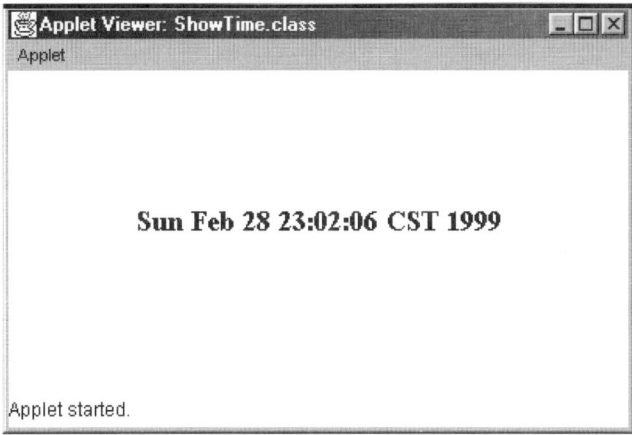

Figure 21.3 *Using a thread to continuously display the current date-and-time.*

The following Java statements implement the *ShowTime.java* applet:

```java
import java.awt.*;
import java.applet.*;
import java.util.*;

public class ShowTime extends Applet implements Runnable
  {
    Thread TimeThread = null;
    Font font = new Font("Serif", Font.BOLD, 18);
    FontMetrics fontMetrics;
    String DateTime;
    Date CurrentDateTime;
    int x, y;

    public void init()
      {
        y = getSize().height / 2;
      }

    public void start()
      {
        if (TimeThread == null)
          {
            TimeThread = new Thread(this);
            TimeThread.start();
          }
      }
```

```
    public void run()
    {
        while (true)
        {
            CurrentDateTime = new Date();
            repaint();

            try
            {
                TimeThread.sleep(500);
            }
            catch (InterruptedException e)
            {
            }
        }
    }

    public void paint(Graphics g)
    {
        g.setFont(font);
        fontMetrics = g.getFontMetrics();
        DateTime = CurrentDateTime.toString();

        x = (getSize().width - fontMetrics.stringWidth(DateTime)) / 2;

        g.drawString(DateTime, x, y);
    }
}
```

As you can see, the format of the *ShowTime.java* applet is very similar to the *MessageMarquee.java* applet. Within the *start* function, the applet creates the *Thread* object. Within the *run* function, the applet performs most of its processing. The applet uses a *Date* object to get the current date-and-time. To access the *Date* object, the applet imports the *java.util* package. Using a *FontMetrics* object and the *getSize* function, the applet centers the date-and-time string within the applet window.

To run the applet, place the following HTML entries within the file *ShowTime.HTML*:

```
<HTML><TITLE>ShowTime Applet</TITLE>
<APPLET CODE="ShowTime.class" WIDTH=400 HEIGHT=200></APPLET></HTML>
```

MINIMIZING SCREEN FLASHING

When you run the applets this lesson presents, you may periodically detect flashing (a choppy screen output). As it turns out, each time your program calls the *repaint* function, *repaint* calls a function named *update*, which blanks the applet window's contents. To reduce such flashing, you can override the *update* function, so that it does not erase the window's contents. The following applet, *LessFlash.java*, overrides the *update* function so that it no longer erases the screen display but, rather, simply overwrites the previous date string by drawing a rectangle. To help you view the rectangle's position, the applet displays the rectangle using yellow, as opposed to the current background color, as shown in Figure 21.4.

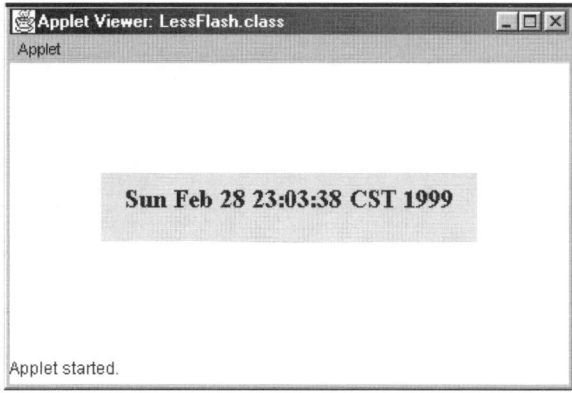

Figure 21.4 *Overriding the* **update** *method to erase only part of the applet window.*

The following code implements the *LessFlash.java* applet:

```java
import java.awt.*;
import java.applet.*;
import java.util.*;

public class LessFlash extends Applet implements Runnable
  {
    Thread TimeThread = null;
    Font font;
    FontMetrics fontMetrics;
    Date CurrentDateTime;
    String DateTime;

    int x, y;

    public void init()
      {
        CurrentDateTime = new Date();
        DateTime = CurrentDateTime.toString();
        font = new Font("Serif", Font.BOLD, 18);
        Graphics g = this.getGraphics();

        g.setFont(font);
        fontMetrics = g.getFontMetrics();

        y = getSize().height / 2;
        x = (getSize().width - fontMetrics.stringWidth(DateTime)) / 2;
      }

    public void start()
      {
        if (TimeThread == null)
          {
            TimeThread = new Thread(this);
            TimeThread.start();
          }
      }
```

185

```
    public void update(Graphics g)
      {
        Color CurrentColor = g.getColor();
        g.setFont(font);
        fontMetrics = g.getFontMetrics();
        g.setColor(Color.yellow);
        DateTime = CurrentDateTime.toString();

        x = (getSize().width - fontMetrics.stringWidth(DateTime)) / 2;
        g.fillRect(x - fontMetrics.charWidth('M'),
                y - fontMetrics.getHeight(),
                fontMetrics.stringWidth(DateTime) + 2 *
                fontMetrics.charWidth('M'),
                2 * fontMetrics.getHeight());

        g.setColor(CurrentColor);
        paint(g);
      }

    public void run()
      {
        while (true)
          {
              CurrentDateTime = new Date();
              repaint();
              try
                {
                    TimeThread.sleep(500);
                }
              catch (InterruptedException e)
                {
                }
          }
      }

    public void paint(Graphics g)
      {
          g.drawString(CurrentDateTime.toString(), x, y);
      }
  }
```

As you can see, the applet overrides the *update* method. Within the *update* method, the code uses the *getColor* method to determine the current color (which is normally black). Next, the function determines information about the current font (the font's metrics) which *update* will use to determine how large a rectangle to draw, as well as the screen locations at which it should draw the rectangle. Note that before the *update* function ends, it calls the *paint* function to update the applet window. To display the rectangle using the current background color, as opposed to yellow, you can use the *getBackground* method.

To run the applet, place the following HTML entries within the file *LessFlash.HTML*:

```
<HTML><TITLE>LessFlash Applet</TITLE>
<APPLET CODE="LessFlash.class" WIDTH=400 HEIGHT=200></APPLET></HTML>
```

TAKING A CYBER FIELD TRIP

As you examine the applets and standalone applications that this book presents, there will be many times when you have questions about specific classes or functions. If you are using Windows, you should take advantage of the online help facility provided with the *JBuilder* compiler that this book provides on its companion CD-ROM. As shown in Figure 21.5, *JBuilder's* online help describes each Java class in detail. For information on installing *JBuilder*, turn to Appendix A, "Using the JBuilder Compiler."

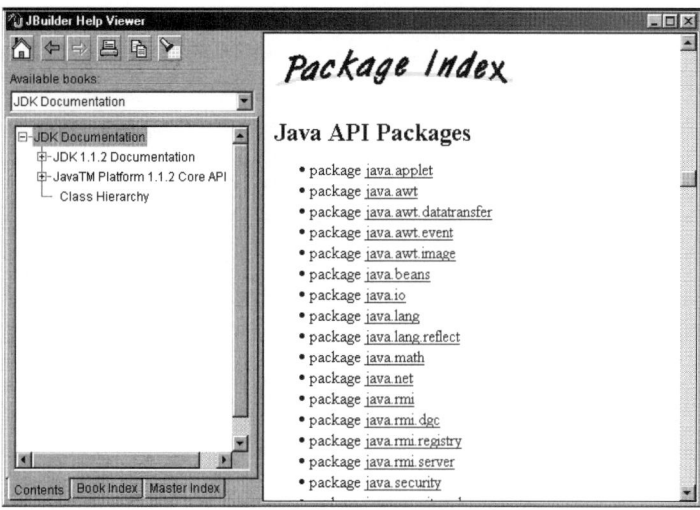

Figure 21.5 The JBuilder compiler provides extensive online help.

WHAT YOU MUST KNOW

As your applets increase in complexity, you will use threads to perform a wide variety of tasks. All animations, for example, take advantage of threads. In this lesson, you learned how to create and start a *Thread* object. In Lesson 22, "Loading Graphics Images," you will learn how to display images within the applet window, such as a photograph. Before you continue with Lesson 22, however, make sure you have learned the following key concepts:

☑ A thread of execution specifies the statements an applet executes to perform specific tasks.

☑ Multi-threaded applets may run two or more threads of execution at the same time.

☑ Threads of execution do not actually run at the same time. Instead, the browser creates the illusion that the threads are running at the same time by quickly switching from running one thread to another.

☑ Using the *Thread* class, an applet can create a thread of execution.

☑ When an applet creates a thread of execution, the applet passes the *Thread* class-constructor function an object whose statements you want the thread to execute.

☑ Using the *Thread* class *start* function, an applet can start a thread's execution. The *start* function, in turn, will call the *Thread* object's *run* function.

LESSON 22

LOADING GRAPHICS IMAGES

As you start creating professional-quality Java applets, you will make extensive use of graphics images, which, for Web-based applications, often reside in GIF files. In this lesson, you will learn that loading GIF images within a Java applet is quite simple—even if you are loading the images from across the Web. By the time you finish this lesson, you will understand the following key concepts:

♦ To use a graphics-file image within your applet, you must first declare an *Image* object.

♦ Most Java applets work with GIF or JPEG files.

♦ To associate a graphics file with an *Image* object, your applets use the *getImage* function.

♦ To display an *Image* object, you use the *Graphics* class *drawImage* function.

♦ To improve the display appearance of images the applet must load, many applets *double buffer* an image by first loading the image into memory and then displaying the image.

♦ Using the *imageUpdate* function, your applets can track how much of an image the applet has loaded into memory.

LOADING A GRAPHICS IMAGE

Java treats graphics images, like most items within your applets, as objects. Before your applet can load a graphics image, your applet must declare an *Image* object, as shown here:

```
Image Picture;
```

Next, your applet must use the *getImage* function to associate the *Image* object with a graphics file :

```
Picture = getImage(getCodeBase(), "ImageFileName.GIF");
```

As you can see, the *getImage* function uses two parameters. The first parameter, which is a call to the *getCodeBase* function, returns the applet's URL (Unique Resource Locator), such as *www.jamsa.com*. The second parameter specifies the name of the graphics file your applet wants to load from the specified URL. If the graphics image resides in a subdirectory beneath the applet, the filename string can include a directory path.

After your applet uses the *getImage* function to load the graphic, your applet uses the *Graphics* class *drawImage* function to display the image, as shown here:

```
g.drawImage(Picture, x, y, this);
```

As you can see, the *drawImage* function's parameters specify the image to display as well as the x-and-y coordinates that correspond to the image's upper-left corner. In addition, the fourth parameter, which in this case is *this*, specifies if the applet (via the *ImageObserver* interface) can receive status information that specifies how much of the image has been loaded. As you will learn later in this lesson, using the *imageUpdate* function, your applets can load an image into a buffer before displaying the image—which makes the image display much smoother. If the parameter is *null*, the applet does not use the image-update information. An applet might use the *null* value within a *drawImage* function call to display an image that it has already loaded:

```
g.drawImage(Picture, x, y, null);
```

The previous two *drawImage* function calls will display the image based on the image size. In some cases, you may want to specify the image's width and height, so you can increase or decrease the image. To control the image size, you specify the width and height you desire as parameters to the *drawImage* method, as shown here:

```
g.drawImage(Picture, x, y, width, height, this);
```

LOOKING AT A SAMPLE APPLET

The following Java applet, *ShowImage.java*, displays the image shown in Figure 22.1.

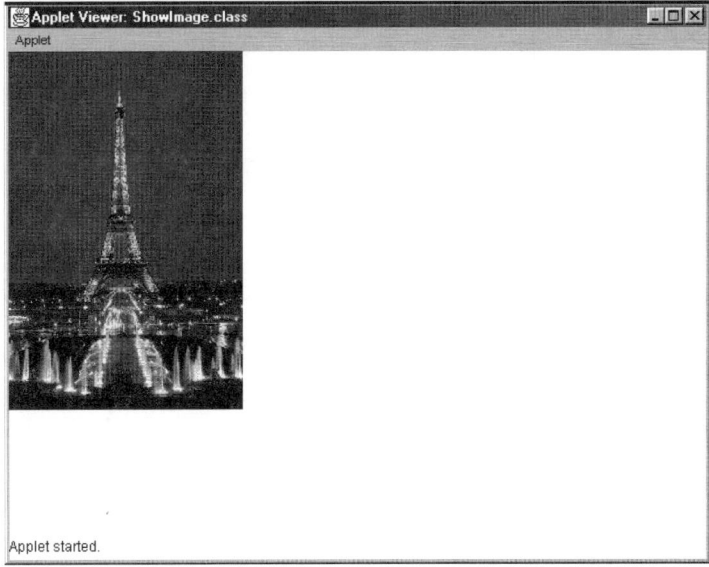

Figure 22.1 Loading a background image within a Java applet.

Before you can run the *ShowImage* applet, you must have a GIF file named *Image.GIF*. If you do not have a GIF file that you can rename to *Image.GIF*, visit the Jamsa Press Web site and download this file from *http://www.jamsa.com/java_demo/ShowImage.html*.

The following statements implement the *ShowImage.java* applet:

```
import java.awt.*;
import java.applet.*;

public class ShowImage extends Applet
  {
    Image picture;

    public void init()
      {
        picture = getImage(getCodeBase(), "Image.gif");
      }
```

```
        public void paint(Graphics g)
          {
              g.drawImage(picture, 0, 0, this);
          }
      }
```

To run the applet, place the following HTML entries within the file *ShowImage.HTML*:

```
<HTML><TITLE>ShowImage Applet</TITLE>
<APPLET CODE="ShowImage.class" WIDTH=600 HEIGHT=400></APPLET></HTML>
```

After you compile and execute this applet, you may be surprised by how choppy the applet draws the image. The applet's display of the image is choppy because the applet does not completely load and display the image before the *drawImage* function completes. Instead, the *drawImage* function creates a thread that loads and displays the image as the applet continues its execution. To improve the appearance of the image display, many applets *double buffer* images by first loading the image completely into memory before displaying the image. In this way, the image's display appears instantaneous.

DOUBLE BUFFERING A GRAPHICS IMAGE

As just discussed, to improve the display appearance of a graphics image, many applets double buffer the image—first loading the image into memory and then displaying the image to the applet window. The following applet, *BackgroundImage.java*, shows you how to double buffer a graphics image in this way:

```java
import java.awt.*;
import java.applet.*;

public class BackgroundImage extends Applet
  {
    Image picture;
    boolean ImageLoaded = false;

    public void init()
      {
        picture = getImage(getCodeBase(), "Image.gif");
        Image offScreenImage = createImage(getSize().width,
                                   getSize().height);
        Graphics offScreenGC = offScreenImage.getGraphics();
        offScreenGC.drawImage(picture, 0, 0, this);
      }

    public void paint(Graphics g)
      {
        if (ImageLoaded)
          {
            g.drawImage(picture, 0, 0, null);
            showStatus("Done");
          }
```

```
      else
        showStatus("Loading image");
   }

   public boolean imageUpdate(Image img, int infoflags, int x, int y,
                              int w, int h)
   {
      if (infoflags == ALLBITS)
        {
           ImageLoaded = true;
           repaint();
           return false;
        }
      else
        return true;
   }
}
```

To start, examine the applet's *init* funtion. The function declares an *Image* object, named *offScreenImage*, to which it assigns the result of the *createImage* function. Next, the function creates a *Graphics* object, named *offScreenGC*, to which it assigns the graphics context of what will become the off-screen image. As you will recall from Lessson 10, "Looking at Several Special Functions," the graphics context specifies such items as the current font and screen color, and provides device-independent graphics functions. Lastly, the function uses the *drawImage* function to display the image. In this case, however, because the applet is drawing the image offscreen, nothing appears within the applet window:

```
public void init()
   {
      picture = getImage(getCodeBase(), "Image.gif");
      Image offScreenImage = createImage(getSize().width,
                                 getSize().height);
      Graphics offScreenGC = offScreenImage.getGraphics();
      offScreenGC.drawImage(picture, 0, 0, this);
   }
```

Earlier in this lesson, you learned that when an applet uses the *this* keyword as the fourth parameter to the *drawImage* function, the applet can get status information about how much of the image Java has loaded. To access the status information, the applet must implement the *ImageObserver* interface, which means the applet implements the *imageUpdate* function. The following statements implement the *imageUpdate* function:

```
public boolean imageUpdate(Image img, int infoflags, int x, int y, int w,
                           int h)
   {
      if (infoflags == ALLBITS)
        {
           ImageLoaded = true;
           repaint();
           return false;
        }
```

```
        else
            return true;
    }
}
```

As it turns out, each time an applet calls the *drawImage* function, *drawImage* creates a thread that calls the *imageUpdate* function, which your applet can use to determine how much of the image the applet has loaded into memory. As you will learn, the thread will continue to call the *imageUpdate* function until the function returns the value *false.*

The second parameter to the *imageUpdate* function, *infoflags,* lets the applet track how much of the image the applet has loaded into memory. When the parameter's value is equal to ALLBITS, the entire image resides in memory. As you can see, after the image resides in memory, the function sets the variable *ImageLoaded* to *true* and calls the *repaint* function to update the applet window. Lastly, the function returns the value *false,* which stops *drawImage's* thread of execution from calling the *imageUpdate* function again.

If you examine the applet's *paint* function, you will find that its processing is controlled by the *ImageLoaded* variable. When the variable becomes *true,* the *paint* function displays the image by using the *drawImage* function, as shown here:

```
public void paint(Graphics g)
  {
    if (ImageLoaded)
      {
          g.drawImage(picture, 0, 0, null);
          showStatus("Done");
      }
    else
      showStatus("Loading image");
  }
```

As you can see, the *paint* function calls the *drawImage* function by using the *null* value as the fourth parameter, which prevents *drawImage* from calling the *imageUpdate* function. Because the image now resides in memory, the image appears instantly within the applet window.

UNDERSTANDING DOUBLE BUFFERING

To improve the display of images the applet must load from a file on disk, many applets double buffer the image by first loading the image into memory, and then displaying the image in one fast step. To double buffer an image in this way, the applet must implement an *imageUpdate* function, which the applet uses to monitor how much of the image the *drawImage* thread has loaded into memory. After the entire image is in memory, the applet can display the image instantly, without the choppy display that appears if the applet tries to load and display an image at the same time.

The applets this lesson presented thus far have displayed images based on the image's size. As you use images within your applets, there may be times when you want to display an image smaller or larger than its normal size. The following applet, *MultiImage.java,* displays the same image using three different sizes, as shown in Figure 22.2.

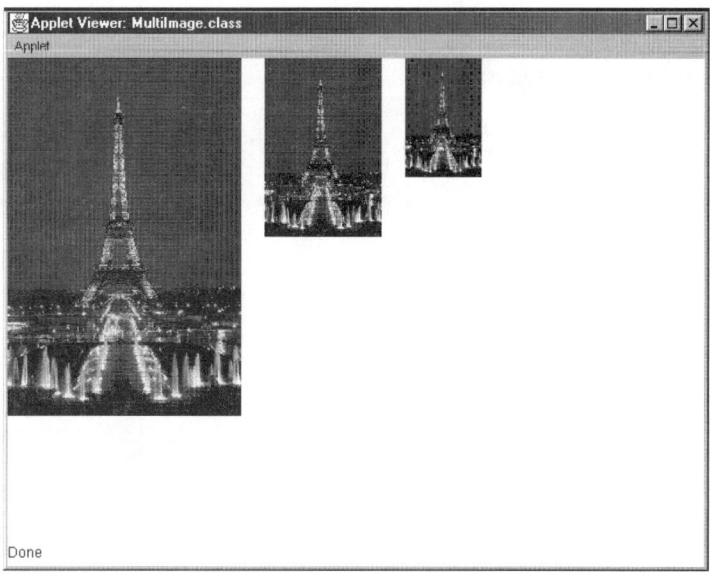

Figure 22.2 Displaying the same image using three different sizes.

The following statements implement the *MultiImage.java* applet:

```java
import java.awt.*;
import java.applet.*;

public class MultiImage extends Applet
  {
    Image picture;
    boolean ImageLoaded = false;

    public void init()
      {
        picture = getImage(getCodeBase(), "Image.gif");

        Image offScreenImage = createImage(getSize().width,
                                 getSize().height);

        Graphics offScreenGC = offScreenImage.getGraphics();
        offScreenGC.drawImage(picture, 0, 0, this);
      }

    public void paint(Graphics g)
      {
        int height, width;

        if (ImageLoaded)
          {
            height = picture.getHeight(this);
            width = picture.getWidth(this);
            g.drawImage(picture, 0, 0, null);
```

```
        g.drawImage(picture, width + 20, 0,
            width/2, height/2, null);

        g.drawImage(picture, width + width/2 + 2*20, 0,
            width/3, height/3, null);

        showStatus("Done");
      }
    else
      showStatus("Loading image");
  }

  public boolean imageUpdate(Image img, int infoflags, int x, int y,
                            int w, int h)
  {
      if (infoflags == ALLBITS)
        {
          ImageLoaded = true;
          repaint();
          return false;
        }
      else
        return true;
  }
}
```

If you examine the program closely, you will find that it is quite similar to the *BackgroundImage.java* applet that double buffers and then displays an image. Within the applet's *paint* function, however, the applet uses three *drawImage* function calls to display the image in various sizes:

```
g.drawImage(picture, 0, 0, null);

g.drawImage(picture, width + 20, 0, width/2, height/2, null);

g.drawImage(picture, width + width/2 + 2*20, 0, width/3, height/3, null);
```

To run the applet, place the following HTML entries within the file *MultiImage.HTML*:

```
<HTML><TITLE>MultiImage Applet</TITLE>
<APPLET CODE="MultiImage.class" WIDTH=600 HEIGHT=400></APPLET></HTML>
```

TAKING A CYBER FIELD TRIP

Because of its platform independence, many developers believe Java is ideal for developing programs that drive smart cards, such as a smart credit card or smart home-control card. To learn more about smart cards and their future, visit the Sun Microsystem's Web site, shown in Figure 22.3, at *java.sun.com/products/javacard*.

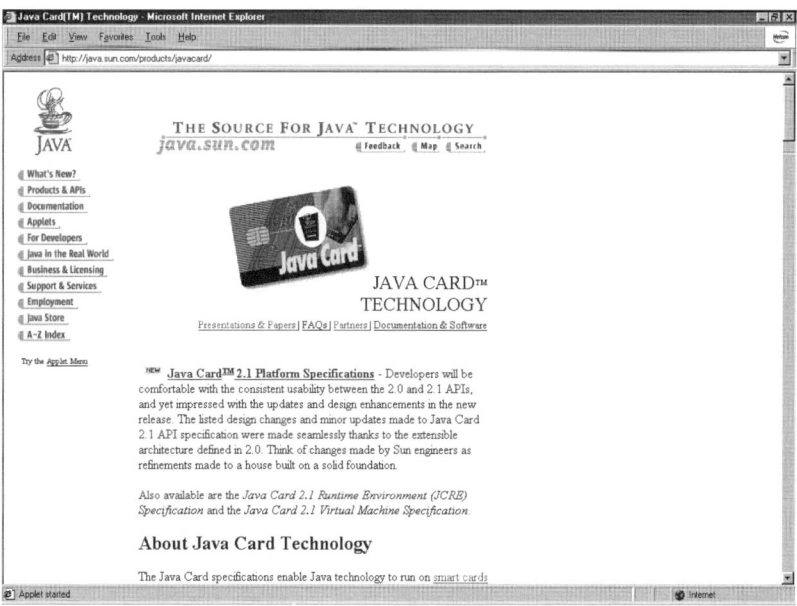

Figure 22.3 Read about smart cards at java.sun.com/products/javacard.

WHAT YOU MUST KNOW

In this lesson, you learned how to load an image file for use within your applet. As your applets become more complex, you will use image files to display background images, company logos, and a wide variety of pictures. In Lesson 23, "Getting Started with Sounds," you will learn how to play back audio files within an applet. Before you continue with Lesson 23, however, make sure that you have learned the following key concepts:

☑ Using an *Image* object, your applets can load and display a graphics image from a file.

☑ Java applets work with GIF or JPEG files.

☑ Using the *getImage* function, your applets associate an *Image* object with a graphics file.

☑ Using the *Graphics* class *drawImage* function, your applets draw the image stored in an *Image* object.

☑ By first loading the image into memory and then displaying the image, Java applets improve the appearance of an image's display.

☑ Using the *imageUpdate* function, applets can track how much of a double-buffered image has been loaded.

LESSON 23

GETTING STARTED WITH SOUNDS

Java provides programmers with the ability to create multimedia-based applets that integrate text, images, animation, and sounds. In this lesson, you will learn how to integrate sounds into your applet. As you will learn, playing sounds within a Java applet is very easy! By the time you finish this lesson, you will understand the following key concepts:

- To use an audio clip within your applet, you first declare an *AudioClip* object.

- To assign an audio clip to an *AudioClip* object, you use the *getAudioClip* function.

- Early versions of the Java compiler only supported AU audio files. Today, most Java compilers support AU, WAV, as well as MIDI files.

- To play an audio clip one time, your applets should call the *AudioClip* class *play* method.

- To play an audio clip continuously, your applets should call the *AudioClip* class *loop* method.

PLAYING AUDIO FILES

Just as you may encounter graphics images in a wide variety of formats, such as BMP, GIF, and JPEG files, the same is true for sound files. The three most common sound-file formats are WAV, MID (for MIDI), and AU files. Early Java compilers only supported AU files, which forced Windows-based programmers to find a utility program they could use to convert WAV files to the AU format. Today, however, most Java compilers support AU, WAV, and MID files.

USING THE AUDIOCLIP CLASS

To load and play back an audio clip within a Java applet, you use the *AudioClip* class, which is defined within the *java.applet.AudioClip* class library. To import this class library, use one of the following *import* statements:

```
import java.applet.AudioClip;          import java.applet.*;
```

Next, to create and initialize an *AudioClip* object, declare an *AudioClip* object, and then use the *getAudioClip* function, as shown here:

```
AudioClip audioClip = getAudioClip(getCodeBase(), "AudioClipFilename.AU");
```

The *getAudioClip* function loads the audio clip from across the net into the applet. The function uses two parameters. The first parameter, the call to the *getCodeBase* function, specifies the URL (the Unique Resource Locator) of the Java applet. In most cases, the audio clip will reside in the same location as the Java applet (such as *www.jamsa.com*). The second parameter specifies the name of the audio file. If the audio file resides in a subdirectory beneath the Java applet, the filename can include the corresponding directory path.

To play the audio clip one time, the applet can use the *AudioClip* class *play* method as shown here:

```
audioClip.play();
```

To play the audio clip continuously, the applet can use the *AudioClip* class *loop* method, as shown here:

```
audioClip.loop();
```

LOOKING AT A SIMPLE APPLET

The following applet, *SoundDemo.java*, loads a sound file named *Sample.AU* from the URL that corresponds to the applet (the applet's directory). Before you can run this applet, you must download the file from the Jamsa Press Web site (at *www.jamsa.com/java_demos/Sounds*) or copy the sound file from this book's companion CD-ROM. The following statements implement the *SoundDemo.java* applet:

```
import java.awt.*;
import java.applet.*;

public class SoundDemo extends Applet
   {
     public void paint(Graphics g)
       {
          AudioClip audioClip = getAudioClip(getCodeBase(), "Sample.AU");

          g.drawString("Sound Demo!", 5, 15);
          audioClip.loop();
       }
   }
```

To run the applet, place the following HTML entries within the file *SoundDemo.HTML*:

```
<HTML><TITLE>SoundDemo Applet</TITLE>
<APPLET CODE="SoundDemo.class" WIDTH=300 HEIGHT=200></APPLET></HTML>
```

After you compile and run this applet, your screen will display an applet window and play an audio file until you close the applet.

The previous *SoundDemo.java* applet plays only the *Sample.AU* sound file in a looping mode. If you want to play a different sound, such as one of the many WAV or MIDI files provided with Windows, you must edit and recompile the applet. The following applet, *SoundParam.java*, lets you specify the sound file you desire, as well as the play back mode (single play or looping) within the applet's HTML file. Within the applet window, the *SoundParam* applet will display a message stating the name of the sound file it is currently playing, as shown in Figure 23.1.

The following code implements the *SoundParam.java* applet:

```
import java.awt.*;
import java.applet.*;

public class SoundParam extends Applet
   {
     public void paint(Graphics g)
       {
          String ClipFilename = getParameter("AudioClip");
          String LoopFlag = getParameter("LoopClip");

          if (ClipFilename != null)
            {
               AudioClip audioClip = getAudioClip(getCodeBase(),
                                         ClipFilename);
```

197

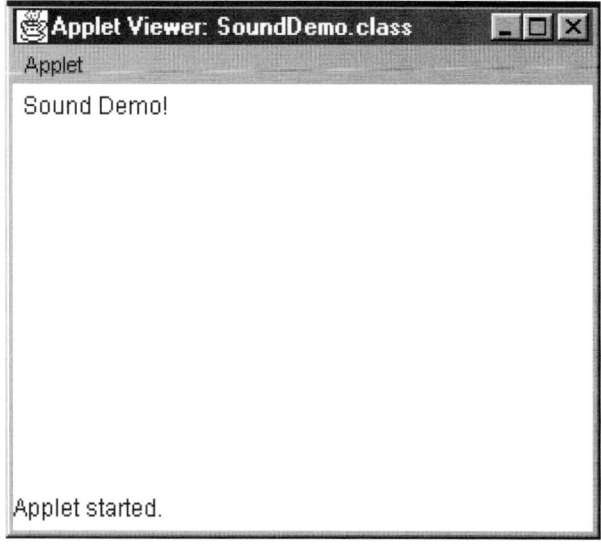

Figure 23.1 Playing a sound while displaying an image within a Java applet.

```
          if (audioClip != null)
            {
                g.drawString("Now playing: " + ClipFilename, 5, 15);
                if (LoopFlag != null)
                    audioClip.loop();
                else
                    audioClip.play();
            }
          else
            g.drawString("Clip: " + ClipFilename + " not found", 5, 15);
        }
      else
        g.drawString("Audio clip not specified in HTML file", 5, 15);
    }
  }
```

As you can see, the applet uses the *getParameter* function to search the HTML file for an *AudioClip* entry as well as a *LoopClip* entry. The following *SoundParam.HTML* file, for example, uses *<PARAM>* attributes to direct the applet to repeatedly loop the sound file *Chimes.WAV* (you can copy the *Chimes.WAV* file from the *Windows\Media* directory into your applet's current directory) one time:

```
<HTML><TITLE>SoundParam Applet</TITLE>
<APPLET CODE="SoundParam.class" WIDTH=300 HEIGHT=200>
<PARAM NAME=AudioClip Value="Chimes.WAV">
<PARAM NAME=LoopClip Value="True">
</APPLET></HTML>
```

If you want to play the sound file one time, as opposed to looping the file's contents, edit the HTML file and remove the *<PARAM>* entry that defines the *LoopClip* entry. Also, note that the previous applet tests the value the *getAudioClip* function returns. If the *getAudioClip* function cannot load the specified audio clip, the function returns the *null* value.

COORDINATING SOUNDS WITH GRAPHICS

As your applets become more complex, there will be times when you will want your applet to play an audio file when a specific event occurs. The following applet, *ShapesAndSounds.java*, continuously draws a randomly-colored square or circle. Each time the applet draws a shape, the applet plays an audio file. The statements implement the *ShapesAndSounds.java* applet:

```java
import java.awt.*;
import java.applet.*;
import java.util.*;

public class ShapesAndSounds extends Applet implements Runnable
  {
    AudioClip audioClip;
    Thread ShapeThread = null;
    Random RandomNumber = new Random();
    Color ImageColor;

    public void init()
      {
        audioClip = getAudioClip(getCodeBase(), "Sample.AU");
      }

    public void start()
      {
        if (ShapeThread == null)
          {
            ShapeThread = new Thread(this);
            ShapeThread.start();
          }
      }

    public void run()
      {
        while (true)
          {
            switch (RandomNumber.nextInt() % 5) {
              case 0: ImageColor = Color.black;
                      break;
              case 1: ImageColor = Color.blue;
                      break;
              case 2: ImageColor = Color.cyan;
                      break;
              case 3: ImageColor = Color.magenta;
                      break;
              case 4: ImageColor = Color.orange;
                      break;
              default: ImageColor = Color.red;
            }
```

```
            try
              {
                  ShapeThread.sleep(3000);
              }
            catch (InterruptedException e)
              {
                  // Ignore the exception
              }

            repaint();
        }
    }

   public void paint(Graphics g)
     {
        g.setColor(ImageColor);
        audioClip.play();

        switch (RandomNumber.nextInt() % 2) {
          case 0: g.fillRect(25, 25, 200, 200);
                  break;
          default: g.fillOval(25, 25, 200, 200);
                  break;
        }
     }
   }
```

The applet's sound processing is quite simple. The applet creates an *AudioClip* object, uses *getAudioClip* to assign the sound file to the object, and then plays the clip by using the *AudioClip* class *play* method. The applet uses a *Random* object to generate random numbers. The applet first uses the random number to determine the object color and, later, within the *paint* function, the applet uses the random number to determine whether to draw a square or circle. The *Random* class *nextInt* function returns a positive or negative value that falls within the range of values for type *int*. Using the modulo division operator (%), which returns the result of an integer division, the applet converts the random number into a value from 0 to 5 (within the *run* function) and a value from 0 to 1 (within the *paint* function).

To run the applet, place the following HTML entries within the file *ShapesAndSounds.HTML*:

```
<HTML><TITLE>ShapesAndSounds Applet</TITLE>
<APPLET  CODE="ShapesAndSounds.class"  WIDTH=300  HEIGHT=300></APPLET></HTML>
```

After you compile and run this applet, your screen will display an applet window that it continuously fills with a different shape or color, as shown in Figure 23.2.

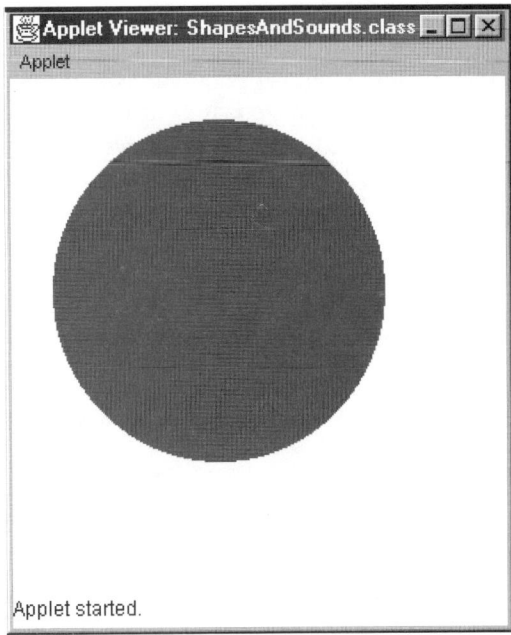

Figure 23.2 Displaying shapes and playing sounds within a Java applet.

TAKING A CYBER FIELD TRIP

Across the Web, programmers make extensive use of Java to implement animations. To help you get started with animations, the Java Development Kit provides an applet named *Animator* that displays an animated graphics image, shown in Figure 23.3, and that continuously plays a sound file. To run the applet or to download the applet's source code, visit the Jamsa Press Web site at *www.jamsa.com/java_demos/Animator.html*.

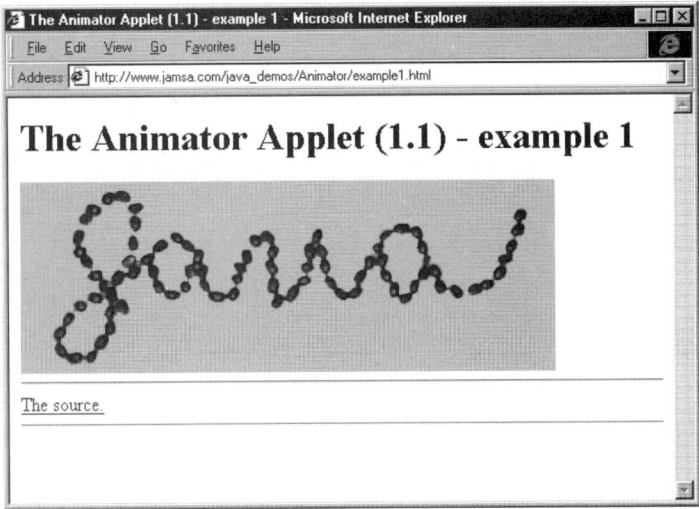

Figure 23.3 The Animator applet provided within the Java Development Kit.

WHAT YOU MUST KNOW

In this lesson, you learned how to play an audio clip within an applet. As you have found, playing an audio clip is actually quite easy. In Lesson 24, "Using Exceptions to Catch Errors," you will learn how to detect and handle errors using exceptions. Before you continue with Lesson 24, however, make sure that you have learned the following key concepts:

☑ Using the *AudioClip* class, your applets can create an object with which you can load and play an object.

☑ Most Java compilers support a variety of audio file formats that include AU, WAV, and MIDI files.

☑ Using the *getAudioClip* function, your applets can assign an audio clip to an *AudioClip* object.

☑ Using the *AudioClip* class *play* method, your applets can play an audio clip one time.

☑ Using the *AudioClip* class *loop* method, your applets can play an audio clip continuously.

LESSON 24
USING EXCEPTIONS TO CATCH ERRORS

After you create and debug (remove the errors from) many applets, you may begin to anticipate the errors the applet may encounter as it runs. For example, if your applet loads a graphics image from a file, the applet must test if the file was successfully located and loaded. Likewise, if your applet uses arrays to store information, your applet must test for and respond to array-index values that are illegal—such as the index value -1 (Java arrays always start at index 0). As your applets increase in size and complexity, you will find that you include many such tests throughout your applet. In this lesson, you will learn how to use Java exceptions to simplify your applet's error testing and handling. By the time you finish this lesson, you will understand the following key concepts:

- An *exception* is an unexpected event (an error) within your applet.

- Within your applet, you define exceptions as classes.

- To direct your applets to watch for exceptions, you use the Java *try* statement.

- To detect a specific exception, your applets use the Java *catch* statement.

- To generate an exception when an error occurs, your applets use the Java *throw* statement.

- Many Java applets catch and then simply ignore exceptions.

- When your applet detects (catches) an exception, your applet calls a special (exception-specific) function, programmers refer to as an *exception handler*.

JAVA REPRESENTS EXCEPTIONS AS CLASSES

Your goal in using Java exceptions is to simplify error detection and error handling within your applets. Ideally, when your applets experience an unexpected error (an exception), your applets can handle the error in a meaningful way—as opposed to simply ending (crashing).

As you will learn, there are two types of exceptions: those that you define yourself and those that another class defines for you. At first, you will be less concerned with the exceptions you define yourself. Instead, you will more likely encounter a situation where your applet must catch an exception that is thrown by another class. For example, as you use Java to create animations, you will often use the *thread.sleep* function to temporarily suspend a thread's execution for a specified number of milliseconds. For example, the following function call would suspend a thread for 500 milliseconds, or one-half of a second:

```
thread.sleep(500);
```

As it turns out, the *thread.sleep* function will generate (throw) an exception named *InterruptedException* if the thread's sleep is interrupted in some way (remember, exceptions are unexpected events). Within your applet, you will detect and catch the exception using the *try* and *catch* statements, as shown here:

```
try
  {
      thread.sleep(500);
  }
catch (InterruptedException e)
  {
```

```
        // Statements you want to execute go here
    }
```

As you can see, the *catch* statement specifies the exception type (in this case, *InterruptedException)* and declares an object of that type named *e*.

In Lesson 21, "Using Threads to Create Simple Animations," you created the *ShowTime.java* applet that repeatedly displays the current system date and time within the applet window. If you examine the applet's run function, you will find that the applet uses the *sleep* function to suspend the thread's processing for 500-millisecond intervals (for one-half second). As just discussed, if the *sleep* function is interrupted before the time interval expires, *sleep* throws the *InterruptedException* exception. In the case of the *ShowTime.java* applet, the *run* method uses the *try* statement to enable Java's exception detection and the *catch* statement to respond to the exception. Within the *catch* statement, the applet does not include any statements, which means the applet simply catches and then ignores the exception:

```
public void run()
  {
    while (true)
      {
          CurrentDateTime = new Date();
          repaint();

          try
            {
                TimeThread.sleep(500);
            }
          catch (InterruptedException e)
            {
            }
      }
  }
```

In the next section, you will examine the *try* and *catch* statements in more detail. For now, understand that the functions you use may generate exceptions, and you must include statements within your applets that catch and detect them.

DIRECTING JAVA TO TEST FOR EXCEPTIONS

Before your applets can detect and respond to an exception, you must use the Java *try* statement to enable exception detection. The following *try* statement, for example, enables exception detection for the *DisplayImage* function call:

```
try {
    DisplayImage("SomeImageFile.GIF");
};
```

Immediately following a *try* statement, your applet should place one or more Java *catch* statements to determine which, if any, exception occurred:

```
try {
    DisplayImage("SomeImageFile.GIF");
};
```

```
catch (FileNotFound e) {
   DisplayErrorMessage("File not found");
   exit_the_applet();
}


catch (FileReadError e) {
   DisplayErrorMessage("Error reading file");
   exit_the_applet();
}
```

As you can see, the code tests for the file-exception errors previously defined. In this case, regardless of the error type, the code simply displays a message and exits. Ideally, your code may respond differently, possibly by trying to eliminate the cause of the error so it can retry the operation. If the function is successful and does not generate an exception, Java simply ignores the *catch* statements.

DEFINING YOUR OWN EXCEPTIONS

Within your applet, you can define your own exceptions by defining classes. For example, the following statements define three file-related exceptions:

```
class FileOpenError extends Exception {}
class FileReadError extends Exception {}
class FileWriteError extends Exception {}
```

As you can see, each of the class definitions extends the *Exception* class that is defined in the package *java.util.**. For now, simply understand that each exception corresponds to a class.

USING THE THROW STATEMENT TO GENERATE AN EXCEPTION

Java itself does not generate exceptions. Instead, your applets (or some of the class-library functions you run) generate an exception by using the Java *throw* statement. For example, the following *ArrayFill* function assigns a value to an array at a specified index. If the caller specifies an index value that falls beneath the array's index range, the function throws an *InvalidIndex* exception:

```
void ArrayFill(int Array[], int Value, int Index) throws InvalidIndex
  {
    if ((Index < 0) || (index > Array.length))
      throw new InvalidIndex();
}
```

As you can see, the applet uses the *throw* statement to generate specific exceptions. Note that the function header specifies that the function throws the *InvalidIndex* exception.

The previous *ArrayFill* function exists to help you understand how a function throws an exception. Ideally, you should use exceptions to handle events you do not expect to happen. It seems reasonable that a function that assigns a value to an array should test for an invalid array index. In the case of the *ArrayFill* function, you should use the function's return statement to indicate errors, such as an invalid index, as opposed to using an exception:

```
int ArrayFill(int Array[], int Value, int Index)
  {
     if ((Index < 0) || (index > Array.length))
        return(-1);   // Invalid index value
  }
```

When you enable exception detection, you increase your applet's overhead (Java has to perform significant behind-the-scenes processing to test for exceptions). Therefore, you should restrict your exceptions to events you cannot reasonably foresee and easily test for within your own code.

How Exceptions Work

When you use exceptions, your applets test for errors and, if necessary, generate an exception by using the *throw* statement. When Java encounters a *throw* statement, Java activates the corresponding exception handler (a function whose statements you define within the *exception* class). After the exception-handling function ends, Java returns control to the first statement that follows the *try* statement that enabled exception detection. Next, using *catch* statements, your applet can determine which exception occurred, and can respond accordingly.

The following applet, *ExceptionDemo.java*, illustrates the process of defining, testing for, throwing, and catching exceptions. The applet defines three exceptions. Within the *paint* function, the object uses a *for* statement to call the *ThrowOne* function three times. The *ThrowOne* function, in turn, based on the value of its parameter, throws one of three exceptions (or does not throw an exception if the parameter's value is not in the range of 1 to 3). Within the *paint* function, the applet catches each exception and displays a message specific to the exception caught:

```
import java.awt.*;
import java.applet.*;
import java.lang.*;

public class ExceptionDemo extends Applet
  {
    class ExceptionOne extends Exception {}
    class ExceptionTwo extends Exception {}
    class ExceptionThree extends Exception {}

    void ThrowOne(int i) throws ExceptionOne, ExceptionTwo, ExceptionThree
      {
        if (i == 1)
          throw new ExceptionOne();
        else if (i == 2)
          throw new ExceptionTwo();
        else if (i == 3)
          throw new ExceptionThree();
      }

    public void paint(Graphics g)
      {
        int i;
        String ExceptionCaught = "Demo";
```

```
      for (i = 1; i <= 3; i++)
        {
          try {
            ThrowOne(i);
          }

          catch(ExceptionOne e)
            {
              ExceptionCaught = "ExceptionOne";
            }
          catch(ExceptionTwo e)
            {
              ExceptionCaught = "ExceptionTwo";
            }
          catch(ExceptionThree e)
            {
              ExceptionCaught = "ExceptionThree";
            }

          g.drawString(ExceptionCaught, 5, 15*i);
        }
    }
}
```

To run this applet, place the following HTML entries within the file *ExceptionDemo.HTML*:

```
<HTML><TITLE>ExceptionDemo Applet</TITLE>
<APPLET CODE="ExceptionDemo.class" WIDTH=300 HEIGHT=200></APPLET></HTML>
```

DEFINING AN EXCEPTION HANDLER

When your applets throw an exception, Java executes an exception handler (a function), whose statements you define within the *exception* class. In most cases, the *exception* class will not provide any method or member variables other than a constructor function. Within the constructor function, the *exception* class normally just calls the *super* class constructor. Lesson 26, "Understanding Inheritance," examines the *super* function in detail. The following statements define an exception class named *NukeMeltdown*:

```
class NukeMeltdown extends Exception
  {
    public NukeMeltdown()
      {
        super();
      }
  }
```

Exceptions in Java extend the *Exception* class that is defined in the *java.util.* * class library. In general, most exceptions will support two constructor functions, one which receives no parameters, and one which receives a *String* parameter that might contain text that describes the exception. The following statements extend the *NukeMeltdown* exception to support both constructor formats:

```
class NukeMeltdown extends Exception
  {
    public NukeMeltdown()
    {
      super();
    }

    public NukeMeltdown(String SomeString)
    {
      super(SomeString);
    }

  }
```

The following applet, *ThrowNukeMeltdown.java*, illustrates the use of the *NukeMeltdown* function. The applet uses a *try* statement to enable exception detection. Next, the applet invokes the *AddU232* function with one parameter. If the parameter's value is less than 300, the function succeeds. If, however, the parameter's value exceeds 300, the function throws the *NukeMeltdown* exception:

```
import java.awt.*;
import java.applet.*;
import java.lang.*;

public class ThrowNukeMeltdown extends Applet
  {
    String NukeStatus = "Status is Safe";

    class NukeMeltdown extends Exception
      {
        public NukeMeltdown()
        {
          super();
        }
      }

    public void start()
      {
        try {
          AddU232(400);
        }
        catch(NukeMeltdown e)
          {
            NukeStatus = "Run! Run! Run!";
            repaint();
          }
      }
```

```
    public void AddU232(int Amount) throws NukeMeltdown
    {
       if (Amount < 300)
         return;
       else
         throw new NukeMeltdown();
    }

    public void paint(Graphics g)
    {
        g.drawString(NukeStatus, 5, 15);
    }
}
```

To run this applet, place the following HTML entries within the file *ThrowNukeMeltdown.HTML*:

```
<HTML><TITLE>ThrowNukeMeltdown Applet</TITLE>
<APPLET CODE="ThrowNukeMeltdown.class" WIDTH=300 HEIGHT=200></APPLET></HTML>
```

Take time to experiment with this applet, changing the value the applet passes to the *AddU232* function to a value less than 300 and one greater than 300.

DEFINING AN EXCEPTION HANDLER

When Java detects an exception within your applet, Java executes a special function called the exception handler. To define an exception handler, you simply create a function within the exception class that has the same name as the exception (similar to a constructor). When your applet later throws an exception, Java will automatically invoke your exception handler. Ideally, the exception handler should perform operations that remedy the error, so your applet can retry the operation that caused the exception. After your exception handler ends, your applet's execution continues at the first statement that follows the *try* statement that enabled exception detection.

STATING WHICH EXCEPTIONS A FUNCTION CAN THROW

When your applets use exceptions, you can use the function definition to specify the exceptions a function can throw. For example, the following function header tells the compiler the *power_plant* function can throw the *melt_down* and *radiation_leak* exceptions:

```
void power_plant(long power_needed) throws melt_down, radiation_leak
```

By including the possible exceptions within the function prototype in this way, other programmers reading your code can readily tell for which exceptions they must test when they use the function.

UNDERSTANDING THE FINALLY CLAUSE

When your applets use the *try* and *catch* statements to test for exceptions, there may be times when you want the applet to perform specific processing, regardless of which exception has occurred. In such cases, your applets can use the *finally* clause. In short, you place the *finally* clause following your last *catch* statement, as a "catch all," so to speak:

```
try {
    DisplayImage("SomeImageFile.GIF");
};


catch (FileNotFound e) {
   DisplayErrorMessage("File not found");
   AppletStop();
}


catch (FileReadError e) {
   DisplayErrorMessage("Error reading file");
   AppletStop();
}


finally {
   DisplayErrorMessage("Exception in processing occurred...applet ending");
   AppletStop();
}
```

As it turns out, if any of the *catch* statements execute, Java will execute the statements that reside in the *finally* clause. Should the statements that correspond to a *catch* statement try to return or branch out of the *try* statement, Java will first pass control to the *finally* clause, and then, after the *finally* clause statements execute, the code will continue at the desired destination.

As you have learned, Java treats exceptions as classes. When you define an exception, you can specify class members. In other words, an exception you define might have data members as well as methods that perform specific processing. The following applet, *ExceptionMembers.java*, shows how you might use class member variables:

```
import java.awt.*;
import java.applet.*;
import java.lang.*;

public class ExceptionMembers extends Applet
   {
     class SomeException extends Exception
       {
         String Message;

         public SomeException()
           {
             super();
             Message = null;
           }

         public SomeException(String SomeString)
           {
             super(SomeString);
             Message = SomeString;
           }
       }
```

```
    void ThrowOne(int i) throws SomeException
    {
      if (i == 1)
        throw new SomeException();
      else if (i == 2)
        throw new SomeException("Demo Exception");
    }


    public void paint(Graphics g)
    {
      int i;

      for (i = 1; i <= 2; i++)
        {
         try {
            ThrowOne(i);
          }

         catch(SomeException e)
          {
            if (e.Message != null)
              g.drawString(e.Message, 5, 15*i);
            else
              g.drawString("Caught exception", 5, 15*i);
          }
        }
    }
}
```

As you can see, the applet defines the *SomeException* class that contains two constructor methods, one that supports a *String* parameter and one that does not support parameters. When the applet throws a *SomeException* exception, the applet can pass or not pass a parameter to the exception. Using the *String* parameter, the applet might pass a text message that details the exception or its cause. When the applet later catches the exception, the applet can test the exception's *Message* member to determine if it contains a value and, if so, use the member in some way.

To run this applet, place the following HTML entries within the file *ExceptionMembers.HTML*:

```
<HTML><TITLE>ExceptionMembers Applet</TITLE>
<APPLET CODE="ExceptionMembers.class" WIDTH=300 HEIGHT=200></APPLET></HTML>
```

TAKING A CYBER FIELD TRIP

In the future, devices throughout your home or office will communicate with one another using a plug-and-play network. To help facilitate the design of such a network, the developers at Sun Microsystems are working on the Jini technology—a Java-based network architecture. To learn more about Jini and the future of device networks, visit the Sun Microsystems Web site at *www.sun.com/jini*, as shown in Figure 24.

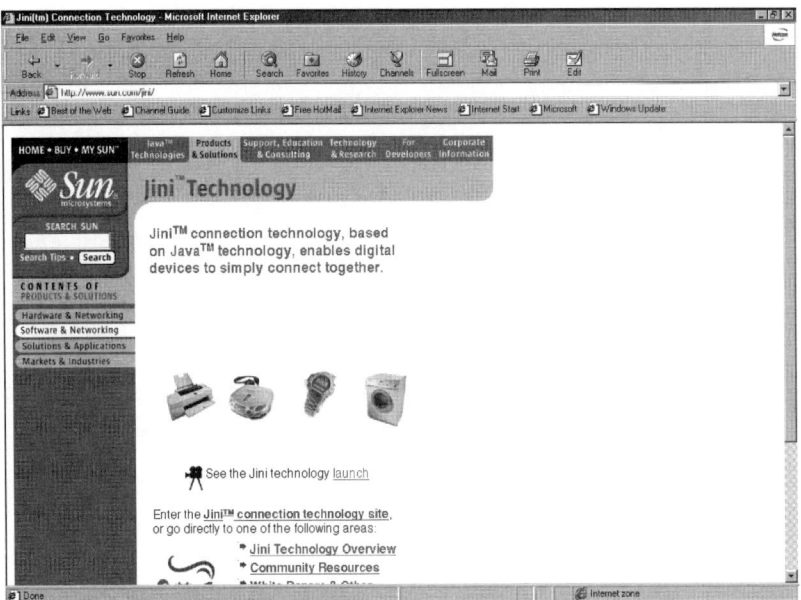

Figure 24 *View information about future device networks at www.sun.com/jini.*

WHAT YOU MUST KNOW

Exceptions exist to simplify and enhance your applet's error-detection and error-handling capabilities. To test for and detect exceptions, your applets use the *try*, *catch*, and *throw* statements. In Lesson 25, "Local Variables and Scope," you will examine an object's scope, the locations within your applet where the object has meaning. You will learn how to control an object's scope using the *public*, *private*, and *protected* keywords. Before you continue with Lesson 25, however, make sure you have learned the following key concepts:

☑ An exception is an unexpected error within your applet.

☑ Your applets should detect and respond to (handle) exceptions.

☑ Within your applets, you define each exception as a class.

☑ You use the *try* statement to direct the Java compiler to enable exception detection.

☑ You should place a *catch* statement immediately after your *try* statement to determine which, if any, exception occurred.

☑ Java does not generate exceptions itself. Rather, your applets generate an exception by using the *throw* statement.

☑ When your applet catches an exception, your applet calls a special function—an *exception handler*.

☑ When your applets use exceptions, you can specify the exceptions a function can throw within a function prototype.

☑ A *finally* clause provides a "catch all," whose statements execute if any of the *catch* statements encounter a matching exception.

LESSON 25

LOCAL VARIABLES AND SCOPE

As you learned in Lesson 9, "Using Functions to Simplify Java Applets," functions let you divide your applets into small, manageable pieces. As your functions perform more meaningful work, the functions must use variables to perform their processing. The variables you declare within a function are *local variables*. The local variable's values, and even the fact that the variables exist, are known only to the function. In other words, if you declare a local variable named *Salary* in the *Payroll* function, other functions do not have access to the *Salary* variable value. Other functions have no idea that the *Salary* variable exists. In fact, two functions can use variables with the same name without a conflict.

Throughout this book, you have created Java classes. Within your classes, you have included the *public* label to provide your applet with access to each of the class members. In this lesson, you will learn how *public* and *private* class members control which members your applets can directly access using the dot operator. As you will learn, your applet can access *public* members from within any function. On the other hand, your applet can access *private* members only within a class's own functions. In this way, *private* class members let objects control how an applet can use its data members. Although your applets have not yet used it, Java also supports the *protected* label which further controls how your applet can access class members. This lesson examines *public, private*, and *protected* members in detail. It will also examine variable scope (the locations within your applet where a variable is known). By the time you finish this lesson, you will understand the following key concepts:

- You declare local variables within a function by specifying the variable's type and name.

- The variable names you use within a function only must be unique to that function.

- A variable's scope defines the locations in your applet where the variable is known and accessible.

- Global variables, unlike local variables, are known throughout your entire applet and are accessible within all functions.

- To control how your applets access class members, Java lets you define members as *public*, *private*, or *protected*.

- *Private* members let a class hide information that an applet does not have to know.

- Classes that use *private* members provide interface *functions* that access the *private* class members.

DECLARING LOCAL VARIABLES

A *local variable* is a variable an applet defines within a function. The variable is said to be *local* because Java restricts knowledge of the variable to that function. You declare local variables at the start of a function, following the function's opening brace, as shown here:

```
void some_function()
  {
    int count;
    float result;
  }
```

When you declare local variables within a function, it is very likely that the name of a local variable you declare in one function is the same as a variable name you are using in another. As briefly discussed, local variables are known only to the current function. Therefore, if two functions use the same local variable name, there is no conflict. Java treats each variable name as local to the corresponding function. The following applet, *LocalName.java*, uses the function *AddValues* to add two integer values. The function assigns its result to the local variable *Value*. Within the class, however, one of the member variables passed to the function is named *Value*. However, because Java treats the function's variable as local to the functions, the names do not conflict:

```java
import java.awt.*;
import java.applet.*;

public class LocalName extends Applet
  {
    int Value = 1001;
    int OtherValue = 2002;          // Class member

    int AddValues(int a, int b)
      {
        int Value;                  // Local function variable

        Value = a + b;

        return(Value);
      }

    public void paint(Graphics g)
      {
        g.drawString("Value: "+ Value + "OtherValue: "+ OtherValue +
                "Result: "+ AddValues(Value, OtherValue), 5, 15);
      }
  }
```

To run the applet, place the following HTML entries within the file *LocalName.HTML*:

```html
<HTML><TITLE>LocalName Applet</TITLE>
<APPLET CODE="LocalName.class" WIDTH=300 HEIGHT=200></APPLET></HTML>
```

UNDERSTANDING LOCAL VARIABLES

Local variables are variables an applet declares within a function. The local variable's name and value are known only to the function within which you declare the variable. You should declare local variables at the start of your functions, immediately following the function's first open brace. The names that you assign to local variables only need be unique to the function. When you declare a local variable within a function, you can initialize the variable using the assignment operator.

UNDERSTANDING GLOBAL (CLASS-WIDE) VARIABLES

If you have programmed with other languages, such as C or C++, you may have used global variables, which are known throughout your entire program (globally to all functions). Because programmer abuse of global variables can lead to errors that are difficult to debug, many programmers do not use global variables. In fact, Java does not let you create them. Instead, each variable you create must be defined within a class. The closest thing to a global variable Java provides is a class-wide variable whose name and value are known throughout the entire class. In the previous *LocalName.java* applet, for example, the variables *Value* and *OtherValue* are class-wide variables.

WHEN CLASS VARIABLE AND LOCAL VARIABLE NAMES CONFLICT

As you have seen, there may be times when a local-variable name defined in a class function conflicts with the name of a class-member variable. When such conflicts occur, Java gives the local variable precedence. In other words, the applet assumes each reference to the name in conflict corresponds to the local variable.

There may be times, however, when you must access a class-wide variable whose name conflicts with a local variable. In such cases, your applets can use the *this* keyword when you want to use the class variable. For example, assume that you have local and class-member variables named *number*. When your functions want to use the local variable *number*, the function simply refers to the variable, as shown here:

```
number = 1001; // Local variable reference
```

When the function wants to reference the class-member variable, on the other hand, the applet uses the *this* keyword, as shown here:

```
this.number = 2002;    // Class member variable reference
```

The following applet, *ShowNumbers.java*, uses a class-member variable named *number*. In addition, the function *ShowNumbers* uses a local variable named *number*. To access the class-member variable, the function uses the *this* keyword:

```java
import java.awt.*;
import java.applet.*;

public class ShowNumbers extends Applet
  {
    int Number = 1001;

    String LocalVariableText;
    String ClassVariableText;

    void ShowNumbers(int Number)
      {
        LocalVariableText = "Local variable: "+ Number;
        ClassVariableText = "Class variable: "+ this.Number;
      }
```

```
    public void paint(Graphics g)
  {
      ShowNumbers(2002);
      g.drawString(LocalVariableText, 5, 15);
      g.drawString(ClassVariableText, 5, 45);
  }
}
```

To run the applet, place the following HTML entries within the file *ShowNumbers.HTML*:

```
<HTML><TITLE>ShowNumbers Applet</TITLE>
<APPLET CODE="ShowNumbers.class" WIDTH=300 HEIGHT=200></APPLET></HTML>
```

After you compile and execute this applet, your screen will display an applet window similar to Figure 25.1.

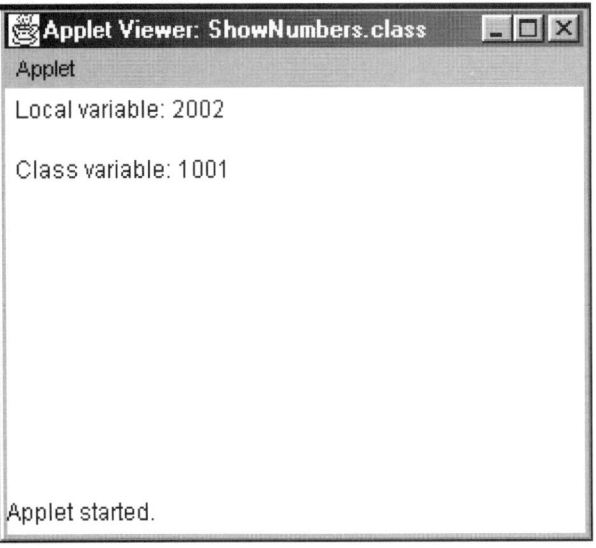

Figure 25.1 *Resolving a name conflict using the **this** keyword.*

As you can see, your applets can select the class-member variable or local variable by using or omitting the *this* keyword. However, note that the use of class-member and local variables that have the same name can confuse another programmer who is reading your code which, in turn, can cause the programmer to introduce errors. As a result, avoid such name conflicts whenever possible.

UNDERSTANDING A VARIABLE'S SCOPE

As you read books and magazine articles on Java, you may encounter the term *scope*, which defines the locations within an applet where a variable's name has meaning (and is therefore usable). For a local variable, the variable's scope is the function within which the variable is declared. Public class-member variables, on the other hand, are known throughout your entire applet. As a result, public class-member variables have a larger scope. As discussed next, you can limit a class member's scope by using the *private* and *protected* keywords.

Understanding Information Hiding

As you have learned, a class contains data and methods (functions). To use a class, your applets simply must know the information the class stores (its data members) and the methods that manipulate the data (the functions). Your applets do not have to know how the methods work. Rather, your applet needs to know only the task the methods perform. For example, assume that you have a *GraphicsImage* class. Ideally, your applets must know only that the class provides the methods *GraphicsImage.print*, which prints the image, or *GraphicsImage.Rotate*, which rotates the image. Your applet does not have to know how these two methods work. In other words, the applet should treat the class as a "black box." The applet knows which methods to invoke and the parameters to the methods, but the applet does not know the actual processing that occurs within the class (the black box).

Information hiding is the process of making available to the applet only the minimal class information the applet needs in order to use a class. Java *private*, *public*, and *protected* class members help you achieve information hiding within your applets. In each of the classes you have created throughout this book, you have used the *public* label to make all of the class members visible to the entire applet. Therefore, the applet could directly access any class member by using the dot operator.

When you create your classes, you might have members whose values the class uses internally to perform its processing, but which the applet itself does not have to access. Such members are *private* members, and you should hide them from the applet. The functions within your applet that are not members of the same class cannot access another class's *private* members using the dot operator. Only a class's methods can access *private* class members. When you create your classes, you will separate the members into *private* and *public* members, as shown here:

```
class SomeClass
  {
    public int SomeVariable;
    public void InitializePrivate(int KeyValue, float KeyNumber)
      {
        this.KeyValue = KeyValue;
        this.KeyNumber = KeyNumber;
      }
    public void ShowData()
      {
        // Statements here
      }
    private int KeyValue;
    private float KeyNumber;
  }
```

As you can see, the *public* and *private* labels let you define easily which members are *private* and which are *public*. In this case, the applet can use the dot operator to access the *public* members, as shown here:

```
SomeClass Object = New Object();                    // Create an object
Object.SomeVariable = 1001;
Object.InitializePrivate(2002, 1.2345);
Object.ShowData()
```

If your applet tries to use the dot operator to access the *private* members *KeyValue* or *KeyNumber*, the compiler will generate syntax errors. As a general rule, you will normally protect class-data members from direct applet access by making the members *private*. In this way, applets cannot directly assign values to members by using the dot operator.

Instead, the applet must call a class method to assign the values. By preventing the applet's direct access to the data members, you can ensure that the data members are always assigned valid values. For example, assume your applet's *NuclearReactor* object uses the member variable named *MeltDown*, which should always contain a value in the range 1 through 5. If the *MeltDown* member is *public*, the applet can directly access the member's value, changing the value in any way it likes:

```
NuclearReactor.MeltDown = 101
```

If, instead, you make the variable *private*, you can use a class method such as *AssignMeltdown* to assign the member value. As shown here, the *AssignMeltdown* function can test the value assigned to ensure that it is valid:

```
public boolean AssignMeltdown(int value)
  {
    if ((value > 0) && (value <= 5))
     {
       MeltDown = value;
       return(true);   // Successful assignment
     }
    else
       return(false);   // Invalid value
  }
```

Class methods that control access to class data members are *interface functions*. When you create classes, you will use interface functions to protect your class data.

UNDERSTANDING PUBLIC AND PRIVATE MEMBERS

Java classes contain data and methods. To control which class members your applet can access directly using the dot operator, Java lets you define *public* and *private* members. Your applets can directly access any *public* member using the dot operator. *Private* members, on the other hand, can only be accessed by class methods. As a rule, you should protect most class-data members by making them *private*. Therefore, the only way your applets can assign a value to a data member is to use a class function that can examine and validate the value.

USING PUBLIC AND PRIVATE MEMBERS

The following applet, *InformationHiding.java*, illustrates the use of *public* and *private* members. To start, the applet defines an object of type *Employee*, as shown here:

```
class Employee
   {
     public void AssignValues(String Name, int Id, double Salary)
       {
         this.Name = Name;
         this.Id = Id;
         this.Salary = Salary;
       }
```

```
    public String ShowEmployee()
    {
        return("Name: "+ Name + "Id: "+ Id + "Salary: $" + Salary);
    }


    public void ChangeSalary(float Salary)
    {
        this.Salary = Salary;
    }

    public long GetId()
    {
        return(Id);
    }


    private String Name;
    private int Id;
    private double Salary;
}
```

As you can see, the class protects each of its data members by making them *private*. To access a data member, the applet must use one of the class's interface functions. The following code implements the *InformationHiding.java* applet:

```
import java.awt.*;
import java.applet.*;

public class InformationHiding extends Applet
{
    class Employee
    {
        public void AssignValues(String Name, int Id, double Salary)
        {
            this.Name = Name;
            this.Id = Id;
            this.Salary = Salary;
        }

        public String ShowEmployee()
        {
            return("Name: "+ Name + "Id: "+ Id + "Salary: $" + Salary);
        }

        public void ChangeSalary(float Salary)
        {
            this.Salary = Salary;
        }
```

```
        public long GetId()
          {
            return(Id);
          }

      private String Name;
      private int Id;
      private double Salary;
    }

  Employee Worker = new Employee();

  public void paint(Graphics g)
    {
       Worker.AssignValues("Happy", 123456, 35000.0);
       g.drawString(Worker.ShowEmployee(), 5, 15);
    }
 }
```

Take time to examine the applet statements in detail. Although the applet is long, its functions are straightforward. The *AssignValues* method initializes the *private* class data. The *ShowEmployee* method displays the *private* data members. The *ChangeSalary* and *GetId* methods are interface functions that provide the applet with *private* data access. After you successfully compile and run this applet, edit the applet and try to directly access a *private* data member by using a dot operator. Because you cannot access *private* members directly, the compiler will generate syntax errors.

To run the applet, place the following HTML entries within the file *InformationHiding.HTML*:

```
<HTML><TITLE>InformationHiding Applet</TITLE>
<APPLET CODE="InformationHiding.class" WIDTH=300 HEIGHT=200></APPLET>
</HTML>
```

After you compile and execute this applet, your screen will display an applet window similar to Figure 25.2.

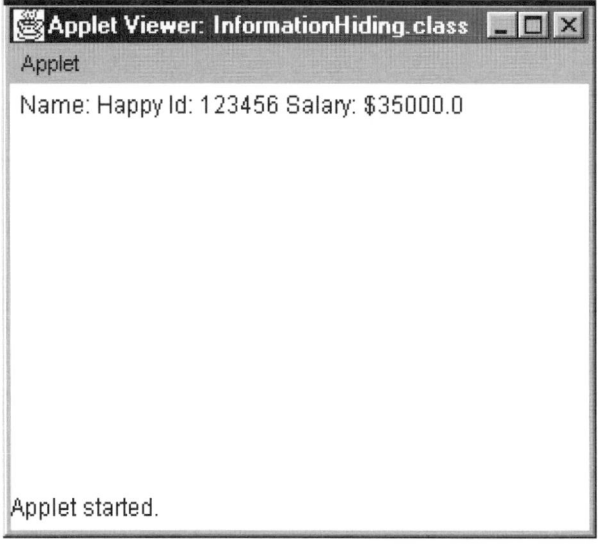

Figure 25.2 Using interface functions to access class-member variables.

UNDERSTANDING INTERFACE FUNCTIONS

To reduce potential errors, you should limit your applet's access to class data by defining class-data members as *private*. In this way, an applet cannot access class-data members by using the dot operator. Instead, the class should define interface functions with which the applet can assign values to *private* members. The interface functions, in turn, can examine and validate the values which the applet is trying to assign.

PRIVATE MEMBERS ARE NOT ALWAYS DATA MEMBERS

In the examples this lesson presents, the *private* members were always data members. As your class definitions become more complex, you might have functions other class methods use that you do not want the rest of your applet to access directly. In such cases, you simply make the method a *private* member. If a class function is not *public*, the applet cannot invoke the function by using the dot operator.

UNDERSTANDING PROTECTED MEMBERS

As you examine class definitions, you may encounter *public*, *private*, and *protected* class members. A *public* member, as you have learned, is accessible by all of the class functions, as well as functions outside of the class. A *private* class method, on the other hand, is only accessible to methods of the class within which the *private* member is defined.

In Lesson 26, "Understanding Inheritance," you will learn how to use an existing class to create a new class. (Java programmers refer to the process of building a new class from an existing class as *extending* the existing class.) If another class extends the class that defines the *private* member, the subclass cannot access the *private* member.

A *protected* class member falls between a *private* and *public* member. A *protected* class member is fully accessible to the functions within which the member is defined. Subclass objects which correspond to a class that extends the class within which the *protected* member is defined can access the *protected* member as if the member were *public*. Likewise, classes in the same package as the class that defines the *protected* class member can access the member as if it were *public*. To the rest of the applet, *protected* members appear as *private*. The only way your applet functions can access *protected* members is by using interface functions.

TAKING A CYBER FIELD TRIP

If you develop Java applets for wide-spread use, you should include an online help facility for your application. To create your online help facility, you can use a program called *JavaHelp*, developed by Sun Microsystems. Like traditional help facilities, *JavaHelp* lets you quickly integrate text and links. In addition, *JavaHelp* lets you integrate applets into your help text. For more information on *JavaHelp*, visit the Sun Microsystem's Web site at *java.sun.com/products/javahelp*, as shown in Figure 25.3.

Figure 25.3 Use JavaHelp to create an online help facility.

WHAT YOU MUST KNOW

A variable's or function's scope controls the locations within your applet where the variable or function has meaning. This lesson examined variable scope in detail. As you learned, a variable's scope can be local to a function, known throughout class functions, or even accessible outside of the class.

In Lesson 26, "Understanding Inheritance," you will learn how you can reduce the amount of code you must write by using an existing class to create a new class. For example, you might create a *Dalmatian* class from an existing *Dog* class. Before you continue with Lesson 26, however, make sure you understand the following key concepts:

☑ Local variables are variables declared within a function.

☑ Local variables are known only to the function within which they are declared.

☑ Two or more functions can use the same local variable name with no conflicts.

☑ A *public* class variable is a variable whose name and value are known throughout your applet.

☑ Class members can be *public*, *private*, or *protected*.

☑ Applets assign values to and access *private* members using interface functions.

LESSON 26

UNDERSTANDING INHERITANCE

A goal of object-oriented programming is to *reuse* a class that you created for one applet within another applet, which saves you programming time. As you define your classes, there may be times when a new class uses many or all the features of an existing class, and then adds one or more data or function members. In such cases, Java lets you build the new object by extending the characteristics of the existing object. In other words, the new object will *inherit* the members of the existing class (called the *super class*). When you extend a new class from an existing class, programmers refer to the new class as a *subclass*. This lesson introduces Java class inheritance. By the time you finish this lesson, you will understand the following key concepts:

◆ When your applets use inheritance, you use a *super* class to derive a new class, in such a way that the new class inherits the *super* class members.

◆ To initialize class members for an extended class (called a subclass), your applet must invoke the *super* class and subclass class-constructor functions.

◆ Using the dot operator, your applets can easily access the *super* class and extended class members.

◆ In addition to *public* (accessible to all) and *private* (accessible to class methods) members, Java provides *protected* members that are accessible by the *super* and extended class members.

◆ To resolve name conflicts between *super* and extended class members, your applet can use the *this* or *super* keywords.

Inheritance is a fundamental object-oriented programming concept. Take time to experiment with the applets this lesson presents. As you will learn, inheritance is very easy to implement and can save you tremendous amounts of programming.

A SIMPLE INHERITANCE

Inheritance is the ability of an extended class (an extended class is the same as a subclass) to inherit the characteristics of an existing *super* class. Assume, for example, that you have the following *Employee* class:

```java
class Employee
   {
     public Employee(String Name, String Position, double Salary)
       {
         this.Name = Name;
         this.Position = Position;
         this.Salary = Salary;
       }


     public String ShowEmployee()
       {
          return("Employee: " + Name + " Position: " + Position +
                  " Salary: " + Salary);
       }
```

```
        private String Name;
        private String Position;
        private double Salary;
    }
```

Next, assume that your applet needs a *Manager* class, which adds the following data members to the *Employee* class:

```
private String Car;
private double Bonus;
private int StockOptions;
```

In this case, your applet has two choices: first, the applet can create a new *Manager* class, which duplicates many of the *Employee* class members; or, your applet can extend the class type *Manager* from the *Employee super* class. By extending the *Manager* class from the existing *Employee* class, you reduce your programming and eliminate duplicate code within your applet.

To begin the class definition, you will specify the *class* keyword, the *Manager* name followed by the *extends* keyword, and the *Employee* class name, as shown here:

```
class Manager extends Employee
  {
     // Members defined here
  }
```

For example, the following statements derive the *Manager* class:

```
class Manager extends Employee
  {
    public Manager(String Name, String Position, String Car,
                   double Salary, double Bonus, int StockOptions)
      {
        super(Name, Position, Salary);
        this.Car = Car;
        this.Bonus = Bonus;
        this.StockOptions = StockOptions;
      }

    public String ShowManager()
      {
        return("Car: " + Car + " Bonus: $" + Bonus +
               " Stock Options: " + StockOptions);
      }

    private String Car;
    private double Bonus;
    private int StockOptions;
  }
```

Note that when you extend a class from a super class, the *private* members within the super class are accessible to the extended class only through the interface functions within the super class. Thus, the extended class cannot directly access a super class *private* member by using the dot operator. The following applet, *ManagerExtendsEmployee.java*, illustrates the use of Java inheritance, extending the *Manager* class from the *Employee* super class:

```java
import java.awt.*;
import java.applet.*;

public class ManagerExtendsEmployee extends Applet
   {
     class Employee
        {
          public Employee(String Name, String Position, double Salary)
            {
              this.Name = Name;
              this.Position = Position;
              this.Salary = Salary;
            }

          public String ShowEmployee()
            {
              return("Employee: " + Name + " Position: " + Position +
                    " Salary: " + Salary);
            }

          private String Name;
          private String Position;
          private double Salary;
        }

     class Manager extends Employee
        {
          public Manager(String Name, String Position, String Car,
                      double Salary, double Bonus, int StockOptions)
            {
              super(Name, Position, Salary);

              this.Car = Car;
              this.Bonus = Bonus;
              this.StockOptions = StockOptions;
            }

          public String ShowManager()
            {
              return("Car: " + Car + " Bonus: $" + Bonus +
                    " Stock Options: " + StockOptions);
            }

          private String Car;
          private double Bonus;
          private int StockOptions;
        }
```

```
    public void paint(Graphics g)
      {
        Manager Boss = new Manager("Happy", "CEO", "Chevy",
                                    35000.0, 10000.0, 500);


        g.drawString(Boss.ShowEmployee(), 5, 15);
        g.drawString(Boss.ShowManager(), 5, 45);
      }
    }
```

As you can see, the applet defines the *Employee* class and then extends the *Manager* class from it. Note the *Manager* constructor function. When you extend a class from a super class, the extended class-constructor function must invoke the super-class constructor. To invoke the super-class constructor, you simply call the super function name with the desired parameters:

```
super(Name, Position, Salary);
```

To run the applet, place the following HTML entries within the file *ManagerExtendsEmployee.HTML*:

```
<HTML><TITLE>ManagerExtendsEmployee Applet</TITLE><APPLET
CODE="ManagerExtendsEmployee.class" WIDTH=300 HEIGHT=200></APPLET></HTML>
```

After you compile and execute this applet, your screen will display an applet window similar to that shown in Figure 26.1.

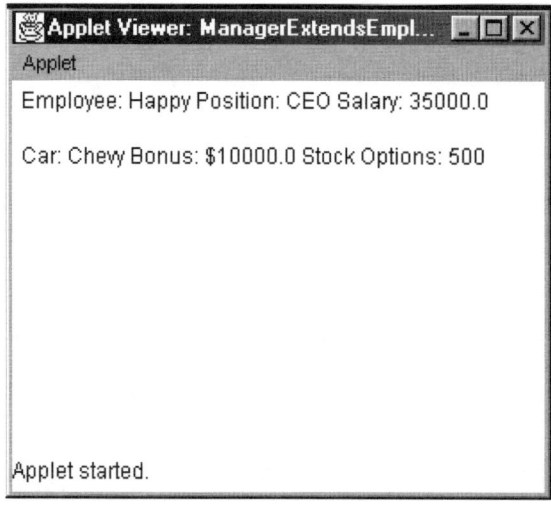

Figure 26.1 Extending an applet class.

UNDERSTANDING INHERITANCE

Inheritance is the ability of an extended class to inherit the characteristics of an existing super class. In simple terms, that means if you have a class whose data or function members a new class requires, you can build the new class (called a subclass) in terms of the existing (or super) class. The new class, in turn, will inherit the members (characteristics) of the existing class. Using inheritance to build new classes saves you considerable time and programming. Object-oriented programming makes extensive use of inheritance by letting your applets build complex objects out of smaller, more manageable objects.

LOOKING AT A SECOND EXAMPLE

Assume, for example, that you are using the following *Book* class within an existing applet:

```
class Book
  {
    public Book(String Title, String Author, int Pages)
      {
        this.Title = Title;
        this.Author = Author;
        this.Pages = Pages;
      }

    public String ShowBook()
      {
        return("Title: " + Title + " Author: " + Author +
              " Pages: " + Pages);
      }

    private String Title;
    private String Author;
    private int Pages;
  }
```

Next, assume that your applet must create a *LibraryCard* class that will add the following data members to the *Book* class:

```
private String Catalog;
private boolean CheckedOut;
```

Your applet can use inheritance to extend the *LibraryCard* class from the *Book* class, as shown here:

```
class LibraryCard extends Book
  {
    public LibraryCard(String Title, String Author, int Pages,
                  String Catalog, boolean CheckedOut)
      {
        super(Title, Author, Pages);
        this.Catalog = Catalog;
        this.CheckedOut = CheckedOut;
      }

    public String ShowLibraryCard()
      {
        return(ShowBook() + " Catalog: " + Catalog +
              " Checked out: " + CheckedOut);
      }

    private String Catalog;
    private boolean CheckedOut;
  }
```

The following applet, *LibraryCardClass.java*, extends the *LibraryCard* class from the *Book* class. As before, note the *LibraryCard* constructor calls the *Book* class constructor (*super*) to initialize members of the *Book* class. Also, note the use of the *Book* class *ShowBook* member function within the *ShowCard* function. Because the *LibraryCard* class inherits the *Book* class methods, the *ShowCard* function can invoke this method without having to specify a dot operator, just as if the method was one of its own:

```java
import java.awt.*;
import java.applet.*;

public class LibraryCardClass extends Applet
  {
    class Book
      {
        public Book(String Title, String Author, int Pages)
          {
             this.Title = Title;
             this.Author = Author;
             this.Pages = Pages;
          }

        public String ShowBook()
          {
             return("Title: " + Title + " Author: " + Author +
                    " Pages: " + Pages);
          }

        private String Title;
        private String Author;
        private int Pages;
      }

    class LibraryCard extends Book
      {
        public LibraryCard(String Title, String Author, int Pages,
                           String Catalog, boolean CheckedOut)
          {
             super(Title, Author, Pages);
             this.Catalog = Catalog;
             this.CheckedOut = CheckedOut;
          }

        public String ShowLibraryCard()
          {
             return(ShowBook() + " Catalog: " + Catalog +
                    " Checked out: " + CheckedOut);
          }

        private String Catalog;
        private boolean CheckedOut;
      }
```

```
   public void paint(Graphics g)
    {
      LibraryCard NewBook = new LibraryCard("Rescued by Java", "Jamsa",
                                         224, "LIB224", true);
      g.drawString(NewBook.ShowLibraryCard(), 5, 15);
    }
 }
```

To run the applet, place the following HTML entries within the file *LibraryCardClass.HTML*:

```
<HTML><TITLE>LibraryCardClass Applet</TITLE><APPLET
CODE="LibraryCardClass.class" WIDTH=600 HEIGHT=200></APPLET></HTML>
```

After you compile and execute this applet, your screen will display an applet window similar to that shown in Figure 26.2.

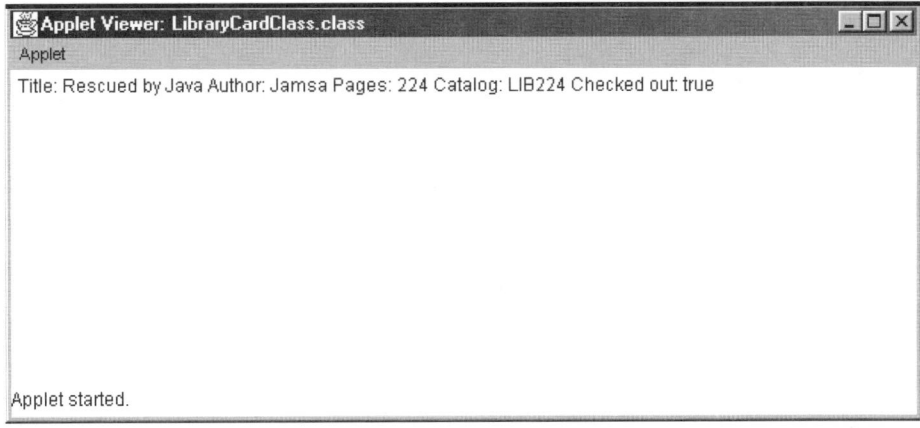

Figure 26.2 Extending the **Book** *class.*

UNDERSTANDING PROTECTED MEMBERS

As you examine *super* class definitions, you may encounter *public*, *private*, *protected*, and *private protected* class members. As you know, an extended class can access *super* class *public* members just as if the members were defined in the extended class. On the other hand, the extended class cannot access *super* class *private* members directly. Instead, the extended class must use a *super* class interface-function to access such members.

A *protected super* class member falls between a *private* and *public* member. If a member is *protected*, extended class objects can access the member as if the member were *public*. Likewise, other classes that are defined within the same package as the class can access the *protected* class members. To the rest of your applet, *protected* members appear as *private*. The only way your applet can access *protected* members is by using interface functions.

RESOLVING MEMBER NAMES

When you extend one class from another, there may be times when a class-member name in the extended class is the same as a member name in the *super* class. If such conflicts occur, Java always uses the extended-class member within the extended-class functions. For example, assume the *Book* and *LibraryCard* classes both use the member *Price*. In the case of the *Book* class, the *Price* member corresponds to the book's retail price, such as $22.95. In the case of the *LibraryCard* class, the *Price* member might include a library discount, such as $18.50. Unless your code tells them to

229

do otherwise (using the *super* keyword), the *LibraryCard* class functions will use the extended (*LibraryCard*) class member. If a *LibraryCard* class function must access the *Price* member of the *super* (*Book*) class, the function can use the *super* keyword, such as *super.Price*.

The following applet, *NameConflict.java*, adds the *Price* member to both the *Book* class and to the *LibraryCard* class. As you will see, to display the *Book* class *Price* member, the *LibraryCard* class will use *super.Price*:

```java
import java.awt.*;
import java.applet.*;

public class NameConflict extends Applet
  {
    class Book
      {
        public Book(String Title, String Author, int Pages, double Price)
          {
            this.Title = Title;
            this.Author = Author;
            this.Pages = Pages;
            this.Price = Price;
          }

        public String ShowBook()
          {
            return("Title: " + Title + " Author: " + Author +
                   " Pages: " + Pages);
          }

        private String Title;
        private String Author;
        private int Pages;
        public double Price;
      }

    class LibraryCard extends Book
      {
        public LibraryCard(String Title, String Author, int Pages,
                    String Catalog, boolean CheckedOut, double Price)
          {
            super(Title, Author, Pages, Price*2.0);
            this.Catalog = Catalog;
            this.CheckedOut = CheckedOut;
            this.Price = Price;
          }

        public String ShowLibraryCard()
          {
            return(ShowBook() + " Catalog: " + Catalog +
                   " Checked out: " + CheckedOut);
          }
```

```
        public void ShowPrice(Graphics g)
         {
            g.drawString("Library price: $ " + Price, 5, 30);
            g.drawString("Retail price: $ " + super.Price, 5, 45);
         }

      private String Catalog;
      private boolean CheckedOut;
      public double Price;
   }

   public void paint(Graphics g)
    {
      LibraryCard NewBook = new LibraryCard("Rescued by Java", "Jamsa",
                   224, "LIB224", true, 25.0);
      g.drawString(NewBook.ShowLibraryCard(), 5, 15);
      NewBook.ShowPrice(g);
    }
 }
```

To run the applet, place the following HTML entries within the *NameConflict.HTML* file:

```
<HTML><TITLE>NameConflict Applet</TITLE><APPLET CODE="NameConflict.class"
WIDTH=600 HEIGHT=200></APPLET></HTML>
```

After you compile and execute this applet, your screen will display an applet window similar to that shown in Figure 26.3.

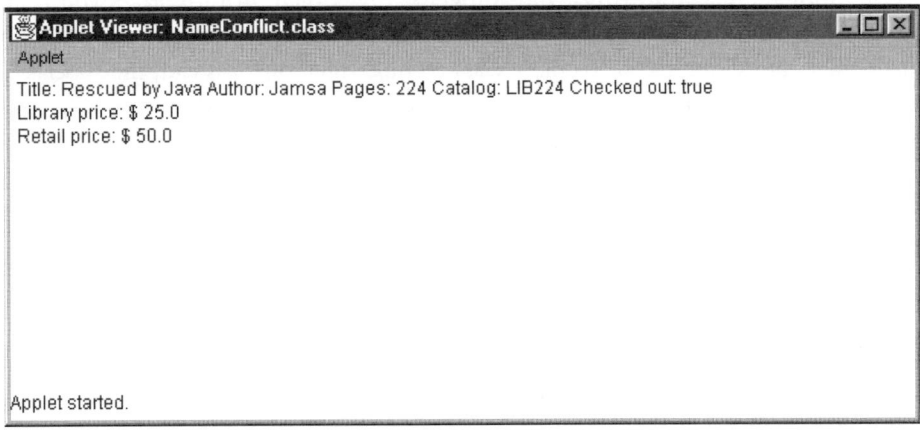

Figure 26.3 Resolving name conflicts within a Java applet.

Taking a Cyber Field Trip

If you develop applications for worldwide distribution, you may need to base your applets character manipulation on the unicode standard that uses two bytes to represent complex international characters. Likewise, as you examine the source code for Java applets you encounter on the Web, you will often find unicode-based operations. To help you understand unicode symbols, the Java Development Kit provides a Unicode applet, as shown in Figure 26.4. Using the applet, you can type in various unicode values for specific fonts and then view the corresponding symbols. To run the applet or to download the applet's source code, visit the Jamsa Press Web site at *www.jamsa.com/java_demos/Unicode.html.*

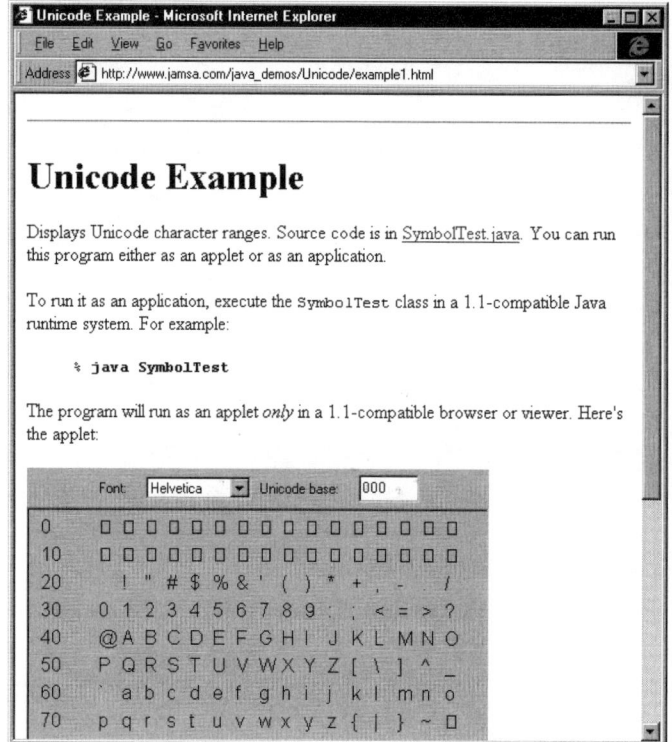

Figure 26.4 *Experimenting with unicode symbols.*

WHAT YOU MUST KNOW

In this lesson, you learned that Java inheritance capabilities let you build (derive) a new class from an existing class. By building one class from another, you reduce your programming which, in turn, saves you time. In Lesson 27, "Understanding and Using Abstract Classes," you will examine abstract class definitions, for which the class does not define the statements that correspond to one or more class-member methods. Instead, the subclass that extends the abstract class must implement the function definitions. Before you continue with Lesson 27, however, make sure that you have learned the following key concepts:

☑ Inheritance is the ability to extend a new class from an existing *super* class.

☑ The subclass is the new class, and the *super* class is the existing class.

☑ When you extend one class from another (the *super* class), the extended class inherits the *super* class members.

☑ To extend a class from a *super* class, you begin your class definition with the *class* keyword, followed by the class name, the *extends* keyword, and the *super* class name, such as *class Dalmatian extends Dog.*

☑ Within an extended class-constructor function, your applet must invoke the *super* class constructor by specifying the *super* function name with the corresponding parameters.

LESSON 27

UNDERSTANDING AND USING ABSTRACT CLASSES

In Lesson 26, "Understanding Inheritance," you learned how to extend an existing class by adding member variables and methods to create a new class. As you learned, by extending a class in this way, you reduce the amount of code you must write for your current applet. In short, by extending a class, you let one class inherit the members of its *super* class.

Depending upon the object which the *super* class implements, there may be times when it does not make sense for a *super* class to implement each of the class methods. For example, assume that the *super* class implements an object named *Shape*. Within the *super* class, you may define a method named *getArea*, which calculates and returns the shape's area. However, as you know, depending on the shape's type, the formula to calculate the area will differ. In this case, the object that extends the *Shape* class (such as a square or circle) should define the *getArea* method. In such cases, when a subclass must provide a method's definition, the *super* class will define the method as *abstract*.

As you will learn, an *abstract method* is a member function whose name appears within the *super* class definition, but whose implementation appears within the subclass. An *abstract class* is a class that contains one or more abstract methods. This lesson examines abstract classes in detail. By the time you finish this lesson, you will understand the following key concepts:

- ◆ An *abstract* class is a class that contains one or more abstract methods.

- ◆ An abstract method is a class function for which the class does not implement the function. Instead, the class simply specifies the function name and type.

- ◆ A class that extends an abstract class must implement each of the abstract methods.

UNDERSTANDING ABSTRACT CLASSES

An *abstract* class is a class that contains one or more abstract methods, which subclasses that extend the class must implement. The following statements, for example, define an abstract class named *Shapes*:

```
abstract class Shapes
{
  public int x, y;                // Coordinates
  public int width, height;

  public Shapes(int x, int y, int width, int height)
    {
      this.x = x;
      this.y = y;
      this.width = width;
      this.height = height;
    }

  abstract double getArea();
  abstract double getPerimeter();
}
```

As you can see, the *Shapes* class definition includes the *abstract* keyword before the class name to inform the Java compiler that the class contains one or more abstract methods. As discussed, an abstract method is a class method for which the class does not provide a function body (the statements the function performs). Instead, an abstract class simply precedes the function name with the *abstract* keyword:

```
abstract double getArea();
abstract double getPerimeter();
```

Because the abstract class does not define all of its methods, your applets cannot create an instance of an abstract class. Instead, your applet must define a class that extends the abstract class. The following applet, *AbstractClass.java*, creates *Square* and *Circle* classes that extend the abstract class *Shapes* class:

```
import java.awt.*;
import java.applet.*;

public class AbstractClass extends Applet
   {
     abstract class Shapes
        {
           public int x, y;                 // Coordinates
           public int width, height;

           public Shapes(int x, int y, int width, int height)
              {
                this.x = x;
                this.y = y;
                this.width = width;
                this.height = height;
              }

           abstract double getArea();
           abstract double getPerimeter();
        }

     class Square extends Shapes
        {
           public double getArea() { return (width * height); }
           public double getPerimeter() { return (2 * width + 2 * height); }
           public Square(int x, int y, int width, int height)
              {
                super(x, y, width, height);
              }
        }

     class Circle extends Shapes
        {
           public double r;
           public double getArea() { return (r * r * Math.PI); }
           public double getPerimeter() { return (2 * Math.PI * r); }
           public Circle(int x, int y, int width, int height)
              {
```

```
            super(x, y, width, height);
            r = (double) width / 2.0;
        }
    }


    Square Box = new Square(5, 15, 25, 25);
    Circle Oval = new Circle(5, 50, 25, 25);

    public void paint(Graphics g)
      {
        g.drawRect(Box.x, Box.y, Box.width, Box.height);
        g.drawString("Area: " + Box.getArea(), 50, 35);
        g.drawOval(Oval.x, Oval.y, Oval.width, Oval.height);
        g.drawString("Area: " + Oval.getArea(), 50, 70);
      }
  }
```

As you can see, the *Square* and *Circle* classes, which extend the abstract *Shapes* class, both implement the *getArea* and *getPerimeter* abstract methods.

To run this applet, place the following HTML entries within the file *AbstractClass.HTML*:

```
<HTML><TITLE>AbstractClass Applet</TITLE>
<APPLET CODE="AbstractClass.class" WIDTH=300 HEIGHT=200></APPLET></HTML>
```

After you compile and execute this applet, your screen will display the applet window shown in Figure 27.1.

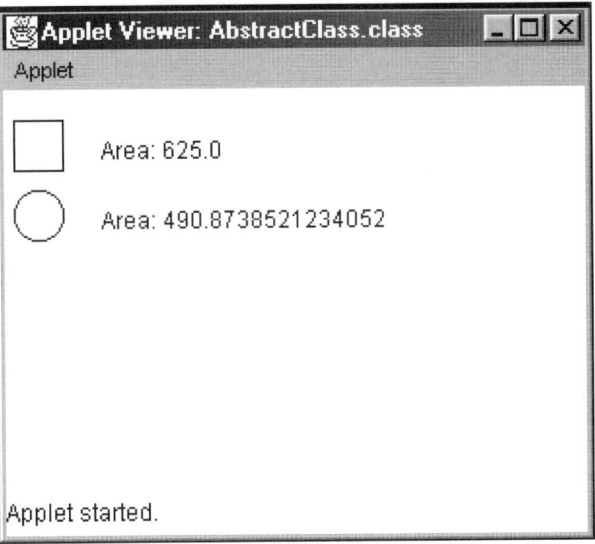

*Figure 27.1 Extending an **abstract** class.*

LOOKING AT A SECOND EXAMPLE

As you have learned, an abstract class is a class that contains one or more abstract methods. A class that extends an abstract class must implement each of the abstract methods. The following applet, *AbstractProduct.java*, defines an

235

abstract *Product* class that contains title, pricing, and cost information. The class, however, does not implement the *ShowProduct* method:

```java
abstract class Product
   {
     double Price, Cost;
     String Name;

     public Product(String Name, double Price, double Cost)
        {
           this.Name = Name;
           this.Price = Price;
           this.Cost = Cost;
        }
     public abstract String ShowProduct();
   }
```

The applet then creates a *Book* class and a *CDROM* class, both of which extend the abstract Product class:

```java
import java.awt.*;
import java.applet.*;

public class AbstractProduct extends Applet
   {
     abstract class Product
        {
          double Price, Cost;
          String Name;

          public Product(String Name, double Price, double Cost)
             {
                this.Name = Name;
                this.Price = Price;
                this.Cost = Cost;
             }

          public abstract String ShowProduct();
        }

     class Book extends Product
        {
          public Book(String Title, double Price, double Cost)
             {
                super(Title, Price, Cost);
             }

          public String ShowProduct()
             {
                return("Book: " + Name + " Price: $" + Price);
             }
        }
```

```
class CDROM extends Product
  {
    public CDROM(String Title, double Price, double Cost)
      {
        super(Title, Price, Cost);
      }

    public String ShowProduct()
      {
        return("CD-ROM: " + Name + " Price: $" + Price);
      }
  }


Book JavaBook = new Book("Rescued by Java", 29.95, 19.95);
CDROM JavaLibrary = new CDROM("Java Programmer's Library", 54.95, 39.95);

public void paint(Graphics g)
  {
    g.drawString(JavaBook.ShowProduct(), 5, 15);
    g.drawString(JavaLibrary.ShowProduct(), 5, 45);
  }
}
```

As you can see, both the *Book* class and *CDROM* class implement the *ShowProduct* method. Place the following HTML entries within the file *AbstractProduct.HTML* to run this applet:

```
<HTML><TITLE>AbstractProduct Applet</TITLE>
<APPLET CODE="AbstractProduct.class" WIDTH=300 HEIGHT=200></APPLET></HTML>
```

After you compile and execute this applet, your screen will display an applet window similar to Figure 27.2.

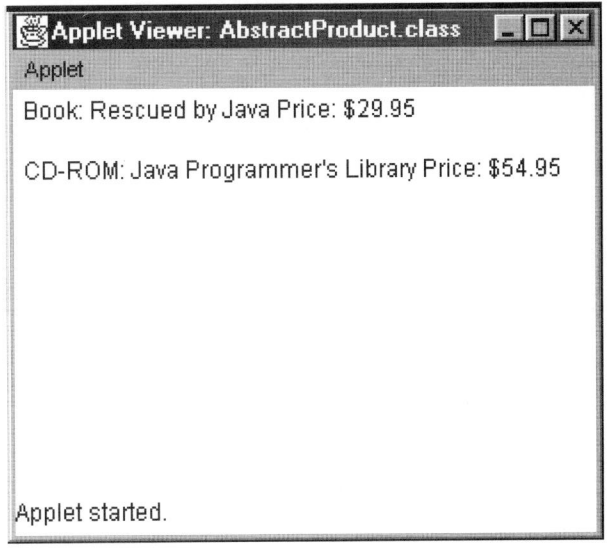

Figure 27.2 Extending the abstract Product class.

TAKING A CYBER FIELD TRIP

If you develop applets for distribution across the Web, you may eventually have to create digitally-signed applets that confirm to the user that you actually created the applet and that the applet has not changed (due to a virus or a hacker) since you posted the applet. Before you can digitally sign your applets, however, you must obtain a digital signature, which you can get from the Verisign Web site, shown in Figure 27.3.

*Figure 27.3 You can purchase a digital signature from Verisign at **www.verisign.com**.*

WHAT YOU MUST KNOW

To reduce your coding, your applets can take advantage of classes written by you or another programmer. By extending an existing class definition, your new class has access to each of the variables and functions the *super* class defines. In some cases, however, it may not make sense for a *super* class to define specific methods. In such cases, the super class can specify the method as *abstract* which means a subclass that extends the *super* class must implement the method. This lesson examined abstract classes in detail. In Lesson 28, "Understanding Class Interfaces," you will learn how to use Java interfaces, which are quite similar to abstract classes. However, using interfaces, your applets can extend multiple classes. Before you continue with Lesson 28, however, make sure you have learned the following key concepts:

☑ An abstract class is a class that contains one or more abstract methods.

☑ An abstract method is a class function for which the class does not implement the function. Instead, the class simply specifies the function name and type.

☑ A class that extends an abstract class must implement each of the abstract methods.

LESSON 28

UNDERSTANDING CLASS INTERFACES

In Lesson 26, "Using Inheritance," you learned that Java lets you create subclasses that inherit member variables and methods from a *super* class. When you extend a subclass from a *super* class in this way, Java lets you extend only one class. In other words, Java will not let a class extend two *super* classes. For example, assume that you have a *Coordinates* class that stores x-and-y coordinates, and a *Shapes* class that stores foreground and background color information, as well as a drawing function. Java will not let you extend both of these classes within a class definition to build a new *Rectangle* class. That is because each Java class can have only one *super* class.

It makes sense, however, that if you have existing classes, such as *Coordinates* and *Shapes,* that you be able to use the classes to build new classes. In this lesson, you will learn that by using Java *interfaces*, you can combine multiple classes as you desire. By the time you finish this lesson, you will understand the following key concepts:

◆ A Java *interface* is similar to an abstract class with the exception that each method within the interface is abstract.

◆ A class that uses an interface must *implement* each of the *abstract* functions.

◆ A class can extend one class while implementing one or more interfaces.

CREATING A JAVA INTERFACE

In Lesson 27, "Understanding and Using Abstract Classes," you learned that an abstract class is a class that contains one or more abstract methods which a class that extends the abstract class must implement. A Java interface is similar to an abstract class, with the exception that with an interface, all the methods must be *abstract*. As you can see here, an interface definition appears very much like a class definition, the difference being that you substitute the keyword *interface* for *class*:

```
public interface InterfaceName
    {
        // Abstract methods
    }
```

An interface, like a class, can have methods as well as variables. The difference between class-member variables and those within an interface, however, is that interface-member variables must be *static* and *final,* as shown here:

```
static final int member = 1001;
```

The *final* keyword in a variable declaration states that a variable contains a constant value that cannot change as the applet executes. The following statement creates a *Shapes* interface that contains two abstract methods:

```
interface Shapes
  {
    abstract double getArea();
    abstract double getPerimeter();
  }
```

To use an interface, a class must implement the corresponding abstract functions. Within the header of the class that uses the interface, the class must specify the *implements* keyword, as shown here:

```
public class ClassName implements InterfaceName
  {
       // Statements
  }
```

The following applet, *ShapesInterface.java*, creates a *Square* class that implements the *Shapes* interface:

```
import java.awt.*;
import java.applet.*;

public class ShapesInterface extends Applet
  {
     interface Shapes
       {
          abstract double getArea();
          abstract double getPerimeter();
       }

     class Square implements Shapes
       {
          public int x, y;
          public int width, height;
          public double getArea() { return (width * height); }
          public double getPerimeter() { return (2 * width + 2 * height); }

          public Square(int x, int y, int width, int height)
            {
               this.x = x;
               this.y = y;
               this.width = width;
               this.height = height;
            }
       }

     class Circle implements Shapes
       {
          public int x, y;
          public int width, height;
          public double r;
          public double getArea() { return (r * r * Math.PI); }
          public double getPerimeter() { return (2 * Math.PI * r); }
```

```
    public Circle(int x, int y, int width, int height)
      {
        this.x = x;
        this.y = y;
        this.width = width;
        this.height = height;
        r = (double) width / 2.0;
      }
  }

Square Box = new Square(5, 15, 25, 25);
Circle Oval = new Circle(5, 50, 25, 25);

public void paint(Graphics g)
  {
    g.drawRect(Box.x, Box.y, Box.width, Box.height);
    g.drawString("Area: " + Box.getArea(), 50, 35);
    g.drawOval(Oval.x, Oval.y, Oval.width, Oval.height);
    g.drawString("Area: " + Oval.getArea(), 50, 70);
  }
}
```

As you can see, the *Square* and *Circle* classes implement the *Shape* interface by defining the *Shape* class abstract methods. To run the applet, place the following HTML entries within the file *ShapesInterface.HTML*:

```
<HTML><TITLE>ShapesInterface Applet</TITLE>
<APPLET CODE="ShapesInterface.class" WIDTH=300 HEIGHT=200></APPLET></HTML>
```

After you compile and execute this applet, your screen will display an applet window similar to Figure 28.1.

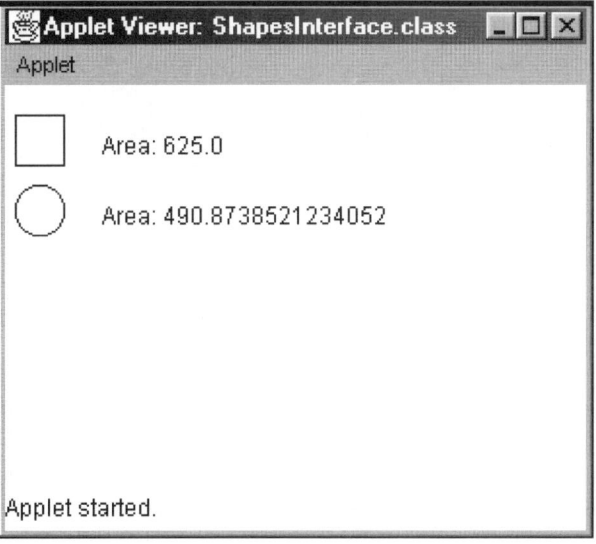

Figure 28.1 Implementing a Java interface.

EXTENDING AND IMPLEMENTING CLASSES

If you examine the previous applet, you will find that the definition for the *Square* class specifies x-and-y coordinates similar to those available within the *Coordinates* class as shown here:

```
class Coordinates
  {
    int x, y;

    public Coordinates(int x, int y)
     {
       this.x = x;
       this.y = y;
     }
  }
```

As you have learned, Java lets a class definition extend only one class at a time. However, Java will let you extend one class while you implement others. For example, the following *Square* class extends the *Coordinates* class while implementing the *Shapes* class:

```
class Square extends Coordinates implements Shapes
  {
    public int width, height;
    public double getArea() { return (width * height); }
    public double getPerimeter() { return (2 * width + 2 * height); }
    public Square(int x, int y, int width, int height)
     {
       super(x, y);
       this.width = width;
       this.height = height;
     }
  }
```

The following applet, *ExtendAndImplement.java*, illustrates the use of the *Square* class:

```
import java.awt.*;
import java.applet.*;

interface Shapes
  {
    abstract double getArea();
    abstract double getPerimeter();
  }

class Coordinates
  {
    int x, y;
```

```
      public Coordinates(int x, int y)
       {
         this.x = x;
         this.y = y;
       }
   }


class Square extends Coordinates implements Shapes
   {
      public int width, height;
      public double getArea() { return (width * height); }
      public double getPerimeter() { return (2 * width + 2 * height); }

      public Square(int x, int y, int width, int height)
         {
           super(x, y);
           this.width = width;
           this.height = height;
         }
   }


class Circle extends Coordinates implements Shapes
   {
      public int width, height;
      public double r;
      public double getArea() { return (r * r * Math.PI); }
      public double getPerimeter() { return (2 * Math.PI * r); }
      public Circle(int x, int y, int width, int height)
         {
           super(x, y);
           this.width = width;
           this.height = height;
           r = (double) width / 2.0;
         }
   }


public class ExtendAndImplement extends Applet
   {
      Square Box = new Square(5, 15, 25, 25);
      Circle Oval = new Circle(5, 50, 25, 25);

      public void paint(Graphics g)
         {
           g.drawRect(Box.x, Box.y, Box.width, Box.height);
           g.drawString("Area: " + Box.getArea(), 50, 35);
           g.drawOval(Oval.x, Oval.y, Oval.width, Oval.height);
           g.drawString("Area: " + Oval.getArea(), 50, 70);
         }

   }
```

As you can see, both the *Square* and *Circle* class definitions extend the *Coordinates* class while implementing the *Shapes* interface. To run the applet, place the following HTML entries within the file *ExtendAndImplement.HTML*:

```
<HTML><TITLE>ExtendAndImplement Applet</TITLE>
<APPLET CODE="ExtendAnd|Implement.class" WIDTH=300 HEIGHT=200></APPLET><HTML>
```

TAKING A CYBER FIELD TRIP

As you create Java programs or examine programs you encounter in books, magazines, or on the Web, you must eventually look up a specific class or function within the Java documentation. To help you find the information you need, Sun Microsystems provides extensive online documentation at their Web site. For information on the Java class libraries, for example, you can visit *http://java.sun.com/products/jdk/1.2/docs/api/index.html* shown in Figure 28.2.

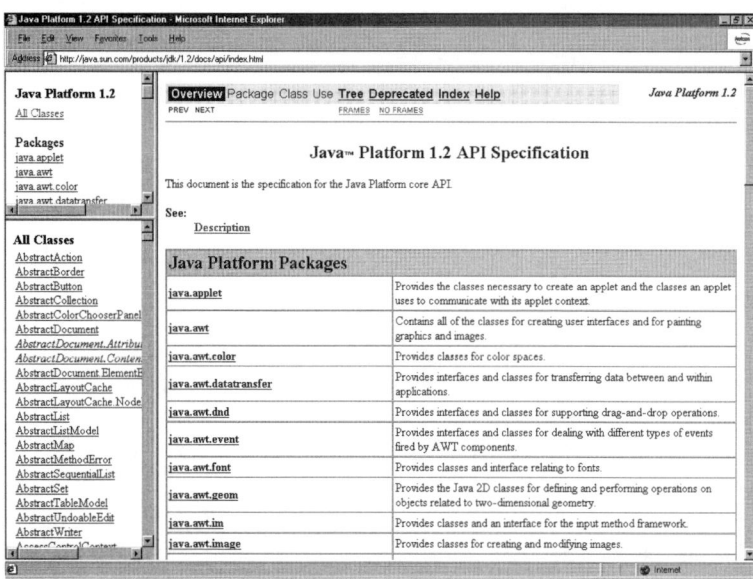

Figure 28.2 *Viewing online documentation at the Sun Microsystems' Java Web site.*

WHAT YOU MUST KNOW

Multiple inheritance is the ability of a class to inherit members from two or more classes. As you have learned, within Java, a class inherits members from its super class by extending the class. Java will let a class extend only one super class. A class cannot extend two or more classes to achieve multiple inheritance. Instead, Java lets an interface extend multiple interfaces. Then, a class can implement the interface and gain access to the members of each interface the interface extended—achieving something similar to multiple inheritance in a roundabout way.

This lesson examined Java interface classes in detail. In Lesson 29, "Understanding Mouse Operations," you will learn how to respond to mouse-click operations and mouse movements within a Java applet. Before you continue with Lesson 29, however, make sure that you have learned the following key concepts:

☑ A Java interface is similar to an abstract class with the exception that each method within the interface is abstract. Abstract classes, on the other hand, can have defined and abstract methods.

☑ Classes that use an interface must implement the interface.

☑ Within your applet, you can define a class that extends one class and implements one or more interfaces.

LESSON 29

UNDERSTANDING MOUSE OPERATIONS

One of the key factors that makes Java applets successful is their user interaction. In a graphical environment, most user interaction occurs through mouse operations. As your Java applets increase in complexity, the applets must let the user click his or her mouse on screen objects and drag objects from one location on the screen to another. This lesson examines how you perform mouse operations in Java. By the time you finish this lesson, you will understand the following key concepts:

♦ When the user performs a mouse operation within a Java applet, Java will generate a mouse event.

♦ Within a Java applet, you can capture mouse movements and mouse click operations.

♦ Within an applet, you can detect three basic mouse-click operations: *mousePressed*, *mouseReleased*, and *mouseClicked*. You can also determine when the user has moved the mouse into or out of an object's (such as the applet window) space.

♦ Within an applet, you can also detect mouse-motion operations that correspond to the user moving or dragging the mouse over an object.

♦ When Java detects a mouse operation, Java generates an event to which your applet can respond. Within your applet, you define functions that correspond to each mouse-event type.

♦ When Java calls an applet's mouse-event function, Java passes the function a *MouseEvent* object whose members specify the x-and-y coordinates of the mouse pointer when the event occurred, a mouse click count, and the object for which the event occurred.

♦ By comparing the x-and-y mouse-pointer coordinates to the coordinates of screen objects, an applet can determine if the user has clicked the mouse on a specific screen object.

UNDERSTANDING MOUSE EVENTS

Within a Java applet, user-mouse operations result in events for which Java calls applet-defined functions. For example, when the user moves the mouse with the mouse-select button held down, Java will automatically call the *mouseDragged* function. When the user holds down the mouse button, Java will call the applet's *mousePressed* function. Likewise, when the user releases the mouse button, Java will call the *mouseReleased* function. In each case, Java passes to the function a *MouseEvent* object that contains information, such as the x-and-y coordinates of the mouse pointer at the time of the event. By comparing the mouse pointer's x-and-y coordinates with the coordinates of screen objects, your applet can determine if the user has clicked the mouse on a specific object.

As a rule, the greater the flexibility programmers build into an object, the more complex the object's code becomes. Mouse operations within Java are a perfect example of such complexity. For example, early versions of Java supported three mouse operations, *mouseUp*, *mouseDown*, and *mouseDrag*, which only the applet could process. As the Java developers expanded Java's user interface, they recognized that within an applet, many different objects may have to respond to mouse operations and perform specific processing. For example, a dialog-box object might respond to a mouse-drag operation differently than a menu object or the applet itself. By expanding the mouse capabilities, the Java developers also increased the complexity of mouse operations.

Before a Java applet can respond to mouse events, you must tell the applet that it should "listen for" such events by implementing the *MouseListener* class within your applet. To implement the *MouseListener* class, you must first include the text *implements MouseListener* within your applet header, as shown here:

```
public class MouseOperations extends Applet implements MouseListener
```

Next, you must define the *mousePressed*, *mouseReleased*, *mouseClicked*, *mouseEntered*, and *mouseExited* functions within your applet. The following applet, *MouseOperations.java*, illustrates how to listen for and respond to mouse operations:

```java
import java.awt.*;
import java.awt.event.MouseEvent;
import java.awt.event.MouseListener;
import java.applet.*;

public class MouseOperations extends Applet implements MouseListener
  {
     String MousePressedEvent = null;
     String MouseReleasedEvent = null;
     String MouseEnteredEvent = null;
     String MouseExitedEvent = null;
     String MouseClickedEvent = null;

     public void mouseReleased(MouseEvent event)
       {
          MouseReleasedEvent = "mouseReleased: " +
             event.getX() + "," + event.getY();
          repaint();
       }

     public void mousePressed(MouseEvent event)
       {
          MousePressedEvent = "mousePressed: " +
             event.getX() + "," + event.getY();
          repaint();
       }

     public void mouseEntered(MouseEvent event)
       {
          MouseEnteredEvent = "mouseEntered: " +
             event.getX() + "," + event.getY();
          repaint();
       }

     public void mouseExited(MouseEvent event)
       {
          MouseExitedEvent = "mouseExited: " +
             event.getX() + "," + event.getY();
          repaint();
       }
```

```
    public void mouseClicked(MouseEvent event)
      {
          MouseClickedEvent = "mouseClicked: " +
            event.getX() + "," + event.getY();
          repaint();
      }


    public void paint(Graphics g)
      {
          addMouseListener(this);

          if (MouseReleasedEvent != null)
            g.drawString(MouseReleasedEvent, 5, 15);

          if (MousePressedEvent != null)
            g.drawString(MousePressedEvent, 5, 45);

          if (MouseEnteredEvent != null)
            g.drawString(MouseEnteredEvent, 5, 75);

          if (MouseExitedEvent != null)
            g.drawString(MouseExitedEvent, 5, 105);
      }
  }
```

As you can see, the *MouseOperations* applet implements the *MouseListener* class and defines functions to process each mouse event.

Within each function, the applet simply creates a *String* that contains the x-and-y coordinates of the mouse event. Then, using the *repaint* function, the applet updates the applet window's contents. In this case, the applet uses only the *MouseEvent* class *getX* and *getY* methods.

If you examine the Java documentation, you will find that the *MouseEvent* class provides additional member variables and methods your applets can use to determine more information about the event, such as the object initiating the event or the current mouse-click count.

To run the applet, place the following HTML entries within the file *MouseOperations.HTML*:

```
<HTML><TITLE>MouseOperations Applet</TITLE>
<APPLET CODE="MouseOperations.class" WIDTH=300 HEIGHT=200></APPLET></HTML>
```

After you compile and execute this applet, your screen will display an applet window similar to that shown in Figure 29.1, which shows the mouse coordinates for each operation.

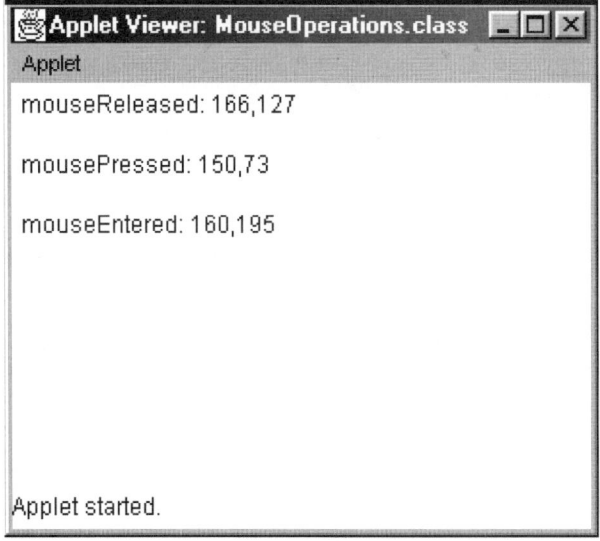

Figure 29.1 *Displaying the x-and-y mouse-pointer coordinates that correspond to a mouse operation.*

DETECTING MOUSE MOTION

In the previous applet, you learned how to respond to mouse events. As you might guess, to respond to mouse movements, such as a mouse drag operation, requires significant processing (and overhead). Each time the user moves the mouse, regardless of how slight the movement, your applet must respond to a series of mouse-motion events. To reduce such overhead, the *MouseListener* class does not respond to mouse movements. Instead, if you want your applet to respond each time the user moves the mouse, your applet must implement the *MouseMotionListener* class. The following applet, *MouseMovements.java*, uses the *MouseMotionListener* class to detect mouse movements:

```java
import java.awt.*;
import java.awt.event.MouseEvent;
import java.awt.event.MouseMotionListener;
import java.applet.*;

public class MouseMovements extends Applet implements MouseMotionListener
   {
   String MouseMovedEvent = null;
   String MouseDraggedEvent = null;

   public void mouseMoved(MouseEvent event)
     {
       MouseMovedEvent = "mouseMoved: " +
         event.getX() + "," + event.getY();
       repaint();
     }

   public void mouseDragged(MouseEvent event)
     {
       MouseDraggedEvent = "mouseDragged: " +
         event.getX() + "," + event.getY();
       repaint();
     }
```

```
    public void paint(Graphics g)
    {
        addMouseMotionListener(this);

        if (MouseMovedEvent != null)
          g.drawString(MouseMovedEvent, 5, 15);

        if (MouseDraggedEvent != null)
          g.drawString(MouseDraggedEvent, 5, 45);
    }
}
```

To run this applet, place the following HTML entries within the file *MouseMovements.HTML*:

```
<HTML><TITLE>MouseMovements Applet</TITLE>
<APPLET CODE="MouseMovements.class" WIDTH=300 HEIGHT=200></APPLET></HTML>
```

After you compile and execute this applet, your screen will display an applet window similar to that shown in Figure 29.2, which shows information about mouse-movement operations.

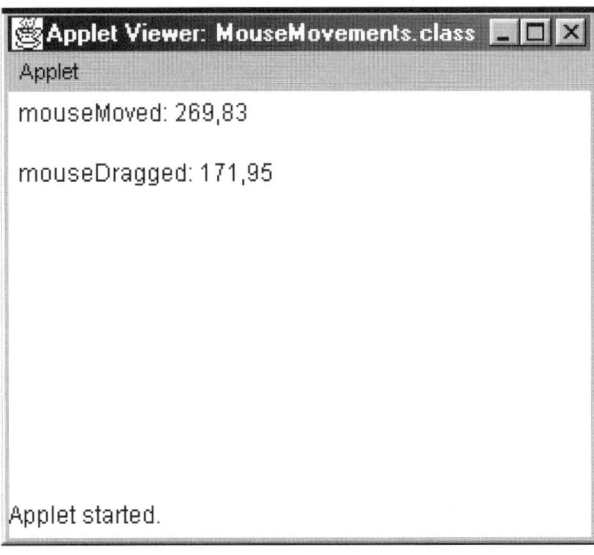

Figure 29.2 Displaying information about mouse-movement operations.

TAKING A CYBER FIELD TRIP

As the programs or class libraries that you create become larger and more complex, you may eventually have to produce documentation other programmers can use to understand your classes or applets. To help you build your documentation from your program's existing comments, the Java Development Kit provides a special program called *JavaDoc*. For information on how to use *JavaDoc*, visit the Sun Microsystems' Web site at *java.sun.com/products/jdk/ javadoc/index.html* as shown in Figure 29.3.

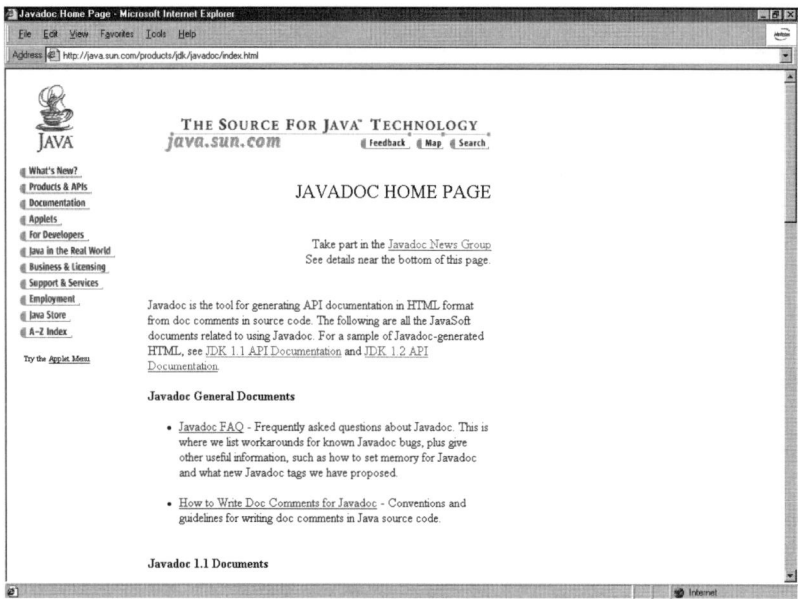

Figure 29.3 The JavaDoc utility helps you automate your program's documentation.

WHAT YOU MUST KNOW

As your applets become more complex, they must let the user click on screen objects or drag an object from one location on the screen to another. In this lesson, you learned how your applets respond to mouse events. Using the *MouseListener* and *MouseMotionListener* classes, your applets can implement most of the mouse operations they will require. In Lesson 30, "Performing Dialog-Box Operations," you will learn how to create dialog boxes which contain text boxes, checkboxes, radio buttons, and pull-down menus. Before you continue with Lesson 30, however, make sure that you have learned the following key concepts:

☑ If your applet implements the *MouseListener* or *MouseMotionListener* classes, Java will generate an event for each mouse operation the user performs for which your applet must respond.

☑ To handle a mouse event, the applet must define a function that corresponds to each of the events.

☑ Each time Java calls an applet's mouse-event function, Java passes to the function a *MouseEvent* object that contains information, such as the x-and-y coordinates of the mouse pointer when the event occurred.

☑ To determine if the user has clicked the mouse on a specific screen object, an applet simply compares the mouse pointer's x-and-y coordinates at the time of the event to the coordinates of known screen objects.

LESSON 30

PERFORMING DIALOG-BOX OPERATIONS

As your applets become more complex, so too will their user input and output operations. Because most users are familiar with buttons, menus, checkboxes, and text fields, you should try to structure your applet's input fields by using these familiar objects. In this lesson, you will learn how to display menus, buttons, checkboxes, and text fields within your applets. By the time you finish this lesson, you will understand the following key concepts:

♦ Java provides several input objects that are similar to those you would find in a dialog box.

♦ To display buttons within an applet window, you create a *Button* object.

♦ To display checkboxes within an applet window, you create a *Checkbox* object.

♦ To display a pop-up menu within an applet window, you create a *Choice* object.

♦ To display a text field within an applet window, you create a *TextField* object.

♦ To respond to *Button*, *Checkbox*, *Choice*, and *TextField* events, your applet must implement an *ActionListener* or *ItemListener*.

DISPLAYING AND RESPONDING TO BUTTONS

Within windows-based environments, users expect to click on buttons, select items from menus, and to type text within a text field. In this lesson, you will learn to use buttons, menus, and text fields within your Java applets. To start, you can use *Button* objects similar to those shown in Figure 30.1.

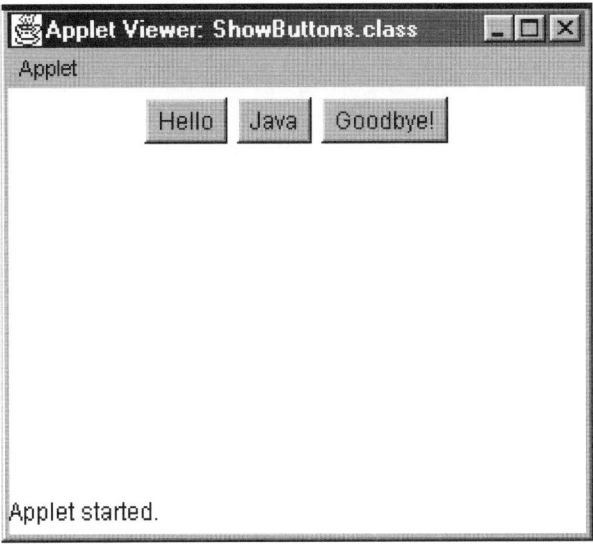

Figure 30.1 Displaying *Button* objects within an applet window.

To display a *Button* object within your applet, you use the *add* function, as shown here:

```
add(new Button("Java"));
```

251

In this case, the *add* function call uses the *new* operator to create a *Button* object that contains the text *Java* as a label. The *add* function then displays the button within the applet window. The following applet, *ShowButtons.java*, uses the add function to display the buttons, as shown in Figure 30.1.

```
import java.awt.*;
import java.applet.*;

public class ShowButtons extends Applet
  {
    public void init()
      {
        add(new Button("Hello"));
        add(new Button("Java"));
        add(new Button("Goodbye!"));
      }
  }
```

As you can see, the applet uses the *add* function to display the new *Button* objects within the applet window. To run the applet, place the following HTML entries within the file *ShowButtons.HTML*:

```
<HTML><TITLE>ShowButtons Applet</TITLE>
<APPLET CODE="ShowButtons.class" WIDTH=300 HEIGHT=200></APPLET></HTML>
```

After you compile and execute this applet, your screen will display an applet window that contains the buttons. Using your mouse, you can click on each button. However, clicking on a button will have no effect. That is because you must tell Java what actions you want the applet to perform when the user clicks on a button, as discussed later in this lesson.

The previous applet displayed buttons within the applet window, but did not create *Button* objects for the code to manipulate. The following applet, *UseButtonClass.java*, changes the previous applet slightly to create *Button* objects. Later in this lesson, you will use *Button* objects to respond to user's mouse clicks:

```
import java.awt.*;
import java.applet.*;

public class UseButtonClass extends Applet
  {
    public void init()
      {
        Button HelloButton = new Button("Hello");
        Button JavaButton = new Button("Java");
        Button GoodbyeButton = new Button("Goodbye!");

        add(HelloButton);
        add(JavaButton);
        add(GoodbyeButton);
      }
  }
```

To run the applet, place the following HTML entries within the file *UseButtonClasss.HTML*:

```
<HTML><TITLE>UseButtonClass Applet</TITLE>
<APPLET CODE="UseButtonClass.class" WIDTH=300 HEIGHT=200></APPLET></HTML>
```

Each of the previous applets displayed buttons within the applet window. However, neither applet processed the button operations. Before your applet can detect and handle button operations, your applet must first tell Java to listen for button events by implementing an *ActionListener* object. The following *MyButtonListener* class implements an *ActionListener* by defining the *actionPerformed* method:

```
class MyButtonListener implements ActionListener
  {
    public void actionPerformed(ActionEvent event)
      {
        // Method statements go here
      }
  }
```

Next, each button must call the *addActionListener* method to register the class the button will use to respond to an *ActionEvent*:

```
HelloButton.addActionListener(new MyButtonListener());
JavaButton.addActionListener(new MyButtonListener());
GoodbyeButton.addActionListener(new MyButtonListener());
```

The following applet, *HandleButtons.java*, displays the buttons previously shown in Figure 30.1. Each time the user clicks his or her mouse on a button, the applet displays a message that contains a count of the number of button operations the applet has processed:

```
import java.awt.*;
import java.applet.*;
import java.awt.event.*;

public class HandleButtons extends Applet
  {
    int counter = 0;

    public void init()
      {
        Button HelloButton = new Button("Hello");
        Button JavaButton = new Button("Java");
        Button GoodbyeButton = new Button("Goodbye!");

        HelloButton.addActionListener(new MyButtonListener());
        JavaButton.addActionListener(new MyButtonListener());
        GoodbyeButton.addActionListener(new MyButtonListener());

        add(HelloButton);
        add(JavaButton);
        add(GoodbyeButton);
      }
```

```
class MyButtonListener implements ActionListener
{
    public void actionPerformed(ActionEvent event)
    {
        ++counter;
        repaint();
    }
}

public void paint(Graphics g)
{
    g.drawString("Button Event: " + counter, 5, 100);
}
}
```

Each time the user clicks his or her mouse on a button, Java generates an *ActionEvent* to which the *actionPerformed* method responds. Within the *actionPerformed* function, the code simply increments a counter and then calls the *repaint* function to update the applet window's contents.

To run the applet, place the following HTML entries within the file *HandleButtons.HTML*:

```
<HTML><TITLE>HandleButtons Applet</TITLE>
<APPLET CODE="HandleButtons.class" WIDTH=600 HEIGHT=200></APPLET></HTML>
```

Normally, when a user clicks his or her mouse on a button, the applet will perform processing specific to the button. The following applet, *SpecificButton.java*, determines which -button the user selected and then displays a message that specifies the button name:

```
import java.awt.*;
import java.applet.*;
import java.awt.event.*;

public class SpecificButton extends Applet
{
    String ButtonPushed = null;

    Button HelloButton = new Button("Hello");
    Button JavaButton = new Button("Java");
    Button GoodbyeButton = new Button("Goodbye!");

    public void init()
    {
        HelloButton.addActionListener(new MyButtonListener());
        JavaButton.addActionListener(new MyButtonListener());
        GoodbyeButton.addActionListener(new MyButtonListener());

        add(HelloButton);
        add(JavaButton);
        add(GoodbyeButton);
    }
```

```
class MyButtonListener implements ActionListener
  {
     public void actionPerformed(ActionEvent event)
       {
          if (event.getSource().equals(HelloButton))
            ButtonPushed = "Hello";
          else if (event.getSource().equals(JavaButton))
            ButtonPushed = "Java";
          else if (event.getSource().equals(GoodbyeButton))
            ButtonPushed = "Goodbye";

          repaint();
       }


    public void paint(Graphics g)
      {
         if (ButtonPushed != null)
           g.drawString("Button Event: " + ButtonPushed, 5, 100);
      }
  }
```

As you can see, within the *actionPerformed* method, the code calls the *event.getSource* method that returns the object that triggered the action. The code uses the *equals* method to determine which button object triggered the action. The *equals* method compares two objects (not the object's contents, but the actual objects) to determine if the object of the objects are one and the same. In contrast, the equal sign operator (==) would compare two object's contents (two *String* objects, for example, could contain the same text).

To run the applet, place the following HTML entries within the file *SpecificButton.HTML*:

```
<HTML><TITLE>SpecificButtons Applet</TITLE>
<APPLET CODE="SpecificButtons.class" WIDTH=300 HEIGHT=200></APPLET></HTML>
```

DISPLAYING AND HANDLING CHECKBOXES

As your applets become more complex, there will be times when you may want the user to select one or more options. In such cases, your applet can display checkboxes, as shown in Figure 30.2.

To display checkboxes within an applet, you use the *add* function to place a *Checkbox* object within the applet window. The *Checkbox* class supports three constructor functions:

```
add(new Checkbox());           // Creates an empty unchecked box
add(new Checkbox("Label"));    // Creates a labeled unchecked box
add(new Checkbox("Label", Group, true);  // Creates a labeled checked box
```

You will examine *Checkbox* groups when you examine radio buttons in the next section. The following applet, *ShowCheckBoxes.java*, uses the *add* function to display the checkboxes as shown in Figure 30.2.

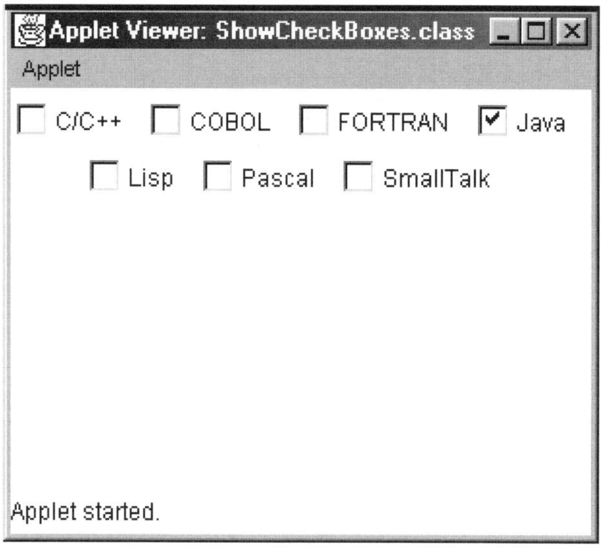

Figure 30.2 *Displaying checkboxes within an applet.*

```java
import java.awt.*;
import java.applet.*;

public class ShowCheckBoxes extends Applet
  {
    public void init()
      {
        add(new Checkbox("C/C++"));
        add(new Checkbox("COBOL"));
        add(new Checkbox("FORTRAN"));
        add(new Checkbox("Java", null, true));
        add(new Checkbox("Lisp"));
        add(new Checkbox("Pascal"));
        add(new Checkbox("SmallTalk"));
      }
  }
```

To run the applet, place the following HTML entries within the file *ShowCheckBoxes.HTML*:

```html
<HTML><TITLE>ShowCheckBoxes Applet</TITLE>
<APPLET CODE="ShowCheckBoxes.class" WIDTH=300 HEIGHT=200></APPLET></HTML>
```

As before, the *ShowCheckBoxes.java* applet displays checkboxes within the applet window without creating *Checkbox* objects the applet can manipulate. The following applet, *UseCheckboxClass.java*, creates several *Checkbox* objects and then displays each object within the applet window:

```java
import java.awt.*;
import java.applet.*;
```

```
public class UseCheckboxClass extends Applet
  {
    Checkbox c_cpp = new Checkbox("C/C++");
    Checkbox COBOL = new Checkbox("COBOL");
    Checkbox FORTRAN = new Checkbox("FORTRAN");
    Checkbox Java = new Checkbox("Java", null, true);
    Checkbox Lisp = new Checkbox("Lisp");
    Checkbox Pascal = new Checkbox("Pascal");
    Checkbox SmallTalk = new Checkbox("SmallTalk");

    public void init()
      {
        add(c_cpp);
        add(COBOL);
        add(FORTRAN);
        add(Java);
        add(Lisp);
        add(Pascal);
        add(SmallTalk);
      }
  }
```

To run the applet, place the following HTML entries within the file *UseCheckboxClass.HTML*:

```
<HTML><TITLE>UseCheckboxClass Applet</TITLE>
<APPLET CODE="UseCheckboxClass.class" WIDTH=300 HEIGHT=200></APPLET></HTML>
```

As before, the previous two applets displayed checkboxes within the applet window, but did not process checkbox operations. As was the case with *Button* objects, before your applet can respond to *Checkbox* operations, your applet must direct Java to listen for *Checkbox* events by implementing an *ItemListener* class. To implement an *ItemListener* class, you must implement the *itemStateChanged* method:

```
class MyItemListener implements ItemListener
  {
    public void itemStateChanged(ItemEvent event)
      {
        CheckboxEvent = event.paramString();
        repaint();
      }
  }
```

In this case, the *itemStateChanged* method calls the *ItemEvent* class *paramString* method that returns specifics about the *Checkbox* operation, such as the *Checkbox* name and whether the user selected or deselected the box.

The following applet, *HandleCheckboxes.java*, displays the checkboxes previously shown in Figure 30.2. In addition, each time the user clicks his or her mouse on a checkbox, the applet displays a message describing the event:

```
import java.awt.*;
import java.applet.*;
import java.awt.event.*;
```

```java
public class HandleCheckboxes extends Applet
  {
    String CheckboxEvent = null;

    Checkbox c_cpp = new Checkbox("C/C++");
    Checkbox COBOL = new Checkbox("COBOL");
    Checkbox FORTRAN = new Checkbox("FORTRAN");
    Checkbox Java = new Checkbox("Java", null, true);
    Checkbox Lisp = new Checkbox("Lisp");
    Checkbox Pascal = new Checkbox("Pascal");
    Checkbox SmallTalk = new Checkbox("SmallTalk");

    public void init()
      {
        add(c_cpp);
        add(COBOL);
        add(FORTRAN);
        add(Java);
        add(Lisp);
        add(Pascal);
        add(SmallTalk);

        c_cpp.addItemListener(new MyItemListener());
        COBOL.addItemListener(new MyItemListener());
        FORTRAN.addItemListener(new MyItemListener());
        Java.addItemListener(new MyItemListener());
        Lisp.addItemListener(new MyItemListener());
        Pascal.addItemListener(new MyItemListener());
        SmallTalk.addItemListener(new MyItemListener());
      }

    class MyItemListener implements ItemListener
      {
        public void itemStateChanged(ItemEvent event)
          {
            CheckboxEvent = event.paramString();
            repaint();
          }
      }

    public void paint(Graphics g)
      {
        if (CheckboxEvent != null)
          g.drawString("Checkbox event: " + CheckboxEvent, 5, 100);
      }
  }
```

To run the applet, place the following HTML entries within the file *HandleCheckboxesHTML*:

```
<HTML><TITLE>HandleCheckboxes Applet</TITLE>
<APPLET CODE="HandleCheckBoxes.class" WIDTH=600 HEIGHT=200></APPLET></HTML>
```

When your applets use *Checkbox* objects, your applets will normally want to perform specific processing when a user chooses a particular checkbox. The following applet, *SpecificCheckbox.java*, lets the applet determine which *Checkbox* the user selected or deselected:

```java
import java.awt.*;
import java.applet.*;
import java.awt.event.*;

public class SpecificCheckbox extends Applet
  {
    String CheckboxEvent = null;

    Checkbox c_cpp = new Checkbox("C/C++");
    Checkbox COBOL = new Checkbox("COBOL");
    Checkbox FORTRAN = new Checkbox("FORTRAN");
    Checkbox Java = new Checkbox("Java", null, true);
    Checkbox Lisp = new Checkbox("Lisp");
    Checkbox Pascal = new Checkbox("Pascal");
    Checkbox SmallTalk = new Checkbox("SmallTalk");

    public void init()
      {
        add(c_cpp);
        add(COBOL);
        add(FORTRAN);
        add(Java);
        add(Lisp);
        add(Pascal);
        add(SmallTalk);

        c_cpp.addItemListener(new MyItemListener());
        COBOL.addItemListener(new MyItemListener());
        FORTRAN.addItemListener(new MyItemListener());
        Java.addItemListener(new MyItemListener());
        Lisp.addItemListener(new MyItemListener());
        Pascal.addItemListener(new MyItemListener());
        SmallTalk.addItemListener(new MyItemListener());
      }

    class MyItemListener implements ItemListener
      {
        public void itemStateChanged(ItemEvent event)
          {
            CheckboxEvent = (String) event.getItem();
```

```
                if (event.getStateChange() == ItemEvent.SELECTED)
                  CheckboxEvent += " Selected";
                else
                  CheckboxEvent += " Deselected";

                repaint();
             }

      }
      public void paint(Graphics g)
        {
          if (CheckboxEvent != null)
             g.drawString("Checkbox event: " + CheckboxEvent, 5, 100);
        }
   }
```

As you can see, within the *itemStateChanged* method, the code uses the *ItemEvent* class *getItem* method to get the *Checkbox* label. Then, the code uses the *ItemEvent* class *getStateChange* method to determine if the user selected or deselected the checkbox. To run the applet, place the following HTML entries within the file *SpecificCheckbox.HTML*:

```
<HTML><TITLE>Specific Checkbox Applet</TITLE>
<APPLET CODE="SpecificCheckbox.class" WIDTH=600 HEIGHT=200></APPLET></HTML>
```

DISPLAYING AND HANDLING RADIO BUTTONS

Radio buttons are a special class of checkboxes for which you define a group of checkboxes, of which a user can select only one button at a time. To define the checkbox group, you create a *CheckboxGroup* object, as shown here:

```
CheckboxGroup RadioGroup = new CheckboxGroup();
```

The following applet, *HandleRadioButtons.java*, displays a group of radio buttons. As the user clicks his or her mouse on a button, the applet displays a message that specifies which button the user selected:

```
import java.awt.*;
import java.applet.*;
import java.awt.event.*;

public class HandleRadioButtons extends Applet
  {
    String CheckboxEvent = null;

    CheckboxGroup RadioButtons = new CheckboxGroup();

    Checkbox c_cpp = new Checkbox("C/C++", RadioButtons, false);
    Checkbox COBOL = new Checkbox("COBOL", RadioButtons, false);
    Checkbox FORTRAN = new Checkbox("FORTRAN", RadioButtons, false);
    Checkbox Java = new Checkbox("Java", RadioButtons, true);
    Checkbox Lisp = new Checkbox("Lisp", RadioButtons, false);
```

```
      Checkbox Pascal = new Checkbox("Pascal", RadioButtons, false);
      Checkbox SmallTalk = new Checkbox("SmallTalk", RadioButtons, false);

   public void init()
      {
         add(c_cpp);
         add(COBOL);
         add(FORTRAN);
         add(Java);
         add(Lisp);
         add(Pascal);
         add(SmallTalk);


         c_cpp.addItemListener(new MyItemListener());
         COBOL.addItemListener(new MyItemListener());
         FORTRAN.addItemListener(new MyItemListener());
         Java.addItemListener(new MyItemListener());
         Lisp.addItemListener(new MyItemListener());
         Pascal.addItemListener(new MyItemListener());
         SmallTalk.addItemListener(new MyItemListener());
      }

   class MyItemListener implements ItemListener
      {

      public void itemStateChanged(ItemEvent event)
         {
            CheckboxEvent = (String) event.getItem();
            CheckboxEvent += " Selected";

            repaint();
         }

      }
   public void paint(Graphics g)
      {
         if (CheckboxEvent != null)
            g.drawString("Checkbox event: " + CheckboxEvent, 5, 100);
      }
   }
```

To run the applet, place the following HTML entries within the file *HandleRadioButtons.HTML*:

```
<HTML><TITLE>HandleRadioButtons Applet</TITLE>
<APPLET CODE="HandleRadioButtons.class" WIDTH=600 HEIGHT=200></APPLET>
</HTML>
```

After you compile and execute this applet, your screen will display an applet window similar to that shown in Figure 30.3.

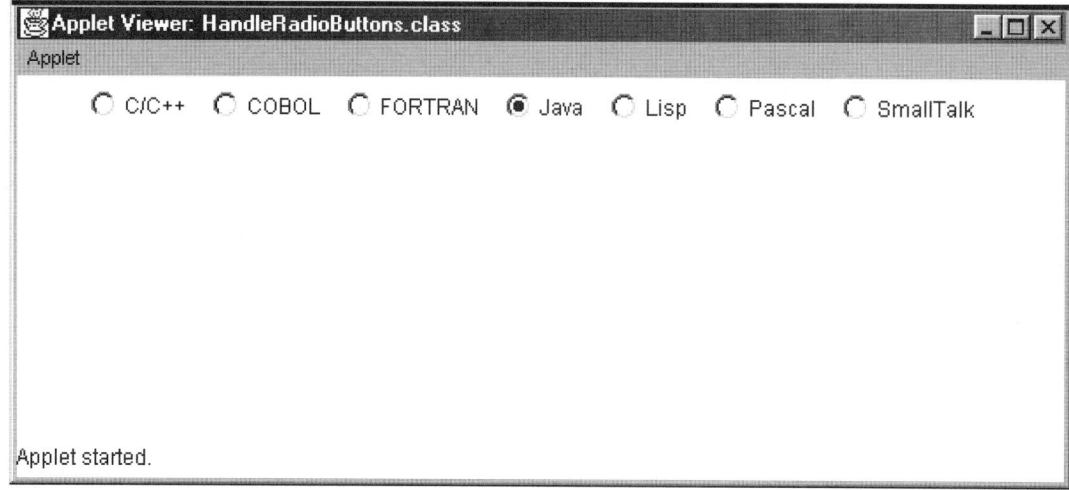

Figure 30.3 *Displaying and handling radio buttons.*

As you click your mouse on one radio button, the *CheckboxGroup* object will automatically select that button and deselect the previous button.

DISPLAYING AND RESPONDING TO MENU CHOICES

Users who work in a Windows or Mac environment are very familiar with pop-up menus. To display a pop-up menu within a Java applet, you create a *Choice* object:

```
Choice menu = new Choice();
```

Next, using the *Choice* class *addItem* method, you add options to the menu, as shown here:

```
menu.addItem("C/C++");
menu.addItem("COBOL");
menu.addItem("FORTRAN");
menu.addItem("Java");
menu.addItem("Lisp");
menu.addItem("Pascal");
menu.addItem("SmallTalk");
add(menu);
```

The following applet, *HandleMenu.java*, displays a menu of options, as shown in Figure 30.4. As the user selects different menu options, the applet displays the corresponding selection.

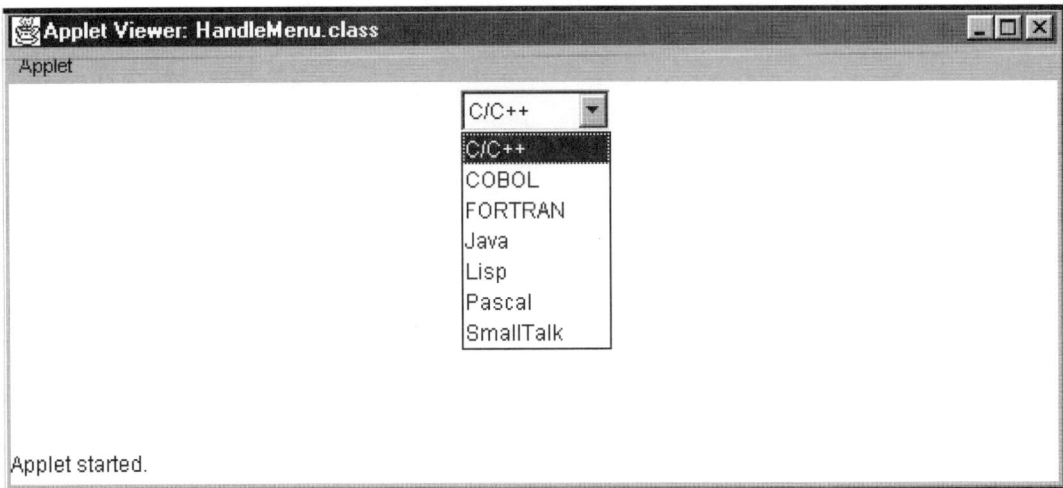

Figure 30.4 *Displaying a pop-up menu.*

The following statements implement the *HandleMenu.java* applet:

```java
import java.awt.*;
import java.applet.*;
import java.awt.event.*;

public class HandleMenu extends Applet
  {
    String MenuEvent = null;

    Choice menu = new Choice();

    public void init()
      {
        menu.add("C/C++");
        menu.add("COBOL");
        menu.add("FORTRAN");
        menu.add("Java");
        menu.add("Lisp");
        menu.add("Pascal");
        menu.add("SmallTalk");

        menu.addItemListener(new MyItemListener());
        add(menu);
      }

    class MyItemListener implements ItemListener
      {
        public void itemStateChanged(ItemEvent event)
          {
            MenuEvent = (String) event.getItem();
            MenuEvent += " Selected";
```

```
        repaint();
      }
   }

   public void paint(Graphics g)
     {
       if (MenuEvent != null)
         g.drawString("Menu event: " + MenuEvent, 5, 100);
     }
   }
```

As you can see, to respond to the user's menu selections, the applet implements an *ItemListener* class by defining the *itemStateChanged* method. Within the method, the code uses the *ItemEvent* class *getItem* method to return the label of the menu item the user has selected. To run the applet, place the following HTML entries within the file *HandleMenu.HTML*:

```
<HTML><TITLE>HandleMenu Applet</TITLE>
<APPLET CODE="HandleMenu.class" WIDTH=300 HEIGHT=200></APPLET></HTML>
```

HANDLING TEXT FIELDS

As your applets become more complex, you must eventually perform complex keyboard input. For example, you may need the user to type in his or her username, a filename, or even a Web address. To perform such input operations, you can display text fields similar to that shown in Figure 30.5.

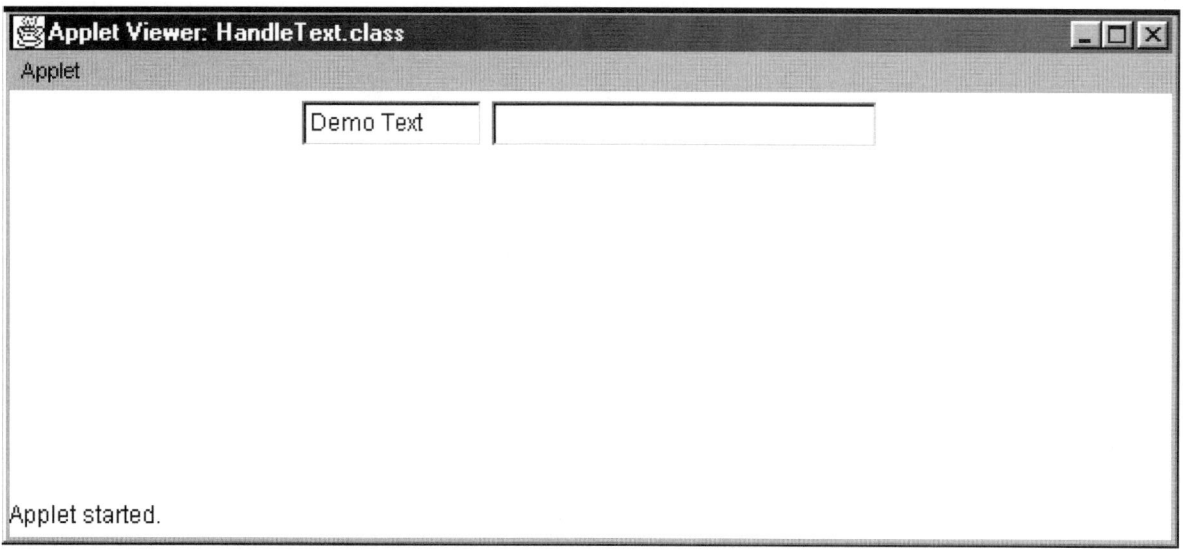

Figure 30.5 *Displaying a text field within an applet window.*

To display a text field, your applet creates a *TextField* object. The *TextField* class supports four different constructor functions:

```
add(new TextField());              // Empty field

add(new TextField(int));           // Creates a text field that can hold the
                                   // specified number of characters

add(new TextField(String));        // Creates a text field that contains the
                                   // specified string as a default

add(new TextField(String, int));   // Creates a text field that contains the
                                   // specified string and that can hold the
                                   // specified number of characters
```

The following applet, *HandleText.java*, displays the text fields shown in Figure 30.5. After the user types in the field's contents and presses ENTER, the applet displays the field's current text:

```java
import java.awt.*;
import java.applet.*;
import java.awt.event.*;

public class HandleText extends Applet
  {
    String TextEvent = null;

    TextField Text1 = new TextField("Demo Text", 10);
    TextField Text2 = new TextField(25);

    public void init()
      {
        Text1.addActionListener(new Text1ActionListener());
        add(Text1);

        Text2.addActionListener(new Text2ActionListener());
        add(Text2);
      }

    class Text1ActionListener implements ActionListener
      {
        public void actionPerformed(ActionEvent event)
          {
            TextEvent = "Text 1: " + event.getActionCommand();

            repaint();
          }
      }

    class Text2ActionListener implements ActionListener
      {
```

```
      public void actionPerformed(ActionEvent event)
        {
          TextEvent = "Text 2: " + event.getActionCommand();
          repaint();
        }
    }

    public void paint(Graphics g)
      {
        if (TextEvent != null)
          g.drawString(TextEvent, 5, 100);
      }
    }
```

As you can see, the applet implements an *ActionListener* for each *TextField* object. In this way, the applet can perform processing specific to a particular text field. To run the applet, place the following HTML entries within the file *HandleText.HTML*:

```
<HTML><TITLE>HandleText Applet</TITLE>
<APPLET CODE="HandleText.class" WIDTH=600 HEIGHT=200></APPLET></HTML>
```

TAKING A CYBER FIELD TRIP

Before you start programming a complex application, you should take time to search the Web for related information. Often, you will find that other programmers have developed software that may make your programming task easier. To start your search for Java components, visit the Jars.com Web site at *www.jars.com* as shown in Figure 30.6.

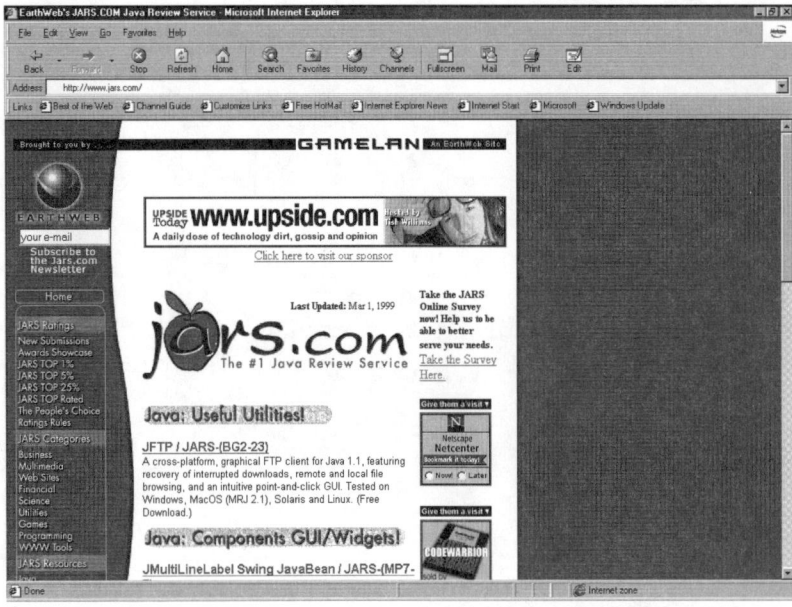

Figure 30.6 *Looking for Java components at **www.jars.com**.*

WHAT YOU MUST KNOW

As your applets become more complex, they must support button-, menu-, and text-based user input. In this lesson, you learned how to perform such operations within your applets. In Lesson 31, "Using Frames to Display Output," you will learn how to display output within a frame that is separate from the applet window. Before you continue with Lesson 31, however, make sure that you have learned the following key concepts:

☑ Using Java objects, your applets can create and use input fields that are similar to those you would find in a dialog box.

☑ Using a *Button* object, your applets can display buttons within an applet window.

☑ Using a *Checkbox* object, your applets can display checkboxes within an applet window.

☑ Using a *Choice* object, your applets can display a pop-up menu within an applet window.

☑ Using a *TextField* object, your applets can display text fields within an applet window.

LESSON 31

USING FRAMES TO DISPLAY OUTPUT

In Lesson 30, "Performing Dialog-Box Operations," you learned how to display buttons, checkboxes, menus, and text fields within an applet window. In this lesson, you will learn how to display an applet's or standalone application's output within a frame, which you can think of as a standalone window. Using a *Frame* object, you can build a graphical-user interface around your standalone Java applications. As you will learn, within a frame, you can display menus, buttons, checkboxes, and text fields. By the time you finish this lesson, you will understand the following key concepts:

◆   To display a frame within a standalone program, your program must extend the *Frame* class.

◆   Before a program can respond to window-based operations, such as the user clicking his or her mouse on the window's Close button, your applet must implement code that listens for window-based events.

◆   To display a frame within an applet, you simply create a *Frame* object.

◆   Within a frame, a Java program or applet can display buttons, checkboxes, menus, and text fields.

◆   To simplify file operations, Java provides a *FileDialog* class that displays a dialog box within which the user can select a file or directory.

DISPLAYING AND CLOSING A FRAME

As briefly discussed, you can think of a frame as a standalone window. The following Java application, *ShowFrame.java*, extends the *Frame* class to display a popup window similar to that shown in Figure 31.1.

*Figure 31.1 Displaying a popup window using a **Frame** object.*

The following statements implement the *ShowFrame.java* application:

```
import java.awt.*;
```

```
class ShowFrame extends Frame
  {
    static public void main(String args[])
      {
        Frame popUp = new Frame("Popup Window");

        popUp.setSize(200, 200);
        popUp.show();
      }
  }
```

In this case, the program simply displays an empty popup window. To close the window, you must end the applet by pressing CTRL-C on your keyboard within the application window (not the applet window). You cannot close the popup window by clicking your mouse on the window's Close button. That is because you have not yet implemented code to listen for window-based operations, as discussed next.

The following program, *CloseFrame.java*, implements the *MyWindowEventHandler* class that implements the *WindowAdapter* that listens for and responds to window-based events, such as the user clicking his or her mouse on a window's Close button:

```
import java.awt.*;
import java.awt.event.*;

class CloseFrame extends Frame
  {
    CloseFrame()
      {
        super();
        Frame popUp = new Frame("Popup Window");

        popUp.setSize(200, 200);
        popUp.addWindowListener(new MyWindowEventHandler());
        popUp.show();
      }

    public class MyWindowEventHandler extends WindowAdapter
      {
        public void windowClosing(WindowEvent event)
          {
            setVisible(false);
            dispose();
            System.exit(1);
          }
      }

    public static void main(String args[])
      {
        new CloseFrame();
      }
  }
```

As you can see, the program uses the *addWindowListener* method to register the class that will respond to window-based operations. Within the *MyWindowEventHandler* class, the code defines the *windowClosing* method which Java calls when the user clicks his or her mouse on a window's Close button. In this case, the method first hides the window (making it invisible) and then disposes of the *Frame* object. Finally, the method ends the application by calling the *System.exit* function.

DISPLAYING A FRAME WITHIN AN APPLET

The previous two programs have displayed a frame from within a standalone application. Java, however, also lets you display a frame from within an applet, which essentially creates a popup window. The following applet, *ShowAppletFrame.java*, displays the popup window, as shown in Figure 31.2.

Figure 31.2 Displaying a popup window from within an applet.

As before, you cannot close the popup window by clicking your mouse on the window's Close button. That is because the applet does not implement a class that listens for window-based events. To close the popup window, you must close the applet window. Note that the popup window contains a warning message that tells the user the window was created by an applet. The following code implements the *ShowAppletFrame.java* applet:

```
import java.awt.*;
import java.applet.*;

public class ShowAppletFrame extends Applet
  {
    Frame popUp = new Frame("Popup Window");

    public void init()
      {
        popUp.setSize(200, 200);
        popUp.show();
      }
  }
```

To run the applet, place the following HTML entries within the file *ShowAppletFrame.HTML*:

```
<HTML><TITLE>ShowAppletFrame Applet</TITLE>
<APPLET CODE="ShowAppletFrame.class" WIDTH=300 HEIGHT=200></APPLET></HTML>
```

USING BUTTONS WITHIN A FRAME

As discussed, you can treat a frame much as you would an applet window, meaning within a frame, you can display buttons, menus, checkboxes, and text fields. The following program, *FrameButtons.java*, for example, displays buttons within a frame, as shown in Figure 31.3.

Figure 31.3 *Displaying buttons within a frame.*

Although the program displays the buttons, the buttons are not yet active, meaning the program does not respond to a user's mouse clicks on a button. To respond to a button-click operation, you must implement an action listener, as discussed in Lesson 30. The following code implements the *FrameButtons.java* program:

```java
import java.awt.*;
import java.awt.event.*;

class FrameButtons extends Frame
  {
    FrameButtons()
      {
        super();
        Button JavaButton = new Button("Java");
        Button BookButton = new Button("Rescued by Java");

        setLayout(new FlowLayout(FlowLayout.LEFT));
        add(JavaButton);
        add(BookButton);

        setSize(400, 400);

        addWindowListener(new MyWindowEventHandler());

        show();
      }
```

```
    public class MyWindowEventHandler extends WindowAdapter
      {
        public void windowClosing(WindowEvent event)
          {
            setVisible(false);
            dispose();
            System.exit(1);
          }
      }

    public static void main(String args[])
      {
        new FrameButtons();
      }
  }
```

If you examine the *FrameButtons* constructor method, you will find that the code calls the *setLayout* method. When you work with *Frame* objects, you can specify a layout format that controls how and where Java displays objects (such as buttons) within the frame. For more information on layout formats, refer to the *LayoutManager* class within the Java documentation.

The following program, *HandleFrameButtons.java*, defines action listeners that respond to a user's button-click operations. Each time the user clicks his or her mouse on a button, the program reverses the order of the characters that appear in the button's label. For example, if the user clicks on the *Java Button*, the applet will change the button's label to *nottuB avaJ* by reversing the label's characters, as shown in Figure 31.4.

Figure 31.4 Reversing the characters that appear within a button's label.

```
import java.awt.*;
import java.awt.event.*;

class HandleFrameButtons extends Frame
  {
    Button JavaButton = new Button("Java Button");
    Button BookButton = new Button("Book Button");
    String ButtonLabel = null;
```

```
HandleFrameButtons()
  {
    super();

    JavaButton.addActionListener(new MyButtonListener());
    BookButton.addActionListener(new MyButtonListener());

    setLayout(new FlowLayout(FlowLayout.LEFT));

    add(JavaButton);
    add(BookButton);

    setSize(400, 400);

    addWindowListener(new MyWindowEventHandler());

    show();
  }

public class MyWindowEventHandler extends WindowAdapter
  {
    public void windowClosing(WindowEvent event)
      {
        setVisible(false);
        dispose();
        System.exit(1);
      }
  }


class MyButtonListener implements ActionListener
  {
    public void actionPerformed(ActionEvent event)
      {
        if (event.getSource().equals(JavaButton))
          {
            if (ButtonLabel == "Java Button")
              {
                ButtonLabel = "nottuB avaJ";
                JavaButton.setLabel(ButtonLabel);
              }
            else
              {
                ButtonLabel = "Java Button";
                JavaButton.setLabel(ButtonLabel);
              }

            JavaButton.invalidate();
            JavaButton.getParent().validate();
          }
```

```
            else if (event.getSource().equals(BookButton))
              {
                if (ButtonLabel == "Book Button")
                  {
                    ButtonLabel = "nottuB kooB";
                    BookButton.setLabel(ButtonLabel);
                  }
                else
                  {
                    ButtonLabel = "Book Button";
                    BookButton.setLabel(ButtonLabel);
                  }
                BookButton.invalidate();
                BookButton.getParent().validate();
              }
          }
      }

  public static void main(String args[])
    {
      new HandleFrameButtons();
    }
}
```

DISPLAYING A DIALOG BOX

In Lesson 33, "Understanding File Operations," you will learn how to perform simple file-based operations, such as displaying a file's contents to the screen. When you perform such operations, you can simplify your programming and improve your program's user interface by taking advantage of a file-based dialog box similar to that shown in Figure 31.5.

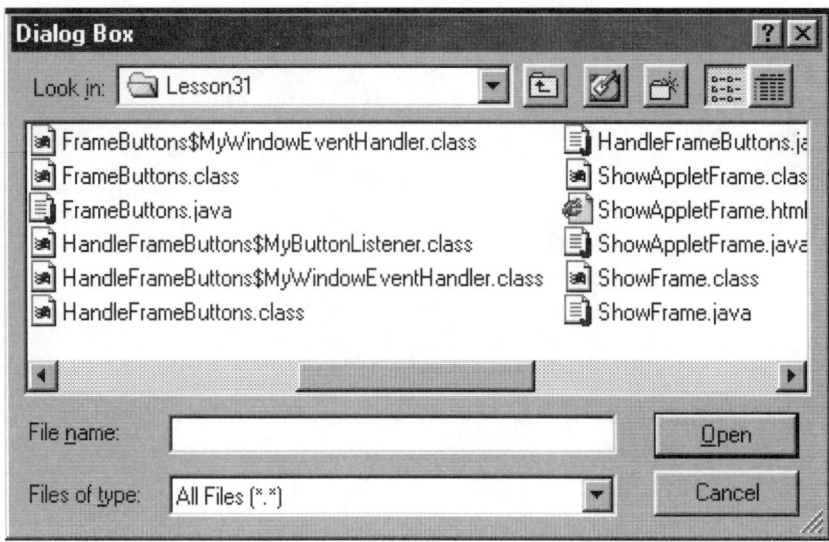

Figure 31.5 Displaying a file-based dialog box.

Using a file-based dialog box, you can let the user specify the name of a file he or she wants to open or the name of the file to which the user wants to store information. The following program, *DialogBox.java*, creates and displays the dialog box previously shown in Figure 31.5:

```java
import java.awt.*;
import java.awt.event.*;

class DialogBox extends Frame
   {
     FileDialog dialogBox;

     String Directory, File;

     DialogBox()
        {
          super();

          dialogBox = new FileDialog(this, "Dialog Box");
          dialogBox.show();

          Directory = dialogBox.getDirectory();
          File = dialogBox.getFile();
          System.exit(1);
        }

     public static void main(String args[])
        {
          new DialogBox();
        }
   }
```

As you can see, the program uses *FileDialog* class *getDirectory* and *getFile* methods to determine the file that the user selected. In this case, the program does not actually use the values but, instead, simply ends. In Lesson 33, however, you will use a *FileDialog* object to get the name of the file that a user wants to display.

TAKING A CYBER FIELD TRIP

As you learned in this lesson, when you place objects within a frame, you can specify a *FlowLayout* object that controls where and how Java will place the objects. To help you get started with *FlowLayout* objects, the Java Development Kit provides the Card Layout applet, as shown in Figure 31.6. When you run the applet, you can select different *FlowLayout* settings and view the effect on the button placement. To run the applet or to download the applet's source code, visit the Jamsa Press Web site at *www.jamsa.com/java_demos/CardLayout.html*.

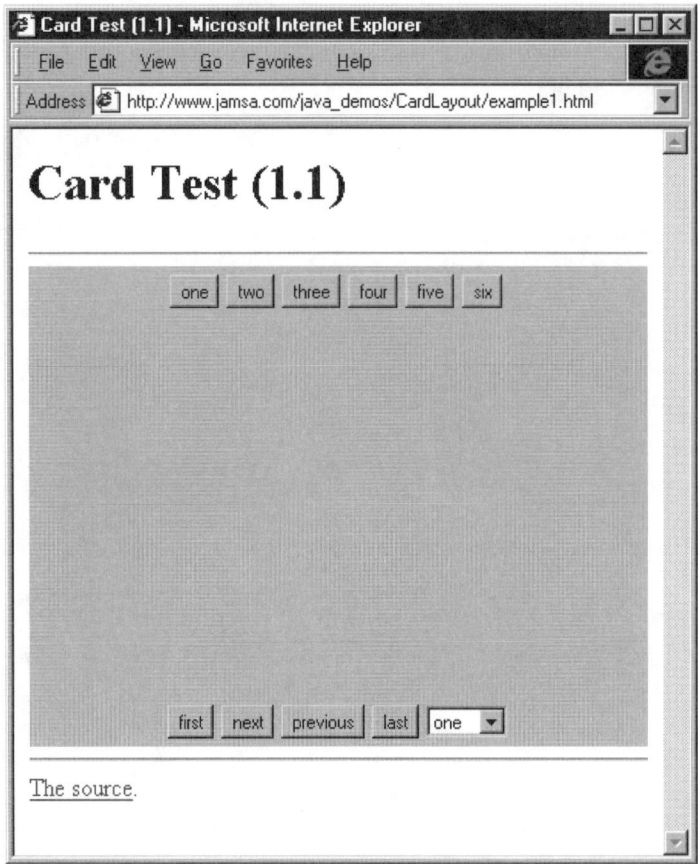

*Figure 31.6 Controlling button placements using a **FlowLayout** object.*

WHAT YOU MUST KNOW

If you use Java to create standalone programs, you can improve your program's user interface by displaying the program's output within a frame. Using frames, your programs can take advantage of buttons, checkboxes, menus, and text fields. Within a Java applet, you can use a frame to create a popup window. In Lesson 32, "Understanding Keyboard Operations," you will learn how to process a user's keystrokes within an applet. Before you continue with Lesson 32, however, make sure that you have learned the following key concepts:

☑ By extending the *Frame* class, a standalone Java program can display a frame object, within which the program can display its output.

☑ Before a user can close a frame by clicking his or her mouse on the frame's Close button, the program must implement code that listens for window-based events.

☑ If you create and display a *Frame* object within an applet, Java will create a popup window.

☑ Within a frame, a Java program or applet can display buttons, checkboxes, menus, and text fields.

☑ Using a *FileDialog* object, a Java applet or standalone application can display a dialog box within which the user can select a file or directory.

LESSON 32

UNDERSTANDING KEYBOARD OPERATIONS

In Lesson 29, "Understanding Mouse Operations," you learned how to handle mouse events within Java applets. As the complexity of your applets increases, there may be times when your applets must respond to keyboard events, such as the user's pressing of a function key. In this lesson, you will examine Java keyboard events. By the time you finish this lesson, you will understand the following key concepts:

♦ When the user performs a keyboard operation within your applet, Java treats the operation as a keyboard event.

♦ Before your applet can respond to a keyboard event, your applet must detect the event by implementing the *KeyListener* class.

♦ To implement the *KeyListener* class, your applet must define the *keyPressed*, *keyTyped*, and *keyReleased* methods.

♦ When Java responds to a keyboard event, Java passes one of the *KeyListener* methods a *KeyEvent* object.

♦ Using the *KeyEvent* class methods and data members, your applet can determine specifics about the key the user pressed.

UNDERSTANDING KEYBOARD EVENTS

Within an applet, Java treats keyboard operations as events to which the applet or Java itself must respond. As has been the case with other types of events, such as mouse or button events, before your applet can detect and respond to keyboard events, you must tell your applet to listen for the events. To direct your applet to listen for a *KeyEvent*, you must implement the *KeyListener* class by defining the *keyPressed*, *keyReleased*, and *keyTyped* methods.

The following applet, *KeyboardEvents.java*, illustrates how an applet listens for and then responds to a *KeyEvent*. When the user presses and releases a key, the applet will display a message that describes the event, as shown in Figure 32.1.

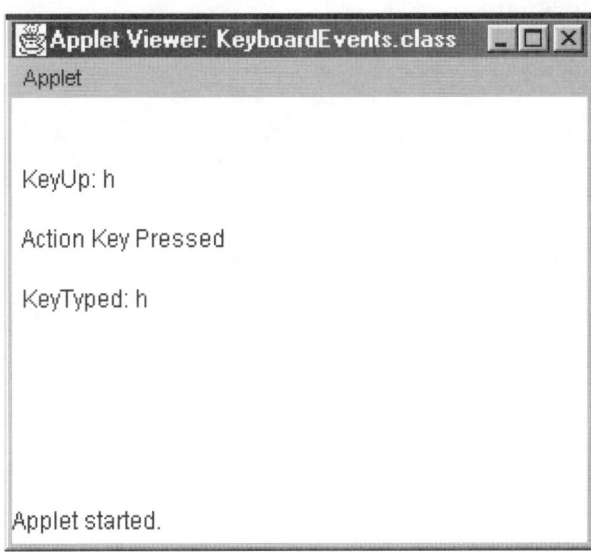

Figure 32.1 Displaying information about keyboard events.

The following statements implement the *KeyboardEvents.java* applet:

```java
import java.awt.*;
import java.applet.Applet;
import java.awt.event.*;
import java.awt.event.KeyEvent;
import java.awt.event.KeyListener;

public class KeyboardEvents extends Applet implements KeyListener
   {
     String KeyPressedEvent = null;
     String KeyReleasedEvent = null;
     String KeyTypedEvent = null;

     public void init()
        {
           addKeyListener(this);
           requestFocus();
        }

     public void keyReleased(KeyEvent event)
        {
           int letter = event.getKeyChar();

           if (KeyPressedEvent == null)
             {
                if (letter == 27) // Esc key
                   KeyReleasedEvent ="Esc key released";
                else
                   KeyReleasedEvent ="KeyUp:" + (char) letter;
             }
           else
             KeyPressedEvent = null;

           repaint();
        }

     public void keyPressed(KeyEvent event)
        {
           KeyPressedEvent ="Action Key Pressed";
           repaint();
        }
```

```
    public void keyTyped(KeyEvent event)
      {
          int letter = event.getKeyChar();

          KeyTypedEvent ="KeyTyped:" + (char) letter;

          KeyPressedEvent = null;

          repaint();
      }

    public void paint(Graphics g)
      {
          if (KeyReleasedEvent != null)
            g.drawString(KeyReleasedEvent, 5, 45);

          if (KeyPressedEvent != null)
            g.drawString(KeyPressedEvent, 5, 75);

          if (KeyTypedEvent != null)
            g.drawString(KeyTypedEvent, 5, 105);
      }
  }
```

As you can see, the applet defines the *keyPressed, keyReleased,* and *keyTyped* functions. In general, Java calls the *keyTyped* and *keyReleased* methods for standard keyboard keys. Java calls the *keyPressed* method for action keys, such as your keyboard's function keys or SHIFT key.

To run the applet, place the following HTML entries within the file *KeyboardEvents.HTML*:

```
<HTML><TITLE>KeyboardEvents Applet</TITLE>
<APPLET CODE="KeyboardEvents.class" WIDTH=300 HEIGHT=200></APPLET></HTML>
```

TESTING FOR FUNCTION KEYS

Depending on your applet's purpose, there may be times when you must distinguish function keys from regular keystrokes. In such cases, your applet can use the *KeyEvent* class *getKeyCode* method to determine the key type. The following applet, *FunctionKeys.java*, changes the previous applet slightly to test for function keys:

```
import java.awt.*;
import java.applet.Applet;
import java.awt.event.*;
import java.awt.event.KeyEvent;
import java.awt.event.KeyListener;

public class FunctionKeys extends Applet implements KeyListener
  {
    String FunctionKey = null;
```

```
   public void init()
   {
       addKeyListener(this);
       requestFocus();
   }

   public void keyReleased(KeyEvent event)
   {
       // Ignore keyReleased events
   }

   public void keyPressed(KeyEvent event)
   {
       switch (event.getKeyCode()) {
       case event.VK_F1: FunctionKey ="F1";
                        break;
       case event.VK_F2: FunctionKey ="F2";
                        break;
       case event.VK_F3: FunctionKey ="F3";
                        break;
       case event.VK_F4: FunctionKey ="F4";
                        break;
       case event.VK_F5: FunctionKey ="F5";
                        break;
       case event.VK_F6: FunctionKey ="F6";
                        break;
       case event.VK_F7: FunctionKey ="F7";
                        break;
       case event.VK_F8: FunctionKey ="F8";
                        break;
       case event.VK_F9: FunctionKey ="F9";
                        break;
       case event.VK_F10: FunctionKey ="F10";
                         break;
       case event.VK_F11: FunctionKey ="F11";
                         break;
       case event.VK_F12: FunctionKey ="F12";
                         break;
       default: FunctionKey = null;
        }

       repaint();
   }

   public void keyTyped(KeyEvent event)
   {
       // Ignore keyTyped events
   }
```

```
   public void paint(Graphics g)
     {
        if (FunctionKey != null)
           g.drawString("Function key:" + FunctionKey, 5, 15);
     }
   }
```

As briefly discussed, Java calls the *keyPressed* method each time the user presses an action key, such as a function. In this case, the *keyPressed* method tests if the key pressed is a function key by using the identifiers *VK_F1* through *VK_F12* that the *KeyEvent* class defines.

To run the applet, place the following HTML entries within the file *FunctionKeys.HMTL*:

```
<HTML><TITLE>FunctionKeys Applet</TITLE>
<APPLET CODE="FunctionKeys.class" WIDTH=300 HEIGHT=200></APPLET></HTML>
```

When you compile and run the applet, your screen will open an applet window within which the applet displays the name of each function key you press.

TESTING THE KEYBOARD STATE

Just as there may be times when your applets must distinguish between function and standard keys, there may also be times when your applets must know the state of keyboard-shift keys. In such cases, your applets can examine the *KeyEvent* class *getModifiers* method. To test the keyboard state, your applets perform a bitwise *AND* operation with specific bits within the *Modifiers* value, as shown here:

```
KeyState ="";

int Modifiers = event.getModifiers();

if ((Modifiers & KeyEvent.SHIFT_MASK) != 0)
  KeyState +=" SHIFT";

if ((Modifiers & KeyEvent.CTRL_MASK) != 0)
  KeyState +=" CTRL";

if ((Modifiers & KeyEvent.META_MASK) != 0)
  KeyState +=" META";

if ((Modifiers & KeyEvent.ALT_MASK) != 0)
  KeyState +=" ALT";
```

In this case, the statements test each of the flags by using a bitwise *AND* operation. If the result of the bitwise *AND* operation is not equal to zero, the corresponding flag is currently set. The following applet, *ShowState.java*, uses the *Event* class *modifiers* field to display the keyboard state:

```
import java.awt.*;
import java.applet.Applet;
import java.awt.event.*;
import java.awt.event.KeyEvent;
import java.awt.event.KeyListener;
```

```
public class ShowState extends Applet implements KeyListener
  {
    String KeyState = null;

    public void init()
      {
          addKeyListener(this);
          requestFocus();
      }

    public void keyPressed(KeyEvent event)
      {
        KeyState ="";

        int Modifiers = event.getModifiers();

        if ((Modifiers & KeyEvent.SHIFT_MASK) != 0)
          KeyState +=" SHIFT";

        if ((Modifiers & KeyEvent.CTRL_MASK) != 0)
          KeyState +=" CTRL";

        if ((Modifiers & KeyEvent.META_MASK) != 0)
          KeyState +=" META";

        if ((Modifiers & KeyEvent.ALT_MASK) != 0)
          KeyState +=" ALT";

        repaint();
      }

    public void keyReleased(KeyEvent event)
      {
        // Ignore keyReleased events
      }


    public void keyTyped(KeyEvent event)
      {
        // Ignore keyTyped events
      }

    public void paint(Graphics g)
      {
        g.drawString("Keyboard State:" + KeyState, 5, 15);
      }
  }
```

To run the applet, place the following HTML entries within the file *ShowState.HTML*:

```
<HTML><TITLE>ShowState Applet</TITLE>
<APPLET CODE="ShowState.class" WIDTH=300 HEIGHT=200></APPLET></HTML>
```

When you compile and run the applet, your screen will open an applet window within which the applet will display a message each time you press the SHIFT, CTRL, or ALT keys, and as shown in Figure 32.2.

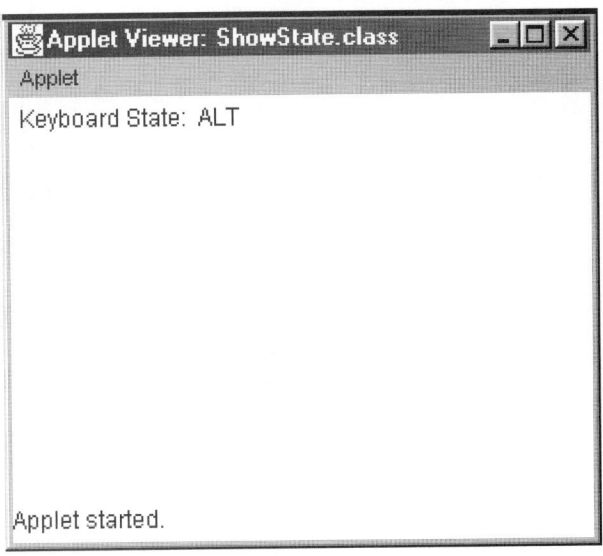

Figure 32.2 *Displaying the keyboard state within an applet.*

SIMPLIFYING KEYBOARD OPERATIONS

By responding to keyboard events, your applets can read user input one keystroke at a time. To perform such input operations, however, your applet must read a character, place the character within a string, display the character in a window by using a function (such as *drawString*), or possibly erase characters if the user presses the BACKSPACE key.

Depending on the amount of keyboard input your applet must perform, you may find it much easier to take advantage of dialog-box text-fields, as discussed in Lesson 30, "Performing Dialog-Box Operations," as shown in Figure 32.3.

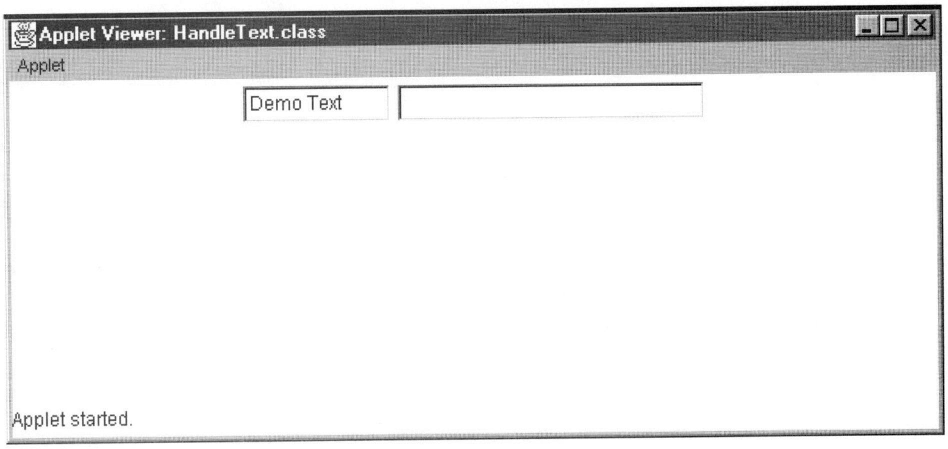

Figure 32.3 *Using text fields to simplify user-input operations.*

TAKING A CYBER FIELD TRIP

As you surf the Web in pursuit of the latest information on Java, two stops you should make are the Java World and Java Developer's Journal Web sites, shown in Figure 32.4. Within these sites you will find source code examples, documentation on the latest APIs, and even job listings for Java programmers. You can visit Java World on the Web at *www.javaworld.com*. Likewise, you can find the Java Developer's Journal at *www.sys-con.com/java*.

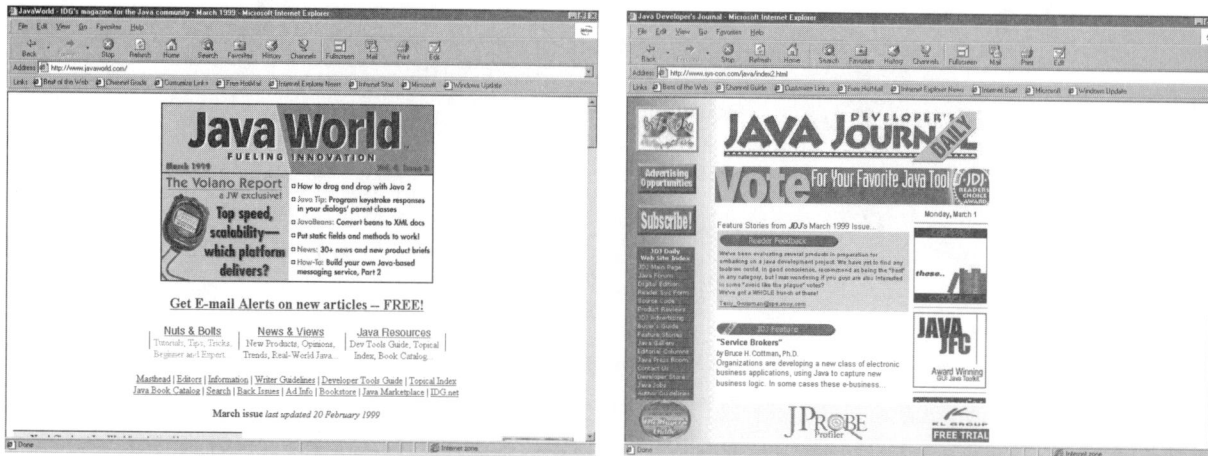

Figure 32.4 *Visit the* Java World *and* Java Developer's Journal *Web sites for the latest Java news.*

WHAT YOU MUST KNOW

As your Java applets become more complex, they must respond to keyboard events. In this lesson, you learned how to direct an applet to listen for and then to respond to keyboard events. In Lesson 33, "Understanding File Operations," you will learn how to store and later retrieve information within a file. Before you continue with Lesson 33, however, make sure that you have learned the following key concepts:

☑ Java treats keyboard operations that occur as your applet executes as a keyboard event.

☑ Before your applets can respond to a keyboard event, you must direct your applet to listen for the events by implementing the *KeyListener* class.

☑ To implement the *KeyListener* class, you must define the *keyPressed*, *keyReleased*, and *keyTyped* methods.

LESSON 33

UNDERSTANDING FILE OPERATIONS

As you know, to store information as they execute, Java programs temporarily store data within variables. To store information from one invocation to the next, programs store information within files. As it turns out, Java supports a variety of file operations, the discussion of which would require a separate book. To help you get started, however, this lesson introduces file operations within Java. By the time you finish this lesson, you will understand the following key concepts:

- For security reasons, Java restricts file operations to standalone programs. Java applets cannot perform file operations.

- Before a program can write information to, or read data from a file, the program must first open the file.

- To open a file, the program can use a *FileOutputStream* or *FileInputStream* object.

- When a program is done using a file, the program should close the file using the *FileOutputStream.close()* method.

- If a Java program experiences an error opening or reading and writing to a file, Java will generate an exception, which your program must catch.

- To store and retrieve non-text data (such as floating-point numbers), your program will use a *DataOutputStream* or a *DataInputStream* object.

OPENING AND CLOSING A FILE

As you learned in Lesson 1, "Introducing Java," to reduce the possibility of Java-based viruses, the creators of Java prevent applets from performing file operations. To read or write file-based information using Java, you must create a standalone Java application. The following application, *OpenFile.java*, creates an *InputFileStream* object, which the program uses to open the file the user specifies within the command line. Before a Java program can read or write a file, the program must open the file. The following command line, for example, would open a file named *Filename.ext* (as you will recall from Lesson 4, "Java Applets Versus Standalone Programs," you run Java standalone programs using the Java interpreter):

```
C:\RBYJAVA\LESSON33> java   OpenFile   Filename.ext   <ENTER>
```

The following statements implement the *OpenFile.java* applet:

```
import java.io.*;

class OpenFile
  {
    public static void main(String args[])
      {
        if (args.length == 0)
          {
             System.out.print("Must specify a filename");
             System.exit(1);
          }
```

```
        try {
            FileInputStream file = new FileInputStream(args[0]);
        }
        catch (FileNotFoundException e)
          {
            System.out.println("Error opening file " + args[0]);
            System.exit(1);
          }


        System.out.println("File opened successfully");
    }
}
```

To start, the program uses the *args.length* member to determine the number of command-line arguments the user specifies in the command line. If the user did not specify a filename, the program displays an error message and exits. If the user has specified a file within the command line, the program creates a *FileInputStream* object which it uses to open the file. If the *FileInputStream* constructor method successfully opens the file, the program displays a message that states it has opened the file. If, however, the constructor method cannot open the file (the file, for example, may not exist), the constructor throws the *FileNotFoundException*, which the program catches.

In this case, the *FileOpen.java* program used a *FileInputStream* object. As you will learn, programs use a *FileInputStream* to read information from a file. Likewise, programs use *FileOutputStream* objects to write data to a file.

CLOSING AN OPEN FILE

As you have learned, before a program can write or read information to or from a file, the program must first open the file. In a similar way, when the program is done using the file, the program should close the file, using the *close* method. The following program, *CloseFile.java*, opens the file that the user specifies within the command line, and then, if it successfully opened the file, the program closes the file using the *close* method:

```
import java.io.*;

class CloseFile
  {
    public static void main(String args[])
      {
        FileInputStream file = null;

        if (args.length == 0)
          {
            System.out.print("Must specify a filename");
            System.exit(1);
          }

        try {
            file = new FileInputStream(args[0]);
        }
        catch (FileNotFoundException e)
          {
```

```
                System.out.println("Error opening file " + args[0]);
                System.exit(1);
            }


        try {
            file.close();
            }
        catch (IOException e)
            {
                System.out.println("Error closing file");
                System.exit(1);
            }

        System.out.println("File opened and closed successfully");
        }
    }
```

DISPLAYING A FILE'S CONTENTS

As briefly discussed, to read a file's contents, Java programs use *FileInputStream* objects. The following program, *ShowFile.java*, opens the file the user specifies within the command line. Then, within a *while* loop, the program uses the object's *read* method to read the file's contents one byte at a time. When the program reaches the end of the file, the *read* method returns the value –1. As you can see, each time the program reads a byte from the file, the program uses the *System.out.print* method to display the byte (as a character) to the screen:

```
import java.io.*;

class ShowFile
    {
    public static void main(String args[])
        {
        FileInputStream file = null;
        byte Letter;
        boolean EndOfFile = false;

        if (args.length == 0)
            {
            System.out.print("Must specify filename");
            System.exit(1);
            }

        try {
            file = new FileInputStream(args[0]);
            }
        catch (FileNotFoundException e)
            {
            System.out.println("Error opening file " + args[0]);
            System.exit(1);
            }
```

```
      try {
        while (! EndOfFile)
          {
            Letter = (byte) file.read();
            if (Letter == -1)
              EndOfFile = true;
            else
              System.out.print("" + (char) Letter);
          }
        }
      catch (IOException ReadError)
        {
            System.out.println("Error reading file");
            System.exit(1);
        }

      try {
        file.close();
        }
      catch (IOException CloseError)
        {
            System.out.println("Error closing file");
            System.exit(1);
        }
    }
  }
```

The previous program, *ShowFile.java*, simply read and displayed a file's contents. The following program, *toUppercase.java*, reads a character from the file, examines the character, and then displays either the character or its uppercase equivalent (provided the character was a lowercase letter). In other words, the program displays a file's contents in uppercase.

```
import java.io.*;

class toUppercase
  {
    public static void main(String args[])
      {
        FileInputStream file = null;
        byte Letter;
        boolean EndOfFile = false;

        if (args.length == 0)
          {
            System.out.print("Must specify filename");
            System.exit(1);
          }
```

```java
    try {
       file = new FileInputStream(args[0]);
       }
    catch (FileNotFoundException e)
      {
        System.out.println("Error opening file " + args[0]);
        System.exit(1);
      }

    try {
      while (! EndOfFile)
        {
          Letter = (byte) file.read();
          if (Letter == -1)
            EndOfFile = true;
          else
            {
              if (((char) Letter >='a') && ((char) Letter <='z'))
                Letter -= (byte) ((byte)'a' - (byte)'A');
              System.out.print("" + (char) Letter);


            }
        }
      }
    catch (IOException ReadError)
      {
          System.out.println("Error reading file");
          System.exit(1);
      }

    try {
      file.close();
      }
    catch (IOException CloseError)
      {
        System.out.println("Error closing file");
        System.exit(1);
      }
    }
  }
```

As you can see, the program uses an *if* statement to determine if the letter is a lowercase letter. To convert the letter from lower to uppercase, the program simply subtracts the difference between a lowercase a and an uppercase A. (If you take a few minutes to examine an ASCII chart, you will understand how this conversion works.)

Finally, the following program, *LineCount.java*, displays a count of the number of lines the file that the user specifies within the command line contains:

```java
import java.io.*;
```

```
class LineCount
  {
    public static void main(String args[])
      {
        FileInputStream file = null;
        byte Letter;
        boolean EndOfFile = false, CharFound = false;
        int Count = 0;

        if (args.length == 0)
          {
            System.out.print("Must specify filename");
            System.exit(1);
          }

        try {
            file = new FileInputStream(args[0]);
          }
        catch (FileNotFoundException e)
          {
            System.out.println("Error opening file " + args[0]);
            System.exit(1);
          }

        try {
          while (! EndOfFile)
            {
              Letter = (byte) file.read();
              if (Letter == -1)
                {
                   if (CharFound)
                     Count++;
                   EndOfFile = true;
                }
              else if (Letter == 13) // Carriage return
                {
                   Count++;
                   CharFound = false;
                }
               else if (Letter != 10) // Linefeed
                 CharFound = true;     // Character found in current line
            }
          }
        catch (IOException ReadError)
          {
               System.out.println("Error reading file");
               System.exit(1);
          }
```

```
      try {
        file.close();
      }
      catch (IOException CloseError)
        {
            System.out.println("Error closing file");
            System.exit(1);
        }
      System.out.println(args[0] + " contains " + Count + " lines");
    }
}
```

The *LineCount.java* program reads characters from a file one character a time. If the program encounters a byte with the value 13, the ASCII carriage-return, the program increments the *Count* variable, which the program uses to keep track of the line count. Depending on the file's environment (such as MS-DOS or Unix), the operating system may use a carriage-return and linefeed (ASCII 10) to signify the end of a line. Also, it is possible for a one-character file to contain a letter immediately followed by the end of the file (in other words, no carriage-return or linefeed). To handle such files correctly, the program uses the *CharFound* variable, which the program sets to *true* each time it encounters a character at the start of a new line.

WORKING WITH NON-TEXT FILES

Each of the previous programs have worked with ASCII text files. Depending on your program's processing, there will be times when you must store integer, floating-point, and other types of values. To write or read such data to or from a file, your programs will use a *DataOutputStream* or *DataInputStream* object. The following program, *CreateDoubleFile.java*, for example, creates a file named *Numbers.dat*, to which the program then writes the floating-point values 0.0 to 100.0:

```
import java.io.*;

class CreateDoubleFile
  {
    public static void main(String args[])
      {
        FileOutputStream file = null;
        DataOutputStream data = null;

        try {
          file = new FileOutputStream("Numbers.dat");
        }
        catch (FileNotFoundException e)
          {
            System.out.println("Error opening file Numbers.dat");
            System.exit(1);
          }

        data = new DataOutputStream(file);
```

```
            try {
              for (double i = 0.0; i <= 100; i += 1.0)
                {
                    data.writeDouble(i);
                }
            }
            catch (IOException WriteError)
              {
                    System.out.println("Error writing file");
                    System.exit(1);
              }

            try {
              data.close();
              file.close();
             }
            catch (IOException CloseError)
              {
                    System.out.println("Error closing file");
                    System.exit(1);
              }
        }
    }
```

To create the file *Number.dat*, the program first creates a *FileOutputStream* object. Then, using the *FileOutputStream* object, the program creates a *DataOutputStream* object. To write data to the file, the program uses the *DataOutputStream.writeDouble* method. It's important that you understand that when you use a *DataOutputStream* object, your program is not writing data in an ASCII format but, rather, in a binary format. If you type to view the contents of the *Numbers.dat* file using a program such as the Windows *Notepad* accessory, the file's contents will appear meaningless.

In a similar way, the following program, *ReadDoubleFile.java*, reads the contents of the *Numbers.dat* file. In this case, the program uses a *DataInputStream* object to read the data. As before, to open the file, the program first creates a *FileInputStream* object:

```
import java.io.*;

class ReadDoubleFile
  {
    public static void main(String args[])
      {
        FileInputStream file = null;
        double value;
        byte Letter;

        boolean EndOfFile = false;
```

```
try {
   file = new FileInputStream("Numbers.dat");
}
catch (FileNotFoundException e)
   {
     System.out.println("Error opening file Numbers.dat");
     System.exit(1);
   }

DataInputStream data = new DataInputStream(file);

try {
   while (! EndOfFile)
     {
        value = (byte) data.readDouble();
        System.out.println("" + value);
     }
}
catch (EOFException EndOfFileException)
   {
      EndOfFile = true;
   }
catch (IOException ReadError)
   {
        System.out.println("Error reading file");
        System.exit(1);
   }

try {
   file.close();
}
catch (IOException CloseError)
   {
        System.out.println("Error closing file");
        System.exit(1);
   }
}
}
```

WORKING WITH FILE-BASED DIALOG BOXES

In Lesson 30, "Performing Dialog Box Operations," you learned how to create a file-based dialog box, such as that shown in Figure 33.1.

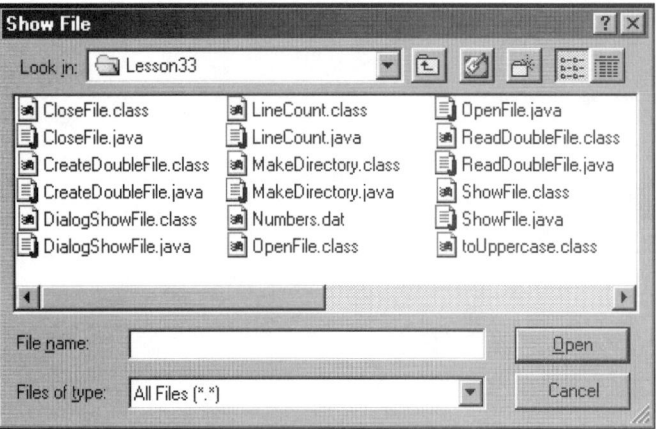

Figure 33.1 *Using a dialog box to specify a directory and file.*

The following program, *DialogShowFile.java*, uses a *FileDialog* object to let the user select the file whose contents the user wants to display. After the user selects a file, the program opens and displays the file's contents, much as the *ShowFile.java* program, presented earlier in this lesson:

```java
import java.awt.*;
import java.awt.event.*;
import java.io.*;

class DialogShowFile extends Frame
  {
    FileDialog dialogBox;
    FileInputStream file = null;
    String Filename;
    boolean EndOfFile = false;
    byte Letter;

    DialogShowFile()
      {
        super();

        dialogBox = new FileDialog(this, "Show File");
        dialogBox.show();

        Filename = dialogBox.getFile();

        try {
          file = new FileInputStream(Filename);
        }
        catch (FileNotFoundException e)
          {
            System.out.println("Error opening file " + Filename);
            System.exit(1);
          }
```

```
          try {
            while (! EndOfFile)
              {
                 Letter = (byte) file.read();
                 if (Letter == -1)
                    EndOfFile = true;
                 else
                    System.out.print("" + (char) Letter);
              }
           }
        catch (IOException ReadError)
           {
              System.out.println("Error reading file");
              System.exit(1);
           }

        try {
           file.close();
           }
        catch (IOException CloseError)
           {
              System.out.println("Error closing file");
           }

        System.exit(1);
        }


   public static void main(String args[])
     {
        new DialogShowFile();
     }
  }
```

It is important to note that using a *FileDialog* object, a user can select a file and change the current directory. In this case, the program assumes the user is selecting the file from the current directory. If the user changes directories within the dialog box, the program will not locate the file. To handle a directory change, the program must use the *FileDialog.getDirectory()* method to get the name of the directory and then append the filename to the string.

WORKING WITH DIRECTORIES

As your program's file operations become more complex, there will be times when you will want the program to manipulate directories. For example, you might want the program to create a new directory within which the program can store a specific file. Using a *File* object, a Java program can perform a variety of directory-based operations. The following program, *MakeDirectory.java*, for example, uses the *File.mkdir()* method to create the directory the user specifies within the command line:

```
import java.io.*;

class MakeDirectory
  {
    public static void main(String args[])
      {
        if (args.length == 0)
          {
            System.out.print("Must specify directory name");
            System.exit(1);
          }

        File Directory = new File(args[0]);

        try {
           if (Directory.mkdir())
             System.out.println("Directory successfully created.");
           else
             System.out.println("Error creating " + args[0]);
        }
        catch (SecurityException e)
          {
            System.out.println("Security error accessing " + args[0]);
            System.exit(1);
          }
      }
  }
```

TAKING A CYBER FIELD TRIP

As your applications become more complex, you may eventually have to access large databases—whose structure requires far more complex file operations than those this lesson presents. To help you perform database operations you can use the JDBC (Java Database Classes) API. For information on the JDBC, visit the Sun Microsystems Web site at *java.sun.com/products/jdbc* as shown in Figure 33.2.

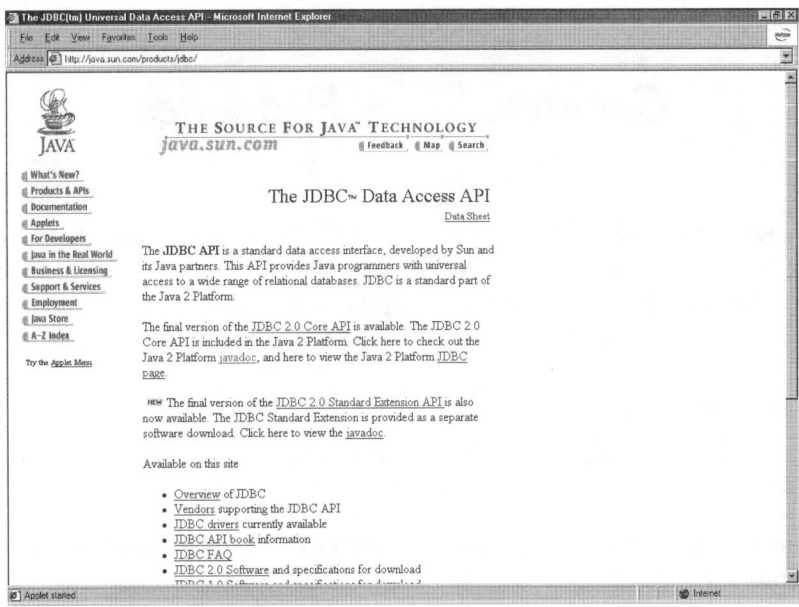

Figure 33.2 *Viewing information on the JDBC API.*

WHAT YOU MUST KNOW

To store information from one invocation to the next, programs must store the data within files. Java supports a variety of file operations, including random-access files. This lesson introduced you to basic file operations within Java. In Lesson 34, "Creating Java Packages," you will learn how to create your own class libraries within Java. Before you continue with Lesson 34, however, make sure you have learned the following key concepts:

- ☑ To reduce the chance of a Java-based virus or an applet reading information from a user's disk, Java restricts file operations to standalone programs.

- ☑ Using a *FileOutputStream* or a *FileInputStream* object, a program can open a file for output or input operatoins.

- ☑ When a program has completed its file operations, the program should close the file using the *FileOutputStream.close()* method.

- ☑ When a Java program experiences a file error (which may be due to opening, reading, writing, or closing a file), Java will generate an exception, which your program must catch.

- ☑ Using a *DataOutputStream* or a *DataInputStream* object a Java program can write data to or read data from a non-text file.

LESSON 34
CREATING JAVA PACKAGES

If you examine a Java applet or standalone program, the first statement you will encounter is typically an *import* statement that directs the Java compiler to use a specific class library. By taking advantage of class libraries, your applets can use existing objects—which saves you time and programming. In this lesson, you will learn how to create your own Java packages. By the time you finish this lesson, you will understand the following key concepts:

- To create a package, you place a *package* statement as the first statement of your source file.

- The *package* statement defines the location of the corresponding class and source files on your disk.

- To use your package within an applet or program, you simply reference the package name using an *import* statement.

UNDERSTANDING PACKAGE NAMES

To create a Java class library, a package, you place the *package* statement as the first statement within your source file—even before the *import* statements. The *package* statement specifies the location of the package files on your disk. For example, the following *package* statement tells Java that you will place the package files (the class files and possibly the source files) within a directory named *myPackage*:

```
package myPackage;
```

In a similar way, the following *package* statement tells Java that you will place the files within a subdirectory named *Shapes* that resides within the *myPackage* directory:

```
package myPackage.Shapes;
```

Later, when a program wants to use one or more classes your package defines, the program will use the following import statements:

```
import myPackage.*;
import myPackage.Shapes.*;
```

CREATING A SIMPLE PACKAGE

The best way to understand Java packages is simply to create and use a few packages. The following source file, *Book.java*, for example, creates a package that will reside within the *myJava* directory. The package will contain a simple *Book* class:

```
package myJava;

import java.awt.*;
```

```
public class Book
  {
    String title;

    public Book(String title)
      {
        this.title = title;
      }

    public void ShowBook(Graphics g, int x, int y)
      {
        g.drawString(title, x, y);
      }
  }
```

To create the package, compile the program as you normally would and then move the source and class files into the *myJava* directory (which you will create beneath your current directory):

```
C:\RBYJAVA\LESSON34> javac  Book.java  <ENTER>
C:\RBYJAVA\LESSON34> mkdir myJava  <ENTER>
C:\RBYJAVA\LESSON34> move Book.* myJava  <ENTER>
```

Next, the following applet, *DemoPackage.java*, uses the *Book* class that resides in the package you just created:

```
import java.awt.*;
import java.applet.*;
import myJava.*;

public class DemoPackage extends Applet
  {
    Book JavaBook = new Book("Rescued by Java");

    public void paint(Graphics g)
      {
        JavaBook.ShowBook(g, 5, 15);
      }
  }
```

Before you compile this applet, make sure you have moved the *Book* class files into the *myJava* directory. If the files reside in the current directory and the *myJava* directory, the Java compiler cannot determine which files you want to use and will generate syntax errors. To compile the applet, you can use the Java compiler, as shown here:

```
C:\RBYJAVA\LESSON34>  javac  DemoPackage.java  <ENTER>
```

Next, to run the program, place the following HTML entries within the file *DemoPackage.HTML*:

```
<HTML><TITLE>DemoPackage Applet</TITLE>
<APPLET CODE="DemoPackage.class" WIDTH=300 HEIGHT=200></APPLET></HTML>
```

When you run the applet, your screen will display an applet window that contains the book title, as shown in Figure 34.1.

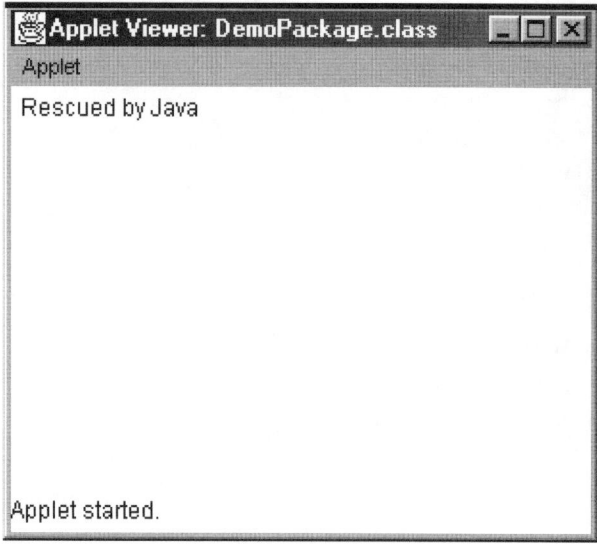

Figure 34.1 Using a class defined within a package.

USING LEVELS WITHIN A PACKAGE NAME

As discussed, the package statement specifies the location on your disk where the package will reside. If the name specified in the package statement contains two or more parts that are separated with periods, the package name specifies levels of subdirectories. For example, the following source code, *Message.java*, creates a package within the *subdir* subdirectory that resides within the *myJava* directory:

```java
package myJava.subdir;

import java.awt.*;

public class Message
  {
    String text;

    public Message(String text)
     {
       this.text = text;
     }

    public void ShowMessage(Graphics g, int x, int y)
     {
       g.drawString(text, x, y);
     }
  }
```

Again, after you compile the source code, create the *myJava* and *subdir* directories and then move the source code and class file to the *subdir* directory.

To use the package, you simply specify the name within an *import* statement. For example, the following applet, *UseMessage.java*, uses the *Message* class that the previous package defines:

```
import java.awt.*;
import java.applet.*;
import myJava.subdir.*;

public class UseMessage extends Applet
  {
    Message Secret = new Message("Hello, Java World!");

    public void paint(Graphics g)
     {
        Secret.ShowMessage(g, 5, 15);
     }
  }
```

To run the applet, place the following HTML entries within the *UseMessage.HTML* file:

```
<HTML><TITLE>UseMessage Applet</TITLE>
<APPLET CODE="UseMessage.class" WIDTH=300 HEIGHT=200></APPLET></HTML>
```

When you run the applet, your screen will display an applet window that contains the message text.

TAKING A CYBER FIELD TRIP

Throughout this book's lessons, you have examined many key Java programming topics. If you are looking for additional information on a specific topic, or additional programming examples, you can find a Java tutorial on the Web at *www.javasoft.com/docs/books/tutorial* as shown in Figure 34.2.

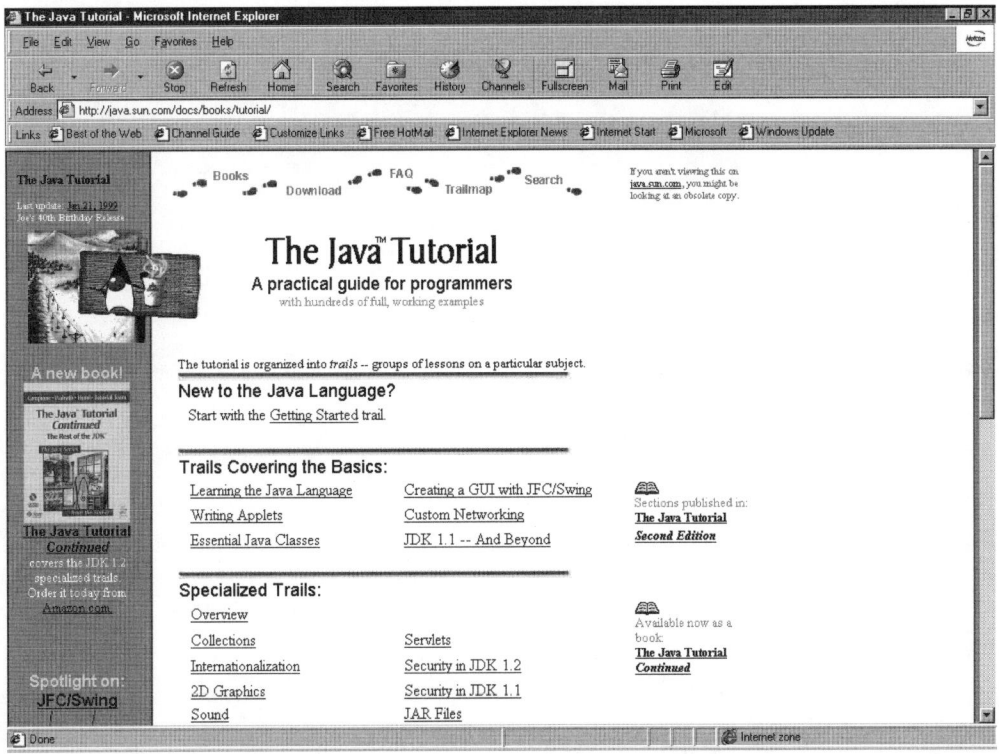

Figure 34.2 Running an online Java tutorial.

WHAT YOU MUST KNOW

Throughout this book, the programs and applets you have created have made extensive use of Java packages. In this lesson, you learned how to create your own packages. In Lesson 35, "Getting Started with Java Beans," you will learn how to create reusable Java objects. Before you continue with Lesson 35, however, make sure you have learned the following key concepts:

☑ Using the package statement, you can create your own class library (package).

☑ The *package* statement must be the first statement in your source file.

☑ The *package* statement defines the location of the corresponding class and source files on your disk.

☑ To use your package within an applet or program, you simply reference the package name using an *import* statement.

LESSON 35

GETTING STARTED WITH JAVA BEANS

Throughout this book, you have read that one of Java's most significant benefits is that your applets or programs can run on a variety of systems, such as the PC, a Mac, or even Solaris, without any programming changes. You have also learned that by creating class-based objects, you can often use code that you write for one program within a second unrelated applet, which saves you time and programming. Programmers often refer to such objects as *reusable components*.

In this lesson, you will examine Java Beans, which are components (objects) you create for use in a variety of programs. In general, Java Beans is a specification that defines how you should create reusable components in Java. To help you get started, Sun Microsystems offers a Beans Developer's Kit (BDK) that you can download and install on your system. The BDK contains sample source files for various reusable components, as well as a program called the *BeanBox*, that you can use to test the components you create. This lesson will introduce you to the Bean Developer's Kit and how you use Java Beans to create an applet. By the time you finish this lesson, you will understand the following key concepts:

- A Java Bean is a reusable component (an object) that you can easily integrate into a variety of applications.

- You can download the Java Bean Developer's Kit from Sun's Java Web site at *java.sun.com*.

- The Bean Developer's Kit provides source code examples of Java Beans and applets that use Java Beans. In addition, the Kit provides a special program, called the *BeanBox*, that you can use to test Java Beans.

- Within the *BeanBox* program, you can demo a Java Bean's processing. You can also direct the *BeanBox* to create an applet that uses the Bean.

DOWNLOAD AND INSTALL THE BEANS DEVELOPER'S KIT (BDK)

To download the Bean Developer's Kit, use your browser to connect to Sun Microsystem's Java Web site at *java.sun.com* and then follow the links to the Java Beans page, as shown in Figure 35.1.

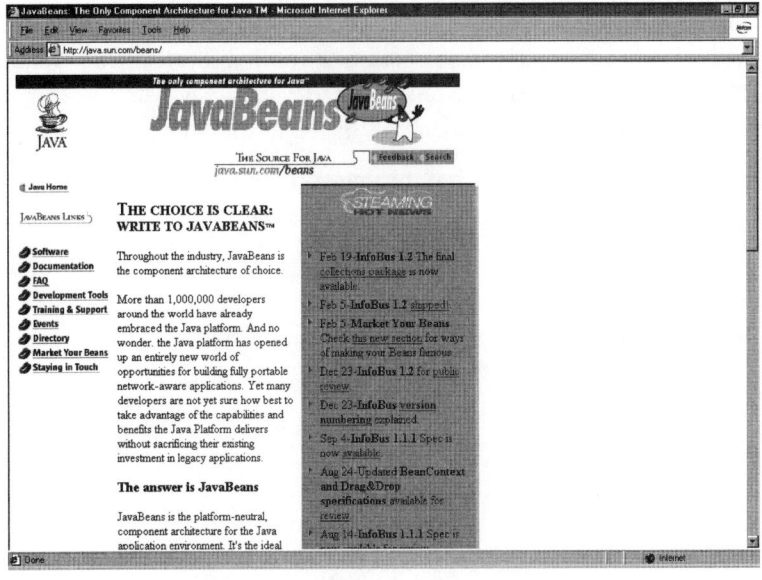

Figure 35.1 *The Java Beans page at Sun's Java Web site.*

From within the Java Beans Web page, download the Beans Developer's Kit that matches your environment, such as Windows. The download operation will place an executable program on your disk that you must later run to install the Beans Developer's Kit.

RUNNING THE BEANBOX

As briefly discussed, the Bean Developer's Kit provides a special program called the *BeanBox*, within which you can test the Java Beans that you create. The Java Beans Web page will provide you with the steps you must perform to run the *BeanBox* on your system. The steps will differ from system to system and may change over time. At the time this book was written, within Windows you select the *BeanBox* sub directory within the directory that contains the Java Beans Developer's Kit, and run a batch file named *Run.bat*. Your screen, in turn, will display three windows, as shown in Figure 35.2.

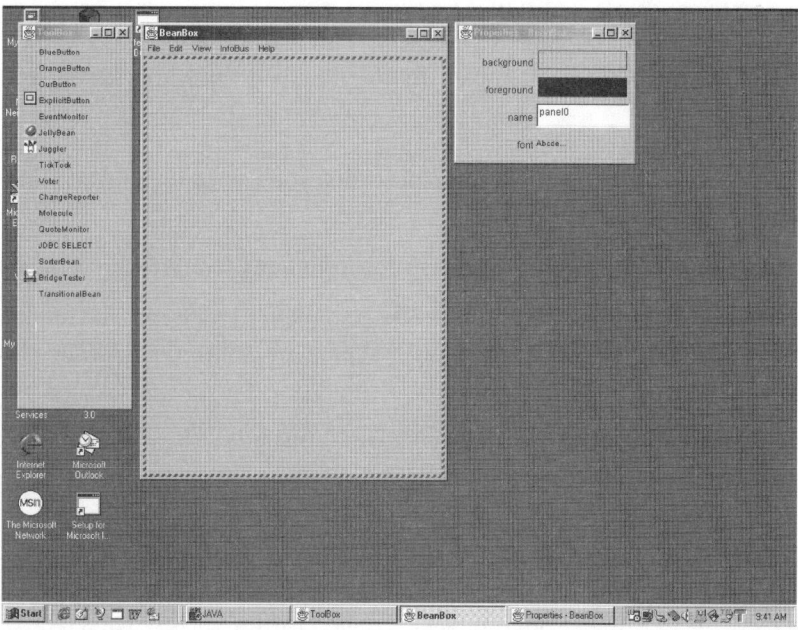

Figure 35.2 Running the **BeanBox** *program.*

The Toolbox window contains a list of Java Beans that you can use within your programs or test within the *BeanBox*. The *BeanBox* window is a container into which you can place and run Java Bean objects. Within the *BeanBox* window, you can click your mouse on an object to select the object. The Properties window, in turn, will display the object's properties you can change (either within a program that uses the object or within the Properties window itself).

To better understand how the *BeanBox* works, click your mouse on the Juggler Bean within the Toolbox. Then, click your mouse within the *BeanBox* window. The *BeanBox*, in turn, will display a Juggler object and the Properties window will display the object's attributes, as shown in Figure 35.3.

When you place a Java Bean within *BeanBox*, the *BeanBox* will use the Bean as if the Bean were running within a program. Using the Properties window, experiment with the Juggler Bean's animation rate, speeding the rate up by typing a value such as 30, and then slowing the rate down using a value such as 500.

Figure 35.3 *Displaying the Juggler Bean within the* ***BeanBox***.

USING BEANS TO CREATE AN APPLET

Depending on the Java compiler you are using, you may be able to drag and drop Java Bean objects into your application's design window and your compiler, in turn, will provide the code your applet must use to interface with the object. In the case of the *BeanBox*, for example, you can direct the *BeanBox* to create the code for the applet that uses the Beans you have currently placed in the box. The *BeanBox*, in turn, will create the Java source files, class files, as well as the HTML file for the applet. To direct the *BeanBox* to create an applet for the current Bean, select the *BeanBox* File menu and choose the Make Applet option. The *BeanBox*, in turn, will display a dialog box asking you to specify the directory within which you want it to write the applet's files. Specify the directory you desire and then choose OK. The *BeanBox* will place the applet's files within the Directory. Figure 35.4, for example, shows the Juggler Bean applet created by the *BeanBox* running within a browser window.

Figure 35.4 *Running the Juggler Bean applet created by the* ***BeanBox*** *program.*

TEST DRIVING A DIFFERENT JAVA BEAN

If your *BeanBox* window currently contains the Juggler Bean, click your mouse on the *Juggler* Bean and then choose the Edit menu Cut option to remove the object from the *BeanBox* window. Next, within the Toolbox, click your mouse on the *Molecule* Bean and then click your mouse within the *BeanBox* window. The *BeanBox* will add a *Molecule* Bean as shown in Figure 35.5.

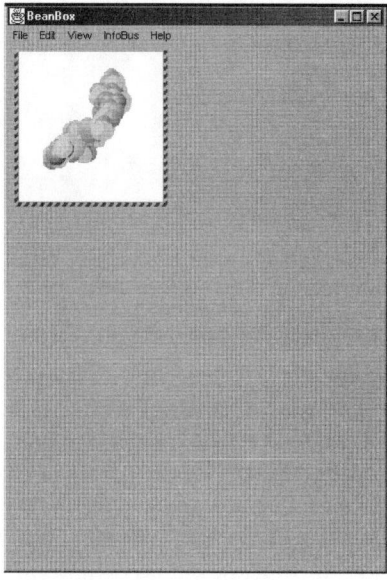

*Figure 35.5 Running the **Molecule** Bean within the **BeanBox**.*

Within the *BeanBox* window, drag your mouse over the *Molecule* Bean's image. As you drag your mouse, the Bean will rotate the molecule's image.

Next, using your mouse, drag the Bean's frame to increase the Bean's size within the *BeanBox* window. Then, click your mouse within the Properties window and use the pull-down list to select a different molecule, as shown in Figure 35.6.

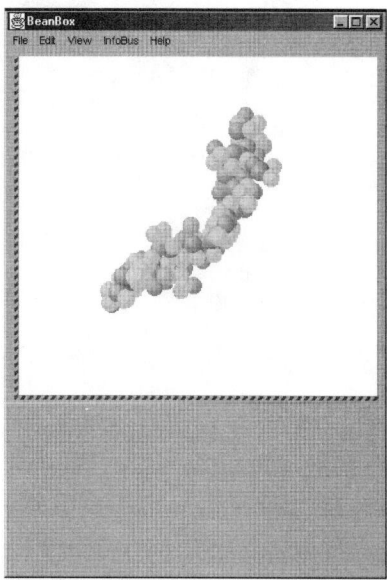

Figure 35.6 Sizing and changing molecules using the Molecule Bean.

WHERE YOU GO FROM HERE

This lesson's purpose is simply to introduce you to Java Beans. Within the Sun's Java Web site, you will find tutorials that discuss the steps you must perform to create your own Java Beans. You will also learn how to bind various Bean attributes, such as exceptions and events, to your application code. In the future, developers will create Java Beans that perform platform-independent operations, such as encryption and telephony support.

JAVA BEANS VERSUS ACTIVEX OBJECTS

If you program within the Windows environment, you may have used ActiveX objects within your programs. Like a Java Bean, an ActiveX object is a reusable component (an object). The primary difference between a Java Bean and an ActiveX object is that a Java Bean is platform-independent and the ActiveX object runs only within the Windows environment.

TAKING A CYBER FIELD TRIP

As you examine books and magazines that discuss Java Beans, you may encounter references to an *InfoBus*. In general, the *InfoBus* is a software-based information channel that lets Java Beans exchange information about one another, which you can use to create data-aware applets. For specifics on the *InfoBus*, visit the Sun Microsystem's Web site at *java.sun.com/products/beans/infobus*, as shown in Figure 35.7.

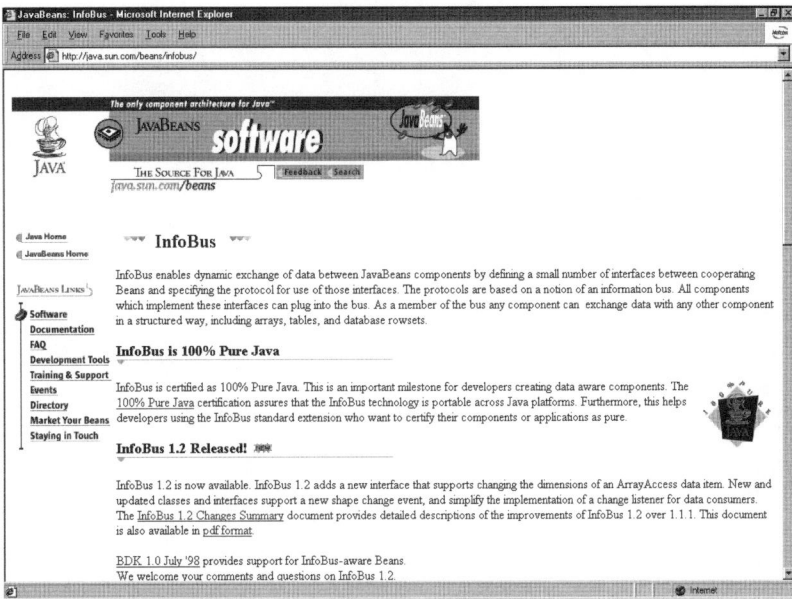

Figure 35.7 Specifics on the InfoBus technology.

WHAT YOU MUST KNOW

A key advantage of object-oriented programming is that you can often use objects you create for one program within a second unrelated program, which saves you time and programming. In this lesson, you examined Java Beans, which are reusable components created with Java. In Lesson 36, "Using the Swing User Interface," you will learn how to display user-interface objects, such as windows, buttons, and menus that have the same look and feel as the user's current environment. In other words, using Swing, a Java program running within the Windows environment will display windows and dialog boxes identical to other Windows-based programs. Before you continue with Lesson 36, however, make sure you have learned the following key concepts:

☑ A goal of object-oriented programming is object reuse. A Java Bean is a reusable component (an object).

☑ Using the Bean Developer's Kit, that you can download from Sun's Java Web site, you can examine Java Bean source code as well as the source code for applets that use Java Beans.

☑ The Bean Developer's Kit provides a special program called the *BeanBox* that you can use to test Java Beans.

☑ Within the *BeanBox* program, you can experiment with a Java Bean's processing by changing the Bean object's attribute values.

☑ The *BeanBox* program can also create an applet that uses the current Bean or Beans. When you use the *BeanBox* to generate an applet, the *BeanBox* will create the Java source code files, the class files, as well as an HTML file you can use to run the applet.

LESSON 36

USING THE SWING USER INTERFACE

In Lesson 31, "Using Frames to Display Objects," you learned how to build standalone applets that use the frames, buttons, and other graphical user interface objects that Java provides within its abstract windowing toolkit (the AWT libraries). In this lesson, you will examine the Swing user interface that lets you display objects that look similar to those you would normally find in your current environment (such as Windows or Solaris). As you will learn, the Swing objects are quite similar to the objects you used in Lesson 31. By the time you finish this lesson, you will understand the following key concepts:

- The Swing user interface lets standalone applications display graphical-user interface objects, such as a window, button, or menu in the format of the user's current environment.

- To use Swing objects, a Java program must import the Swing class libraries using the *import javax.swing.*;* statement.

- Java distinguishes Swing objects from the objects you examined in Lesson 31 by preceding the object names with the letter J, such as *JFrame*, *JButton*, and so on.

LOOKING AT A SIMPLE EXAMPLE

To use the Swing interface, you must first import the *swing* class libraries, as shown here:

```
import javax.swing.*;
```

The following program, *SwingDemo.java*, uses Swing objects to display a window similar to that shown in Figure 36.1. In this case, the screen shot was taken on a Windows-based system. Note that the program's frame (window) appears the same as a standard window.

Figure 36.1 *Using Swing to display a window.*

The following statements implement the *SwingDemo.java* application:

```java
import javax.swing.*;
import java.awt.event.*;

public class SwingDemo extends JFrame
   {
     public SwingDemo(String WindowTitle)
       {
         super(WindowTitle);

         class WindowEventHandler extends WindowAdapter
           {
             public void windowClosing(WindowEvent event)
               {
                 dispose();
                 System.exit(1);
               }
           }

         addWindowListener(new WindowEventHandler());
       }

     public static void main(String args[])
       {
         JFrame frame = new SwingDemo("Swing Demo Window");

         frame.setSize(400, 400);
         frame.setVisible(true);
       }
   }
```

The program first imports the *javax.swing* class libraries. Next, the program's class extends the *JFrame* class, much as the programs in Lesson 31 extended the *Frame* class. As you will learn, Java programs precede the Swing object names with the letter J (such as *JFrame*, *JButton*, and so on).

As you can see, the program implements a *WindowEventHandler* class that extends the *WindowAdapter* class. The program uses the *WindowEventHandler* object to listen for window-based events, such as the user closing the program window.

ADDING A TEXT LABEL

The previous *SwingDemo.java* program was actually quite simple in that it created only a blank window. The following *LabelDemo.java* application changes the previous program slightly to display a label within the window, as shown in Figure 36.2.

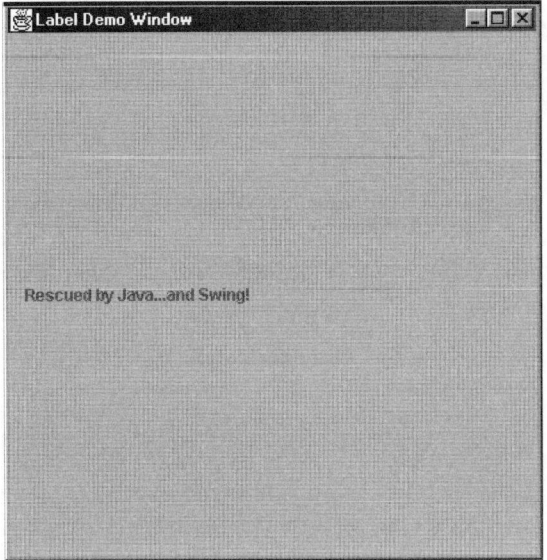

Figure 36.2 *Using the Swing interface to display a label object.*

The following code implements the *LabelDemo.java* application:

```java
import javax.swing.*;
import java.awt.event.*;

public class LabelDemo extends JFrame

  {
    public LabelDemo(String WindowTitle)
      {
        super(WindowTitle);

        class WindowEventHandler extends WindowAdapter
          {
            public void windowClosing(WindowEvent event)
              {
                dispose();
                System.exit(1);
              }
          }

        addWindowListener(new WindowEventHandler());
      }

    public static void main(String args[])
      {
        JFrame frame = new LabelDemo("Label Demo Window");
        JLabel label = new JLabel("    Rescued by Java...and Swing!");
```

```
        frame.getContentPane().add(label);
        frame.setSize(400, 400);
        frame.setVisible(true);
    }
}
```

Again, note that the program precedes the Swing object names with the letter J. Because the *JLabel* object is not an active object (upon which the user can click his or her mouse), the program does not have to implement an action listener for the object, as it would for a *JButton* object, discussed next.

ADDING A BUTTON

The following *ButtonDemo.java* application uses the Swing interface to add a button to the user window. Each time the user clicks his or her mouse on the button, the program increments a counter, which it then displays within the program's title bar, as shown in Figure 36.3.

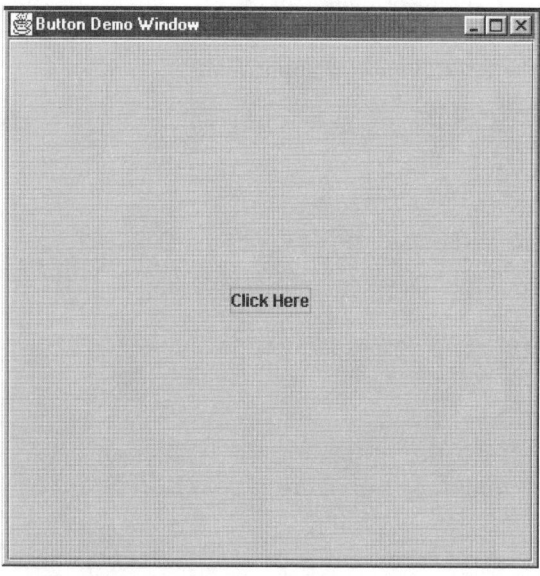

Figure 36.3 Using the Swing user interface to display a button.

The following code implements the *ButtonDemo.java* application:

```
import javax.swing.*;
import java.awt.event.*;

public class ButtonDemo extends JFrame
    {
    int Count = 0;
    String Title;
```

```
    public ButtonDemo(String WindowTitle)
     {
        super(WindowTitle);

        JButton SwingButton = new JButton("Click Here");

        class WindowEventHandler extends WindowAdapter
          {
            public void windowClosing(WindowEvent event)
              {
                dispose();
                System.exit(1);
              }
          }

        class MyButtonListener implements ActionListener
          {
            public void actionPerformed(ActionEvent event)
              {
                ++Count;
                Title = "Current Count: " + Count;
                setTitle(Title);
              }
          }

        addWindowListener(new WindowEventHandler());
        SwingButton.addActionListener(new MyButtonListener());
        getContentPane().add(SwingButton);
     }

  public static void main(String args[])
     {
        JFrame frame = new ButtonDemo("Button Demo Window");

        frame.setSize(400, 400);
        frame.setVisible(true);
     }
  }
```

As you can see, the program implements a *WindowEventHandler* to listen for window-based events and an *ActionListener* to respond to button operations.

TAKING A CYBER FIELD TRIP

In this lesson you looked at several simple examples of the Swing interface. To help you get started, the *Java Development Kit* provides a simple StylePad application shown in Figure 36.4. Using the StylePad program, you can edit text, change fonts, change colors, and work with images. To the download the StylePad application's source code, visit the Jamsa Press Web site at *www.jamsa.com/java_demos/StylePad.html.*

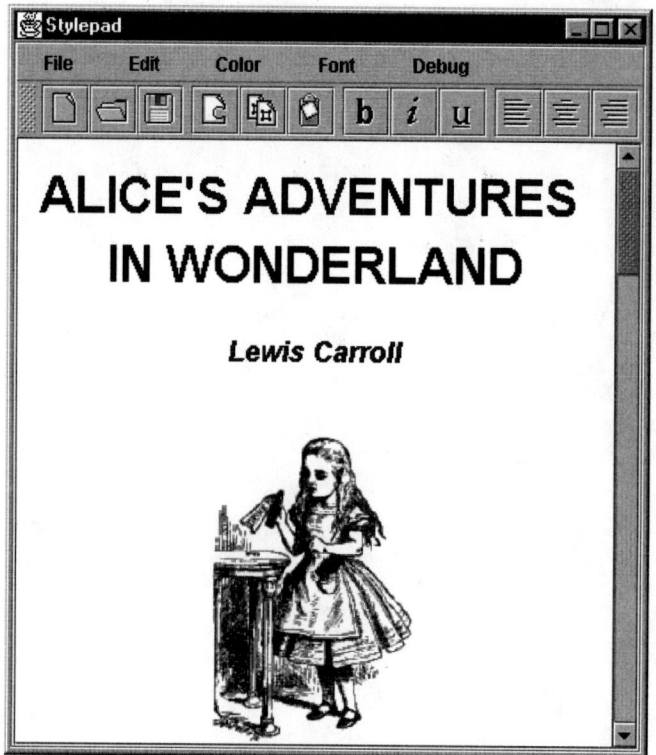

Figure 36.4 Using Swing to build the StylePad application provided with the Java Development Kit.

WHAT YOU MUST KNOW

When you create Java applets, the user will normally run the applet from within a browser, such as the *Internet Explorer* or the *appletviewer*, which provides the applet with a windows-based interface. When you create standalone applications, however, the user will normally run the program from the command line. In this lesson, you learned how to use the Swing interface to display user-interface objects in the same format as your current graphical-user environment. In Lesson 37, "Using the Personal Web Server," you will learn how to test your applets on the Web using the Personal Web Server software that Microsoft bundles with Windows 98. Before you continue with Lesson 37, however, make sure you have learned the following key concepts:

- ☑ Java provides the Swing user interface so that standalone applications can display graphical-user interface objects in the same format as the user's current environment.

- ☑ Java places the Swing objects within the *swing* class libraries. To use the Swing class libraries, place the statement *import javax.swing.*;* at the start of the program.

- ☑ To distinguish swing objects from the objects you examined in Lesson 31, Java precedes the Swing object names with the letter J, such as *JFrame*, *JButton*, and so on.

LESSON 37

USING THE WINDOWS 98 PERSONAL WEB SERVER

Throughout this book, you have used the *appletviewer* or your Web browser to run your Java applets. If you are developing Java applets for the Web, you should test your applets in a Web-based environment before you bring your applets online. If you are working at a company that has an Internet connection, your network administrator can create a directory on the Web server within which you can place your programs for testing. If, however, you do not have access to a large Web server, you can use the Personal Web Server that Microsoft bundles with Windows 98. This lesson examines the steps you must perform to install and use the Personal Web Server. By the time you finish this lesson, you will understand the following key concepts:

◆ To install the Personal Web Server, you must run the Setup program that resides in the \add-ons\pws folder on the Windows 98 CD-ROM.

◆ After you install the Personal Web Server on your system, you must start the software by running the Personal Web Manager program that you will find in the Start menu's Programs submenu *Internet Explorer* options.

◆ To access your PC across the Net, you or another user must know your PC's Internet Protocol (IP) address. To determine your PC's IP address, you can run the *WinIPcfg* program provided with Windows 98.

◆ After you connect to the Net and start the Personal Web Manager software, you (or another user) can access Web files by typing the letters http:// followed by your IP address, a forward slash, and the HTML filename, such as *http://111.222.112.112/TestSite.HTML*.

INSTALLING THE PERSONAL WEB SERVER

As discussed, after you install and run the Windows 98 Personal Web Server and then establish an Internet connection, you or another user can test your Java applets from across the Internet. To install the Windows 98 Personal Web Server, perform these steps:

1. Click your mouse on the Start button. Windows, in turn, will display the Start menu.

2. Within the Start menu, click your mouse on the Run option. Windows will display the Run dialog box, as shown in Figure 37.1.

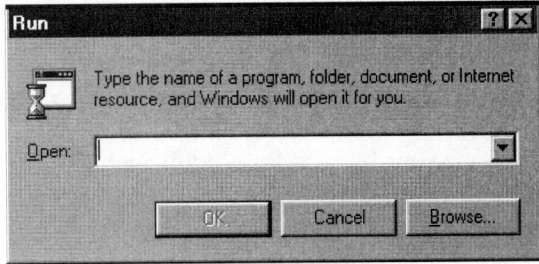

Figure 37.1 The Run dialog box.

3. Insert your Windows 98 CD-ROM into your CD-ROM drive.

4. Within the Run dialog box, click your mouse on the Browse button, then select the \add-ons\pws folder within the CD-ROM and choose the *Setup* program.

315

5. Click your mouse on the OK button. Windows, in turn, will install the Personal Web Server on your system.

DETERMINING YOUR PC'S INTERNET PROTOCOL (IP) ADDRESS

Across the Internet, every computer has a unique address, called its Internet Protocol or IP address. When you receive e-mail, for example, the e-mail program sends information across the Net to your PC's IP address. Likewise, when you browse the Web, a remote site's server downloads text and graphics to your PC by sending the data to your PC's IP address.

An IP address consists of four numbers, separated by periods, such as 111.211.221.112. Each time you connect your PC to the Internet, your Internet Service Provider (such as America Online) assigns your PC a unique IP address. To determine your PC's IP address, you can run the *WinIPcfg* program as shown in Figure 37.2.

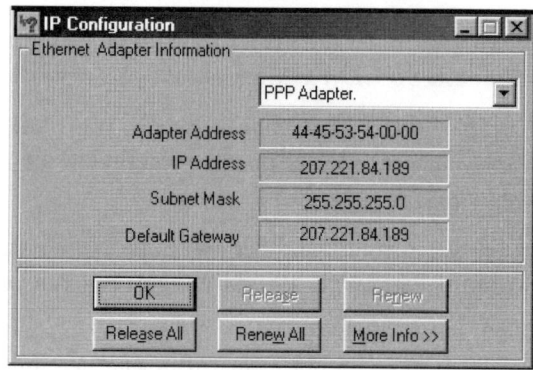

Figure 37.2 *The WinIPcfg program.*

To run the *WinIPcfg* program within Windows 98, perform these steps:

1. Click your mouse on the Start button. Windows, in turn, will display the Start menu.
2. Within the Start menu, click your mouse on the Run option. Windows will display the Run dialog box.
3. Within the Run dialog box, type **WinIPcfg** and press ENTER.

Within the *WinIPcfg* window, you will find your PC's IP address. Write down the IP address; you (and other users) will need it to access your PC's Web server. Each time you connect to the Internet, you must perform these steps to determine your PC's IP address.

RUNNING THE PERSONAL WEB SERVER

To use the Personal Web Server, perform these steps:

1. Connect to the Internet using your Internet Service Provider.
2. Move the HTML files and Java class files you want to test to the folder *\InetPub\wwwroot* folder (which normally resides on drive C).
3. Click your mouse on the Start button. Windows, in turn, will display the Start menu.
4. Within the Start menu, click your mouse on the Programs option and choose *Internet Explorer*. Windows will display a menu of additional options.
5. Within the *Internet Explorer* menu, click your mouse on the Personal Web Server option and then choose Personal Web Manager. Windows, in turn, will display the Personal Web Manager, as shown in Figure 37.3.

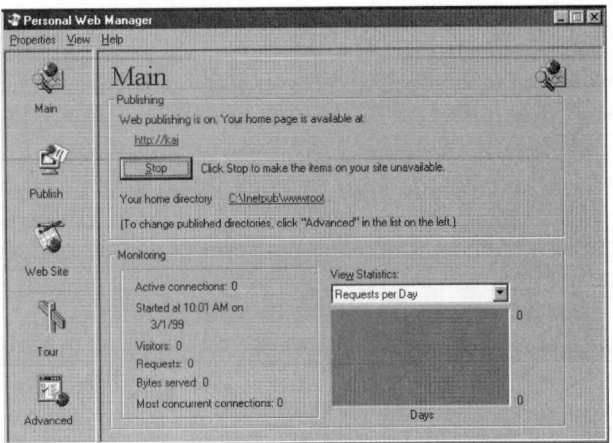

Figure 37.3 *The Personal Web Manager.*

After the Personal Web Manager is running, you (and other users) can view HTML documents from your PC, as discussed next. You can tell other users your IP address by sending them an e-mail message or by simply calling them on the phone!

VIEWING HTML DOCUMENTS USING THE PERSONAL WEB SERVER

After you have the Personal Web Server running, you (or another user) can view Web documents on your PC by typing the letters http://, followed by your IP address, a forward slash, and the HTML file name. For example, if your IP address 207.221.84.189 and you want to view the file *TestSite.html*, you would type *http://207.221.84.189/TestSite.html*, as shown in Figure 37.4.

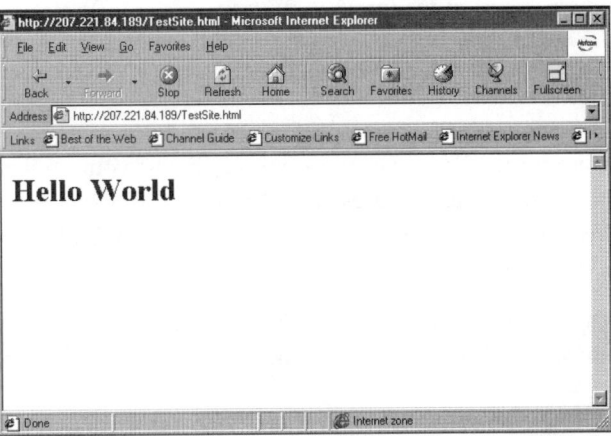

Figure 37.4 *Viewing an HTML document by specifying an IP address and file name.*

DOMAIN NAMES ELIMINATE YOUR NEED TO WORK WITH IP ADDRESSES

As you surf the Web, you normally use domain names, such as *www.jamsa.com* or *www.microsoft.com*, as opposed to IP addresses. When companies (or some users, for that matter) register a domain name, they receive a permanent IP address that is then stored in a database on the Net. Later, when a user specifies a domain name within his or her browser, the browser (behind the scenes) contacts a special site on the Web called a *domain-name server* (DNS) and asks the site for the IP address that corresponds to the domain name. Then, using the IP address, the browser can send information to the site. By letting users specify domain names, the software eliminates the user's need to work with IP addresses, which the user would find difficult to remember and to type.

TAKING A CYBER FIELD TRIP

In this lesson, you learned how to use the Personal Web Server and your PC's Internet Protocol (IP) address. As you have learned, having to work with IP addresses is error prone and time consuming. If you are interested in obtaining your own domain name, visit the InterNIC Web site at *www.internic.net*, as shown in Figure 37.5. The Web site will explain the steps you must perform, and fees you must pay, to get your own domain name.

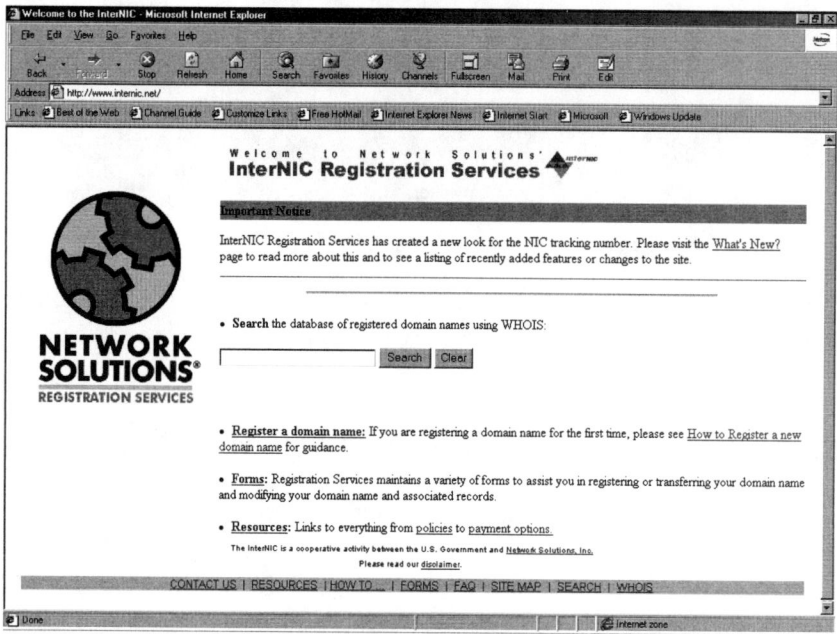

Figure 37.5 Learning about domain names at the InterNIC Web site.

WHAT YOU MUST KNOW

When you develop applets for use on the Web, you must eventually test your applets within a Net-based environment. In this lesson, you learned how to create and use the Personal Web Server that Microsoft bundles with Windows 98. Using the Personal Web Server, you or other users can access HTML files (and the Java applets the HTML files reference) from across the Web.

Since you created your first Java applet in Lesson 2, "Creating Your First Java Applet," you have learned a great deal about Java. Before you continue on your way with Java, however, make sure you have learned the following key concepts:

☑ The Windows 98 CD-ROM contains the Personal Web Server that you can install by running the *Setup* program that resides in the \add-ons\pws folder.

☑ To start the Personal Web Server software, you must run the Personal Web Manager program that you will find in the Start menu's Programs submenu *Internet Explorer* options.

☑ To access your PC across the Net, you or another user must know your PC's Internet Protocol (IP) address.

☑ Using the *WinIPcfg* program provided with Windows 98, you can determine your PC's IP address.

☑ After you connect to the Net and start the Personal Web Manager software, you (or another user) can access Web files by typing the letters http://, followed by your IP address, a forward slash, and the HTML filename, such as *http://111.222.112.112/TestSite*

APPENDIX A

USING THE JBUILDER COMPILER

The companion CD-ROM that accompanies this book contains the Java source code for each applet and program this book presents. In addition, the CD-ROM contains Borland's *JBuilder* Java Development Environment. If you are running Windows 95 or higher, you can use *JBuilder* to create, compile, and test your Java programs.

INSTALLING JBUILDER ON YOUR SYSTEM

To install *JBuilder* on your system, perform these steps:

1. Insert this book's companion CD-ROM into your CD-ROM drive.
2. Click your mouse on the Start menu and choose Run. Windows, in turn, will display the Run dialog box.
3. Within the Run dialog box, click your mouse on the Browse button and then locate the *JBuilder* folder on the CD-ROM.
4. Within the *JBuilder* folder, click your mouse on the Setup program and choose OK. Windows will start the *JBuilder* installation program.

RUNNING THE JBUILDER JAVA DEVELOPMENT ENVIRONMENT

To run *JBuilder*, perform these steps:

1. Click your mouse on the Start menu and choose Programs. Windows, in turn, will display the Programs submenu.
2. Within the Programs submenu, click your mouse on the Borland *JBuilder* option and choose *JBuilder*. Windows will start *JBuilder*, as shown in Figure A.1.

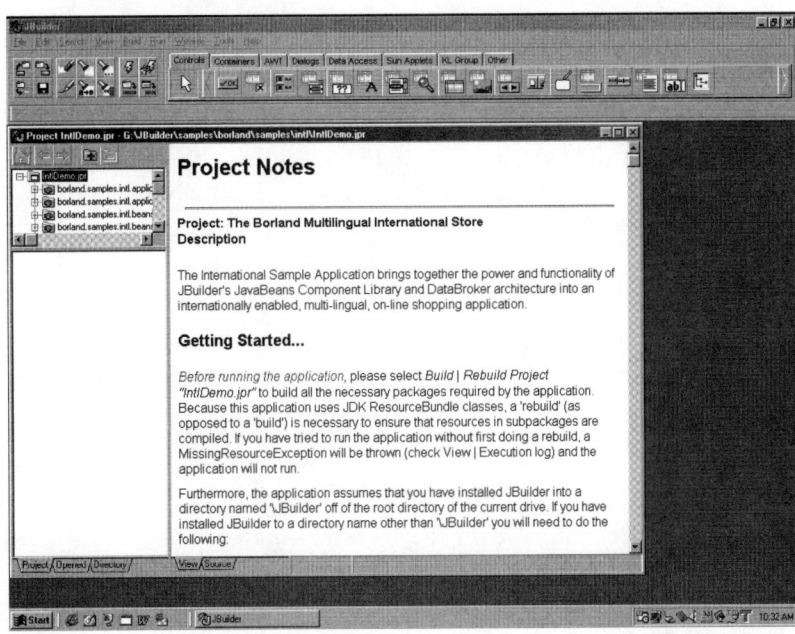

Figure A.1 The JBuilder Java Development Environment.

UNDERSTANDING JBUILDER PROJECTS

When you use *JBuilder* to create Java programs, you store your source code and HTML files within a project file. For example, to build the *MathOverflow* applet which Lesson 5, "Java Applets Store Information in Variables," presents, you might create a project file named *MathOverflow.jpr* that contains the *MathOverflow.java* source file as well as *MathOverflow.HTML*.

To better understand the process of creating a project file within *JBuilder*, perform these steps to create a project file for the *MathOverflow* applet:

1. Using the Windows Explorer, create a folder on your disk called *JBDemo*, such as *C:\JBDemo*.
2. Again, using the Explorer, copy the *MathOverflow.java* and *MathOverflow.HTML* files from *LESSON05* folder of this book's companion CD-ROM into the *JBDemo* folder.
3. Within *JBuilder*, click your mouse on the File menu New Project option. *JBuilder*, in turn, will display the Project Wizard dialog box, as shown in Figure A.2.

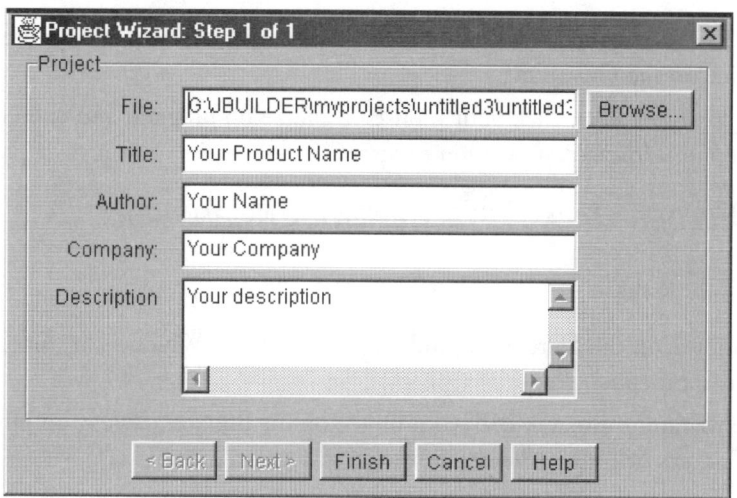

Figure A.2 *The JBuilder Project Wizard.*

4. Within the Project Wizard dialog box File field, type in the directory and filename for your project, in this case, *C:\JBDemo\MathOverflow.jpr*. Next, complete the Wizard's remaining fields and then click your mouse on the Finish button. *JBuilder* will display a message telling you that the file *MathOverflow.HTML* exists and asking you if it can overwrite the file. Select No.
5. Within the *JBuilder* project window, click your mouse on the *MathOverflow.jpr* icon to select the project and then click your mouse on the large plus-sign button. *JBuilder* will display the Open/Create dialog box, as shown in Figure A.3.
6. Within the Open/Create dialog box, click your mouse on the file *MathOverflow.java* and choose Open to add the file to the project.
7. Within *JBuilder*, click your mouse on the Run menu and choose the Run applet in the *MathOverflow.HTML* option. *JBuilder*, in turn, will compile the applet's source code and then display the HTML file's contents within its *appletviewer* program, as shown in Figure A.4.

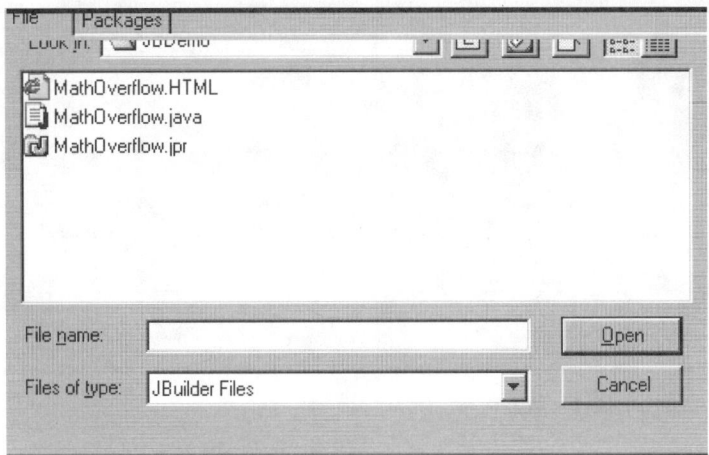

Figure A.3 *The Open/Create dialog box.*

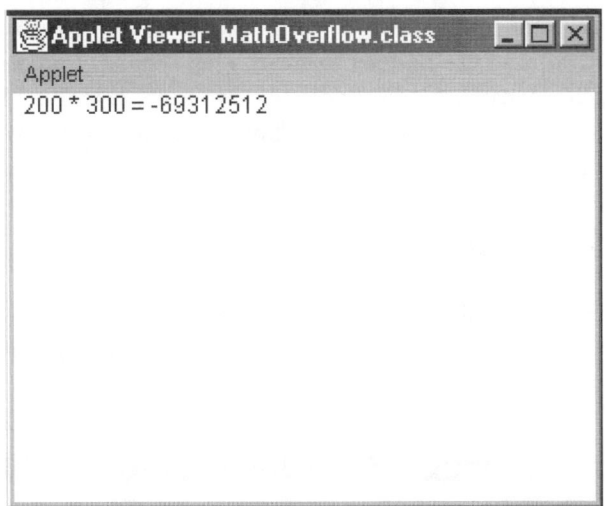

Figure A.4 *Running an applet within JBuilder.*

8. Within *JBuilder*, use the File menu Save option to save your project files.

Note: *If you find that* **JBuilder** *will not let you edit a source file, the file may have its readonly attribute set. To clear the file's readonly attribute, right click your mouse on the file within the Windows* **Explorer** *and then choose Properties from within the popup menu. Windows, in turn, will display a Properties dialog box within which you can clear the readonly attribute.*

USING THE JBUILDER DEMO PROJECTS

To help you get started, *JBuilder* provides several demo projects you can open using the File menu Open option. *JBuilder* places the demo programs within its *Java\Demos* folder. For example, Figure A.5 shows the *Animator* applet running from the project file *Animator.jpr*.

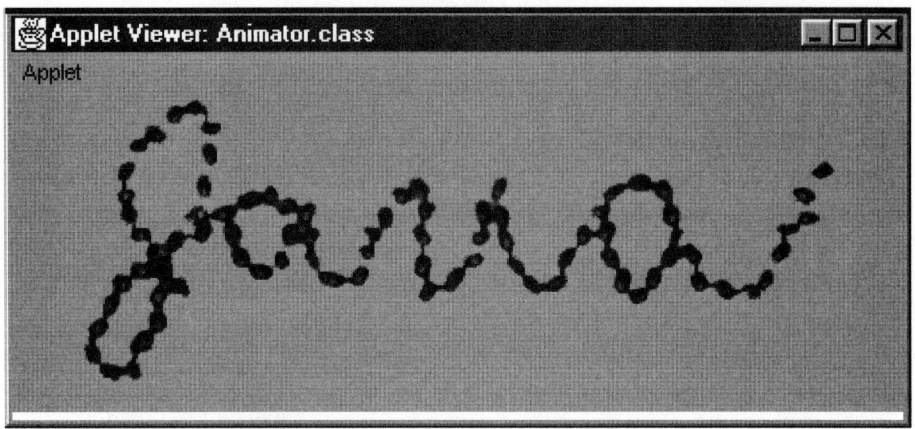

Figure A.5 *Running a **JBuilder** demo project.*

USING THE JBUILDER WIZARDS TO CREATE AN APPLET OR STANDALONE APPLICATION

As you have learned throughout this book, most Java applets have several common attributes. First, most import common files, such as *java.awt.** and *java.applet.**. Next, most define *init, run,* and *paint* functions. Using the *JBuilder* File menu New option, you can use *JBuilder* to create a new applet. *JBuilder*, in turn, will predefine some Java source for your applet which you can use, edit, or delete, as your needs require. In a similar way, if you use the File menu New option to create an application, *JBuilder* will provide code that lets your application take advantage of *Frame* objects. Take some time to experiment with *JBuilder* and examine the source code it predefines for you.

USING THE JBUILDER TUTORIAL

To help you make the best use of its capabilities, *JBuilder* provides a tutorial that you can start from the Help menu by selecting the Welcome Project option. *JBuilder*, in turn, will display the Welcome Project, as shown in Figure A.6, that walks you through various operations.

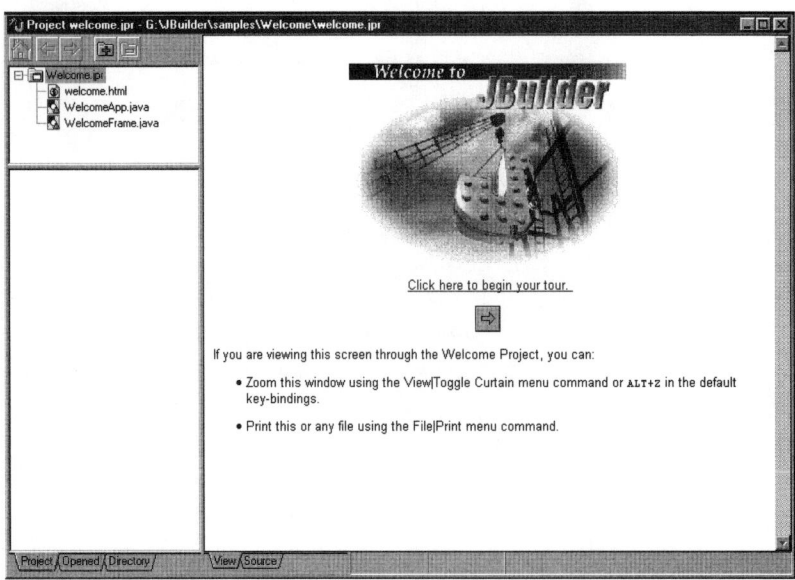

Figure A.6 *Using the **JBuilder** Welcome Project to learn common operations.*

For more information on *JBuilder*, or to order the latest version, visit the Borland Web site at *www.borland.com.*

Sun Microsystems, Inc.
Binary Code License Agreement

READ THE TERMS OF THIS AGREEMENT AND ANY PROVIDED SUPPLEMENTAL LICENSE TERMS (COLLECTIVELY "AGREEMENT") CAREFULLY BEFORE OPENING THE SOFTWARE MEDIA PACKAGE. BY OPENING THE SOFTWARE MEDIA PACKAGE, YOU AGREE TO THE TERMS OF THIS AGREEMENT. IF YOU ARE ACCESSING THE SOFTWARE ELECTRONICALLY, INDICATE YOUR ACCEPTANCE OF THESE TERMS BY SELECTING THE "ACCEPT" BUTTON AT THE END OF THIS AGREEMENT IF YOU DO NOT AGREE TO ALL THESE TERMS, PROMPTLY RETURN THE UNUSED SOFTWARE TO YOUR PLACE OF PURCHASE FOR A REFUND OR, IF THE SOFTWARE IS ACCESSED ELECTRONICALLY, SELECT THE "DECLINE" BUTTON AT THE END OF THIS AGREEMENT.

1. LICENSE TO USE. Sun grants you a non-exclusive and non-transferable license for the internal use only of the accompanying software and documentation and any error corrections provided by Sun (collectively "Software"), by the number of users and the class of computer hardware for which the corresponding fee has been paid.

2. RESTRICTIONS. Software is confidential and copyrighted. Title to Software and all associated intellectual property rights is retained by Sun and/or its licensors. Except as specifically authorized in any Supplemental License Terms, you may not make copies of Software, other than a single copy of Software for archival purposes. Unless enforcement is prohibited by applicable law, you may not modify, decompile, reverse engineer Software. You acknowledge that Software is not designed or licensed for use in on-line control of aircraft, air traffic, aircraft navigation or aircraft communications; or in the design, construction, operation or maintenance of any nuclear facility, Sun disclaims any express or implied warranty of fitness for such uses. No right, title or interest in or to any trademark, service mark, logo or trade name of Sun or its licensors is granted under this Agreement.

3. LIMITED WARRANTY. Sun warrants to you that for a period of ninety (90) days from the date of purchase, as evidenced by a copy of the receipt, the media on which Software is furnished (if any) will be free of defects in materials and workmanship under normal use. Except for the foregoing, Software is provided "AS IS". Your exclusive remedy and Sun's entire liability under this limited warranty will be at Sun's option to replace Software media or refund the fee paid for Software.

4. DISCLAIMER OF WARRANTY. UNLESS SPECIFIED IN THIS AGREEMENT, ALL EXPRESS OR IMPLIED CONDITIONS, REPRE- SENTATIONS AND WARRANTIES, INCLUDING ANY IMPLIED WARRANTY OF MERCHANTABILITY, FITNESS FOR A PARTICULAR PURPOSE, OR NON-INFRINGEMENT, ARE DISCLAIMED, EXCEPT TO THE EXTENT THAT THESE DISCLAIMERS ARE HELD TO BE LEGALLY INVALID.

5. LIMITATION OF LIABILITY. TO THE EXTENT NOT PROHIBITED BY LAW, IN NO EVENT WILL SUN OR ITS LICENSORS BE LIABLE FOR ANY LOST REVENUE, PROFIT OR DATA, OR FOR SPECIAL, INDIRECT, CONSEQUENTIAL, INCIDENTAL OR PUNITIVE DAMAGES, HOWEVER CAUSED REGARDLESS OF THE THEORY OF LIABILITY, ARISING OUT OF OR RELATED TO THE USE OF OR INABILITY TO USE SOFTWARE, EVEN IF SUN HAS BEEN ADVISED OF THE POSSIBILITY OF SUCH DAMAGES. In no event will Sun's liability to you, whether in contract, tort (including negligence), or otherwise, exceed the amount paid by you for Software under this Agreement. The foregoing limita- tions will apply even if the above stated warranty fails of its essential purpose.

6. Termination. This Agreement is effective until terminated. You may terminate this Agreement at any time by destroying all copies of Software. This Agreement will terminate immediately without notice from Sun if you fail to comply with any provision of this Agreement. Upon Termination, you must destroy all copies of Software.

7. Export Regulations. All Software and technical data delivered under this Agreement are subject to US export control laws and may be subject to export or import regulations in other countries. You agree to comply strictly with all such laws and regulations and acknowledge that you have the responsibility to obtain such licenses to export, re-export, or import as may be required after delivery to you.

8. U.S. Government Rights. If Software is being acquired by or on behalf of the U.S. Government or by a U.S. Government prime contractor or subcontractor (at any tier), then the Government's rights in Software will be only as set forth in this Agreement; this is in accordance with 48 CFR 227.7201 through 227.7202-4 (for Department of Defense (DOD) acquisitions) and with 48 CFR 2.101 and 12.212 (for non-DOD acquisitions).

9. Governing Law. Any action related to this Agreement will be governed by California law and controlling U.S. federal law. No choice of law rules of any jurisdiction will apply.

10. Severability. If any provision of this Agreement is held to be unenforceable, this Agreement will remain in effect with the provision omitted, unless omission would frustrate the intent of the parties, in which case this Agreement will immediately terminate.

11. Integration. This Agreement is the entire agreement between you and Sun relating to its subject matter. It supersedes all prior or contemporaneous oral or written communications, proposals, representations and warranties and prevails over any conflicting or additional terms of any quote, order, acknowledgment, or other communication between the parties relating to its subject matter during the term of this Agreement. No modification of this Agreement will be binding, unless in writing and signed by an authorized representative of each party.

For inquiries please contact: Sun Microsystems, Inc. 901 San Antonio Road, Palo Alto, California 94303